MASS MEDIA

THE INVISIBLE ENVIRONMENT REVISITED

MASS MEDIA

THE INVISIBLE ENVIRONMENT REVISITED

ROBERT J. GLESSING

Cañada College
Redwood City, Ca.

WILLIAM P. WHITE

California State University
Chico

SRA

SCIENCE RESEARCH ASSOCIATES, INC.
Chicago, Palo Alto, Toronto, Henley-on-Thames, Sydney, Paris, Stuttgart

A Subsidiary of IBM

It is impossible to acknowledge all of the persons who directly or indirectly assisted us in the preparation of this volume as well as the first edition. Special recognition must, however, be accorded to Howard Nathan, Mark Hall, Sharon White, and Janet Burkett. Particular thanks must be extended to Barbara Carpenter at SRA for her patience and skill in the production of these texts.

R.J.G. and W.P.W.

We wish to thank the following for permission to reprint materials quoted within articles and to reproduce illustrations:

p. 91 Superman comics, © 1971 National Periodical Publications, Inc. *p. 92* Green Lantern comics. ©1971 National Periodical Publications, Inc. *p. 92* Li'l Abner comics. © N. Y. News-World, rights reserved. *p. 93* Jules Feiffer. Reprinted by permission of Robert Lantz of the Lantz Office. *pp. 106, 111* Photographs reprinted by permission of photographer Peggy Barnett and NBC News. Originally published in *Audience* Magazine, July–August, 1972. *p. 123* Courtesy of Rice Council of America. *p. 126* Courtesy of Helene Curtis Inc. *p. 126* Courtesy of Kenwood and the Albert Frank-Guenther Law agency. *p. 127* Courtesy of Munsingwear, Inc., Vassarette Division. *p. 128* Courtesy of artist Hall Stebbins. *p. 130* Photograph courtesy of *Playboy* magazine. *pp. 135, 139* Photographers Richard Kapp and Ron Appelbe. Courtesy of *Business Week*. *p. 144* Shulamith Firestone, from her book *The Dialectic of Sex*, by permission of William Morrow and Company, Inc. *p. 144* Robin Morgan, reprinted by permission. *p. 145* Franchellie Cadwell, by permission of *Advertising Age Magazine*.

p. 161 Jerome Holtzman, The Chicago Sun-Times. *p. 161* Tom Fitzpatrick, The Chicago Sun-Times. *p. 162* Gene Ward, Courtesy of the New York News. *p. 163* Bill Gleason, The Chicago Sun-Times. *p. 163–64* C. C. Johnson Spink. *p. 164* John Steadman. *p. 165* Harry Caray. *p. 167* Roone Arledge, from *TV Guide*. *p. 167* James Roach, © 1972 by The New York Times Company. Reprinted by permission. *p. 167* Earl Cox, The Courier-Journal and Louisville Times. *p. 219* Fred Rogers, from his song "It's You I Like." *p. 246* J. Edward Gerald, "What the AEJ Can Do With the Press Council Idea," *Journalism Quarterly*, Spring 1968 (Vol. 4, No. 1), p. 83. *pp. 246, 249, 251* William L. Rivers, Stanford University. *pp. 249, 250* Robert W. Chandler. *pp. 249, 250* Ray Spangler.

© 1976, Science Research Associates, Inc.
All rights reserved. Printed in the United States of America.

Library of Congress Cataloging in Publication Data

Glessing, Robert J.   comp.
  Mass media.

  Includes index.
  1. Mass media—United States—Addresses, essays, lectures. 2. United States—Popular culture—Addresses, essays, lectures. I. White, William Paul, 1935– II. Title.
P92.U5G55   1976   301.16′1   75-44488
ISBN 0-574-22700-8

CONTENTS

THE FIRST WORD   2

Introduction   4
Communications and Society
    Douglass Cater   6

MEDIA FORMS   16

Electronic   18
Humanistic Claim on the Cable
    Richard Adler   19
TV Debases Everything It Touches—and TV Touches Everything   *Harry J. Skornia*   26
Television, the Only Truly Mass Medium Remaining Today: Its Role in Our Society
    D. Thomas Miller   36
Radio, or "Come On, Let Me Show You Where It's At"   *Don R. Pember*   42

Print   46
The American Newspaper Is Neither Record, Telegram, Examiner, Observer, Monitor...   *Ben H. Bagdikian*   47
Newsroom Revolution
    Robert C. Achorn   53
Unspecialized Publications Step Aside
    Jean-Louis Servan-Schreiber   56
PW Interview with Jean-Louis Servan-Schreiber   *John F. Baker*   63

Film   65
On the Future of Movies   *Pauline Kael*   66
The Docudramatelementary
    Norman Corwin   71
Films, Movies, and Audiences
    Penelope Houston   73

Music   77
Rock on the Rocks or Bubblegum Anybody?
    Irving Louis Horowitz   78
It's a Family Affair (Parts 1 and 3)
    Michael Shain   82
The Strange Death of Rock and Roll
    Langdon Winner   87
Return to Good-Times Rock
    Time Magazine   88

Comics, Graffiti, and Clothing   90
The Comics on the Couch
    Time Magazine   91
Comix   *Charles-Gene McDaniel*   94
Graffiti Lives   *Bonnie O'Boyle*   97
Clothing: Our Extended Skin
    Marshall McLuhan   100

MEDIA CONTENT   103

The News and Newspersons   104
Versions of National News
    Edward Jay Epstein   105

Post-Watergate Reconstruction—Media (from *Commonweal*)   Sisyphus   110
from *All the President's Men*   Bob Woodward and Carl Bernstein   114
from *The New Journalism*   Tom Wolfe   116
Bad News (Judgment?) Drives Out the Good   Ray McHugh   118
What's News   Marty Glass   119

Advertising   121

Sex and Advertising   Charles Winick   122
Advertising—Parity and Peter Pan   Isadore Barmash   127
Culture Is Our Business   Marshall McLuhan   130
To Sell Your Product, Admit It's Not Perfect   Gary Gregg   131
Advertising—Its Own Worst Enemy?   Joe Cappo   132
Madison Avenue's Response to Its Critics   Business Week   133

Minority Voices and Media   142

Is Television Making a Mockery of the American Woman?   Edith Efron   143
Speeding Down the Wrong Track   Frederick Breitenfeld, Jr.   146
Women's Pages: You Can't Make News Out of a Silk Purse (from *Ms.*)   Lindsy Van Gelder   147
What Do Black Journalists Want?   Dorothy Gilliam   150

Sports   156

How Television Has Changed Sports   Wells Twombly   157
The Secret Reasons Why Men Watch Football on TV   A. M. Watkins   159
The Shame of the Sports Beat   Bill Surface   161

MEDIA ENVIRONMENTS   170

Politics, Censors, and Media   172

Power Struggle: President Versus Press   Theodore H. White   173

How "Fair" Should TV Be?   Nat Hentoff   185
TV in Election Campaigns—a Call for Change   Robert D. Squier and Jane M. Squier   192
Has Public Broadcasting Lost Its Nerve?   Harry J. Skornia   193
The Decision Is Tentative   Benno C. Schmidt, Jr.   202

Minds, Manipulators, and Media   208

Contamination: Propaganda and the News   Dale Minor   209
TV Violence: How It Changes Your Children   Victor B. Cline   212
Saturday's Kidvid Ghetto   F. Earle Barcus   216

Ownership, Economics, and Media   222

The Rush to Chain Ownership   Robert L. Bishop   223
A Third Force in Broadcasting: The Group Owner   Westin C. Pullen, Jr.   232
Media Monopolies: Is Bigness a Curse?   Walter Pincus   234
It's a Family Affair (Part 2)   Michael Shain   237

Educators, Media Watchers, and Media   241

The Sword in the Stone   Martin T. Ducheny   242
How Community Press Councils Work   Donald E. Brignolo   245
Students as Media Critics: A New Course   Nat Hentoff   252

THE LAST WORD   256

What Can We Do About Television?   Nicholas Johnson   258
Cable TV, Videophones, Satellites, and Data Networks Will Soon Change the Way You Live, Work, and Play   Peter C. Goldmark   264
How Communications May Shape Our Future Environment   Ben H. Bagdikian   267

INDEX   273

Messages are the medium in which human beings exist. Precisely how human behavior and attitudes are shaped by the multifarious forms of mass communication is now beginning to be investigated.

George Gerbner

from "Communication and Social Environment"
(1972)

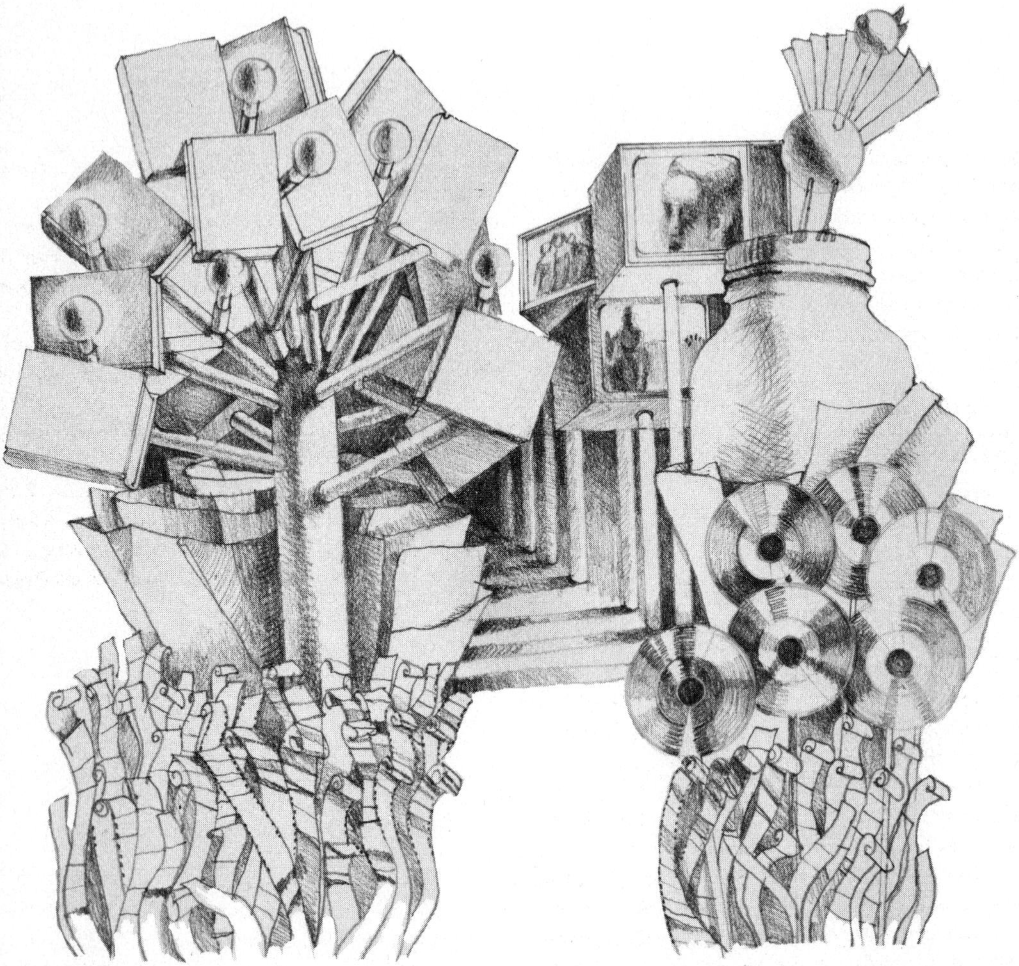

THE FIRST WORD

The title for this section of the book has been chosen for two reasons. The first and most obvious is to provide a balance with the closing section entitled "The Last Word." A second, more significant purpose is to emphasize *The Word* as a basis for mass communication in all forms.

A **Pogo** cartoon strip once featured a poem that read in part:

There high in the wind
   rides a star my own . . .
And the Star in the wind
   is a word

Using the word as a vehicle for communicating ideas is precisely what media analyst Douglass Cater accomplishes in his opening essay, "Communications and Society: Toward a Public Philosophy." Here Cater's broad observations establish the position and role of the press in a nation ever watchful of the erosive tendencies of big government to regulate more and more of our mass media systems.

Cater raises a fundamental question about whether the mass media **reflect** or **shape** the world in which we live. He believes that because the press quite decidedly shapes contemporary society, it has a responsibility to that role. He agrees with esteemed social critic Walter Lippman in arguing that, since the mass media help shape us, one of their basic responsibilities is "to provide a picture of reality on which man can act."

The ongoing problems of fairness in broadcasting and the public's right to free access to our precious media time and space are other issues covered in the opening article.

And so "The First Word" in this timely new collection becomes, at least figuratively, a word that describes what the press is, can be, and should be in an ever-changing society of which that press must provide an accurate picture.

Mass media began with Gutenberg's printing press which in a sense preceded radio, followed by television, which preceded satellites. But it all started with and depends upon the use of *words*. Or as Pogo would have it *The Word*.

There's a star in the wind
   and the wind blows high
Blowing alight
   thru fog, thru night
Thru cold, thru cold
   and the bitter alone . . .
There high in the wind
   rides a star my own . . .
And the Star is a word
   of white, of white
And the Star in the wind
   is a *Word*.

INTRODUCTION

ROBERT J. GLESSING
WILLIAM P. WHITE

The first edition of this reader stated that Americans are media junkies, addicted to some 60 million newspapers per day, 300 million radios in cars and homes, and 97 percent of those homes equipped with television sets. The average consumer totalled 50 hours of media consumption per person per week. That's quite a habit.

As media philosopher Marshall McLuhan has observed, our media environments are as pervasive as water is to a fish. Just as the fish functions largely unaware of its environment, we too are relatively unaware of the impact and importance of mass media environments in and on our lives. But strong indications are that public awareness of the media and their impact is changing. Recent events suggest that such awareness, sparked by a new public consumer interest, is increasingly altering the contents and environments of major media systems. The era is probably over when the political powers could explain away disturbances such as the ones accompanying the 1968 Democratic National Convention simply as contrived media performances. The strident voice of Spiro Agnew might have struck fear and prompted a review of performance by major media owners and managers, but Americans everywhere began to realize that what we see and the form in which we receive it are vital ingredients in how we as a people interpret and know our world. Indeed, the revelations of Watergate included an enhanced public awareness of the potential and real powers of the media—an awareness that makes the media's invisible environment much more visible, if less predictable.

Information flows through our environment in such overwhelming quantities that even the most intelligent minds have difficulty sorting it out and separating the worthwhile from the worthless, the truths from the untruths and the half-truths. But the range of freedoms and the quality of life in this information-laden society may well depend on the alternatives we select. In order to choose wisely we must be aware of the forms the mass media take, the content they present, and the environments with which they interact.

The readings in this revised edition reflect the level of media awareness of today's students, who have logged their lifetimes in our modern media environments and whose knowledge of media content is generally extensive. Thus, we have tried to present readings that will increase students' ability to consume modern media wisely and, in so doing, to extend their awareness of modern mass culture.

Our nation has undergone significant economic, political and social changes these past few years, and American mass media reflect these changes. Many observers emphasize the strength of our free press as demonstrated by the "lonesome gallantry" of Kathryn Graham's *Washington Post* in its relentless reporting of the Watergate break-in. Included in this edition is a significant excerpt from the Woodward and Bernstein book, *All The President's Men*, capturing the flavor of that historic journalistic effort and presenting a vivid picture of how investigative journalism works. Also included is a masterfully designed segment from Theodore White's *The Making of the President 1972* explaining how and why the press was inevitably cast in the role of watchdog and protector of the American people's fundamental right to know.

While all this melodrama was unfolding in our print and electronic media, other significant changes were taking place. Television maintained its increasing dominance in the lives of media audiences. While people spent more and more time in front of the tube, they saw less and less of significance. Dr. Harry Skornia's biting critique of commercial television ("Television Debases Everything It Touches—and It Touches Everything") provides an indictment of what specifically is wrong with television and offers a constructive script for what can be done about it. Defending the increasingly widespread attacks on commercial television is D. Thomas Miller, a CBS executive, who paints a broad picture of how television has enriched our lives with its abundance of news, information, and entertainment ("Television, the Only Truly Mass Medium Remaining Today"). Richard Adler's article on cable television explains CATV's history and presents the status of this promising, but economically troubled new medium. ("Humanistic Claim on the Cable"). If there is an old standby in media, it must be AM radio. Much the same, but always changing, it is described in an article on radio ("Radio, or 'Come on, Let Me Show You Where It's At' " by Don R. Pember).

As women become more and more aware of their individuality, the media either lead or respond to this awareness. A thoughtful article on the changing nature of "women's news" reflects the need for lifestyle newspaper sections geared to people—both male and female—to replace the stereotyped, outdated, and often sexist traditional women's pages ("Women's Pages: You Can't Make News Out of a Silk Purse" by Lindsy Van Gelder).

Every institutionalized industry in the history of American business has had to include both stability and the capacity for change, and over the past five years the mass media have demonstrated these paradoxical characteristics. While books continue their historic dominance as a major source of conveying important ideas and information, the film industry appears to be killing off any opportunity it might have gained in providing the nation with meaningful and thought-provoking film fare ("On the Future of Movies" by Pauline Kael). While much of what is offered on commercial television is self-perpetuating game shows and soap opera reruns, the networks' and public television's airing of the Senate Watergate Hearings provided an unprecedented demonstration of just how and why our political systems function as they do in contemporary society.

The continuing conflict over media access and program control is reviewed by critic Nat Hentoff ("How Fair Should TV Be?") in an attempt to infuse change in an industry that has long been characterized by sameness and monotony.

Included in this revised edition is an article on revolutionary technology as it applies to newsgathering ("Newsroom Revolution" by Robert C. Achorn), and a definition of the new journalism ("The New Journalism" by Tom Wolfe). Also included is an opening article discussing several

> It's the primary America we're in. It hit the night before last in Prineville Junction and it's been with us ever since. There's this primary America of freeways and jet flights and TV and movie spectaculars. And people caught up in this primary America seem to go though huge portions of their lives without much consciousness of what's immediately around them. The media have convinced them that what's right around them is unimportant. And that's why they're lonely. You see it in their faces. First the little flicker of searching, and then when they look at you, you're just a kind of an object. You don't count. You're not what they're looking for. You're not on TV.
> from *Zen and the Art of Motorcycle Maintenance* by Robert Persig

forms of mass media and their relationship to the larger society ("Communications and Society: Toward a Public Philosophy" by Douglass Cater).

An update on the newsperson's right to withhold confidential information from the courts is covered in "The Decision Is Tentative" by Columbia law professor, Benno C. Schmidt, Jr. Also included is new material on advertising, minority programming, and television violence and children.

In recent years the size, scope, and complexity of our mass media systems have both widened and deepened. Now, more than ever before, our capacity to develop and govern ourselves is inextricably bound to those systems. This collection attempts to provide the student of media with a visible picture, complex but valid, of the media that permeate our environment and our existence.

COMMUNICATIONS AND SOCIETY

DOUGLASS CATER

The First Amendment set up a separation, zealously guarded over nearly two centuries, between government and the press. There is need to examine the present condition of that separation. While our conventional wisdom holds to the proposition that the media should be free and independent from government, it fails to account for the growth of entangling relationships beyond the purview of the First Amendment.

Government and the media engage in daily and intimate intercourse, regularly accusing each other of mortal offenses. Conflict between the official right to secrecy and the press's right to publish is waged in a no-man's land; Congress shies away from legislative interpretation and Court rulings leave vast areas of uncertainty. The government official does not hesitate to disclose classified information when it promotes his purposes. Reporters exploit biased confidences frequently without attempting to search out the fuller facts. This temptation to manipulate the communication process saddeningly lacks self-correctives. It leads to increasingly harsh and dogmatic confrontations between government and the media. Cumulatively, it contributes to a growing crisis of public understanding which affects the credibility of both.

Even greater public confusion arises over issues of media regulation. Once upon a time, government exercised little regulatory power beyond its prerogative to allocate official advertisements among competitive publishers. Today, government power goes wide and deep. The licensing authority of the Federal Communications Commission creates ambiguity about First Amendment rights of the broadcaster. The Newspaper Preservation Act grants special privilege—and vulnerability—for the publisher. Postal rate regulation can mean life or death for periodicals. Public Broadcasting's future is being shaped by annual appropriation after the most searching review by the White House and Congress. Franchising and rule-making are setting the fundamentals for satellite and cable development in America. The new technologies open the prospect of greatly expanded diversity in our communications system. But here, too, government must determine the policy by which diversity is achieved.

We enter the era of "television of abundance" at a time of growing public concern over television's impact on social behavior. Congressional leaders show an inclination to hold network heads responsible for pollution of the air waves. But will government pressure against certain types of broadcast programming—cigarette advertisements, televised violence, X-rated pornography—be extended to the multiple channels of the cable? Who will be held accountable? And to whom? How will government deal with the question of regulating newsprint when it is delivered by facsimile over the TV set?

Organized publics are keenly aware that our nation's media constitute a *de facto* fourth branch of government. Through communication, there is power. This has brought growing citizen demands for the *right to communicate*. Those range from petitions by counter-advertisers to lawsuits by the opposition party seeking network time to respond to the President. Recent court and regulatory commission decisions have tended to expand First Amendment doctrine by setting off the citizen's against the broadcaster's rights, and raising perplexing issues of how to arbitrate "access" and "fairness."

Amid the disputations between media and government there is danger of ignoring the common obligation they share—to provide "a picture of reality on which men can act." This phrase was of Walter Lippmann's coinage but concern about the role of communications in society goes back at least as far as Plato. In *The Republic* Plato related the parable of the underground cave where human beings have been chained since childhood, positioned so they see

---

Prologue entitled "Toward a Public Philosophy on Government-Media Relations" by Douglass Cater, in *Aspen Notebook on Government and the Media,* edited by William L. Rivers and Michael J. Nyhan. © 1973 by Praeger Publishers, Inc., New York. Excerpted and reprinted by permission.

only the shadows projected against the cave's inner wall. Plato concluded, "And if they were able to talk with one another, would they not suppose that they were naming what was actually before them?"

We might find it challenging to attempt to explain to Plato how our Republic keeps its citizenry informed. We would say first off that news is free—or nearly free—for the citizen. How then is it paid for, he might ask? We would reply that news is supported by our merchants who have products to sell. By their advertisements, they subsidize our print news and totally support our broadcast news. Doesn't this, asks Plato, distort the communications? Not so serious distortion as letting the government pay and control, we would reply. But we would be obliged to confess that merchandizing does determine the amount of news the citizen receives. Newspaper column inches rise and fall in proximate ratio to advertising content. Television's public affairs programs must compete for time with the higher-earning fictional dramas. For the newsweeklies the size of world-wide staffs depends not so much on what is happening as how Madison Avenue ad agencies allocate their accounts. No one can be certain whether the coming competition of the cable for the advertising dollar will increase or diminish the total revenues and resources devoted to projecting the image on the cave's wall.

Is each citizen equally informed, Plato might inquire? Not really, we must answer. If the citizen lives in certain metropolitan communities—New York, Washington, Los Angeles—his newspapers bulge with the latest national and international events. In other communities—Denver, San Francisco, Tucson—he must content himself with a thin diet of more than local happenings. His broadcast fodder similarly varies depending on where he lives and who owns his community's media.

Plato might consider this to be a most peculiar arrangement for a Republic where public opinion is the ultimate ruler. Natural law does not decree that what the citizen needs to know should be in continuing balance with what the merchant needs to sell. But can anyone devise a better alternative? Lacking one, we regularly insist that our media are "affected with the public interest." We demand that they be governed by more than profit motive. We exhort them to do a better job.

But enough of Plato and on to Agnew. In his critique of the media, the Vice President essentially made two points: One, they fail to communicate the picture of reality that accords with the picture he holds. Two, the picture communicated by the media is controlled by a small mysterious group known as "they." Mr. Agnew didn't get very specific about who "they" are; but "they" are to blame for our communication failures. Now the interesting thing about Agnew's analysis is that Stokely Carmichael and Jerry Rubin and other leaders of the radical left would agree with both points. So would George Wallace. The devil theory of the mass media rallies a diverse band of brothers.

More disturbing to serious critics is that Agnew stirred a response among a much wider public than the extremists on the right and the left. He apparently touched a sensitive nerve. We need to study this phenomenon. It is not enough to respond in the fashion of the bumper sticker I once saw in Los Angeles: "Will the silent majority please shut up."

Do the communications media present an adequate picture of reality to the American public? One media critic, who is widely quoted but little read and even less understood, suggests that this is not a proper question. The question ought to be turned around, according to Marshall McLuhan. He argues that the media are not reflecting but shaping society. In an interview carried in *Playboy*, which is the clearest explication of his theories that I have come across, McLuhan states;

All media, from the phonetic alphabet to the computer, are extensions of man that cause deep and lasting changes in him and transform his environment. . . . But most people, from truck drivers to literary Brahmins, are still blissfully unaware of what the media do to them; unaware that because of their pervasive effects on man, it is the medium itself that is the message, *not* the content, and unaware that the medium is also the *massage*—that, all puns aside, it literally works over and saturates and molds and transforms every sense ratio. The content or message of any particular medium has about as much importance as the stenciling on the casing of an atomic bomb.

McLuhan is a controversial and frequently confusing critic. I am not certain that he himself fully understands the full implications of his various insights. But he was not the first to contemplate the shaping role of the media. E. B. White, that sensitive observer of mankind, wrote a short essay in the *New Yorker* back in 1938 after he had witnessed a demonstration of television. He concluded, "I believe television is going to be the test of the modern world, and that in this new opportunity to see beyond the range of our vision we shall discover either a new and unbearable disturbance of the general peace or a saving radiance in the sky. We shall stand or fall by television—of that I am quite sure." White went on to explain:

> Television will enormously enlarge the eye's range, and, like radio, will advertise the Elsewhere. Together with the tabs, the movies, it will insist that we forget the primary and the near in favor of the secondary and the remote. More hours in every twenty-four will be spent digesting ideas, sounds, images—distant and concocted. In sufficient accumulation, radio sounds and television sounds may become more familiar to us than their originals. A door closing, heard over the air; a face contorted, seen in a panel of light—these will emerge as the real and the true; and when we bang the door of our own cell or look into another's face the impression will be of mere artifice.

This interplay of image and reality long fascinated me as a reporter in Washington. For I observed that the image of government, projected by the media, was being accepted as the reality not only by the people but by those involved in government. In 1958, I wrote in my book, *The Fourth Branch of Government*, that the news of government

> ... has been known to assume a generative spirit of its own—in turn recreating the people and policies being publicized even as the Hollywood starlet is remade to fit the public stereotype. The reporter in Washington has witnessed on numerous occasions the phenomenon described by the psychologist when the mask of the man takes possession of the true self. More than witness, he has helped to shape the mask which transforms the public figure.

After serving four and a half years inside the White House, I can only say "amen" to this analysis. Communication media have a vast power to shape government—its policies and its leaders. This is not a strictly editorial power. It is the power to select—out of the tens of thousands of words spoken in Washington each day and the tens of dozens of events—which words and events are projected for mankind to see. Equally powerful is the media's capacity to ignore. Those words and events which fail to get projected might as well not have occurred.

My criticism of the media is that they don't take themselves and their role seriously enough. A number of my colleagues in the press were offended by the title of my book assigning the communicators to a fourth branch of government. They felt contaminated by the phrase. They refuse to admit that those who are involved in the communications of a democracy play a major role in its governance.

The media project the shadows by which American society judges itself—whether we are pretty or ugly, healthy or sick. In the age of television, we are all more aware that each of us lives in a cubbyhole of direct experience. We all spend more and more of our lives, in E. B. White's phrase, viewing the secondary and the remote, digesting ideas, sounds, images—distant and concocted. How can any one of us judge whether the images we see are an adequate picture?

We are more image-conscious than our forefathers. Marshall McLuhan argues that we need to be conscious not only of images but how the images are made and their impact on us. He writes:

> In the past, the effects of media were experienced more gradually, allowing the individual and society to absorb and cushion their impact to some degree. Today, in the electronic age of instantaneous communication, I believe that our survival, and at the very least our comfort and happiness, is predicated on understanding the nature of our new environment, because unlike previous environmental changes, the electric media constitute a total and near-instantaneous transformation of culture, values, and attitudes. This upheaval generates great pain and identity loss which can be ameliorated only through a conscious awareness of its dynamics.

These are abstract words but they may help explain some of the hostility toward the media which has been displayed by the silent and the not-so-silent majority. We don't know for sure what the media are doing to us but we are damned uncomfortable about it.

At the risk of being charged with bias, I would like to present two examples of faulty communication for which the media at least partly share the blame:

As the decade of the 1950s came to a close, the dominant image of America held by most Americans was of a quiet society afflicted with faint fears of being stagnant. Our great concern was to achieve a higher economic growth rate. J. K. Galbraith, a pace setter among idea men, had in 1958 published his book *The Affluent Society*. He devoted only a limited amount of attention to the poverty in our midst and pretty well confined even that, as Michael Harrington later pointed out, to "insular" rather than "endemic" poverty. John F. Kennedy found a convincing campaign theme in pledging to get America moving again. But when he talked of millions of people going to bed hungry at night, even close supporters thought he was laying it on a bit thick.

The reality of that period was quite different. The American economy may have been stagnant but American society was in tremendous ferment. During that decade alone, there was a migration of over 8 million Americans into the metropolitan areas. Since the start of World War II, nearly two and a quarter million blacks left the South and crowded into the northern cities. Urban America was feeling the tremendous strain on its facilities—schools, hospitals and clinics, welfare. There was a rapidly growing crisis in the finance and governance of the cities. Prosperous Americans were fleeing to the suburbs.

And that crisis was not being adequately communicated. I was a reporter during that decade and share the blame. To refresh my memory, I dispatched a researcher to the Library of Congress to review the record. My conclusion is that the media did not serve as an early warning system for the crisis. Poverty, as Harrington wrote in 1962, was "invisible." It was not being heard, not being communicated.

Let us turn to my second example. As the decade of the 1960s drew to a close, there were some rather startling statistical changes in America. The economy had achieved an unparalleled period of rapid growth. The increase in gross na-

> The mass media molds everyone into more passive roles, into roles of more frantic consuming, into human beings with fragmented views of society. But what it does to everyone, it does to women even more. The traditional societal role for women is already a passive one, already one of a consumer, already one of an emotional nonintellectual who isn't supposed to think or act beyond the confines of her home. The mass media reinforce all these traits.
> —Alice Embree

tional product during the first eight years of that decade, measured in constant dollars, was greater than the entire GNP of 1938. To put it succinctly, in less than a decade, a second economy had been built as large as the national economy prior to World War II. At the same time, there was unprecedented spending by federal, state, and local governments on poverty-related programs. More families were moving out of poverty and at a faster rate than at any time in our nation's history.

Yet, if we looked at the projected images of our communication system, we saw unmitigated misery. There was widespread public concern that we had become a sick society. Spokesmen, from George Wallace on the right to the extremists of the left and a good many in between, found agreement in the slogan: "We never had it so bad." The picture we were seeing of ourselves led to growing despondency among many citizens over whether our society, as presently organized, can cure its ills.

I suggest that this, too, represents a failure of communication. It is, paradoxically, an opposite failure from my first example. During the late fifties, our communication media failed to serve us as an adequate early warning system for troubles already on the horizon. During the late sixties, the media failed to discriminate adequately among the troubles in our midst. Like a stuck alarm in a crowded theater, the jangling of the media threatened to stimulate either public panic or public apathy or both.

These are blanket and highly subjective indictments, I realize. They provoke impatient reactions from reporters and editors. So why blame the media for all the sins of society? What about the experts in and out of the universities? What about politicians who claim to represent the people? Haven't they contributed to the faulty picture of American society? The answer is that they certainly have. But our concern here is the media.

A more serious objection is that the mere statement of these inadequacies puts impossible demands on our communications media. Am I, to use Walter Lippmann's phrase, asking the reporter to serve as "the umpire in the unscored baseball game?" A half century ago, in his classic book *Public Opinion*, Walter Lippmann raised the question whether "news"—the product of the media—could ever be made to serve as the vehicle for communicating the "truth" about government or society. He reached a pessimistic conclusion. "If we assume . . . that news and truth are two words for the same thing, we shall, I believe, arrive nowhere," he wrote. The function of news, Lippmann pointed out, is "to signalize an event" whereas the function of truth is "to bring to light the hidden facts, to set them into relation with each other, and make a picture of reality on which men can act." Lippmann thus dismissed the communications media as the means to present an adequate picture of American society to the public. Instead, he advocated the creation of new institutions of "organized intelligence" which would serve as the purveyors of truth.

Looking at the situation fifty years later, I am inclined to doubt that the roles of news and truth can be that neatly divided. I do not believe that the leaders of the communications media wish to abdicate the task of bringing to light the hidden facts, setting them into relation with each other, and making a picture of reality on which men can act. That has been the main thrust of the best investigatory journalism.

There have been some noteworthy new organizations of intelligence since Lippmann wrote his book. The Council of Economic Advisors, the Bureau of Labor Statistics, and the Bureau of the Census supply vital and impartial statistics which have vastly improved the reporting on the nation's economy. Economic communications are no longer like umpiring an unscored baseball game. Similarly, a private institution such as Congressional Quarterly has provided better yardsticks for measuring and communicating an adequate picture of the legislative branch. Numerous other enterprises—the Drug Abuse Council, the Urban Institute, the Fair Campaign Practices Committee, etc.—have sprung up to provide organized intelligence on complicated problems of American society. They have helped to create a more adequate picture. Many of them have been subsidized by foundations. I sometimes wonder what would be the condition of our communications if the media were not aided by this particular form of philanthropy.

But I do not believe it is the job of government or philanthropy to take over completely the organizing of intelligence. Our communications media are not paupers. They can afford to do a larger share of the digging and the fitting together and the reporting in depth. I learned in my journalist days that the really important reporting is expensive in time and money. It is easier and much cheaper to play follow-the-leader journalism—to read the clipping files, think up a gimmicky new lead and practice armchair reporting. I watched a great deal of that variety while I was in the White House.

I marvel at the maldistribution of reportorial resources. Scores of reporters are dispatched to ride the candidate's campaign plane. Less than a handful give any systematic coverage to the education crisis in America which affects the lives of millions of children. Education and health appear to stand only slightly higher than religion as journalistic beats.

To organize intelligence and present a more adequate picture of reality is going to require initiative by those involved with communications. It is time for them to be more than at best grudging, at worst hostile recipients of other people's ideas about taking up new responsibilities in a new era. I will be impressed when I see leaders from the press and television media, individually or in association, approach the universities and research institutes on better ways to organize intelligence about our society. We know, for example, that economic indicators have only limited value in revealing the social condition. Why aren't the media leading the effort to develop a set of social indicators that will provide reporters with meaningful yardsticks?

We live in an era when all our traditional institutions are under attack. The Establishment is suspect. Old and private arrangements can no longer be easily defended. The credibility gap looms before all who exercise power in our society, not simply the politicians. Universities, foundations, churches—no institution has been exempt from searching reexamination by those who challenge the way our society works.

There is no reason why the institutions of the communications media should be exempt. They are crucially affected with the public interest. This does not call for government regulation in the manner of the public utilities. Far from it. But it does mean that there is a right of public review of how well the media are fulfilling their role.

Several ways occur to me for helping close the credibility gap and perhaps even improve media performance:

First, it is time for more public accounting of the problems of the media. How the news is managed has been kept in dark mystery even as the press strives to throw the fierce light of publicity on decision-making elsewhere. It would be refreshing, first of all, for the public to know that the collecting, processing, and distributing of news require judgments all along the line. Human judgments. It would be even more helpful to credibility if there were more frank discussions and mutual criticism of human error in the managing of news. For too long the communicators have operated according to Randolph Churchill's dictum that "Dog don't eat dog." When one of them commits folly, everyone else looks the other way.

One cannot expect self-criticism to be too rigorous. But there is no reason why the newspapers can't be sharply critical of television and television of the print media. And there is good reason to encourage more young men to follow the footsteps of A. J. Liebling and Ben Bagdikian as thoughtful critics of the media. Where are their successors?

A heartening prospect is the recent decision of the Twentieth Century Fund to take the lead in sponsoring a national Council on Press Responsibility and Press Freedom. Urged by a distinguished task force, including leading representatives of the media, such a Council can investigate grievances, urge higher news standards, and build better public understanding of the complexity of communications.

the relative credibility of media: most believable

television 51%	newspapers 20%	
Radio 8%	magazines 8%	Don't know/no answer 13%

The First Word

A second area of public accounting goes to the structure of communications. It is time for an institution looking at the system as a whole. How is the health of the media? Why are there so many exits and so few entrances to the newspaper business? Must one national magazine after another die without a public accounting for their failure? Should the tax laws allow conglomerates to bid for media properties with different kinds of dollars than individual entrepreneurs? How can we provide new incentives to maintain diversity in media ownership?

All these questions and others are worthy of serious inquiry. We need to know more how government impacts on the media with its ad hoc and random policies. A system's analysis, perhaps including an econometric media model, could in turn contribute to shaping sound public policy.

A non-governmental Institute for Communications Policy would not have a humble assignment. It might start from the bottom up by examining exactly what is the picture that reaches the citizen. Then it could proceed to define areas of organized intelligence which are missing in that picture that reaches the citizen. Then it could proceed to define areas of organized intelligence which are missing in that picture. And, finally, it would come to the question of what role the media might be expected to play—the existing media and possibly newly created media.

I don't believe we should jump to the conclusion that our existing media represent the last word in communications. There is room for innovation. Yardstick media such as public television should be given a fair and well-financed opportunity to prove their worth. Just as "Sesame Street" has demonstrated marvelous new techniques for stimulating preschoolers, there may be untried ways of reaching adults with a more adequate picture of the world beyond their immediate horizons.

It was my privilege to ride herd for the President on the legislation that created the Public Broadcasting Corporation. I believe it to be one of the more helpful initiatives in the communications field during the past few decades. But I am full of fears for public television. Hand-to-mouth appropriations as a means of financing it could lead to all sorts of hidden pressures that would destroy its integrity.

In making this suggestion for a new institution, I am well aware of the derisive greeting it will receive from many veterans in the communications field. I remember the abuse heaped on the Hutchins Commission nearly a quarter century ago. Reread this many years later, the Hutchins Report does not seem like such a radical document. Its main message was that the press could best maintain its freedom by becoming more accountable. Its most daring proposal was to create an agency, independent of government and of the press, to appraise and report annually upon the press.

The Hutchins Commission listed society's five expectations of the communications media:

1. A truthful, comprehensive and intelligent account of the day's events in a context which gives them meaning;
2. A forum for the exchange of comment and criticism;
3. The projection of a representative picture of the constituent groups in the society;
4. The presentation and clarification of the goals and values of the society;
5. Full access to the day's intelligence.

These are hardly a very startling set of expectations. It would be helpful if a new commission took a look to see whether we have moved closer or farther away from realizing them.

But the fact is that the communications business is often treated by its spokesmen as the last preserve of rugged individualism. Even as media have grown into vast corporate enterprises, its spokesmen keep up the pretense. The First Amendment is treated as an ironclad bar against probing into the adequacy of communications, even as the publishers pushed through an act of Congress exempting them from the Antitrust Act.

Let me be clear. When I argue that the communications media are affected with the public interest, I am not talking about the official government's interest. They do not belong within Spiro Agnew's interest. Indeed the media should probe more relentlessly into the significant business of government and hold public officials to stricter accounting on issues of public concern. A press with true grit would not docilely accept the decline of the Presidential press conference as a rigorous and regular institution for putting the Chief Executive on the spot. Government leaders must not be relieved of their obligation to help create the picture of reality on which men can act.

More threatening than the frontal confrontation between government and the media is the subtle blackmail which affects the flow of news without the public's awareness. Within the White House now exists an Office of Telecommunications Policy. A predictable bureaucratic effort to coordinate policymaking, it nonetheless heightens the danger of invisible pressures for caution and conformity by the media managers.

Concern for communications should not be left solely to government or the media. Others have a role to play in setting the goals, defining the problems, and keeping check on shortcomings. Freestanding institutions need to be created to maintain countervailing powers.

For we are dealing with the most critical function that holds a free society together—how it communicates. And the challenge in a society grown as big and vulnerable as ours is formidable. There is a story, perhaps apocryphal, that the dinosaur did not go out of existence because he was too big or too clumsy. What really happened was that his communication system did not create an adequate picture of reality on which the dinosaur could act. That story holds a lesson.

> Women in America occupy a special position in the American consumer economy; they are exploited in a particular way, just as their exploitation takes on a particular form in the society at large. In the technological economy, women are particularly alienated. Men, at least, are brought up to have some kind of working knowledge of the technological produce that surrounds them.... But, more important, men occupy the jobs that put them in touch with the assembly line and managerial work of the new technology. Women are traditionally brought up to know only the skills of the household. Cooking, sewing, cleaning are eighteenth- and nineteenth-century skills, not contemporary ones.... Women's roles are especially divorced from the overriding mythology of a highly technological America. Women are the neglected orphans of the technological age.
> —Alice Embree

MEDIA CONSUMPTION DIARY

More of our time is spent consuming media than any other major activity in our lives—with the exception of sleeping.

Can you account for, and justify, this expenditure of time as a necessary part of your life? Compare it to other major activities in your life. In the light of your personal goals and values in life, to what degree do your media usage patterns support or detract from achieving these goals and values?

The following media consumption diary can be used as an aid to assist you in determining your media consumption patterns. For a week log the amount of time you spend (in 15 minute units) consuming each medium listed in the column at the left. At the end of the week, total your consumption and compare your log with other class members.

	SUN	MON	TUES	WED
Newspapers				
Magazines				
Television				
Radio (home)				
Radio (car)				
Stereo				
Film				
Books (college or work assigned)				
Books (unassigned)				
Other Media				
Total Units				

THUR	FRI	SAT	(15 min. = 1 unit) UNITS

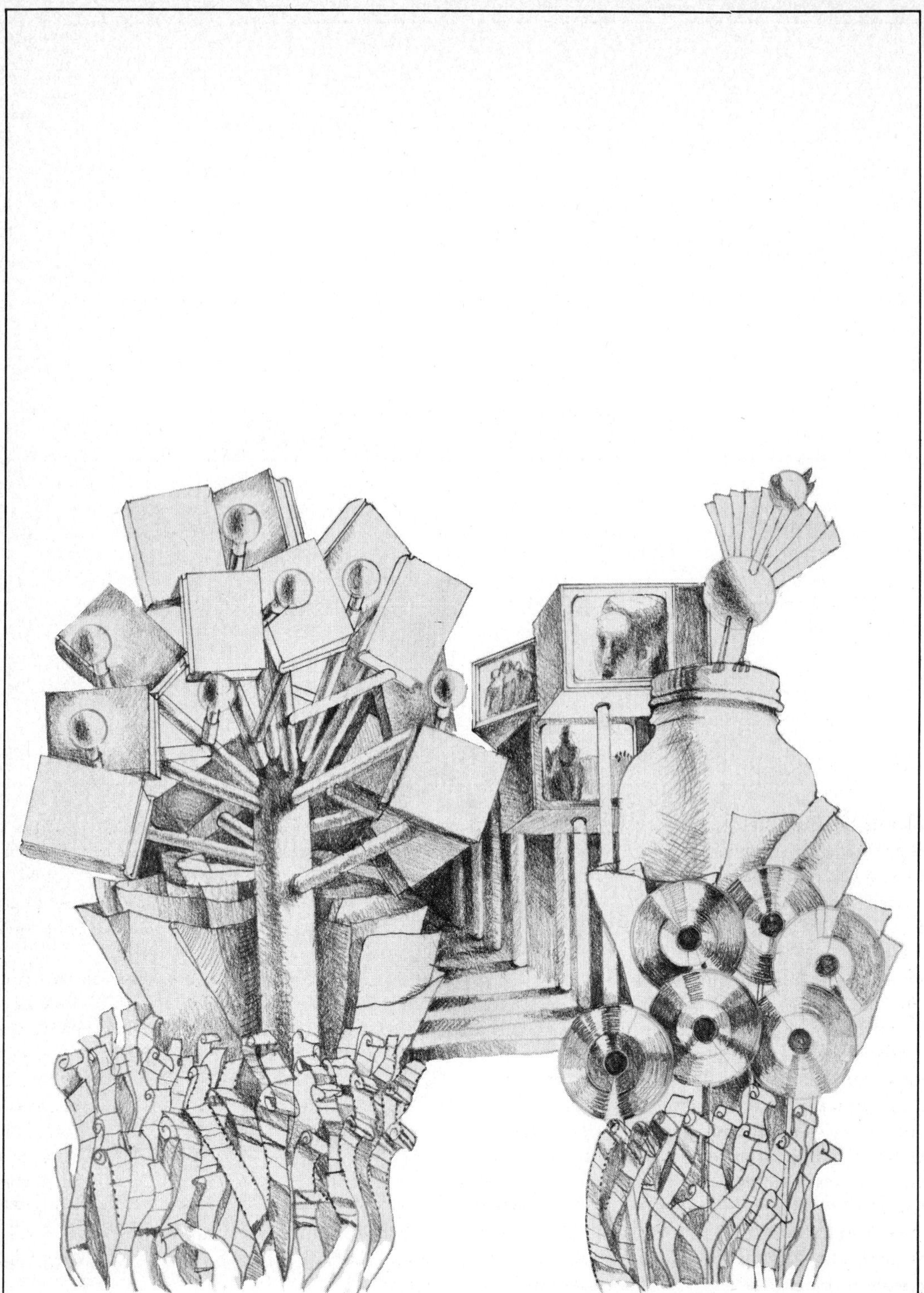

MEDIA FORMS

Media forms are systems through which people receive information. As you travel on the first leg of the journey through mass media's invisible environment, examine each form, noting its strengths and weaknesses, its biases and unique qualities. Consider clothing, comics, and graffiti as less massive and more personal systems of transmitting and receiving information. Reflect on the subtle, pervasive, and at times overwhelming flow of material, both informational and entertaining, that is directed at you—material designed to gain your attention, motivate you, and direct your activities. The media may provide a backdrop to your daily activities as music flows from jukeboxes, cars and home radios, stereo records and tape cassettes; or media may be in the foreground, demanding the time and attention required to digest print or television.

The process of transmitting and receiving information is continuous, and the effort expended may be as great as that required to operate a broadcast network or as limited as that needed to write on a wall. Whatever the medium, the information transmitted has been selected by an individual or institution that has programmed an interpretation into the message you receive.

Information flow is a much more complex process than the mere transportation of messages. It involves not only our eyes, ears, and minds but the totality of our human experience. In short, the way we receive a message is largely determined by the method or form through which it is sent. As you thread your way through the complexity of electronic and print media forms in this section, be aware that this very book and its method of presentation—words and images printed on paper—determine the effectiveness of its communication. What we know is shaped in part by how we learn it.

ELECTRONIC

HUMANISTIC CLAIM ON THE CABLE

RICHARD ADLER

The first community antenna television system was constructed in 1948, only a few years after the beginning of commercial television broadcasts in the United States. According to CATV lore, the builder of the first system was a small-town television dealer in Pennsylvania who wanted to provide better reception in his community so that he could sell more sets. From that modest beginning, CATV systems spread steadily over the next two decades in reception-poor areas, providing their subscribers with better quality signals and additional television channels.

Until recently, this growth attracted little public interest outside of the communities directly involved in CATV. Of late, however, cable has become the subject of considerable attention. One reason for this is simply the significant increase in the number of cable systems and subscribers. From the single small system in 1948, cable had grown by 1973 to more than 3000 systems serving some 7.5 million subscribers, or nearly 12 percent of all television households. In the next few years, cable systems are expected to increase by approximately 10 percent per year.

Another reason for the heightened interest in CATV is the recent technological developments which have broadened the capabilities of cable. Early systems could relay no more than five to seven channels of broadcast television. Modern systems can carry twenty-five to thirty channels per cable, and two-way communication via cable, although still not perfected, has been demonstrated in several experimental projects. The possibility of linking cable systems nationally via satellites is also under active investigation by the industry. These developments have suggested that cable may be the vehicle for bringing about yet another communications revolution in this century.* A great variety of innovative cable applications in education, health and other community services have been proposed, and these ideas have generated the hope that cable could become a means for increasing the dissemination of information and a new tool for dealing with social problems.

A final reason for interest in cable—and the one most pertinent here—is dissatisfaction with the quality and diversity of programming currently available on conventional broadcast television in this country. Commercial television is clearly an enormous financial success and has amassed audiences of unprecedented size. However, this success has been achieved primarily by ignoring the tastes and interests of many different minority segments of the population. The larger the audience, however minimal its attention or satisfaction, the more successful the commercial television program.

As the most successful and powerful of the media, television is a principal social resource. Its value and responsibilities must be judged by a more demanding standard than simple audience size. I would argue that a primary responsibility of television in a civilized society must be broadly educational. Inescapably, its function is nothing less than "the maintenance, extension and transmission of a culture."† The structure and content of such national systems as the British Broadcasting Corporation, the Canadian Broadcasting Corporation and Japan's NHK all manifest well-established commitments to these goals and responsibilities. By contrast, American commercial TV has either ignored or given only passing attention to them. In fact, as it has

---

From article entitled "The Humanistic Claim on the Cable" by Richard Adler in *The Electronic Box Office: Humanities and Arts on the Cable* by Richard Adler and Walter S. Baer. © 1974 by the Aspen Program on Communications and society. Excerpted and reprinted by permission of Praeger Publishers, Inc., New York.

*A number of studies deal with the non-broadcast services cable may offer. See, for example, Richard Adler and Walter S. Baer, *Aspen Notebook: Cable and Continuing Education* (Praeger, 1973); and the 1973 Rand Corporation reports on cable television, including Walter S. Baer, *A Handbook for Decisionmaking* (R-1133-NSF); Robert K. Yin, *Applications for Municipal Services* (R-1143-NSF); and Polly Carpenter, *Uses in Education* (R-1143-NSF).

†The phrase is from John Scupham, *Broadcasting and the Community* (D.A. Watts and Co., London, 1967).

grown and become more prosperous, American television has demonstrated ever-increasing reluctance to innovate, to experiment or to do anything that might disturb the loyalties of its vast audience. . . . It may be that the development of cable gives us a second, and perhaps the last chance to determine whether television will be used not merely to provide diversion or immediate information but to teach, to inspire, to enhance the quality of American life.

The task will be demanding and expensive, and it is not at all certain that such an enterprise can be financially self-supporting. It *is* certain that the cable industry itself cannot and will not meet this responsibility unaided. But before we consider cable's prospects for providing high quality programming, it will be useful to look more closely at the institution of television as it exists today.

THE PRESENT STATE OF AMERICAN TELEVISION

Whatever else may be said about television, the statistics of its omnipresence in American life are stunning. At least 97 percent of all American homes have television sets; over 60 percent now have color receivers. These households currently average over 40 hours of television usage each week, or over six hours per day. At the peak of prime-time viewing (around 9:30 p.m.) during the winter months, the television sets will be on in nearly 65 percent of all homes in the United States.*

Nearly 90 percent of those sets will be tuned to one of the three national networks, for "television" means the networks for the great majority of the population. Even the independent (non-network affiliated) "local" stations mainly offer syndicated re-runs of programs originally made for network showings. Cable television systems also exist largely because of the desire of people in remote areas for access to network programming. Canada became the most heavily cabled country in the world in order to import American network programming.

There are a number of things that network television can and does do extremely well. Network news has become a major force in American journalism and has profoundly altered our view of the world. Undoubtedly, television's great power has been its ability to "take us there"—to Moscow and Peking, to the streets of Chicago, to the funerals of dead leaders, to the drama in Congressional hearing rooms, even to the moon. Television has enabled us to become participants in history as it occurs. In addition, network television has also done a remarkable job in the coverage of sports events, perhaps the most sophisticated technical use of the medium.

Another area in which broadcast television has clearly demonstrated its potential as a humanistic medium has been the development of documentary programming. Television's dramatizations of historical events and personages (*The Andersonville Trial, Elizabeth R.*), interpretations of new developments in science and society (*60 Minutes, NET Journal*), and presentations of man's artistic and intellectual accomplishments (Sir Kenneth Clark's *Civilisation*, Alistair Cooke's *America*, Jacob Bronowski's *The Ascent of Man*) are all examples of how the medium can be used to "maintain, extend and transmit a culture."

Beyond these areas, however, the great bulk of television bears out all too well the new cliché image of a "vast wasteland." Although the medium does periodically offer programs of merit, its staple fare has become almost entirely light entertainment. Original drama has almost entirely disappeared; opera and dance are rare; serious music has been even more thoroughly excluded. Why? In attempting to account for the absence of artistically significant programming on television, commentators have offered two explanations: first, the aesthetic limitations of the medium and, second, the economic structure of the television industry. Both merit examination before we turn to cable's potential.

The aesthetic argument. Several critics have suggested that the nature of the medium itself is responsible for the failure of artistic and humanistic programming to attract large audiences. Martin Mayer, for example, claims that the environmental context in which television is watched restricts the degree of viewer involvement with its content.

---

*Broadcasting Yearbook 1973 (Broadcasting Publications, Inc.), p.12.

Watching television is an activity that excludes doing anything else than eating and knitting. The requisite minimum level of attention is fairly high. At the same time, unlike films or plays in a properly designed theater, television pictures do not absorb the peripheral vision; and it may be the attainable maximum level of attention is fairly low. At best, the spread between minimum and maximum is much reduced from that experienced in the use of other media.*

Mayer concludes that this is a serious but not insurmountable problem. To "overcome the homogenizing qualities of the medium," he contends, will require "a content so strongly different from normal programming that it probably can appeal only to minorities too small to carry the costs of production under an advertiser-supported system."

Other critics have cited the technical standards of television as destructive to the involvement of the audience in artistic and, particularly, musical works. The audio performance of most television receivers is especially poor—today's sets have a dynamic audio range far below that available on phonograph records or FM-radio broadcasts. Thus, symphony and opera performances on television may not satisfy even the most undemanding audiences under present technical conditions.

Upgrading audio reception on television by adding higher quality components and speakers to present receivers would be simple enough. "Simulcasting" of the audio portion of television programs on FM is even simpler. But improving another technical inadequacy—the visual quality of television—is not so easy. A number of technical schemes exist for increasing picture resolution and enhancing visual signal quality, but these innovations would require a new set of technical standards and a complete re-design of television receivers to accommodate high-resolution pictures. Cable has the frequency bandwidth to carry high-resolution television signals and still offers the opportunity—perhaps the only opportunity in this country—to develop a high-quality television service. However, current FCC rules for cable establish reception-quality standards so minimal that they fall well below the level for broadcast television in most communities.

Perhaps the most fundamental objection to television as a conveyor of the performing arts has been made by the English stage and film director Peter Hall. He contends that TV is simply unable to "capture the original experience" of a performance because it destroys the illusory nature of the stage. Hall explained his objections in responding to a proposal from television producer Humphrey Burton to carry opera performances from Covent Garden on the BBC:

When Humphrey Burton, who is a great man of television, says that this medium can nearly capture the original experience, I must listen to him. But I don't believe it. I have never seen it happen. I have always found that the unengaged and unimpressed eye of the camera betrays and finally ridicules the essential nature of the theatre and opera.

A piece of theater is not a physical act like a horse race, but an imaginative game agreed on between the performer and the audience. The camera finds difficulty in participating in this game unless it is itself the audience. If a good actor walks on to a bare rostrum and informs the audience with words of sufficient quality that they are in ancient Rome, they will believe him. An act of the imaginative has been provoked. But if a camera photographs this, it will reveal nothing but a bare rostrum, and the disappointing visual image can even make the words seem ludicrous. It is at this moment that we, as viewers, notice the ancient naiveté of the theatre and the "unreal" nature of its settings.*

In a report on cable and the arts, Richard Roud responds to the critics of television aesthetics, pointing out that television has its own requirements for successful presentation and that drama or opera for television must be produced with those requirements in mind. He grants that smaller, more intimate theater pieces may be most appropriate for the television screen and that a televised performance cannot fully capture the experience of live theater, but he argues that such loss is more than made up for by the greatly increased audience which would otherwise have no access to such experiences.†

---

*Martin Mayer, *About Television* (Harper and Row, 1972), p.394.

*Richard Roud, *Cable and the Arts* (Sloan Commission on Cable Communications, March 1971.)
†Roud, pp. 10-14.

Objections such as those of Martin Mayer or Peter Hall should be seriously considered, but it seems premature to write off television *per se* as an artistic medium. It is not particularly difficult to recall the occasional programs which have demonstrated television's dramatic power. The BBC's *Forsyte Saga*, for example, was a distinguished, if not very adventurous, drama which worked splendidly on television by adopting one of the medium's most humble genres, the soap opera. Its strength and wide appeal were based on the fact that it was not a movie nor a play but a literate, entertaining and well-done television production.

Following the success of this series, the BBC has gone on to adapt a succession of more demanding works: *Vanity Fair, Candide, Emma, Pere Goriot, A Room with a View, Nana,* and *The Golden Bowl*. Most impressive of all was the nine-part version of *War and Peace* shown in this country on public television in the fall of 1973. There has been wide critical agreement that the BBC version was artistically superior and more faithful to the original than the earlier film versions. The success of *War and Peace* suggests that the medium of television is better able than cinema to give sufficient time (the series runs for a total of 15 hours) to match the massive scale of such a work. And what is lost by not having the cinematic sweep of the wide screen can be more than made up by television's ability to focus on details and on the human interactions.

The past few years have also seen an energetic exploration of television as an art form in its own right. Some of the most advanced work of this kind is being carried out at experimental laboratories at Boston's WGBH and New York's WNET and at the National Center for Experiments in Television in San Francisco. These facilities are serving as places where artists—filmmakers, painters, writers, dancers and composers—can learn the unfamiliar technology of television and participate directly in the creation of video-taped works. Little of this work has been shown on broadcast television, and it is too early to judge whether the work of these centers will lead to anything more than an expanded range of optical and visual special effects for conventional television. However, their work so far suggests that the affective, aesthetic dimensions of television have only begun to be explored. . . .

The economic argument. There is a good deal of evidence to suggest that it is the economic structure of the broadcasting industry, rather than the nature of the medium itself, which is primarily responsible for the content of American television. The argument can be stated briefly. As has been frequently pointed out, the real customers of television are not the viewers but the corporate sponsors. The revenues of commercial television are based directly on the size of the audiences its programs attract. The producers of programming are concerned, therefore, not with whether their viewers are enlightened or stimulated or even fundamentally interested in what they see, but only with whether they can be kept watching week after week. Since it is the business of broadcasters to maximize revenues, there can be only a single criterion for evaluating the worth of a program:

> The function of the television program is to make the commercial break valuable. A good show is one that is important enough to the advertiser that he will pay a premium for the minute breaks within; a bad show is one that sells at distress prices. Accordingly, the system thrives on "The Beverly Hillbillies" and will not support a "Playhouse 90."*

It is easy, in retrospect, to overestimate the achievements of the "golden age" of the early days of television. But the fact remains that there was an abundance of original and quality drama on television, and drama seemed an area where the promise of television seemed brightest. Les Brown, currently television correspondent for the *New York Times*, notes that "It was the only time in the history of the medium that program priorities superseded all others." However, the reasons for this "golden age" had more to do with economic expediency than with idealism or cultural responsibility. Since television programming first originated from New York, the skills and talent of the theater world—playwrights, directors, stage actors—were most readily available. Even more important, as Brown points out, was the need to

---

*Les Brown, *Television: The Business Behind the Box* (Harcourt-Brace-Jovanovich, 1971), p. 66.

sell enough television sets to create a market for advertising:

> If there was an abundance of original and quality drama at the time ("Studio One," "Philco Playhouse," "Goodyear Playhouse," and later "Playhouse 90"), it was in large part because those shows tended to appeal to a wealthier and better-educated part of the public, the part best able to afford a television set in those years when the price of receivers was high.*

As the cost of television sets declined and affluence increased during the 1950s and 1960s, television ownership became nearly universal, and programming had to attract and hold a large portion of the entire American population to survive. This led inexorably to program schedules made up almost entirely of light entertainment. Television became the pre-eminent mass medium.

The significance of an advertiser-supported television system can be seen clearly in contrast with the well-financed, publicly supported systems of such countries as England and Japan. These systems have developed strong traditions of bringing humanistic programming to their populations. Japan's NHK system, for instance, operates a nationwide "educational" channel which devotes 18 percent of its time to cultural programming, as well as offering instruction ranging from foreign languages to violin lessons to college-level courses. A second, "general" channel allots fully one-third of its air time to cultural programming:

> The NHK spares no cost to bring first-class kabuki, noh and bunraku productions into millions of homes in prime time. It has its own 120-member symphony orchestra, the oldest and one of the finest in Japan. To introduce foreign culture, it regularly imports award-winning scholars for invitational lecture tours which are telecast and broadcast. These have included Ralph Bunche, Werner von Braun and John Kenneth Galbraith. In addition, the network sponsors, and televises, concert-hall events, such as the New York City Ballet Company.†

American public television has striven valiantly to provide an alternative to the banalities of most commercial offerings and to manifest a commitment to the medium as a cultural force. Unfortunately, the history of public television has been marked by persistent problems which have retarded its development: an uneasy relationship with its governmental sponsors, confusion over its mission and intended audience, and, above all, chronic under-financing. It is persuasive testimony for the value of an American public television system that despite the continuing problems of PBS and its affiliates, the system has managed to offer so much excellent programming. Certainly, with the means available to it, public television has been unable to fulfill the promise of the medium. But it has—more than any other single source in this country—demonstrated how great the promise of the medium is.

In light of public television's continuing difficulties and commercial television's twenty-five year history as a willing servant of big business and mass taste, it is logical to ask whether American television will ever be capable of fulfilling its promise as a humanistic medium. If its potential is to be realized, it will probably be necessary to look beyond the structural and economic limitations of broadcasting to that abundance of outlets which cable can provide. Cable, of course, offers no panaceas. It brings its own set of problems, and so far has given us only more of what we already have. However, it also presents important new opportunities for innovation which deserve to be explored.

THE PRESENT STATE OF CABLE TELEVISION

Looming in the background of all speculations about the potential of cable television has been the vision of a wired nation in which the cable is as ubiquitous as the telephone and as necessary a means of communication as the postal service. The development of cable technology, coupled with American entrepreneurial know-how, seemed about to provide us all with an abundance of remarkable and valuable social and economic services. The prestigious Sloan Commission generated some of this speculation in 1972 when it concluded that CATV promises to bring about yet another communications revolution whose "impact on society's most immediate needs might be enormous."* The commission's

---

*Brown, p.154.

†Sloan Commission on Cable Communications, *On the Cable: The Television of Abundance* (McGraw-Hill, 1971), p.4.

*Sloan Commission, p. 4.

Electronics 23

optimism was based in part on their belief that 40 to 60 percent of all American homes would be "on the cable" by 1980.

By 1974, however, it became clear that this enthusiasm about cable was somewhat premature. The high hopes have been considerably diminished by the impact of regulatory limitations, higher costs, difficulties in attracting urban subscribers, and other economic problems. Most cable industry representatives would now be cheered by assurances that cable would reach even half of the number of homes predicted by the Sloan Commission for the end of the decade. Moreover, even if cable were to grow as rapidly as its most enthusiastic supporters hope, there is no certainty that it will contribute significantly to the improvement of life in America.

Shortly after the appearance of the Sloan Commission report, Kas Kalba (who had worked on the commission staff) warned of uncritical acceptance of the vision of "cable systems which will be to network television what newsletters, community newspapers and specialty magazines are to *Life, Reader's Digest* or *Playboy*."*
The difficulty with this vision is that too often it obscures the conditions essential to its realization. Before considering the use of cable for programming in the humanities and arts, let us take a look at the realities of cable today and the manner in which it is likely to develop in the near future.

The FCC Rules. The FCC cable rules of March 1972 defined the regulatory context in which cable will have to grow. Although the rules were supposed to permit *measured* growth, the thrust of much of the regulation is clearly to protect the interests of commercial broadcasters. The introduction to the rules states unmistakably that it is the commission's basic objective "to get cable moving so that the public may receive its benefits, and to do so without jeopardizing the basic structure of over-the-air television."† To date, the rules have proved more successful in preserving the health of broadcast television than in moving cable forward.

---

*Kas Kalba, "The Cable Fable," *Yale Review of Law and Social Action* (Spring 1972), p.196.

†Federal Communications Commission, "Fourth Report and Order," *Federal Register* (February 12, 1972, Vol. 37, No. 10, Part II).

The principal areas of regulation in which these protectionist concerns appear are the limitations of the number of distant signals cable systems may carry and the so-called "exclusivity" provisions, which require cable operators to black out programs on imported stations that duplicate local programming. The effect of these regulations is to restrict substantially the major selling point for CATV in the past—the ability of cable systems to offer additional off-the-air programming not available to non-subscribers.

In other areas, the FCC has provided positive guidelines intended to motivate cable systems to offer more than clearer views of conventional broadcast programs. The guidelines require that all new systems in the 100 largest television markets have

- at least a 20-channel capacity;
- one channel reserved for non-broadcast use for each broadcast signal carried;
- three free channels—one for educational use, one for municipal government, and one for public access;
- channels available for lease at "non-discriminatory rates";
- a built-in two-way capacity, although actual two-way service is not now required.

The commission's rules also state that cable systems will be permitted to carry pay television—that is, programs provided for an additional charge beyond that for the basic cable service. However, a series of "anti-siphoning" provisions restrict the kinds of programming which may be offered on pay cable—particularly in regard to series programs and to movies and sports events now carried on broadcast television. . . .

Finally, in an earlier ruling, the commission had also required that all systems with more than 3500 subscribers must originate their own programming. However, the FCC is not now enforcing this requirement.

Other Problems in Cable Development. Federal regulation is only one factor which affects the growth of cable. There are also a number of political and economic obstacles which lie on the path between cable today and the "wired nation" of the future. They represent serious barriers which must be overcome if cable is to become a major force. Among these problems are the following:

24 Media Forms

1. *Cable's entry into the cities.* As we have noted, cable began developing, quite naturally, in the remote areas where off-the-air reception was poor or where few broadcast signals were available. As a rule, the nation's major population centers do not present these problems of poor reception or few channels, and therefore the cities are a difficult market for cable to enter. While cable is serving approximately 12 percent of all homes nationally, cable penetration in the largest urban centers is only slightly more than 2 percent. Urban cable systems also face the further problem of the very high costs of wiring the densely populated and developed cities.

2. *Financing cable growth.* Because of the twin problems of attracting urban subscribers and financing the development of urban systems, the future growth of cable is very likely to be slower and more costly than it has been in the past. The combined effects of inflation and of meeting the FCC design specifications have also caused sharp increases in the capital requirements for further cable expansion. As these costs continue to rise more quckly than new subscribers are added, the industry faces increased difficulties in obtaining financing to build new systems. And so long as the industry is short of funds, it will be difficult for it to undertake support of new programming, which is essential for attracting subscribers. The industry is already looking to the FCC for relief from this vicious cycle through a liberalization of the cable rules, particularly the commission's restrictions on the use of movies and sports for pay programming.

3. *Developing new services and programming.* A shortage of funds within the industry is not the only barrier to the development of new cable programming. As described earlier, the growth of cable in the past has been based on the construction of systems designed to improve broadcast-television reception. The industry as a whole has had little experience as producers and distributors of original programming and knows surprisingly little about such a basic matter as what kinds of new programming will attract a significant audience. Moreover, because cable represents a completely new medium for program distribution, a large number of questions about legal and copyright arrangements and union agreements remain to be worked out.

Although original cable production is not now an important source of revenue, it may be in

> Television is one of the strongest industries in this country. It has forgotten about audiences. It laughs at all those stupid dopes out there—unsophisticated, gullible, unfulfilled. It laughs all the way to the bank with your money. The point is who is allowed to have the last laugh.
> —Sheila Smith Hobson

time, and arrangements which are made now will set precedents for the future. Arriving at workable agreements with copyright owners, program producers, performing artists and other unionized personnel will continue to be difficult until there is greater certainty about the ultimate scope of the cable marketplace.

4. *Problems of local regulation and control.* While cable has become an issue of national concern, the FCC rules leave the franchising power in local hands, so that the granting of franchises and the enforcement of their provisions remain largely the responsibility of municipal governments. Cable is regarded by most municipal officials mainly as a potential source of additional revenue and, therefore, as a political issue. Few are equipped to deal with the social and cultural implications of a new communications system. And, certainly, they should not be concerned with the content, *per se*, of cable programming. Yet their decisions bear directly on the uses and future development of cable.

5. *Assuring access to cable systems.* In its first 20 years, cable television was a highly fragmented business of many small, independent system owners. Today, growing financial and managerial demands on the industry have led to substantial consolidation under multiple-system operators (MSO's). Although slowed by recent Justice Department anti-trust actions, the merger trend is likely to continue and to lead to the emergence of a few cable MSO's who will dominate the industry. The cable systems in the major cities—each requiring a capital investment of tens of millions of dollars—will very probably be controlled by the largest MSO's.

Concentration of cable ownership in a few

hands creates the obvious problems of the control by a small number of people over programming and access. On the other hand, the large MSO's may provide regional and national markets for high quality programming that otherwise would be very difficult to amass. The degree to which cable system operators will be permitted to control both the sources of programming and the means of distribution is an issue that will receive increased attention in the next few years.

A major new element in the debate over control was added in January 1974, with the release of a report to the President from a special Cabinet committee on cable.* Several years in preparation, the report recommends that ownership of cable systems and control over programming be separated. Cable, as envisioned by the committee, would ultimately become a partial common carrier† obliged to lease channels at standard rates. With the threat of monopoly control diminished, access to cable for all potential programmers would be encouraged, and the need for regulation of content should be minimal. However, the report also recommends that these changes not be implemented until cable reaches half of all American homes—which is unlikely to happen for a number of years.

To sum up this overview of the present cable situation:

1. Cable systems will continue to grow and develop, although probably at a slower rate than predicted a few years ago.

2. Cable today remains essentially a reception service. To date, it has added little of substance to the diversity (or lack of it) offered by broadcast television.

3. The cable industry alone will be financially and artistically unable to exploit the full capabilities of cable. Its ultimate success may depend heavily on the degree to which it is willing and able to work cooperatively with others who are interested in using the distribution channels cable can provide.

---

*The Cabinet Committee on Cable Communications, *Cable: Report to the President* (Office of Telecommunications Policy, 1974).

†The Cabinet committee report recommends that cable operators be allowed to continue providing programming on one or two channels.

TV DEBASES EVERYTHING IT TOUCHES – AND TV TOUCHES EVERYTHING

HARRY SKORNIA

Harry Skornia, well-known analyst and critic of broadcasting, reviews the numerous facets of American society that are subject to the pervasive and often negative influences of television. His arguments, conclusions, and recommendations are striking and controversial and should receive close scrutiny by persons seeking to understand the forces that shape our society.

We are being told through the media today that we are headed toward another great depression. In fact, it is a double depression: partly economic and partly spiritual. To the degree that the leaders of the broadcast media serve as the gatekeepers of reality (every survey shows that at least 60 percent of the people in America today get most of their "news" from television), the impact of television on our ability as a democratic society to define problems, perceive options, and choose solutions is critical.

I came through the Great Depression of 1929, losing everything I'd saved to get an education in a bank that failed. I fear that in the next depression, which may not be far off, the hungry and oppressed will never again line up meekly for handouts and relief checks. For twenty years, television has shown Americans how to loot, burn, kill, and burglarize.

TV has produced the gospel of Consumerism, fanned the flames of the revolution of rising expectations, dulled our senses with repetition, turned a nation of viewers into zombies who expect to be entertained in everything, who see

---

Reprinted by permission of Chicago Journalism Review and Dr. Harry J. Skornia.

17A

JOSEPH RUZICKA-SOUTH, INC.
911 Northridge Street　　Greensboro, N. C. 27420

Instructions by:	Phone No.:	Date Sent to Binder
Durham T. I.	598-9368	2/28/86

ALL INSTRUCTIONS ON BINDING TICKET WILL BE FOLLOWED EXPLICITLY

LETTER SPINE EXACTLY AS FOLLOWS:

Title:

Mass media: the invisible environment revisted

Vol.:

45758   22

Year

Call No.:

P92
U5G55
1976
c.3

INSTRUCTIONS TO BINDER

___ Bind as is (with covers & ads)
___ Remove front covers
___ Remove back covers
___ Remove ads (front & back)
___ Remove all ads (extra charge)
___ Bind title page/contents in front
___ Bind index in front
___ Bind index in back
___ Hand sew if necessary (extra charge)
_____ Cover Color
Letter in: ___gold; ___black; ___white

LIBRARY BOOKS:
___Decorated covers; ___plain covers;
___picture covers (extra charge)

SUPER-FLEX (economy binding) Uniform height, white lettering. Covers & ads bound in. Cover color for **periodicals only** _____
Books & Paperbacks — cloth colors random selected by binder; binder's choice of black or white lettering.
Paperbacks: ___Mount front cover; ___Bind in covers; ___Discard covers.

Special Instructions:

Send two copies of binding slip with volume; retain one copy for your files. If item returned for correction because of binder's error, original binding slip **must be** returned with volume.

BINDERY COPY

force and violence exalted over reason as the means of resolving conflict, whose capacity to believe and trust has been impaired by disingenuous commerciality.

TV has told us "you deserve the best," "pamper yourself," "spoil yourself," "help yourself to the good things of life," "get yours."

In a Latin American city, with Frankensteinian justice, an enraged populace a few years ago burned down a broadcast station which played them for fools with a repeat of "Invasion from Mars." There may be ugly, tragic days ahead for America, made far more dangerous as a result of television's last twenty years of "lessons" in violence—among other things.

Television, as it exists today, has played a key role in producing a spiritual depression in our nation—a depression which I fear may have seriously eroded our ability to respond creatively to the economic depression on the horizon.

This isn't a very pleasant period for an American to attend international radio and television conferences, as I frequently do.

The chief source of embarrassment is the low estate to which U.S. commercial television has fallen abroad. Nation after nation is erecting barriers (they call them quotas) to U.S. programs because of violence and other ingredients. Nations that a few years ago declared they were going "the American way" and planning commercial television now add "but not the way it's done in the U.S." We are now the ghastly example of "how not to do it"!

Most new commercial systems follow the Italian or West German examples in which the only commercials are those grouped in usually five-to-twenty minute periods, not more than four or five times a day, with no commercials *within* any programs, *between* any programs, or at any time other than during the allocated periods. No "sponsoring" is permitted, and spots are rotated among the various commercial time slots. With such a "civilized" approach, television commercials—which are never repeated more than a small, specific number of times—are *not* resented. Since you can take them or leave them, these periods are in fact often among the highest rated in listenership. TV advertising can be a welcome, pleasant service instead of the interruptive, intrusive, repetitive irritation it is in the U.S.

Finally, there are the decisions of the juries of two of the principal world television awards, the Prix Italia and Japan Prize. Though Britain won several, and there are Australian, Iron Curtain, Canadian, African, Latin American, and two U.S. awards, the only U.S. winners were "The Electric Company" and "Carrascolendas" (a Texas Latin American production), both public television programs. U.S. commercial winners are rarer and rarer these days, even though our system is the richest in the world.

Since many of U.S. commercial television's top-rated programs are borrowed from other nations (*All in the Family* is a copy of the BBC's *Till Death Us Do Part*, *Sanford and Son* comes from *Steptoe and Son*, and so on), it is of course understandable why most of them are not even entered in foreign competition.

Although violence is one of the principal characteristics of U.S. programs which causes foreign broadcasters to avoid them (and this violence will be discussed more fully later), a more subtle value system also disturbs them. American television, like Watergate, seems to teach: "The end justifies the means. Get *yours* while you can. To hell with sportsmanship. Winning is everything. Nice guys finish last. Money, power, and products are everything. Lying is often justified. Christian (or Jewish or Buddhist or Mohammedan) ideas of morality, ethics, fairness, and humanity are now out of date and impractical."

Many nations do not agree. Hence the disenchantment and the increasing "Yankee Go Home" signs, often aimed at our TV programs, our films, and our values as well as at our bombers and soldiers. This is a great change for those of us who recall the open-armed genuine welcome and love for Americans of not too long ago, when we lived in France, Germany, and Austria.

Many of the objections listed above are of course valid in the U.S. as well. However, all too few people realize that this way is not necessarily the way things have to be. I have devoted much of my life to building an awareness of what individuals can do to bring about desirable change. Let's look at a few of those problems at home, and then see if we can't do something about those aspects of U.S. television which must be changed.

TURNING WATERGATE INTO PROFITS

If you've been trying to keep up on the news by watching more TV lately, but enjoying it less, here is part of the story.

It was, as you know, the free press of America which finally exposed the Watergate scandal. No wonder the entire national press system of the U.S. is in a state of euphoria.

Perhaps the most self-congratulation heard is that from the broadcast industry, although, unless I missed some major revelation by TV or radio, it was *not* TV or radio which rescued us from police-state arrogance. It appears to have been the print media which dug out the facts and published them. TV merely quoted them.

Ironically, it is the broadcast media which are profiting most. While Canadian newsprint was in increasingly short supply, newspapers and magazines had to cut down on their press runs and number of pages. This meant a great reduction in advertising and in profits. (It is to the credit of papers like the Chicago *Daily News* that they *did* cut *advertising* most, rather than *news* as some more selfish papers in the U.S. have done.)

But television stations suffered no such fate. Here was a bonanza for them. Since TV keeps reminding us it is part of the great U.S. free press, you wouldn't think of suspecting it of anything, would you, or watching it too closely in this tragic period in our history? Well, while we have had our eyes half closed in thanksgiving for a free press and good guys to save us, television has "shafted" us.

Where a year ago there was already a deadening barrage of commercials, their number has now been virtually doubled so they can make hay while the print media can't compete. Where there were five or six commercials in a row a year ago (already far too many), there are now often nine or ten in a row with no program to intervene. As one of our more expert monitors, Sharon Zurek, observed after monitoring and logging program segments and commercials on all three network stations: "Between 10:52 and 11:02 the Johnny Carson show averages approximately ten commercials in a row, broken up only by a short pause in which a card is held up to remind the television audience that they really *are* watching the *Tonight Show*, and not some brand-new program called *The Commercial Marathon* or an updated version of *Can You Top This* by the advertising industry."

Another cluster of commercials (though you're never far from five or six of them) occurs between 11:25 and 11:35 pm, and again around midnight. If you "hang on," as they urge you to, all you get is a "We're out of time, goodnight," in most cases. "As for the night movies," Miss Zurek concludes, "it will have to be an epic film if I am expected to sit back and watch an extra 10 or 15 minutes of commercials just to see the end of a movie. CBS averaged nine commercials in a row during each break. That's correct: *nine!*"

I personally have timed CBS from midnight to 12:30, and found four minutes of mangled movie and credits, four minutes of fragmented and interrupted news, and 20 to 22 minutes of commercials and "promos" in this half-hour.

No wonder they only rarely and shamefacedly show the window-dressing TV Code symbol. Weasel-worded as the Code is, they still violate it. Many self-respecting stations, like the Westinghouse group of TV stations, have withdrawn from the Code because the hypocrisy of it turns even their stomachs.

Network stations that were making only a 100 percent profit a year ago have doubled their own profits. Lacking any restraint on their greed, the money machine is racing out of control. All the pent-up latent greed of TV leadership is being manifested in this rape of the goodwill of loyal listeners. How do you like it?

Each year for over twenty-five years I have assigned students to monitor various types of programs, jotting down each commercial and segment of a program with approximate timing. Several thousand present and former students are now doing this. Their figures and mine are stopwatch figures, not unfair accusations or even "estimates," as the Nielsen ratings must legally admit to being in view of the small "sample" they use to reveal the "tastes" of the nation.

But don't take our word for these figures. Even with a sweep-second-hand electric clock or wristwatch, you can see for yourself what is happening.

As you begin your monitoring I urge you to start with a soap opera, football game, or news program and work up to the late-night talk shows and movies. Otherwise you'll find the commercials coming too fast and continuously for you to count and record them.

If you watch closely, you'll see commercials packed in so close to each other that they tread on each other's heels and clip each other's words. Time is money, Man! Or you'll hear a news clip cut into, with the first portion clipped so badly you don't know what it's about.

Since the public are too disoriented, unorganized, and groggy to know when they're being "screwed," there is no longer any hesitancy by TV networks to mangle their own products if this results in more money.

TV LEADERSHIP:
SOME DISTURBING EXAMPLES

In many of the most advanced countries in the world, the leadership of broadcasting is in the hands of intellectuals, educators, philosophers, religious leaders, and the like. In several countries, like West Germany, where I had the honor of helping design the national system after the war, all the various components of society (religion, labor, agriculture, business, education on various levels, and so on) are represented equally, with the Federal Government completely excluded. Not so in the U.S. Here broadcasting is a business, in the hands of advertisers and salesmen, with the other groups treated as outsiders.

TV is, and should be, so much more. TV leaders may not intend to, but they are teaching the nation what are acceptable behavior patterns, fashions, and values. Where money and power are their principal goals and lessons, the public interest suffers. Let us look at two case histories in which the integrity and sense of responsibility of TV leadership have been challenged to see how our TV leadership has measured up. We shall then survey more briefly additional characteristics of U.S. commercial TV under present management and policies. In many cases a strange resemblance will be noted between TV administration and the U.S. executive branch of government.

THE SURGEON GENERAL'S STUDY
ON TELEVISION AND SOCIAL BEHAVIOR

In 1969 a Surgeon General's committee was appointed to investigate the possible harmful or dangerous effects of TV violence in causing crime, delinquency, and other social problems.

This committee was to be similar to that which had reported earlier on the connection between cigarette smoking and lung cancer and heart attacks.

A strange thing happened in the choice of this *later* committee, however, a tribute to the power of the TV networks and industry to control even who would be allowed to serve on the committee. For some reason, the then Surgeon General submitted the names of the forty distinguished researchers proposed to the three networks and the National Association of Broadcasters, inquiring "whether the industry felt that any of the scientists had already determined that there was a link between televised violence and subsequent anti-social behavior." Two of the networks and the NAB vetoed seven of them—the ones who had in most cases done research on this problem. And on the final committee itself, of twelve scientists, the networks and the NAB managed to get "two industry representatives, one former industry employee, and two consultants to one of the networks." This was the equivalent, for a cancer committee, of blackballing the scientists who were expert in the problem and stacking the committee with cigarette and network people, thereby turning the whole project into a whitewash. That is what happened.

By 1970 a protest arose among research scholars and critics, including myself. However, the appointments stood and the study was published.

It should come as no surprise that the press release issued by the committee resulted in headlines such as "TV CONTRIBUTES LITTLE TO VIOLENCE IN SOCIETY, U.S. STUDY SAYS." In addition to rigging the committee, industry employees and friends rigged the press release.

This scandalous procedure finally caused Senator John Pastore, who had been the one to call for the study in the first place, to hold four days of hearings in March 1972 in which most of the blackballed scientists (Bandura, Berkowitz, Eisenberg, Garry, Larsen, and Tannenbaum) were heard. Also heard were the three network presidents, two spokesmen for the Federal Communications Commission, and spokeswomen for such groups as Action for Children's Television.

As the hearings got started, it was obvious that a great cover-up of the now-proven fact that there is abundant evidence that TV violence is indeed dangerous to our nation was being exposed. TV's own Watergate was being uncovered.

Dr. Leo Bagart, vice-president of the American Newspaper Publishers Association, himself a distinguished ad-agency researcher and hardly anti-business, declared: "The idea that an industry should not only be represented directly in a scholarly inquiry into its activities, but also exercise a veto over the membership of the investigating panel, is too stupid and scandalous to escape commentary."

Though the rigged press release (which is all most Americans have heard about the study to this day) was reassuring, the testimony was not.

At the hearings themselves, the Surgeon General declared, on the record: "Certainly my interpretation is that there is a causative relationship between televised violence and subsequent anti-social behavior, and that the evidence is strong enough that it requires some action on the part of responsible authorities, the TV industry, the Government, the citizens. . . . There comes a time when the data are sufficient to justify action. That time has come."

The whitewash report and press release were being exposed before our very eyes in these hearings. However, you have never seen—and probably never will see—these hearings on network TV. When it is television's scandals that are being exposed, the hearings are not broadcast. The cameras were there. You could see them. Senator Pastore declared at one point "I want to say the news media have been very generous in this matter. I hope we have accomplished something." Little did he know that the videotapes made by the networks would never see the light of day. Network chiefs and their hired "researchers" continue to this day to declare that "no connection has been proved," and continue to program scores of hours of violence (see "Kojak," "Cannon," "Mannix," "Barnaby Jones," "Hawaii Five-O," and so on).

Fortunately a camera of the Canadian Film Board was also at these hearings. Much of the U.S.'s TV violence is broadcast across the border to them, and they are concerned. Determined to defeat the efforts of the networks to "bury" this story (only one of hundreds like it), I personally sent out a mailing promoting the showing of this Canadian film to a few hundred colleagues and institutions to break the stranglehold effort of the networks to bottle it up. It has now been shown widely on the East and West Coasts, along the Gulf Coast, and in the Chicago area. But not on television.

I personally offered the film six months ago to WTTW Chicago's public television station. Perhaps they needed the "goodwill" of the network stations for fund-raising too much to dare to show it. In any case, they never did.

In the film are appearances by the three network presidents. They do not show up to particularly good advantage, which may be an additional reason for the networks' decision not to carry *these* significant Senate hearings, some of the most crucial of recent years. Over a year after their appearance—and promises to be more responsible—I invite you to determine for yourself whether violence on TV has been significantly reduced. (Not until this year have I personally become so super-saturated with violence that I become physically ill and have to turn such programs off.)

Also on the film is Commissioner Nicholas Johnson of the FCC. He was disowned by the FCC's Chairman Dean Burch and "dressed down" by Senator Baker (later of Watergate Committee fame). Under sharp questioning, Johnson declared to Senator Baker: "I feel, Senator, after I have been here for over five and a half years and witnessed what this industry has done, that there are no words that would be too strong to describe the outrage that you ought to feel, as I do, over what these gentlemen are doing, and what they are failing to do, with the responsibilities that we have given them as government, to serve in the public interest." I hereby endorse that statement.

These, then, are two of the most revealing and disturbing case histories of recent television leadership. But these are only the most scandalous. Let us look at a few other performance records which also raise some questions.

DRUG PUSHER TO THE NATION

Visitors to our shores are often aghast at the drug, medication, and nostrum advertising on

30   Media Forms

TV. Medicine men in their worst pitchman excesses never matched this. It's pretty hard to prove what a mature and advanced nation we are, and how sound we are, when quack nostrums and pitchmen including all sorts of news, entertainment, and sports individuals willing to prostitute their talents for money fill the air. Are we as sick as TV indicates in its millions of commercials?

Better-qualified specialists than I (doctors, psychiatrists, criminologists) have accused TV of a large share of the blame in developing the belief that pills are the answer to nearly every problem, and thereby developing a drug problem in the U.S.

As one of the most flagrant of the many examples we could discuss here, let us look at the advertising for aspirin and aspirin-related products. In spite of repeated warnings, the dangers of this drug to many people are well known. It is a disgrace that there is no warning on the label, or in advertising. Low platelet conditions (that is, low coagulation or clotting factors, and hence danger of bleeding to death) are multiplying in number and intensity. Yet the orgy of aspirin pushing goes on.

TV's tolerance for the ridiculous claims and counter-claims of aspirin (versus Bayer aspirin) versus Anacin, versus Bufferin, versus all the others is of course already inexcusable tolerance of the deliberate confusing of the consumer, because it is profitable. Bayer proves its superiority by its own tests. Or states that aspirin alone is as good as combinations (such as Anacin). Then why does Bayer manufacture such combinations (Vanquish, Cope)? What kind of an industry will tolerate such lies?

The FTC (Federal Trade Commission), of course, supposedly bans advertising "which is misleading in a material respect . . . or fails to reveal facts material to the *consequences* which may result." What are the likely consequences of pushing drugs on America simply because it means billions of profits to TV? Or of showing, in a TV ad, a mother with a child in one arm and a corrosive toilet-bowl cleaner in her hand, a few inches away from her child's eyes or prying hands? No wonder there are household accidents in which children are poisoned and blinded.

How long will TV continue to push, as an over-the-counter all-purpose cure-all, a product which is in effect a deadly poison to many people? Until we stop it—with laws! For there is no practice that TV seems *ever* to have stopped (cigarette advertising being the most conspicuous) as long as it was profitable. It has always taken a law. No wonder TV presses daily for more freedom from laws and regulation.

TV'S ROLE IN MALNUTRITION

Closely related to TV's record in drug advertising is its role in pushing on the nation soft drinks, sugared cereals, potato chips, pizza, and other snack foods which are enemies of adequate nutrition unless balanced by an adequate diet. How can our educational system be effective in the face of the drowning out it receives from the mass media?

One of the greatest causes of inadequate nutrition, as well as of high incidence of dental caries and predisposition to diabetes and obesity, is the profit TV makes out of the products you see most advertised on TV.

Judge for yourself, from food and beverage commercials on TV, what your diet should be. Is it any wonder that malnutrition is higher in the U.S., as found in draft and health-care figures, than in nearly any other developed country? Has TV leadership no shame in its greed? Will it push any product or practice which is profitable, regardless of the danger to human beings, our environment, or our enlightenment? Let us look at an even more disgraceful illustration which seems to indicate that the answer is yes.

MOCKING THE ENERGY CRISIS

TV tells us how it is helping in the energy crisis. Yet there seem to have been few documentaries on this problem in the years since 1969, when informed authorities—and some of the print media—warned us of the coming crisis and begged for TV time to warn the nation. Instead TV seems to have intensified that crisis, and is still doing so today.

In programs and spots TV and radio harangue us to "dial down," resign ourselves to lower temperatures, and so on.

For every program urging us to turn off lights, slow down, and save energy, TV shamefully pushes on the nation the most sinfully energy-wasting devices you can imagine. I invite you to check instances of this for yourself. How compatible with America's survival in the energy crisis are TV's present practices? Greed will apparently cause TV to cancel with spot announcements what it preaches with programs.

Here are a few examples in only one product line which I have chosen from the many available. Lady Shick's Time Machine Hair Dryer is really fast. It should be. Its capacity is 1400 watts—the same as 14 hundred-watt bulbs. And TV tells you to turn off these little bulbs.

Of course there are also Mist-Stylers, Styler-Dryers, Porta-Quick Dryers, Mist Hairsetters, Create-A-Curl Dryers, Hugger Hair Dryers, Gillette's Super Max, Clairol's Steam Hair Dryers, the Sunbeam Mist-Stick Curler-Styler being pushed by Billie Jean King (demonstrating the value of athletics to daily life), and any of the twenty other varieties. Enough such devices are being pushed to increase our energy consumption greatly. "There really isn't a crisis," TV tells you with these commercials.

There are now perhaps a million high-wattage hair dryers in America—mostly in beauty shops. According to television, there should be one in every home! And, in case the *women* won't buy enough, ads push them for men's use too, along with other high-energy users like Hot Lather Makers. And to make sure the dryers are used *often*, women are now urged by TV (in commercials like those devoted to Johnson's Baby Shampoo) to shampoo *daily*. These companies' profits—and the mass media's—are more important than our energy crisis, it seems. What a mockery and hypocrisy!

More importantly: what an example of corporate irresponsibility (including TV's) when it conflicts with the national interest!

TV ABDICATION TO ADVERTISING: THE NAME OF THE GAME

In many countries I find the advertising to be some of the finest material on the screen—that is where it is grouped in blocks, where repetition is strictly limited, and where it does not fragment, interrupt, or trivialize programming.

If newspapers and magazines had abdicated to advertising, working it into the "program" content, you would today have news and feature stories in which six or seven lines would be the story... then, without a change of type, a plug of a line or two for one or more products... then a continuation of the story. That is how intrusive radio and television ads have become, while *newspapers and magazines have kept advertising separate*—out of the content, where you can skip it.

To use another analogy: If the owner-managers just turned parks and playgrounds over to the people using them, there would be widespread violence and dope peddling. A few bullies would run the show, and the whole tenor of the place would be set by the lowest, least responsible elements. That is what TV and radio management have allowed to happen, and their media are a jungle of deceit, shouting and screaming, and other unsavory practices.

Advertising is a great profession. The fact that nowhere else—in no other country or medium—is it in the disfavor it's in in broadcasting,—is not the advertisers' fault. It is the fault of TV and radio big business—where Ed Murrow long ago placed the responsibility. Where TV leadership should have set and maintained high standards, it sold out. It abdicated, not to advertising in general, but to the lowest type of advertising.

As it is, in both broadcasting and advertising, the most unscrupulous, dishonest, and greedy have been allowed to set the tone. No wonder we're a worldwide disgrace of greed, violence, materialistic values, dishonesty, and pitchmen.

One last analogy—and some of you aren't going to like this. I invite better analogies, but for now must go with this:

To me it seems that TV network and station management has become merely a kind of panderer. If you're an advertiser, you pay your money and management lets you directly at its viewers, to "work them over" again and again and again. The prostitute knows what the panderer is up to. But TV has told *us* that it is our friend, shielding us against bad old government, the nasty critics, and pay TV, which would take away your "free" (that's a laugh) programs. You, the viewer, have been wheedled into trusting TV. So you agree and nod, and suddenly "whammo"—you've been had, right up to the hilt.

I don't like this analogy. It's indelicate. But how would *you* describe an industry management that turns its loyal supporters, its people, over to the manhandling of pitchmen, poison peddlers, and pushers of drugs, soft drinks, and other items to get you hooked on, because product producers—friends of the boss—are making him rich?

A usual defense of the industry, when accused of over-commercialization and a too-long succession of commercials, is to say "Yes, but look at the time. It was only five minutes of commercials."

My reply: How long does a rape take? How long does it take an "expert" bully to beat up a victim? How many rapists need to jump on you before you're exhausted, even if the time is only ten minutes in a half-hour?

It's the intensity, the hundred-fold repetition, the inability to avoid it, the friendly, hypocritical guise in which the "villain" visits you in your own home—where you should set the tone—that makes the present system so outrageous.

Let's look at a few more of the several scores of consequences of this abdication of leadership to the most obnoxious product pushers.

THE ULTIMATE CONTEMPT: TURN IT OFF IF YOU DON'T LIKE IT

The usual answer to people who object to TV excesses is to turn the program or set off if you don't like it. Since the average viewer has several thousand dollars invested in TV, this reply is nothing but insolent. Suppose a car dealer told you to just "park it" if you don't like its performance? Who is paying for this medium?

Most TV fare is an insult to the national intelligence. What sly satisfaction the managers of the media must feel at keeping people, who might be doing great and educational or spiritual things, digging for clues or engaging like idiots in other childish, petty activities needed to win on cheap TV game shows.

Or what contempt to say it's the parents' fault if children's viewing is not supervised adequately. How can parents know, or have standards? Twenty years ago we appealed to the industry to help set up courses in discrimination standards for viewing. The media sabotaged this. Present parents might now be qualified. Keep the parents ignorant, and then blame *them*—that's the way TV serves the public interest.

Even the auto industry helped finance driver-training courses to help the public "manage" the tools they foster. What, except to obstruct such an effort, has TV done?

The Ratio of the Unwanted to the Wanted. This is the crux of a serious problem today. To illustrate: If you wish entertainment you must first tolerate commercials; if you wish news or weather you must tolerate sports; if you wish world news you must first listen to the descriptions of accidents, crimes, and scandals. No wonder the frustration level of American citizens has risen so high as to result in irrational acts which result only from fury or resentment. Adlai Stevenson II once siad, "The media more and more separate the wheat from the chaff—then broadcast the chaff." The ratio of this irritating chaff to what we should know, or even wish to know, has now passed into the danger zone. Our mental health is in danger and our minds are dulled beyond belief....

Permissiveness. Not only is TV a drug pusher, a pusher of millions of tons and gallons of nutritionless food and beverages, and a pusher of energy-wasting gadgets, but it is a pusher of discontent, whetting appetites for things that the poor often cannot afford, and that many people should not have for their own good.

For some reason TV feels that "freedom of the press" should give it the right to engage in whatever non-press freedoms it likes, in its ignorance shaking society to its roots—as if it had some sacred right to destroy human motivation for higher values.

Consumerism. American broadcasting's financial life blood is consumerism. This has become the burden of nearly its every word.

It is consumerism which has exhausted our natural mineral and energy resources. Millions of tons of now-exhausted metals lie rusting and rotting in land fills and city dumps where the cosmetic packaging and aerosol containers for which they were used were thrown away as nuisances. Many were used up not even for products—only for packages for products.

Thanks to consumerism we have an energy crisis (a shortage) at the same time that we have pollution (a glut or surplus) and inflation.

To promote consumerism, materialism has become our religion. TV models declare "You have made me truly happy—Diet Rite."

Greed has become our fetish. "Throw it away," "Spoil yourself," "You deserve it," and the like are the Bible texts of this insane religion, bred and spread by broadcasting, which is now bringing our nation to its knees and to shame.

Political Havoc. TV has inflated political costs several thousandfold, pricing out of the possibility of even becoming a candidate virtually anyone not a millionaire or beholden to monied interests.

As long as *any* money, private or public, has to be paid to the private broadcast industry for showing a nation its potential leaders (so they may make the crucial decision of democracy—the election of those leaders), we are not a democracy.

Recommended are the models of virtually any civilized democracy you care to mention: Britain, West Germany, Japan, Scandinavia, and so on. Until money is taken out of the process, our democracy can never be a real one.

Vulgarity. No matter how suave the executives in striped pants may be, or how beautiful their words, they have defiled our homes in their greed.

Never before have our homes been flooded by such vulgarity. Snot, children's bare butts, itching rectums, constipation, whining voices of people with colds and other afflictions have been let into *our* homes by TV's gatekeepers. How can they again claim to be outraged by any obscenity, vulgarity, or selfishness? What kind of picture of America do they offer?

The human armpit, dirty hair, stringy locks awaiting high-wattage treatment and useless beautifiers sold to unsuspecting shopgirls—all in living color in our living rooms.

Ethics. The ethics taught by TV, as by Richard Nixon and John Mitchell (who said that *nothing* was more important than re-electing Mr. Nixon) seem similar. Why, then, are Mitchell and Watergate made to look exceptional? Because it is public rather than broadcast practice?

Whether in fiction or in sports, the lesson of TV is: Winning is everything. To that end, no violence or ruthlessness is too much. No matter how unfair the tactics, use them if necessary, if you can get away with them. Watergate demonstrated the same lesson. As on TV programs nightly, robbery and other crimes are acceptable if they are for a good cause. In Watergate, as on TV, the end justifies the means. The good cause is profits.

Sports. Once TV found that sports was its greatest moneymaker, the nation was doomed. Regardless of the diversity of interests of the population, there are many times when nothing but spectator sports is available to most areas.

TV comes to shape all sports in its own image. As the auto racers' association official said: "If ABC wants a 40-minute (75-mile) race, that is what ABC (or TV) will get."

Sports used to be something you did. It's now something you watch—preferably with a beer or other consumer product at your side.

THE PERVERSION OF THE WORDS: "PROOF" AND "EVIDENCE"

Since the eighteenth century Western civilization has promoted what Voltaire so greatly advanced: the cause of rationality. Our schools, step by step, teach us to recognize valid proof, evidence, argument, and so on.

TV—and the advertising it promotes—tries to destroy this. Anything that helps the consumer to be a wise buyer is taboo. Just as large corporations can "buy" immunity from exposure of their less savory practices, advertisers can purchase the co-operation of TV in putting a fast one over on TV's loyal audience.

Why buy Courant Perfume by Helena Rubinstein? "Because I like myself?" What kind of sense is that? Can you say anything if you bribe TV? The answer seems to be yes. "What is Sony? No Baloney."

You don't believe Bayer's ads? They prove it. Read the label! Bayer's own tests (!) (rigged as "TV's own research" seems to have been) find Bayer superior. That proves it! (When I was younger I worked at a chemical plant where they made aspirin for anybody. Only the mold stamp was different.)

Arthritis Pain Formula is especially for arthritis. Great stuff. Oh yes: It's great for headache too. "If you don't believe it, read the label." What is the effect of Binaca mouthwash? An orgasm-like explosion. What does Pfeiffer's salad dressing do? Spill the salad all over the table, in "surprise."

This is proof? No wonder we can't prove to these TV leaders that TV violence is dangerous. *This* is what *they* call proof. They are taken in by their own brainwashing.

As with the emperor's new clothes, they see what is not there, deny what is, and expect Americans to believe the same.

The cost of this perversion of proof and evidence is matched only by the mangled grammar ("Winston tastes good, like a cigarette should," large "amounts" of people, new "words" like "Wee-oo" and "gasid") and deteriorated language which teachers daily try to cope with in our unfortunate and dismal schools. These delicate bastions are wholly incapable of stemming the flood and correcting the false values and practices forced on America by powerful mass media.

TRIVIALIZATION

Perhaps one of TV's most shameful accomplishments is the trivialization of the medium. To look at prime-time color TV, you would think that America's greatest problems were not energy, political corruption, world leadership, or humane law enforcement, but milady's hair, smell, and feel. Lotions, potions, and twelve billion dollars' worth of cosmetic advertising say *that* is America's greatest problem. TV puts it in prime time, where it does *not* put news, for example.

The dialogue is largely about cosmetics, detergents, coffee breaks, sports, canned and frozen foods, and appliances. The arts have been largely "amateurized." Anyone can play. Disciplined musicians are history.

All ideas and conversation are trivialized. How sustained a thought can you work in between commercials? Thinking is broken into such small bits that even Sesame Street must imitate the "short bit" approach, taking children from where they are (*short* attention spans). The most significant idea is fragmented and defused when put between commercials, gags, bosoms, gossip, and violence. The nation's brain power has been criminally trivialized and "kitschified." The quantification of quality prevails. There is no large talk; all is, indeed, small talk

and small thought—about celebrities, money, and "things."

Since proof has been perverted and evidence re-interpreted, of course a Nixon is elected. Real qualification or evidence is no longer recognized. If people had been thinking, there would have been no Watergate—and probably no Nixon in the White House. TV encouraged us not to think, to "believe the label."

ALTERNATIVES: SOME COURSES OF ACTION

While profitable broadcasters have been busy counting their money and fighting off regulation, they may not have noticed the huge flurry of citizen dissatisfaction, outrage, and activity. I myself am connected with at least half a dozen action groups, like ACT (Action for Children's TV) and NABB (National Association for Better Broadcasting), which recently challenged renewal of a large station on the West Coast and got it to produce a list of violent old programs it agreed never again to use, and to announce before other violent programs—in times when children may be up—a warning of their unsuitability.

We must all become activists. Here are a few such activities to pursue:

(1) Join national organizations and help form local action groups.

(2) Participate in hearings on CATV and ask for hearings on local station renewals.

(3) Learn to monitor and log, even roughly, programs and commercials. You'd be surprised what they're doing to you. Then badger stations, sponsors, the authorities.

(4) Become a short-wave listener. Hundreds of my former students have learned that on short wave they can get (from Britain, Germany, the Netherlands, and a dozen other countries) real news—not just a list of the disasters, crimes, fires, and scandals our stations call news.

(5) Abandon network-station news programs, especially their local operations. You'll only miss a dozen or so of the same stories each day anyway, and you'll be more sane.

(6) Turn to non-publicized news sources like WFMT, WBEZ (the Chicago School Station, with public radio sources), and even WTTW news breaks. Strangely, some of the best news, with-

out interruption, is on WMBI, the Moody Bible Institute station. (This station is also recommended for something other than irritating fare during drive time.) Certain other stations, like WCLR (on FM), also have only three or so commercial breaks per hour. You don't *need* to take the commercial "beating" that the big-money stations administer to you.

(7) Demand that Public Television—and WTTW—undertake to serve this unserved need.

(8) Do a little reading about other systems, so you can see in what form civilized nations operate, and in some cases even broadcast commercials. Don't believe "ours is the greatest."

(9) Promote pay TV, and don't believe the distortions the NAB has set up a budget of nearly a million dollars to feed you.

(10) Join, support, and sponsor all kinds of pressure for "smallness" and "localness" in TV and radio; guerrilla TV, new 10-watt educational FM, cable studios, and so on.

(11) Watch cable TV: It could be a benefit. But with the political football it is becoming in Chicago, it will need popular participation to keep honest. Otherwise it will only mean that we'll be mauled by different millionaires.

(12) Press for basic change: more regulation, more public TV and radio, a change in licenses. Having helped create from the ground up one national system, the West German (called by some one of the best in the world, with Japan's NHK and Britain's BBC), I know we don't have to put up with *this*.

(13) Write, protest, phone. Raise hell. Don't let stations get away with the mockery they now call service.

(14) If you have children, and TV is wrecking your life, get rid of your set—as thousands are already doing. See past issues of the *National Enquirer* for case histories of *life without television*, in which many families are happier than they had been in years.

There are terrible, bloody days ahead. As consumers begin to be unable to buy so much and accounts begin to be canceled, the hysteria will deepen. The intensity, the shrillness, the repetition will become even more desperately intolerable. Don't take it. TV should be operated for "the public interest, convenience, and necessity." That is not what is happening now.

TELEVISION, THE ONLY TRULY MASS MEDIUM REMAINING TODAY: ITS ROLE IN OUR SOCIETY

D. THOMAS MILLER

Mr. Miller has been president of the CBS Television Stations Division since September 1970 and responsible for the operation of the five CBS-owned television stations—WCBS-TV New York, KNXT Los Angeles, WBBM-TV Chicago, WCAU-TV Philadelphia, and KMOX-TV St. Louis. He has been active in local, national, and international broadcasting since 1950.

I am delighted to discuss with you broadcasting and its role in our society. It is perhaps healthy, from time to time, to defend that which should require no defense, and to explain that which should not require an explanation.

But television does need its defenders and its champions. Man has always sought someone—or something—to blame for his errors, his foibles and his problems. Historically, this has been so. For example, let me read a couple of quotes to you:

> The tendency of children to imitate the daring deeds seen upon the screen has been illustrated in nearly every court in the land. Train wrecks, robberies, murders, thefts, runaways, and other forms of juvenile delinquency have been traced to some particular [program.]* The imitation is not confined to young boys and girls but extends even through adolescence and to adults.

© Columbia Broadcasting System, Inc., 1971. All rights reserved. Reprinted by permission of the Department of Communication Arts, College of Agriculture and Life Sciences, Cornell University.

Now, here's another quotation:

> The [programs]† are so occupied with crime and sex stuff and are so saturating the minds of children the world over with social sewage that they have become a menace to the mental and moral life of the coming generation.

Do they sound familiar? They may well be sentences from today's magazines complaining about violence on television. Actually, only one word change in each quote made them "relevant." Both statements were made about motion pictures. They first one appeared in the magazine *Education*—in December 1919. The second is from the magazine *Christian Century* —in January 1930.

Similar complaints are available about books dating back to the publication of "The Tales of King Arthur" and continue through movies, comic books and radio. Now television is the new boy in town. What better whipping boy is there available than television? In practice, almost any pervasive influence finds itself the subject of some form of public attack. Other major whipping boys include religion, the Government, and of course, education.

Television is the most pervasive medium known to modern man. It reaches more people than newspapers, books, magazines and motion pictures. More time is devoted by the average American to watching television than to any other form of leisure time spectator activity. The most recent surveys show that Americans spend approximately 2600 hours per year with all forms of spectator entertainment. Nearly one-half of that time—1200 hours—is spent in front of the television set. Another 900 hours is given to another form of broadcasting—radio.

THE GOOD AND THE BAD

What happens to the balance of the time, about 500 hours? We spend about 218 hours reading newspapers and 170 hours with our magazines. Unfortunately, we set aside only about 10 hours a year to read books. As to the balance of the leisure time activity, 68 hours are spent listening to tapes and records, nine hours at the movies and three hours at sporting events. Finally, all cultural events combined—plays, operas and the like—account for only three hours of our time annually.

Is it any wonder, then, that having spent so much time with television we also devote an inordinate number of hours to complaining about what we see?

For many years, our principal contact with the outside world was the newspaper and the magazine, and we were reasonably content—at least from the public point of view, although politicians had their complaints. We referred to "the good gray *Times*" (a reference to *The New York Times*), an appellation which I can assure you is not applied to any radio or television station. Newspapers were solid members of the community, with acerbity only a sometime thing. Perhaps the reason for that situation may be found in the words of the late Frank Moore Colby, written about half a century ago: "Journalists have always been our most old-fashioned class, being too busy with the news of the day to lay aside the mental habits of 50 years before." That may have been true with the print media, but then came radio, closely followed by television.

Television opened new vistas, new horizons, and it brought the good and the bad of the entire world into our living room. It also became a catalytic social instrument, for better or for worse. It created an awareness that did not exist before.

We are now engaged in the first televised war in history. We have fought bigger wars and wars that were far more important. In the past, we learned of battles through the printed or spoken word. The action we saw was primarily in the weekly newsreel. Most graphics, however, were in the form of still photos, not always of the best quality, that appeared in our newspapers and magazines. This was true up through the Korean War. Now, however, all the bloodshed of Vietnam shows up on the screen in our living room. We see the fighting and the bombing and the deaths. We are engaged in a spectator war, something new to all of us.

WINDOW TO THE WORLD

Television, no doubt, has contributed greatly to the anti-war feeling that is so prevalent today.

---

*In original: film
†In original: movies

There were no major peace marches during the Korean fighting, for example, although the same pacifistic feelings might well have been expressed then as are heard today. Then we knew war; today we *see* it. If we ever see an end to war, it may be because a global television network brings these same newsfilms to every nation and village with the same results that we see here.

In addition to awareness, television has also brought to the American people forms of culture and entertainment that would otherwise have been totally unattainable. Television is not perfect, and rare is the individual in the broadcasting industry who would claim that it is. But how many people who have never attended a concert in person have done just that through television? How many Americans who have never attended a play have seen one on television? How many whose world was circumscribed by the boundaries of his own community now know what life is like in other parts of the United States and in the world *through television?* How many people have learned something about life while being entertained, through watching such broadcasts as *Medical Center* and *Men at Law?* They have not become experts in such matters through watching, but they have learned something about how others live and the problems of their fellow man. I would also suggest they've learned something about the warning signs of cancer and maybe a little about their civil rights.

THE PRIMARY SOURCE OF NEWS

Television has also become the primary source of news for the American people. According to the famous Roper study conducted in January of this year, when asked where they got most of their news, 60 percent of the public said television; only 48 percent said newspapers. In analyzing the results, Roper reported 31 percent of the respondents mentioned *only* television as the source of news, while 21 percent mentioned only newspapers. When it came to believability, 49 percent opted for television, while 20 percent picked newspapers.

All this may sound a bit defensive and self-serving. But it is a necessary preamble to the basic point that I wish to make today. Before I get to that let's speak for a minute about our detractors.

There are many self-styled "experts" who would tear down what has been accomplished, who would virtually start again with some sort of amorphous medium. As to many—although not all—of these "experts," I am reminded of a definition offered years ago by the late Nicholas Murray Butler, when he was president of Columbia University. "An expert," he said, "is one who knows more and more about less and less." Perhaps today that definition might be updated to saying, "An expert is someone who knows less and less about more and more." Let's take a look at some of the major complaints that we hear.

Many of those who complain contend that the overall fare on television is puerile pap, that it's all *Beverly Hillbillies* and *Green Acres*. It isn't, of course. But these are the people who feel that we should be devoting more time to Shakespeare and concerts. Actually we do both. But let's examine the complaint a little closer. It is true that there should be millions of people willing to watch cultural offerings on television. Unfortunately, people have a tendency to tell you what *should* be on television—not what they would actually be willing to watch themselves.

Public television does, indeed, offer more cultural events and broadcasts than the commercial stations do. Therefore, Shakespeare, Kenneth Clark's *Civilisation* and a host of other "good" programs are offered. According to the latest Nielsen surveys, only 60 percent of those households able to receive public television admit to tuning in during the course of a week. Now we come to the heart of the matter. Nielsen reports that the mean household that tuned in at all, did so for an average of 1.1 hours per week—and that *Sesame Street* was far and away the most popular program scheduled on public television. Please note that *Sesame Street* is education disguised as entertainment.

SPECIALS AND SPECIALTIES

Do people want more cultural events on television? They may *say* that they do—but they still opt for entertainment. It would seem that the only means by which culture can be sold to the public is by offering it on entertainment pro-

38   Media Forms

grams or at least in an entertaining way. After all, Ed Sullivan brought ballet to Muscatine, Iowa.

Then there are the many who contend that television has gone downhill in the area of news coverage, that things were much better back in the golden age of television, back in the fifties. Critics contend that television carried more news and more searching documentaries in the fifties. Is that complaint warranted?

We recently did a quantitative and qualitative analysis of the CBS News output in 1968 and 1969 and 1956 and 1957. We found that in the two years of the 1960s we carried 1354 hours of news compared with 675 hours in the fifties, or almost twice as much now as then. In the prime time hours of the sixties we carried 192 hours of news—about six times more than the 34 hours carried in the fifties. In all categories, the survey showed, the sixties far outstripped the fifties in the measurable amounts of news carried.

Then we come to the question of "hardness" versus "softness" in the documentaries that we broadcast. Today we often hear of our news specials being compared in a denigrating way with the broadcasts of the fifties. In the same two years of the fifties mentioned earlier—the benchmark of the golden age of television news—CBS carried 13 specials and 22 *See It Now* broadcasts. By today's standards, probably only one of these would be considered "hard"—a broadcast called "The Farm Program: The Crisis of Abundance." In those golden years we had CBS News studies of Grandma Moses, Danny Kaye and Marian Anderson, plus broadcasts devoted to the problems of the post office, automation and feudal Japan.

GOLDEN OR GOLD-PLATED?

Compare these offerings with our recent *The Selling of the Pentagon,* which has resulted in a direct CBS confrontation with the Vice President, the Department of Defense and the Congress itself. Or consider our specials on Vietnam, on civil rights, on hucksterism. I can assure you that if we were to rebroadcast some of those much-vaunted specials of the golden age—the 1950s—there would be a public outcrying about CBS having caved in to the pressures

> I am satisfied that the incessant depiction of violence on TV has contributed significantly to the appalling levels of crime and vandalism in our country. It is a cop-out to say that young people always have been exposed to violence in reading matter; printed violence is not the same. Voluntarily, without censorship, responsible program directors can greatly improve the present situation.
> —Sen. Frank Church

of the administration to avoid controversy. The so-called golden age of television was, at best, only gold-plated. Please note what I said at the opening of my remarks, the more pervasive we get the worse we seem to be regardless of the facts. What I'm saying is, we're learning.

The major practical problems facing broadcasters today come from two areas: the Government, and the pressure groups in various communities. Both stem from the same difficulty inherent in broadcasting. We are a licensed medium, using what is constantly referred to as the public airwaves and legally serving what is called the public interest.

Many areas of government affect television—the FTC, the Congress, the Justice Department—but the one agency charged directly with regulating broadcasting is the Federal Communications Commission. The FCC acts on its own and in response to the public. In March of this year, the FCC set a new record for complaints, comments and inquiries received from the public. There were 3010 complaints in March plus 5087 comments and inquiries, the highest number in FCC history. Many of these are passed along to the broadcaster, who must respond—not to the complainant—but to the FCC itself.

WHO MAKES THE DECISIONS?

To many broadcasters, actions of the FCC go far beyond looking out for the public interest and good. If the situation has not already reached the harassment stage, it is dangerously close to it.

The Congress is heard from rather directly. Last week, for example, congressional hearings were held on alleged racial and ethnic slurs in motion pictures and television. In essence, several congressional resolutions would give these industries a year to eliminate any references that might be considered demeaning to any racial or ethnic group. If this isn't accomplished, then the House and the Senate would step in, in a regulatory fashion.

This seems to presuppose that the television industry, either intentionally or through inexcusable negligence, is engaged in demeaning various groups. More important, such decisions about slurs must be a purely subjective appraisal. Who will make those decisions? And will it also mean that we would be unable to offer on television *The Adventures of Huckleberry Finn*, *The Merchant of Venice*, *The Confessions of Nat Turner*, because all of these have at one time or another been attacked for stereotyping or attacking racial or ethnic groups?

Finally, how far could such regulation go? A student group, for example, might object to our depiction of life in a university town. That's not as farfetched as it may sound. When CBS presented the play *The Death of a Salesman* a few years ago, we received a demand from a sales group to permit a spokesman time on the air after the play to explain that not all salesmen were like Willy Loman.

WOULD-BE JUDGES AND JURIES

At least as serious a problem stems from the community groups who feel that stations are not serving the public interest. These groups often set themselves up as would-be judges and juries, telling us what is wrong with television and what should be done. They profess to speak for the many, when often they represent only a small segment of the community. The phrase "public interest" has been both ill-defined and over-defined. The groups that challenge station licenses are often poorly informed about our broadcasts, our responsibilities and their own involvement.

Let me tell you about one actual example of a challenge situation which we found ourselves faced with only a few months ago. There, the

> Television should be a reflective medium—accurately reflecting America and her people. It should show Americans as they really are—in their homes, at their jobs, in their daily lives.
>
> Real life is not a situation comedy, although it has much humor. It is not a tragedy, although there is much tragedy in everyday life. Much of it is not news—except to those who live it. . . .
>
> . . . television should mirror the needs of people, their wants and aspirations, their dreams and their problems.
> —George Meany

challenge groups started with census figures covering the racial composition of the city of license, not the total area served. They found that the city had a 34.2 percent Black population, 8.7 percent Spanish-surnamed and .6 percent Orientals. Therefore, they said, all of our programming, all of our employment, should accurately reflect these percentages. Not only that, they wanted our programming, for example, to reflect accurately the life-style of these minority groups.

First of all, the employment quotas are illegal. Secondly, programming for special interests is divisive. I feel it would exacerbate the growing separatism in many of our cities. If we started passing out portions of the broadcast schedule to the various interests it wouldn't be long before George Wallace types would demand their share. As far as depicting accurately the lifestyles of minorities, it has been our experience that social realism is of least interest to those people who are depicted.

Through broad appeal programming the total audience becomes aware of problems and situations that might otherwise be totally alien to it. We cannot create understanding and tolerance by legislative fiat, but we can display all aspects of all life styles and hope that native intelligence will do the rest.

As you are no doubt aware, everyone from the

Vice President on down has seemingly set himself up as the news editor for the nation and the arbiter of entertainment fare for all of us. The problems of television have, happily, also reached the humorous stage. One story has it that if a modern-day Moses came down from Mt. Sinai with the Ten Commandments, he would be met by the lights and cameras of the television crews. That night, the fourth item in the late news broadcast might read something like this: "Moses came down from Mt. Sinai today with the Ten Commandments. The top three were ... "

And I am sure that no matter which three we picked, someone would be in total disagreement.

Unfortunately, all is not humorous in the feeling of the public about television.

THE ONLY TRUE MASS MEDIUM

Television has accomplished much in reaching the public. The words of criticism coming from the constant viewer or the unhappy public official do not constitute a mark of failure or shortcoming, but rather of success and achievement. The public expects much and wants more. Television, with all its accomplishments in so short a period of time, has become an unhappy victim of its own achievements.

Unfortunately, television is under serious attack. I say "unfortunately" for reasons that go far beyond my own personal involvement. My interest is only slightly greater than yours ought to be.

We now reach the basic thought that I would like to convey. Slowly but inexorably the mass media have been dying off. Motion pictures now reach relatively small audiences. Magazines, once courting national audiences, now are far more limited, appealing to specialized audiences in most cases. Even major metropolitan newspapers no longer reach far into the suburbs. For instance, there are some 30 papers in the greater Los Angeles area. Early this year, *The New York Times* quoted NBC officials as saying that "radio, except for newscasts and occasional special events, is economically no longer a mass medium." In fact, radio's recent resurgence can be attributed to its appeal to specialized audiences—news, talk and various music formats. *Only television remains today as a truly mass medium.*

The men of television were to outlast Agnew as they outlasted Taft and Eisenhower, Kennedy and Johnson, Goldwater and Nixon. In the twenty-two years between 1952 and 1974, their electronic magic would change American politics. Television would free national candidates more and more from dependence on, or discipline by, their parties; the tube could sway more swing votes than any party organization. A candidate's hopes could be destroyed by television in a single unguarded moment, as George Romney's were to be in 1967. Or a man could use it to appeal over his party, over its managers, even over the head of the ticket. One must mark 1952 as the date that Richard Nixon discovered how spectacular the influence of television could be, when, with his masterful and era-marking "Checkers speech," he reached for the first time, nationally, to stir the emotions of Middle America. . . .

The Checkers speech was a primitive one, in modern terms—hastily produced, amateurishly assembled—but its success scored the mind of every realistic politician. Television would change the mechanics of all future American campaigning, inviting in the manipulators. The new system would require new professionals, image merchants, market analysts, psephologists, artist-producers in a managerial enterprise divorced from party structure, responsible to one man only—the candidate. To use television effectively would require huge sums of money, an extravagance of campaign financing unimagined in 1952. But the Cain-and-Abel brotherhood of television and politics began there in Chicago, in 1952, on July 8th.

—Theodore H. White

Excerpted from *Breach of Faith–the Fall of Richard Nixon*. Copyright © 1975 by Theodore H. White. Reprinted by permission.

RADIO, OR "COME ON, LET ME SHOW YOU WHERE IT'S AT"

DON R. PEMBER

Announcer: The Columbia Broadcasting System and its affiliated stations present Orson Welles and the "Mercury Theater of the Air" in *The War of the Worlds* by H.G. Wells. Ladies and gentlemen, the director of the Mercury Theater and star of these broadcasts, Orson Welles.

Welles: We know now that in the early years of the twentieth century this world was being watched closely by intelligences greater than man's. . .

Jingle: More muuuuuuuuuusic, K*O*Mmmmmm
DJ: Welcome back to boss radio number one, the top sound in the top city. Cousin Brucie layin' 'em on you til seven when brother Jack B. Nimble rocks in with more of the hits on the big eleven. (Cue music) And now more outtasight sounds, far-reaching wails and good vibes with Dental Floss and the Cavities, the first of eighteen nonstop hits in a row from your man Bruce.

American radio has changed dramatically in the past 30 years. And all the important changes can be discovered just by reading closely the two passages above. The first contains the opening lines of Orson Welles' famous production of *The War of the Worlds*. The second represents what might be heard on at least one radio station in almost any American city today.

The differences are striking. The Welles' production was a dramatic presentation given in an era when radio was filled with drama, comedy, and variety programs. As Cousin Brucie says, recorded music is about all that's programmed on modern radio. *The War of the Worlds* originated in New York City and was broadcast to millions of Americans over a radio network—a linking of several hundred stations. In the seventies nearly all radio programming is produced (if that word is accurate) locally by individual radio stations.

The Welles' production was broadcast in the evening hours, prime radio listening time, to a vast audience of all ages. Nighttime radio today is generally regarded as the domain of young people. Prime radio time is early in the morning and late in the afternoon as millions of commuters, momentary captives of their radio hosts, wend their way along crowded freeways to and from their jobs. Finally, the quality of radio broadcasting has shifted dramatically from what was once considered a fairly high-class entertainment medium to a barren desert of commercial messages, dotted here and there with musical oases.

A tight program scheme or format dictates what music will be heard on most radio stations. And within the music format genre there are a wide variety of different approaches, ranging from classical to hard rock on a musical scale. Yes, there are a few AM stations that still play classical music—about a dozen at last count. FM has become the new retreat of classical music. This represents a distinct change in American broadcasting for there was a time, not too long ago, when AM radio not only broadcast classical music but supported it financially as well. NBC, CBS, and Mutual all supported respected symphony orchestras at one time. But radio has gotten out of that business, at least in the United States. The respected British Broadcasting Corporation still has its own widely renowned symphony orchestra. And the Japanese broadcasting network, NHK, financially supports three symphonies as well as several light orchestras. In fact, NHK has succeeded in a little more than a generation in giving a large portion of the Japanese people an appreciation for Western classical music. In the United States, radio tends to play music, but not directly support it.

Moving down the musical spectrum from the classics, one encounters the *good music* stations that tend to steer away from the heavier rock sounds. This kind of format rarely attracts large numbers of listeners, but those that do listen tend to be better educated and more affluent, which gives the station an edge in advertising

---

From *Mass Media in America* by Don R. Pember. © 1974, Science Research Associates, Inc. Used by permission.

rates, because it appeals to an audience that is more likely to buy. WJR in Detroit, for example, counts among its listeners many of the major executives of the automobile industry and carries commercial messages aimed specifically at them. Ads for roller bearings and for tool works companies, for example, are often aired. There aren't many people in the market for roller bearings, but purchasing agents at Ford, GM, and Chrysler do buy millions of them. Few cities can support more than one or two "good music" stations.

The *middle-of-the-road* or *"MOR"* station falls between the good music and the rock categories. The MORs play the softest of the rock and the loudest of the "good" music. This kind of station frequently attempts to build up a personality cult around its record spinners, and sometimes it appears that music is secondary. These friends of the housewife and buddies of the commuter often carry high ratings during drive time, 6 to 10 A.M. and 3 to 7 P.M., when adult radio listening is at its peak. The MOR station sounds a lot like radio sounded when the disc jockey first emerged—unplanned and rather hectic at times. But usually it is as tightly programmed as the prototype rock stations.

The contemporary sound in radio (that's what the programmers like to call it) is the *rock* station, the battleground for the jingle warfare of the airwaves. Within the rock format there are variations, but they appear important only to those who know and love radio. Critics call the stations "screamers" and describe the format as one "with an extreme foreground treatment, playing only the top tunes with breathless and witless striplings making like carnival barkers."

The heart of the rocker is the chart—top 30, top 40, top 50, and so forth. Record sales, or jukebox plays, are charted each week. These are songs with proven appeal: someone has paid money to hear them. The records are scheduled in sequence and played over and over during the week. A few album cuts are sometimes thrown in, and a few new songs are featured as well. But the charted records are the heart of the scheme.

One variation in the rock format is the *personality rocker* which is a station like the MOR mentioned earlier that attempts to create listener interest in the disc jockey himself. WMCA in New York rode the crest of popularity for years with the "Good Guys" format, and at KHJ in Los Angeles the "Real Don Steele" captured the ears of teenyboppers throughout Southern California. The most successful prototypes for this kind of personality appeal were Alan Freed and Murray the K, both of whom broadcast from New York in their heyday.

Some rock stations have successfully integrated tunes that were formerly popular— golden oldies, blasts from the past—into their format and capitalized on the nostalgia craze of the early seventies. Often the format is one of half oldies, or two to one from the "vault of gold." In 1972, stations like WCAU in Philadelphia, WIXZ in Pittsburgh, KWIZ and KNEW in Southern California and KUUU in Seattle all significantly boosted their ratings with the "where have all the good songs gone" format.

Other "contemporary" radio stations have attempted to capture a soul sound, with heavy emphasis on blues and ethnic music. Scores of AM radio stations in America are programmed primarily for black audiences, although they frequently have listeners outside this group. (Tragically, most of the soul stations aren't owned by blacks. Surely one of the great dilemmas facing the electronic media is the lack of the means to increase black and other minority-group economic participation in broadcasting.)

Some AM stations have even successfully programmed "hard rock" or "acid rock" or "underground rock." The audience for this kind of pure rock is small; the heavy sounds turn off most listeners. The greatest success for such a format has been in the FM field. KDAY in Santa Monica, California, first succeeded with this format on AM. It featured a long play list (meaning that it played lots of different records), limited commercials to eight minutes each hour, and tried to create personality DJs who were knowledgeable about the music they played but not "jivers" like those on the screamer stations. The successful format was quickly copied elsewhere.

Perhaps the most interesting concept in rockers is the *more music* format, first promulgated in the sixties by men like Bill Drake. Drake was born Philip Yarbrough in 1937 and cut his teeth in radio spinning country and western tunes on backwater southern radio stations. In 1961 the owner of KYA radio in San Francisco gave Drake a chance at overhauling his rock station, which was at that time running behind the pack in the

Electronics 43

ratings sweepstakes. When he began work at KYA it was the prototype rocker, with music coming last, after the commercials, DJ chatter, jingles, air horns, and gongs. Drake's formula was to clean up the station and clear away the clutter on the airwaves. He toned down the station's rock image and began playing softer—but still popular—music. His theory was if you don't like it, don't play it. He depersonalized the disc jockey and emphasized music instead. Split-second timing was the key to his format, with a plethora of mini-jingles announcing what was coming up next. Disc jockeys were instructed to talk over both the intros and endings of records and often commercials were spaced to allow two and three record sweeps. Time was told only with numbers—it was 12:30, not half past the hour. And news was used to gain a strategic advantage in the battle for listeners. Drake's theory was that many listeners will tune out news. If station KOMM carried its five minutes of news at twenty-five minutes after the hour, a Drake station would carry the news at twenty minutes after the hour. Listeners would switch their dial when the news came on KYA at 12:20, but switch back when KOMM news came on at 12:25 and then stay with KYA until the next news cycle began. A Drake trademark was 20/20 news, twenty minutes before and after the hour.

The Drake format is a superslick sound. Most disc jockeys hate it and say that Drake is turning his back on what's really happening in music—progressive rock and soul. (But although the criticism may be valid, we must remember these are the same DJs Drake told to stop talking and play more music.) And the formula has been successful. In the early seventies there were at least forty stations that had the Drake sound and paid the young man more than $100,000 annually for his programming service, which includes weekly play lists and predictions of new records. He has attained such importance in the record industry that many recording companies don't feel a record has a chance to succeed if the song doesn't appear on the Drake play list. Drake's success with the AM format has pushed him into even more programming in FM, which we will talk about shortly.

Probably the one remaining important subgroup in the variety of music formats is the country and western station, or what many people used to call "hillbilly" music. Following a decrease in the number of C & W stations during the past ten years, a renaissance of sorts has taken place and new "country" stations are popping up in many parts of the nation, including some large sophisticated eastern urban centers such as New York City. Country music is adult music, and its popularity might be a reaction to the youth orientation of pop music in the past three decades. Bill Sherrill at Columbia records calls it humanitarian music, music that talks about human problems at a very mundane level—about love and cheating, about drinking and the daily frustrations most people share. Rock, on the other hand, confronts issues on a grander scale—war, ecology, and racism are popular themes. One reason the number of country music stations have decreased is because country and western sounds have begun to infiltrate popular music. (At the end of this chapter, when we talk about pop music, we will try to point out the extent of this infiltration.) The remaining "barefoot" radio stations have adopted a top-forty kind of format, using C & W charts rather than pop music play lists.

Although music remains the basic AM format, it is not the only one. In recent years two innovations have been introduced, neither of which has been an overwhelming success. Phone-in programming was very popular for a while. Some stations went almost exclusively to this scheme, while others just used it an hour or two each night. This kind of format adopts two of America's basic rural pastimes as its attractions—listening in on the party line and talking at the town meeting. The premise is simple: the average citizen probably has something to say about most issues, so let him call the station and give his ideas over the air. A fairly glib host is required, as well as some special tape-recording equipment that permits the station to broadcast the callers on a five- or eight-second tape delay (to give the station the chance to censor obscenity, libel, or other noxious remarks). But the program still retains the spontaneity of a live broadcast. With a good host and a good topic, this kind of programming was often popular. But after a while listeners got tired of hearing generally uninformed people, most of whom had a petty complaint or a plan to save the world. Also, the same callers tended to monopolize the lines.

In any case, the format began to fade.

But it didn't die completely. In fact, in 1973 call-in radio was given a new breath of life when several stations shifted the flavor of the telephone discussions from social, political, and economic issues to more earthy subjects—mainly sex. During discussions that the radio hosts described as "frank and honest but not dirty," listeners were asked to give their views on extramarital relations, premarital sex, group sex, and so forth. Many listeners have responded favorably to a limited amount of this kind of programming, especially when the phoned-in comments are interspersed between records.

The other innovation was kind of a throwback to early radio as many large-city stations went to a 24-hour all-news format. Although it sounds exciting, public interest-oriented and all those good things, in fact it was usually a bore. The idea was fine, but most stations refused to put out the cash to hire enough newsmen to do the job. So listeners would hear about the same news with maybe twenty minutes of new material, in one-hour cycles. The first hour was great, the second hour was even okay, but by the third hour listeners began to know the news headlines as well as the readers at the radio station. Only large cities can support such stations, and few all-news stations still exist.

Music remains as the staff of life for the AM radio station, and there is nothing to suggest that this will change in our lifetimes. If we begin with the premise that the medium of radio tends to be background rather than foreground, music is an inexpensive, noncontroversial, and usually profitable programming concept. In the years to come we will probably see program formats play an even more significant role. The old-timers of radio despise the format; it means a loss of freedom to them. But the younger generation of radio hands understand it, have a feel for it. As Arnold Passman wrote in his book, *The DeeJays*, "It speaks their language. If they have a sense of freedom, and they are no way near their politically active and socially experimenting peers, it may be in the vocal furor they are asked to create. The medium's message (any medium's) seems to be: Out of passion comes chaos, and out of chaos comes order." In comtemporary radio it is often the listener who creates the order.

QUESTIONS FOR DISCUSSION

1. Review the arguments Miller makes for TV and contrast them with the arguments cited by Adler that summarize some of its shortcomings. Who has the stronger case?

2. Reveiw the Skornia article listing the areas of discontent that he asserts are directly related to television. Based on your own viewing experience, defend or oppose his allegations.

3. Regulation of CATV requires the franchise holder to provide a variety of public services not required of over-the-air broadcasters. What are the specific requirements in your community? Why do you think CATV has been given these obligations?

4. Can CATV reasonably be expected to fill the void of programming for the many different minority segments of the population? Consider its financial base in contrast to commercial, over-the-air stations and networks.

PROJECTS

1. Watch prime time television (7:30 p.m. to 11:00 p.m.) one evening to determine:
    (a) the number of minutes per hour of news/entertainment versus advertising messages
    (b) the time slots in which commercials are run
    (c) the percentage of time spent on advertising message per show
    (d) the number of commercials per show
    (e) the number of violence-oriented shows as opposed to nonviolent programming

2. Prepare a report comparing programming formats on at least four different local AM and FM radio stations. Tabulate the following over a four-hour period:
    (a) commercial messages per hour
    (b) public service announcements per hour
    (c) ratio of talk to music per hour
    (d) network programming as compared with material originating locally

3. In addition to the data compiled in Project No. 2, determine which station(s) emphasizes the following:
    (a) identifiable announcer personality
    (b) local talent
    (c) involvement in local public affairs
    (d) editorial statements
    (e) live vs. pre-prepared program materials

PRINT

The American Newspaper Is Neither Record, Telegram, Examiner, Observer, Monitor . . .

BEN H. BAGDIKIAN

Although this article was written in the 1960s, most of what is argued holds true today. The narrow leadership and the excessive influence exerted by government and big business continue to characterize far too many contemporary dailies. Unless corrective measures are taken, Bagdikian asserts, the ultimate loser is the public.

Last April [1966] several hundred editorial workers on New York newspapers received mimeographed sheets that began "Dear employee."

The first paragraph announced that three New York dailies were merging into one successor, the World Journal Tribune, Inc. The second paragraph began with one of the more bizarre formulations in the English language:

"Your employment will be continued by the successor enterprise. We regret to inform you, however, that this employment will be terminated...."

It was signed, "World Journal Tribune, Inc., The Hearst Corporation, New York Herald Tribune, Inc., New York World-Telegram Corporation."

Three major American papers, operating in the largest city with the most sophisticated citizenry, during a period of unprecedented increases in spending, literacy and hunger for news, had stumbled into homogenized oblivion.

Copyright © 1967 by Ben H. Bagdikian. Reprinted by permission of Sterling Lord Agency, Inc. First published in *Esquire* Magazine.

The owners, impelled by an irrepressible death wish, permanently buried the best of the three, the New York *Herald Tribune*, while mating the remaining two, the former *Journal-American* and *World-Telegram,* in an ingenious hybrid that preserved the worst traits of both parents. Newspapers as a whole are in no such shaky corporate or semantic shape, nor have most shown such monumental ineptitude in labor relations as the New York publishers. But most papers are stumbling into the future, though at the moment they are stumbling all the way to the bank.

Even the worst newspaper has a life of its own that becomes intertwined in an intimate way with the lives of men who write for it. When the paper dies it carries part of its staff with it. But in New York, as elsewhere, the ultimate loser is the public, which has been exhibiting an historic thirst for information on public affairs that has been met by the typical American paper by a reduction in the amount of news it prints.

Considering the great new market for news and the reaction of most papers, the most kindly comment about contemporary American newspaper proprietors can be borrowed from a panhandler who used to hang around Piccadilly Circus behind dark glasses, a tin cup and a semi-scrupulous sign that read, "Nearly Blind."

The newspaper trade literature is a litany of complaints about rising costs, but the newspaper industry makes profits quite a bit higher than the steel industry. Publishers have a standardized outrage at their obstinate unions, but most newspaper operators don't know enough about their own economics to realize where their long-range self-interest lies. There are real problems for the metropolitan papers confronted with sprawling suburbs, yet it was only recently that a few brighter publishers perceived the uses of scientific analysis to solve their technical problems. Dailies will remain free and creative not as printing industries but as social institutions with a commanding purpose, like the local college, art museum or bawdy house, yet most of them organize their corporations no differently than textile mills.

The unique strength of the American daily is its roots in its own community, yet indifferent and narrow local leadership of papers has encouraged galloping consolidations so rapidly

Print 47

> The unique strength of the American daily is its roots in its own community.
> —Ben Bagdikian

in the last ten years that by now forty-four percent of all dailies are controlled by chains and fifty-four percent of all papers sold daily are published by a multi-paper corporation operating in more than one city.

In their slow response to rising popular standards, publishers seem haunted by H. L. Mencken's aphorism, "No one ever went broke underestimating the taste of the American public."

Mencken was wrong. Since World War II a lot of papers have gone broke that way, among them the Boston *Post*, the Los Angeles *Mirror*, the Houston *Press*, the St. Petersburg *Independent*, the New York *World-Telegram*, the New York *Journal-American*, and most of the other petrified specimens in the old Hearst empire.

Mencken's own paper, the Baltimore *Sun*, has been a cornucopia of profits because it provided thorough national reporting, though it only recently woke up to its own community. The New York *Times* is the most solid property in that journalistically unhappy city for about the same reason with the same exception. The Los Angeles *Times* has turned handsome profits since it ended its career as a strident family trumpet and began being a good newspaper. The Louisville *Courier-Journal*, a high-quality paper in a small city in a poor state, has a balance sheet to gladden the heart of the Internal Revenue Service. The Washington *Post*, loaded with sophisticated if disorganized talent, has been making so much money that its late proprietor, Philip Graham, used to tell people he bought the stock of *Newsweek* magazine just to get rid of the profits jamming the *Post*'s cash register.

The source of the profits is obvious: the country is rich, it is reading, and it is interested in public affairs.

The source of underlying trouble with newspapers is almost as obvious: most of them are riding this easy tide, complacent in their monopoly status, without making basic reforms that they and the readers deserve.

Some of the needed changes are relatively easy. Newspaper technology needs to be brought up-to-date, using science, engineering and rational problem-solving in mechanical and distribution problems. This requires a top-level, industry-wide working relationship with the craft unions, a project just recently started after years of chaos.

The most fundamental reform is not so easy. Leadership and policy control on newspapers need to be made more responsive to the body politic, but sensitive to social and economic reality as a good university is to learning. Yet there is no organizational mechanism in newspapers to keep leadership responsive, as there is in higher education and in other large social enterprises like the better foundations and private agencies.

The problem has peculiar agonies for the newspaper because it has to be a godless corporation run for profit and at the same time a community institution operated for the public good, with the two functions largely insulated from each other. This requires the good publisher to have the mixed qualities of John Jacob Astor and Albert Schweitzer, which would try the ingenuity of the most conscientious board of directors. Yet this crucial national institution is run by a multitude of mostly parochial businessmen selected by worse-than-conventional corporate happenstance. Colleges and shoe factories select their leaders with more care than is shown in the process by which men come to operate daily papers.

The good papers today are run by strong men, almost never by a committee or by trustees or by absentee owners. Their papers mean more to them than any other enterprise in the world and these men are driven by the obsession that whatever important happens in the world must be told to the readers by their local paper and that paper alone.

Most American dailies fail this standard. A few are excellent, most are mediocre, and many are wretched. The quality of reporting and editing has increased markedly in the last generation but this is no contradiction of the fact that most newspapers are failing their present duty. The new urgency in local and national public events, the faster reaction time of all social movement, and the dramatic change in the nature of the American audience is widening the gap between the responsibilities of the press and its performance.

The newspaper audience today is unrecognizable from the one in the Twenties. Since that time people with family incomes over $6,000 (in constant dollars) increased from 18,000,000 to 90,000,000. Men and women voting for President went from 29,000,000 to 71,000,000; white-collar and skilled workers from 16,000,000 to 42,600,000. Just since World War II the number of adults with better than eighth-grade educations rose from 29,000,000 to 67,000,000.

Newspapers congratulate themselves for keeping up with the change in size of the adult population, and this is largely true. But in the last ten years book sales have doubled; the number of new books on social and economic subjects has increased more than six times.

Social change, which provides the most dramatic materials for newspapers—or should—has accelerated at dizzying speed. The amount of knowledge is said to double every ten years. Political evolution that used to take decades is sometimes measured in months. Its personal impact is enhanced by instant communication. The involvement of men in social affairs and the world at large is magnified; men who in childhood could travel no farther than from Kansas City to Chicago in eight hours now can go from Kansas City to Paris in the same amount of time. The enlarged concern with national and global news is obvious.

Less noticed, especially by foreign observers and most nonprofessional American ones, is the deep involvement of the reader in community news, which, contrary to the European tradition, is not a sign of provincialism. The United States lacks true national papers not primarily because of its vast geography but because it, unlike any other modern country, organizes some of its central institutions—schools, police powers, property taxes, etc.—on a local basis, voted on by the local citizen. Increasingly the American citizen has children in the public

> Everybody's seen the flicks: Bogart or Gable with a press card in his fedora, catching the killers and whipping out his deadline exclusive. Guys in green eyeshades yelling "Scoop." Hot tips, hard drinking, and undercover disguises. The cub reporter sneaking into the jury room, rifling the waste basket, and stuffing the secret ballots into his trench coat pocket.
>
> Newspapers have changed a great deal since the days when reporters functioned largely as cops without badges. Today we have press secretaries and public relations men, and our biggest everyday occupational hazard is getting clobbered by a television camera at a press conference. But the myths live on. The newspaper city-room is still the place where you sit in your shirtsleeves, flick your cigarettes on the floor, and keep a bottle in the desk drawer.
>
> —Lindsy Van Gelder

schools and worries about them, owns his own house, drives his own car, fights over zoning and City Hall. No national paper, magazine or broadcasting network can tell him what he wants to know about such things.

How have American papers responded?

Most of them still cover their local governments wretchedly. It is common to have the primary ruling body hold open meetings without personal press coverage. Over half the papers in state capitals get most of their statehouse coverage from sources outside their own staff, like wire services, outside papers, or press releases. Some quality coverage has been outstanding, but a mass of indifferent local papers remain.

In the face of enormously increased interest in public affairs, newspapers have reduced their average space devoted to news. In 1940 the average American daily had twenty-seven pages. In 1965 it had fifty pages. Of the additional twenty-three pages, three went to "news" and twenty to advertising. But during that same period the reader lost more than three pages of live news. Type size was enlarged and white space used more liberally, to make papers more readable. There was a radical increase in the number and size of photographs used. Syndicated features ranging from comics to political columns took vastly more space. Some of these elements have advantages for the serious reader but because they and the ads have eaten into former news space the result is a decrease in live news. One rule-of-thumb of some editors is that it is impossible to tell the news adequately without a minimum of forty columns of "hard news"—what is left after subtracting ads, features, specialized information and entertainment. In some large cities the readers get an average of twenty columns.

Yet the modern audience is a collection of specialists, each looking for comprehensive information in his field; they include the baseball fan with his insatiable appetite, the P.T.A. leader, the zoning fighter, the man who owns stocks, the man who drives a car, the new political activists. Mostly they look elsewhere because their paper fails them. News magazines, for example, tend to sell more copies where the local paper has inadequate news. *Time* magazine sells twice as many copies per capita in Boston, San Francisco and Manchester, New Hampshire, as it does in Louisville, Nashville and New York.

Since World War II, sales of newspapers per family have dropped eighteen percent. There are more cities than ever and fewer papers. Community growth has become volatile as newspapers have become more ponderous. In 1910 there were twenty-two-hundred dailies published in twelve-hundred cities; fifty-three percent of all urban places had their own paper. Today only twenty-four percent of urban places have their own paper, mostly because there are many more cities, partly because the number of papers is down to 1760. The lack of a local paper and its function of tying together urban populations has increased the lack of community identity in urban America.

In 1910 the majority of cities with papers had competing ones; today only four percent have.

One reason the newspapers have moved slowly and adapted clumsily is that most of them blind themselves with paranoid secrecy. Basic statistics common to other industries are clutched jealously by individual papers. Publishers probably have the least accurate picture of themselves of any major economic activity in the country. Accounting methods are archaic and variable. Advertising rates are a Byzantine morass so arcane that often both paper and advertiser have trouble figuring out how much is being paid for what kind of space. Drifting in a forgiving economy, papers survive this with profit, but when their environment changes they are uncomprehending and sometimes unviable.

This is a contributing cause of monopoly. "The old monopoly"—domination of one city by one newspaper management—is just about complete. There are fourteen cities left (out of fourteen hundred newspaper cities) with face-to-face competition, a morning paper against a morning paper, or an evening against an evening. At last count forty-five papers with two managements had divided their spheres of influence, one taking the morning, the other the evening. Half of these forty-five are semi-married in joint operations in such areas as printing and in the selling of ads. The remainder of the fourteen-hundred cities have one newspaper.

"The new monopoly" is that of groups, a word evolved from the old-fashioned "chain," as "funeral director" is from "undertaker." A group, or chain, consists of a single management that controls papers in more than one city. They are growing like wildfire. Ten years ago there were ninety-four groups that controlled 491 papers. Today there are 154 groups (or 161 depending on whether you bother with twin groups controlled by the same stockholders) that control 752 dailies. This does not include Sunday papers.

Papers in trouble, because their hierarchs are at each other's throats or living in Majorca, are candidates for the chains. This is the secret of Samuel Newhouse who controls eighteen papers. He keeps dossiers on papers that are not well run or are torn by dissension; when the inevitable time of trouble comes, he makes his offer. Newhouse appears to be uninterested in the local editorial product; his purchase agreement usually keeps in office the same crew that allowed the paper to drift. He brings in essentially national caliber credit, rational management, accounting, purchasing and marketing. By applying ordinary modern business methods he makes money where others threw it away. Editorially his papers usually are neither better nor worse than before. He makes it easy for them to be better in some ways. He maintains a fairly enterprising Washington bureau whose output is available but not mandatory for member papers. The best reporting in depth from this bureau is regularly picked up by only two members of the chain.

The primary danger of chains is not that their operators are evil but that absentee owners are bad for American papers. So is ordinary corporate management.

Chains increase absentee ownership. And they deepen the tendency for monolithic politics in an institution already suffering from severe ideological ossification. Thirty chains own 308 papers controlling forty percent of all daily papers sold in the country. The seven largest chains (in average daily circulation, in decreasing size, Chicago Tribune, Scripps-Howard, Hearst, Newhouse, Knight, Gannett and Ridder) control twenty-four percent of all daily papers sold. In leadership and in editorial views they are something less than a representative spectrum of American thought and values.

They tend not only to present single editorial views on any national issue but also enlarge their corporate size on political grounds. When the conservative Chicago *Tribune* bought the Fort Lauderdale *News* in Florida it was in political camaraderie. The chief executive of the *News*, R. H. Gore, said "There isn't another newspaper organization with whom I would have entertained negotiations.... Our basic philosophy on government ... for community progress and civic upbringing is almost identical." If that part of Florida expected ideological relief they were wrong.

In 1962 a controversy between the Du Pont ownership of one of their Delaware papers and the paper's executive editor provoked the question of whether it would be better to avoid embarrassment by having the Du Pont holding company, Christiana Securities, sell the paper. In an internal memorandum, editor-publisher Charles L. Reese, Jr., told Lammot du Pont Copeland, president of the Du Pont Company, that one way out would be:

> Outright sale to an outside newspaper organization whose political and economic views closely parallel those of the present ownership. There are a number of such organizations. To avoid having the papers fall into unfriendly hands through a second sale, the sales agreement should give Christiana or its successors the first opportunity to purchase the papers if they should be again put up for sale.

The Du Ponts did not sell their papers but the conflict continued, causing the executive editor, Creed Black, now managing editor of the Chicago *Daily News*, to quit in protest.

The chains will probably continue to grow. Eighty percent of all newspaper sales since the war have been to other newspapers. The Internal Revenue Service has a rule against "unreasonable" accumulation of corporate income without taxation, but the Tax Court has ruled that using accumulations of newspaper profits to buy more newspapers is a "reasonable need of the business."

The underlying cause for both the old and the new monopolies is mass production and mass consumption, which favors the big operator. The best hope of the reader is to keep pressure on existing monopolies, not to bifurcate from sheer corporate guilt, but to be more responsive to the

> The newspaper trade literature is a litany of complaints about rising costs, but the newspaper industry makes profits quite a bit higher than the steel industry.
> —Ben Bagdikian

community. The history of newspapers in modern times is that survival tends to go to the paper most serious about news. The Chicago *Tribune* is the best nineteenth-century newspaper in America; it thrives because it has always been diligent about news, even eccentric news.

The New York *Times* and The New York *Herald Tribune* entered World War II with roughly the same circulation. When wartime newsprint restrictions went into force, each had to make a decision: with a fixed size of paper, would they give more space to the advertisers who were clamoring to buy, or to the readers who wanted war news? The *Herald Tribune* decided it would solidify its financial position by selling more ads. The *Times* made a good, grey decision to put its space into news. The late Orvil Dryfoos, publisher of the *Times*, said he thought this was a crucial decision that sent the *Times* into the postwar era in an unassailable position and the *Trib* into a decline.

> Leadership and policy control on newspapers need to be made more responsive to the society at large, not as a mirror image of the body politic, but sensitive to social and economic reality as a good university is to learning.
> —Ben Bagdikian

Newsroom Revolution

ROBERT C. ACHORN

In this highly informative essay Achorn points out that the quality of the newspaper is finally determined by the men and women who report, write, and edit the publication, not by the machinery that produces it. The article discusses many of the current technical changes taking place in newspaper production.

James Reston observed a half-dozen years ago: "Change is the biggest story in the world today, and we are not coping adequately with it."

Certainly change is the biggest story in the newspaper world today. We are just beginning to appreciate its dimensions.

Ben Bagdikian calls it a revolution. The word is appropriate. . . .

A survey ten years ago showed 80 newspapers—out of 1,750 dailies in the United States—using photo composition. Last year, 4,100 phototypesetters were sold world-wide.

Ten years ago, manufacturers of hot-metal line-casting machines sold 453 of them in this country. Last year they sold only 55—and manufactured none in the United States.

Computers, video editing terminals, optical character recognition machines, plastic plates, and other forms of new technology get all the attention.

The age of lead in newspapers is dying. The age of gold may replace it.

That depends on what we do with our ability to set type faster and more accurately and more economically. The reader doesn't know whether the type he is reading was set by hand, using tweezers, or whether it was set by computerized equipment racing along at 500 lines a minute. He does care what it says—how important the information is, how fresh it is, how accurate it is.

From *The Quill,* published by The Society of Professional Journalists, Sigma Delta Chi.

There is no point in throwing away the soft pencils and cans of rubber cement and bringing in cathode ray tubes unless the result is a product of higher quality. It can be. Whether it will be depends on how publishers and editors use the system—and the savings. "System" is the key word. Every newspaper needs a system, it is said. The truth is that every paper has a sytem of sorts for turning news into type. The question is how much electronic efficiency can be introduced into the system.

A good many large newspapers are still trying to come to grips with what the system should be.

Meanwhile, other newspapers, small and large, have gone ahead. For technical and economic reasons, the smaller newspapers led the parade toward offset printing. A few have pioneered in electronics.

One striking example is the *Breeze Courier* (circ., 8567) in Taylorville, Ill. Jim Cooper, the president-publisher-editor-etc., spoke of the incentive: "We had come to a point where, if we didn't do something, we just wouldn't be around very much longer."

In 1971, he installed an OCR scanner, a VDT terminal and a couple of phototypesetters. He linked them, with paper tape as a backup. There, in one small package, was his system to provide news and advertising for his offset press.

News is written on electric typewriters. The scanner "reads" the words on the typewritten sheet and gets them into the computer as electronic impulses. They can be called up on the video terminal screen for editing. When everything is just right, the push of a button sends that story to the typesetting machine, which produces printing on paper to be pasted up, photographed and sent to the press as an offset plate.

There are fancier systems on larger papers. They all have a similar purpose: to capture as many of the original keystrokes as possible.

A substantial and lasting part of each story published is created by the reporter at his typewriter. The Los Angeles *Times* once installed some new technology on the theory that only 15 percent of the lines in a reporter's copy are changed by editing corrections. That estimate proved low. Ronald White of Gannett has estimated that the figure is closer to 50 percent for local copy and 15 percent for wire copy.

The more of those original keystrokes that can be used to set type, the faster the process will be and the fewer errors there will be. The error rate drops even faster when stories are photocomposed—set in "cold type"—because phototypesetters make far fewer mechanical errors than do hot metal linecasters.

If the typewritten copy is relatively clean and is typed in the proper face, it can be read by one of the various scanners on the market and converted into type on a composition machine.

Scanners aren't new. They have been around for a couple of decades. But it is only recently that they have become cheap enough and simple enough for general newspaper use.

The prototype of the ECRM Autoreader was installed at the Worcester *Telegram* and *Gazette* in September 1970. The Compuscan and Datatype units were field-tested and were introduced at the ANPA/RI Production Management Conference in June 1971. By 1972, 155 scanners were in newspaper use. More are being added regularly.

They are an excellent device for volume input. They convert copy into type at rapid rates of speed, up to 1500 words a minute. They handle deletions easily, and some insertions.

But the general experience seems to be that they are not ideal tools when a lot of editing is required. They tend to slow the editing process and the thought process in the newsroom. The material may even have to be retyped, which means another keyboarding—more time, more cost, more chance of introducing error.

Enter video display terminals. They permit a reporter or editor to "massage" the story quite rapidly. At the push of a button, the story appears on the video screen from its computer storage. An editor, working on a keyboard at the screen, can make all needed changes to get the story into final form. The handling of paper can be eliminated.

According to Collier Elliott, a consultant, the first upper and lower case VDT displaying 2400 characters on its screen for newspaper use appeared in May 1969.

Since then, the Associated Press and United Press International have led the way. Between them, they are using 150 video editing terminals.

The Detroit *News* has installed half that many in its system. That system provides for reporters to write their stories at the keyboards of VDTs. Then editors do their work on similar machines.

A recent trend, seen at the Detroit *News* and at *Today*, the Gannett paper in Cocoa, Fla., is toward VDTs with somewhat smaller screens than the early models. These machines show 15 or 18 lines on the screen at one time. They are cheaper and less bulky than the first newspaper VDTs. They make it economically and physically feasible to tie a large number of VDTs into one system.

Can editors function effectively in front of screens? Tippen Davidson of the Daytona Beach *Journal* and *News* has said VDT editing is 80 percent slower than pencil editing. But Davidson, a pioneer in the field, points out the vast time savings once the editing has been completed.

Jim Jesse, from *Today*, says his young staff has taken enthusiastically to the system. There is still, however, in every newsroom the human problem of working out the individual's relationship to the machine. A total VDT system leads to a quiet newsroom. OCRs do not. OCR copy must be prepared on electric typewriters, which produce their own special kind of noise. The evidence is not all in yet but, for a guess, VDTs as general input devices are not yet as economical for most newspapers as are OCRs. But VDT editing is more efficient than the sort of pencil, pen and typewriter editing required by OCRs. The total system should be designed around a combination of scanners and video terminals.

Jesse is studying the installation of an OCR for volume input. The Detroit *News* is designing its system to provide for inexpensive OCRs in its outlying news bureaus. The Richmond *Times-Dispatch* and *News Leader*, the first large newspaper to move toward a total system, designed it around a combination of scanners and video terminals.

The scanners are great for volume input. The video terminals are outstanding for selective input and for editing. Moreover, they provide access to the computer in which all sorts of wire news, as well as local news, may be stored.

AP and UPI are girding for high-speed transmission of news—computer talking to computer. The old 60 words a minute is prevalent but obsolete today. The video terminal is the magic device for getting this news out of the computer and getting it into the newspaper.

Moreover, newspapers are beginning to recognize the computer as a source of news, in this sense: the computer can compile and arrange information in a way that a battery of reporters, working many hours, could not match. Computers are already invaluable for keeping track of election results. The Miami *Herald*, along with newspapers in Philadelphia, New York and some other cities, has used a computer to compile facts on crime rates, school rankings and other complex subjects.

What does all this new technology mean to the reporter, the editor and the one who really matters, the reader?

A good system can provide greater flexibility and speed. Together with offset printing, it can provide higher quality reproduction. Within a few years, technology will make it possible to bypass the cumbersome page pasteup system, although the cost may put that out of reach of many newspapers for awhile.

The main product of the changing newsroom may be economy. If original keystrokes need not be duplicated, then the manpower that goes into duplication and into correction of errors introduced during dupl cation will not be needed in that role.

Newspapers spend from perhaps 8 to 20 percent of their budgets on news. More spend 8 percent than spend 20 percent, it seems safe to say. In a sense, the reader who pays a dime for his paper is putting less than two cents of his money toward the gathering and editing of the news. He would probably be shocked, if he knew it.

The new electronic systems lend hope that a higher proportion of a newspaper's spending can go into original work, rather than duplication. For some newspapers, greater efficiency means survival. For others, it means improvement.

Ben Bagdikian, the newspaper critic, has said: "The dream of all journalists and conscientious owners has been to free the American newspaper from being mostly a factory. That liberation has begun."

That is the significance of the revolution. It gives reporters and editors and publishers the means to do a better job.

How effectively those means will be used depends on journalists themselves. In October 1969, an editor speaking at the UPI Edicon urged editors to "make their voices heard, and fast." Otherwise, he suggested, the production experts will tell us what to do and how to do. He was only echoing what John Diebold, the automation expert, had suggested six years earlier.

Editors have begun to take an interest. Somewhat ironically, the APME New Technology Committee may have been one of the results of the UPI meeting. L. William Hill of the Washington *Star-News* was prominent in both.

A good many editors have filled themselves in on the basic elements of the new technology. But the record is mixed. The picture will be clearer in a couple of years, when the systems now in planning are in operation. Then we shall see how effective a role editors, and reporters, have played in designing the newsroom of the second half of the '70s.

As the one who sounded the call for editor involvement at UPI in 1969, I think the time has come for a word of caution. There is no doubt that an efficient, effective newsroom—in a paper of almost any size—needs a reliable electronic input and editing system. Newspapers that don't have it will not be able to put out competitive products by 1980.

But there is a real danger, for some of us at least, of being bemused and blinded by machinery, just because it is the first new equipment in the newsroom since the Woodstock replaced the pen. To describe the editor of the future as the supervisor of input or the principal manager of composition systems ignores his central responsibility to manage the creation of that input. The quality of the newspaper is finally determined not by the machinery but by the men and women who report and write and edit for that newspaper.

And all the reader cares about is performance.

Unspecialized Publications Step Aside

JEAN-LOUIS SERVAN-SCHREIBER

Specialization—social, vocational, and so forth—is accelerated by modern media systems. The abundance of media channels encourages social specialization and individual isolation. The process is well outlined by Servan-Schreiber in this analysis of modern publications that rely increasingly on a specialized slice of the audience instead of the something-for-everybody publications of the past.

If in 1967 anyone was taught a bitter lesson by the difficulties of publishing it was thirty-eight-year-old John Veronis, then president of Curtis Publishing's magazine division. After the anguished demise of the *Saturday Evening Post*, his crown jewel, one might have thought he would switch to a more stable line of business. On the contrary, he not only decided to remain in publishing but did so with the daring of the captain of an ocean liner who banks his future on an experimental pedalboat: he went into partnership with Nicholas H. Charney, a twenty-five-year-old psychologist fresh out of college, and launched with him a psychology monthly based in San Diego, five hours by plane from New York and its concentration of media and ad agencies. The two immediate major questions were: was there enough of an academic audience for a specialized publication of this sort, and could the publishers assemble a readership that would attract advertisers?

Three years later, Veronis and Charney had not only succeeded in launching *Psychology Today* but they had also made a fortune selling the infant publication (and its large book publishing and book club operation) to a major conglomerate, Boise Cascade, for the eyebrow-raising sum of $21.3 million. The same man who had had a hand in one of the biggest failures in the history of contemporary publishing had, in record time, totted up an equally unprecedented capital gain (which he and his partner lost later in the equally daring, but this time unsuccessful, venture of revamping the *Saturday Review*).

Certainly the *Psychology Today* episode indicated Veronis and Charney's considerable talents as innovators, entrepreneurs, and businessmen; more importantly, it demonstrated the potential vitality of an industry that many were already referring to in the past tense. However, the only thing that Veronis' *Saturday Evening Post* and *Psychology Today* ventures had in common was the fact that they both involved publishing magazines. The marketing approach between the two had undergone a radical change. General magazines were dead, long live specialized publications!

A FRAGMENTING SOCIETY

On the evening that *Look*'s folding was announced, in September 1971, one of the most noteworthy commentaries on the end of the "general interest publications" came from television commentator Eric Sevareid. Predicting that the changes evolving in the communications field would bring about even greater fragmentation in a society that had already become too diversified, Sevareid claimed that the real hazard was not a monopoly of information but, rather, a Tower of Babel.

In so saying, he first of all made a plea for the cause of television, which had been accused by Agnew and others of having too strong an influence on public opinion. But Sevareid was also underscoring the swift acceptance of heterogeneity in place of social coherence and conformity. Americans today find that, as a result of an era of progress from which their country benefited before any of the other industrialized nations, their immense, reputedly homogeneous society of 200 million individuals is fragmenting. What are the basic causes of the profound evolution that has forced the media to diversify?

Job Specialization. The more complex a society is, the more necessary it becomes for

From *The Power to Inform.* Copyright © 1974 by Jean-Louis Servan-Schreiber. Used with permission of McGraw-Hill Book Company.

everyone in that society to play a role in a restricted area he knows thoroughly, so that things are kept functioning smoothly. The preference for teams of competent specialists over the intuition of an exceptional generalist is at the foundation of American management. Today this specialization has created subgroups which barely speak a common language when one of them has to communicate with another. Within the same business firm, engineers and researchers, moneymen and management live in different worlds. At the same university, history professors are out of touch with biologists, professors of literature are unlikely to meet with mathematicians. To meet the needs of these subgroups, publications strictly tailored to their fields of interest are required.

> A study of characters in American magazine fiction from 1890 to 1955 found a decline in the number of older women appearing as characters.... The middle-aged woman almost never sees herself and her problems depicted in print or on the screen. When they are, she sees mostly negative sterotypes. Her dilemma is very similar to that of the black ghetto child who finds ... a world that is irrelevant at best, invidious at worst. To have oneself and one's experiences verified in the mythology and art of one's culture is a fundamental psychological need at every stage of the life cycle.
>
> —Inge Powell Bell

The Assertion of New Freedoms and Tastes. As American society became more "permissive," magazines developed to cater to the interests of different groups that were asserting their potential for new markets in magazines. Sexual, class, age, regional, and spare-time differentiation in tastes made themselves felt. A new type of women's magazine emerged in *Ms.*; the special services and delights of a major city were catalogued in *New York*; mildly sex-oriented magazines like *Playboy* began to receive serious competition from the more forthright *Penthouse* and started a similar magazine, *Oui*; *Rolling Stone* serviced the youth culture beyond paying particular attention to rock music; the *National Lampoon's* extraordinary success rested in the appeal of *Mad* magazine's type of humor for college graduates. The list is long and will continue to change as additional segments of American society demand a magazine to fit their needs. Magazines specifically aimed at a black audience, for example, continue to spring up—ranging from journals with a definite political or social orientation, to slicks.

Liberal Education. For one thing, a greater interest in culture and increased knowledge of the world have played a strong role in the diversification of Americans' tastes. And for another, since World War II, the education system has tried to cope with the problems of a greater influx into the schools for a longer period of time. In other words, Americans have had to cope with all the problems of mass education. This has led to the diffusion of learning norms and values, and the concomitant multiplication of varied curricula and standards at schools and universities. Perhaps few Americans under forty years of age today have received an identical education.

The Consumer Paradise. In a market as vast and prosperous as that of the United States, any well-presented idea can create a limited but highly lucrative submarket for itself. The era of standardization corresponded to a time when all families were concurrently equipping themselves in durable goods. Today they can afford to be more fussy. The era of the 15 million Model-T Fords belongs to the past. Chevrolet, one General Motors line of cars, may display as many as forty different models on a single page of advertising. One of the main attractions of the eternal Volkswagen beetle could be the fact that, for the purchaser of this anti-Detroit car, it is a way of showing independence from the traditional American overemphasis on large size as a symbol of prestige.

Increased Leisure. Confined to jobs which bring them little satisfaction other than earnings, the great majority of Americans—affluent by world standards—seek to express themselves in their leisure activities. Thanks to the thirty-five- to forty-hour work week, weekends off (and, in the near future, more four-day work weeks), Americans have embraced a wide variety of sports, from bowling to scuba diving, from surfboards to pleasure boats, all of which have created new markets. Also, the ability to take vacation and business trips abroad—on a scale undreamed of by previous generations—has helped to diversify American interests in food, wine, art, and architecture, making the United States one of the most sophisticated markets in the world for a great variety of products.

People with the means and desire to do so have found new ways to express their interests by identifying and joining together with others of similar interests, which gives them the feeling that they are leading more meaningful lives.

Advertising caught on to the new consumer trend and adapted itself accordingly. While it had already been acknowledged that it was inadequate to run the same January tire ad in Chicago, which is covered with snow at that time of year, and in Miami, where crowds tan on the beach, now it was recognized, for instance, that for certain items it is more productive to use different sales pitches and media to reach black and white women. Surfers would be too expensive to reach if it were necessary to run an advertisement intended exclusively for them in a general interest publication like *Reader's Digest*. Also, the same individual will not react to a liquor ad found in *Life* as he would to one in *Gourmet*. Marketing and advertising have forced the media to do the same.

THE PUBLIC AS A SALAMI

Facing competition from smaller, more specialized means of communication, in response to advertisers' demands, the mass media realized that it was no longer possible to sell their audience as a whole and devised techniques for cutting it into slices. . . .

Many of my friends who read *Time* or *Newsweek* in Paris have come to the erroneous conclusion that "There really isn't much advertising in American magazines." The slim, sixty-page publication which they buy in Paris actually contains no more than ten pages of advertising. Unfamiliar with the sophisticated methods used to slice up the readership like a salami, they are unaware that the same week the New York edition carried perhaps sixty pages of advertising and the San Francisco edition forty-five, and that the Italian edition of *Time* may have four fewer pages of advertising than the French one.

At the end of the 1950s magazines discovered that many advertisers could no longer afford advertising rates which, as millions of subscribers continued to be recruited, had become astronomical.

By publishing editions for different parts of the country, magazines were able to offer business firms the choice of advertising only in editions destined for specific geographical areas covering several states, a single large city, or, in the case of the weekly newsmagazines (which are the only ones with sufficient worldwide circulation), Africa, all of Europe, or simply Ireland. The largest publications put out up to fifty regional editions. Not all of these were profit-making, since regional advertising pages brought in, at best, only 10 to 20 percent of a publication's revenues. National advertising continued to be by far the main source of revenue for magazines.

True, up to now magazines have not on the whole tried to offer regionally adapted editorial content along with regionally adapted advertising. In the future, though, if they wish to compete with television's increasing trend toward regional area programming, some magazines may have to think about revising this policy of standardized editorial content, which was originally dictated by cost factors. A newsmagazine such as *Newsweek* could increase reader following in California appreciably if, in addition to its national pages, it provided Californians with four to six pages of more local news that concerned them more directly. After all, with a population equal to half that of France, California certainly merits a few pages of weekly news.

Publishing separate editions with regional advertising makes sense only in those countries where different parts of the nation are comparable in wealth. Up to now, no French magazine has dared to take this step. Paris holds such a dominant place in the country's economy that publishers fear—and, for the moment, rightly so—that special advertising editions would be so heavily concentrated on the Paris market that regional editions would be deadly thin.

In recent years, the computer's infinite flexibility has made it possible for American magazines to acquire more precise statistical breakdowns of their readership. With the aid of zip codes, the country's wealthiest neighborhoods and suburbs (according to census figures) can be grouped in such a way as to provide advertisers with an audience that enjoys better-than-average purchasing power.

Demographic information enables a magazine such as *Time* to direct itself to the several hundred thousand students, doctors, or businessmen who are among its 4.25 million readers. In this case, specialization creates internal competition problems: with its "businessmen's" edition alone, *Time* can offer advertisers more readers than *Fortune*, published by the same corporation. *Business Week*, whose advertising rates had grown at a faster pace than many of its advertiser's budgets, introduced in 1972 an industrial edition (thus excluding bankers, insurance men, and professionals in other service fields), which ran additional pages in the editorial section. Nevertheless, by slicing up the readership in this way, the publisher runs a risk: if, in the future, the majority of advertisers find that their needs are satisfied by only one of these slices, the new editions, instead of bringing in additional advertising, could show a net loss for the magazine. . . .

UNLIMITED SPECIALIZATION

The advantages of slicing up the public by region has its limits, especially if little more is known about readers than their zip codes. For instance, the impact of an advertisement for certain products or services may be diffused in a general interest magazine. The editorial "environment" can play a critical role in the directness and intensity of the reader's response to a specific ad. It is not necessary to have studied marketing for three years and to have a computer at one's disposal to be aware that an ad for a new book is more effective in a literary review, that an ad for car seat-covers does best in an automobile monthly, that one for an anti-flea product belongs in a pet magazine, that one for a fishing reel gets the most action if run in a sports fishing journal, and that an ad for machine tools should be placed in an engineering publication.

Engineers, doctors, and sports enthusiasts make careful distinctions between editorial content and advertising when looking through a newspaper or general-interest magazine, but tend to be more receptive when they have a periodical that covers their specialty or hobby.

The specialized press, which focuses its articles and illustrations on a small number of sub-

> The mass media reinforce this perception [that the only criterion for feminine success is attractiveness of men]. . . . **Seventeen, Glamour,** and **Mademoiselle** provide endless pages of fashion, make-up, and dating advice. The girl learns that she must know how to attract, talk to, kiss, keep (or get rid of) a boy, depending on the circumstances. The magazines suggest which eye shadow, hair spray, lipstick, and blusher to use to accomplish these all-important ends. While fashion magazines tell her how to dress and use cosmetics, movies instruct on how to undress—and on the explicit use of sexuality.
> —Lenore J. Weitzman

jects, has a considerable psychological advantage over generalized magazines: it talks to readers about themselves, about things that really matter to them, about professional success stories, the problems and issues that are unique to their particular area of interest. In these ways, the specialized press mirrors very important facets of the reader's personality and thus holds his attention. Discovering that there is a magazine which deals with one's specific tastes, profession, social group, or city gives certain importance to one's own existence. . . .

Hobbies—There are monthlies for archers, numismatists, butterfly chasers, and modern jazz enthusiasts. *Age*—There are magazines for children of different age groups, as well as those that meet the needs of teenagers, college students, and young working people who identify with the youth culture. And certain magazines are aimed in large part at the interests of the more affluent retired people. *Sex*—One of the major categories under this heading is women's magazines. *Seventeen* is one of the most prosperous women's magazines in the United States despite the fact that its readership, by virtue of its name, is limited to a small sector of the public. From the feminist magazine *Ms.* to *Cosmopolitan* (which preaches sexual liberation for women without social emancipation), there exists a feminine press which is far more specialized than that of the traditional large women's magazines. Certain of these specialized women's magazines, such as *Marriage*, must obviously constantly renew their supply of readers. Many magazines are thought of as male-oriented because of subject matter that has traditionally been considered as falling within the masculine domain—sports, technology, business, etc. In this way, a general magazine like *Argosy* is fully cognizant of the "masculine mystique." Magazines like *Oui*, *Penthouse*, *Playboy* and *Genesis* all say on their covers that they are directed toward men, and only in this sense may they be considered specialized. There are magazines for both sexes (*Man and Woman*, *Sexology*) and for those who are single or divorced (*Single* and *Singles*, for example). *Ethics*—As the great waves of immigrants came to America, there were publications for people of Irish, Swedish and German descent as well as journals published in Spanish, Chinese, Hebrew, Yiddish, and Portuguese, or English-language publications addressed to specific ethnic audiences—all destined for Americans of diverse origins. The black press has gone through several periods of strong development. And, of course, the audience for specialized publications is further broken down into smaller categories: *California Pilot*, *Black Sport*, and *Business West* are only a few examples.

There are 9,000 different periodicals published in the United States and more than 2,000 in France. These figures remain fairly constant, but they do not always stand for the same 9,000 or 2,000 publications. Every year a certain number fold as a result of the decline of various specializations and a great number of journals are introduced to attract new subgroups.

ONLY THE ONES WE NEED

For publishers of specialized magazines, the most important consideration is not obtaining maximum circulation but servicing a homogeneous audience in order to maintain advertiser interest. If *Golf* magazine found that a high proportion of its readers took winter vacations and decided to add a winter sports column, it would run the risk of attracting skiers who may not play golf, thus diluting the total readership's interest in editorial content and ads directed toward golfers. Therefore, it would be wiser to create another magazine directed to skiers alone, if there are enough of them to constitute an audience for such a magazine.

The way to preserve the value of a magazine's readership is to refuse subscriptions to readers who are not within the magazine's target area. McGraw-Hill's *Business Week*, which is directed exclusively toward executives with responsible positions, asks subscription "candidates" to fill out a questionnaire concerning their work status. If the prospective subscribers are doctors, retired persons, students, or accountants, they receive a carefully worded letter explaining that *Business Week* is reserved for business executives. Obviously it would be a bit awkward to have to tell them that the real reason they have been turned down is that they would not be valuable advertising "prospects." Indeed, there are few doctors who can place orders for cranes or computers. . . .

A drawback of the selective subscription list is that it all too easily stirs discontent among those who are refused. Take, for example, a man who, because his name appears on a list of American Express card holders, receives a subscription solicitation from *Business Week*, which relies heavily on such lists of people with high purchasing power. The man decides he is interested in subscribing and sends back the order card. Fifteen days later the postman brings him an embarrassed letter from the magazine, which has turned down his subscription request because he is a dentist. Even if the man no longer has any illusions about the bizarre workings of postindustrial society, he still probably would not calmly accept the turndown ("First they beg me to subscribe and now they don't want me"). The management of *Business Week* does admit that if an individual insists, they would let him subscribe.

Selected subscribers bring more advantages to magazines than the creation of a specific market for their advertising salesmen. By the use of detailed questionnaires, specialized publications can gather (and record on computers) precise information about their subscribers and can, for example, produce lists of their readers who work in the aeronautic industry or are under thirty-five years old. This is exactly what *Business Week* did when it began renting, at a substantial price, tailored subscriber lists to mail-order companies whose products were of interest only to narrow groups of clients.

Magazines whose specialization is geographical come up against still another problem involved in reader specialization. The most prosperous among the specialized regional magazines is *Sunset*, a monthly unread outside the Western part of the United States for the simple reason that *Sunset* does not want circulation except in that part of the country. Dealing solely with "life style" (gardening, travel, decoration, cooking), *Sunset* is a mass-circulation magazine; with sales over 1 million, it surpassed *Life's* circulation figures for that section of the country. The members of the Lane family, owners and operators of *Sunset* for two generations, have warded off any attempt to enlarge the magazine's distribution by refusing to sell it throughout the country or to seek subscribers beyond the boundaries they set up. In spite of this restrictive policy—or, more likely, because of it—*Sunset* ranks twenty-fifth in the nation for advertising revenue.

A new arrival on the publishing scene, *New York* magazine, made a similar decision when it was introduced in 1967. Observing that the venerable *New Yorker* had long overstepped the boundaries of the city whose name it bears, *New York* decided to concentrate its sales solely in the New York metropolitan area which, with over 10 million inhabitants, constitutes one of the wealthiest advertising markets in the world. As a result, no newsstand sales were made and no subscriber solicitations were conducted outside metropolitan limits. *New York* even went so far as to charge a significantly higher subscription rate to anyone living outside the designated area who nevertheless wanted to receive the magazine. In contrast to *Sunset*, articles in *New York* are written by some of Americas's best bylines, which gives the magazine increased general interest and importance. Finally, however, a tearful letter from an exiled New York woman who complained about the financial discrimination of her high subscription price moved George Hirsh, then the magazine's publisher, to do away with the costlier "out-of-area" rate. This was of little consequence, though, because the very fact that the magazine conducts no national promotional campaigns keeps its circulation restricted to the New York area, just as its orginators had intended.

All of the publishers of specialized magazines did not have the foresight to limit their circulation targets. A good example of the risks involved in indiscriminate growth is *Scientific American*. This excellent monthly was transformed by Gerard Piel with the aim—admittedly quite difficult to meet—of presenting the scientific discoveries and issues of our time in language that would be understandable to laymen while avoiding cheap popularization. The task was immense, making it necessary for journalists to spend days on end with the scientist-authors, men who were far more at ease with a test tube than an inkwell, rewriting their words in readable form without distorting their thoughts. The goal was met, and today *Scientific American* is considered the best scientific magazine in the world.

However, the magazine's editorial success seriously jeopardized it financially. As long as *Scientific American's* circulation remained modest, advertisers of scientific equipment (microscopes, scientific calculators, etc.) flocked to the magazine, lured by the quality of its audience and its reasonable advertising rates. But *Scientific American* readership grew steadily, and, once it had reached the point where it was putting out several hundred thousand copies per issue, advertising rates had to be raised, making it out of reach for manufacturers of small equipment to continue advertising in the magazine. In addition, businessmen, students, commercial engineers—all of little interest to scientific equipment firms—now made up a large proportion of its readers.

Alarmed by the sudden loss of advertisers, *Scientific American* tried to give itself a new look, launching promotional campaigns which purported that its readers were, on the whole, decision-makers. This was an attempt to get in on the lucrative business advertising market. There, however, *Business Week*, *Fortune*, and others offered advertisers more concentrated groups of middle- and top-management readers, and the results were disappointing. By aiming at a fairly general readership, *Scientific American* compromised its very existence. In an ideal world this would not happen to a publication whose educational value is unquestionable. But, alas, the rules of the economic game prevail.

Ultimately, the logic of specialization and the desire for an undiluted market led some publishers to make a stab at free distribution. Today ever-increasing lists of the members of any given profession are available. Anyone who wants to can secure the names and addresses of all the physicians in a nation. Why, then, spend a fortune trying to sell subscriptions to doctors when, at the most, only 20 to 50 percent of them will respond? It is far more profitable simply to send them copies of the magazine free. Even the system of free distribution will still result in a modest print-order (there are 40,000 doctors in France; 200,000 in the United States). This makes it possible for the publishers to guarantee pharmaceutical manufacturers that the group they wish to reach is 100 percent covered. The situation would also hold true for electronic engineers or urban planners. The major problem, of course, is that other publishers may have the same idea and thus there is a strong possibility that the unwitting engineer whose name appears on an alumni list will receive three or four free magazines in his field. Editorial quality then becomes crucial. The publisher must be able to prove—through reader surveys—that the magazine is not only received but read as well. Magazines that do not meet this conclusive test will have trouble finding advertisers. The paradox is that the editorial quality of free periodicals may be higher than in those that charge a cover price. Advertising agencies, however, wonder just how seriously interested readers are in something they have not paid for, and it is this factor which is the major rein on the proliferation of free professional magazines.

When the groundwork has been carefully prepared, this method of controlled circulation (a euphemism for "free") makes highly precise marketing possible. Take the example of Gilbert Kaplan who, in 1967 at the age of twenty-five, launched *Institutional Investor*, a magazine of top editorial quality designed exclusively for those engaged in the newly developed business of managing huge stock investment funds. Firms of this type are few in number, but handle considerable sums on Wall Street. Kaplan put together a list of only 20,000 names, sent them the magazine, and pulled in financial advertising from corporations, banks, and stockbrokers. A year later, he repeated his success by creating *Corporate Financing*, a publication which also dealt with money management but which was designed only for financial directors of major firms. In 1972, he refined his target area further by introducing *Pension*, a periodical available only to managers of powerful retirement funds. Obviously, none of these magazines is known to the general public, but the professionals who happily receive them constitute an exceptional advertising market.

The advantages of specialization in a

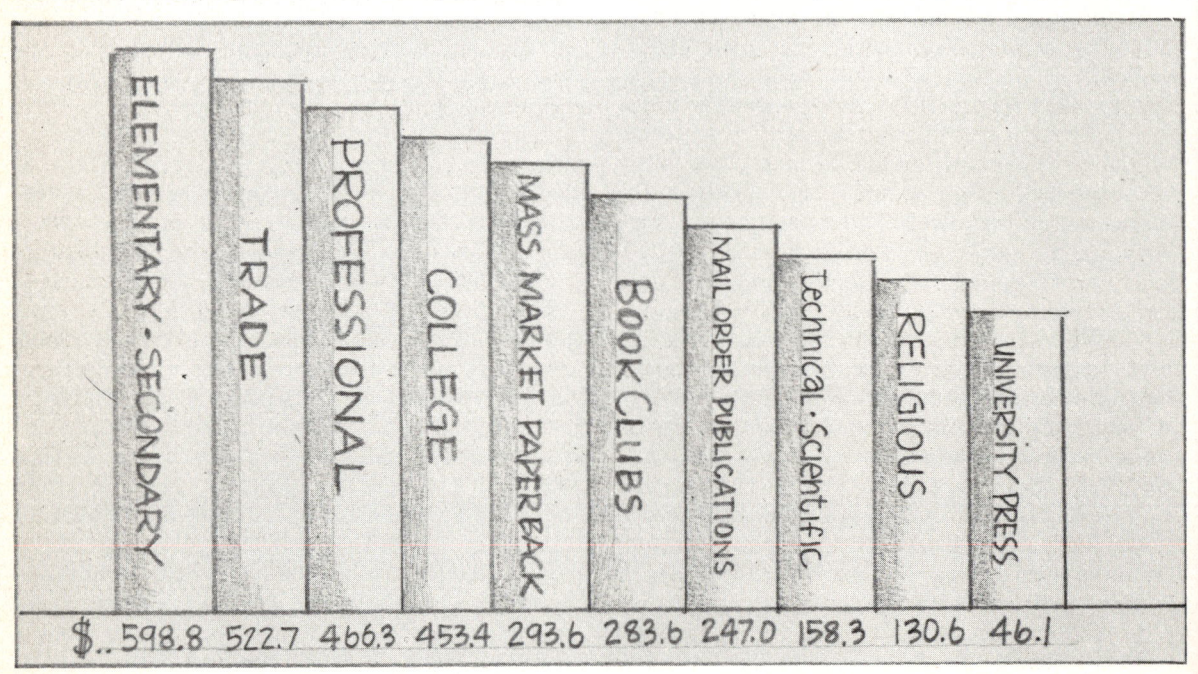

ELEMENTARY-SECONDARY	TRADE	PROFESSIONAL	COLLEGE	MASS MARKET PAPERBACK	BOOK CLUBS	MAIL ORDER PUBLICATIONS	Technical-Scientific	RELIGIOUS	UNIVERSITY PRESS
$598.8	522.7	466.3	453.4	293.6	283.6	247.0	158.3	130.6	46.1

magazine are not limited to advertiser appeal. If a publication can create a bond between itself and its devotees it will benefit from reader enthusiasm when it lends its name to other enterprises.

This trend marks a new departure in publishing, which began by selling news, information, and dreams to readers. Later publishers began to sell readers to advertisers. Now they have started to sell products and services to their readers. Two main business functions of a journal have become establishing a publication's market and image, then capitalizing on that to cement relations with readers. This favorable condition can be used to advantage in creating spin-offs such as other, more specialized publications, which benefit from public trust in the parent magazine or firm.

Another facet of publishing widely practiced today is selling to subscribers the product which most complements a magazine: books. The greatest successes in this area have been achieved by *Reader's Digest*, which publishes condensed books (the literary critics find them loathsome, but the public adores them), and Time, Inc., whose science, nature, geography, and cookbook series are put together with editorial techniques drawn from the magazines. Enormous success and huge profits are available to those publications that inspire great reader confidence in products bearing their name.

As was at first true of advertising, ten years or so ago the selling of related products was considered to be an adjunct of a magazine's principle activity and an opportunity for supplementary profit. But as the decline in advertising revenue and mounting production costs made journals less profitable, supplementary income from the sale of related products has become essential for some journals. In several countries of the world, local editions of *Reader's Digest* would lose money if book profits did not exist.

Today's generation of publishers on the whole deal in marketing-oriented conceptions and count on selling books, posters, games, records, audio-visual cassettes, seminars, conferences, packaged tours, and, of course, other publications to their readers. And why not? If *Time*, the pet of genial, austere Henry Luce, can go into the pots and pans business, the practice can't be all that bad.

PW Interview with Jean-Louis Servan-Schreiber

JOHN F. BAKER

. . . [Jean-Louis] Servan-Schreiber has thought deeply about the role of the information media and responded gladly to *PW*'s suggestion that he think aloud about the book publishing business as part of the picture.

The book is today almost certainly the best vehicle for the communication of important ideas. . . . Nothing else is nearly as effective if you have a message. Whatever is printed in a book automatically commands more respect and attention than anything in newspapers and magazines. An article, a speech, a TV appearance, produces no echo, no fallout. But an author of a book can be sure that the right people will read what he has to say. Reviewers, often experts in the same field, will discuss his ideas. Perhaps he will be interviewed, and therefore can expand on them further for a wider audience. As a result, a book's message is very widely dispersed, and in that sense it is the most modern and efficient of media.

He warms to one of the themes of his book, which is that most people today are surfeited with information, and find it increasingly difficult to select what is useful and relevant to them from among the barrage of words and pictures.

You know how obsessed we are with diet. Well, too many people are gaining too much weight in the brain today. What they need is more protein and less carbohydrate. And a good book is nearly all protein; what is more, if you don't need it, you won't read it. People do not casually nibble at books the way they

Reprinted from the September 2, 1974, issue of *Publishers Weekly*, published by R. R. Bowker Company, a Xerox company. Copyright © 1974 by Xerox Corporation.

Print 63

> Today the meaning of the book for young people in their TV environment is exotic indeed. The printed book, by its stress on intense visual culture, is the means of detachment and civilized objectivity in a world of profound sensuous involvement. The printed book is thus the only available means of developing habits of private initiative and private goals and objectives in the electric age.
>
> —Marshall McLuhan

nibble at newspapers, TV, and magazines. A book also helps you exercise your mind much more than any other form of reading. I'm thinking only of nonfiction in what I'm saying, of course.

No one can survey the publishing scene without sooner or later getting around to overproduction and Servan-Schreiber is no exception. "It's depressing to go into a bookstore. So many books, and they all look so interesting and attractive. They're like cakes. You want them all, and then you buy too many, and can't read them all, and you feel guilty." One of the problems of a potential book buyer, Servan-Schreiber suggests, is that he is not well informed as a consumer.

A reader needs an analysis of what's in a book, so that he can decide if it's something he wants to read. Obviously there's not nearly enough room to review enough books. Perhaps the answer might be a computerized system, regularly updated, which gives a brief analysis of the contents of current books, so that people could consult it for what interests them.

He feels that if such careful analysis of book contents was widely available, it would lead to fewer books, because it would make publishers much more selective. "It's too easy to publish too many books. There should be a much higher premium placed on good books." Servan-Schreiber is not speaking here as an outsider. *L'Expansion* has its own book publishing division in France (in which Mc-Graw-Hill is a partner), producing business and management books.

QUESTIONS FOR DISCUSSION

1. Ben Bagdikian contends that most newspapers are not serving society as effectively as they might. What changes do you think should be made? What can newspaper readers do to bring about desired change?

2. How has television affected the print industry? What other cultural, social, or technological changes have affected people's reading habits?

3. Why are specialized magazines replacing mass magazines? Choose two or three specialized magazines and list some characteristics that you assume fit the audience for each.

4. In his interview, Jean-Louis Servan-Schreiber states that "the book is certainly the best vehicle for the communication of important ideas." Why in this area are books superior to documentary films, magazine articles, or newspaper stories?

PROJECTS

1. Develop a map indicating the population clusters in your area. Identify the newspapers serving those regions and draw circles to indicate the approximate geographic areas served by each newspaper. From the library, obtain copies of those various newspapers and determine the differences among them in the emphasis placed on each of the following:
   (a) national news and local news
   (b) features
   (c) editorials
   (d) agricultural and business news
   (e) sports
   (f) entertainment

2. Analyze the content of a weekly news magazine and a metropolitan daily newspaper. Compare the following:
   (a) hard news vs. features
   (b) ratio of advertising space to editorial space
   (c) use of color vs. black and white
   (d) non-news vs. news items

3. Prepare a class profile to determine the time class members spend reading in the following categories:
   (a) newspapers
   (b) news magazines
   (c) special interest magazines
   (d) books (not including textbooks)

FILM

On the Future of Movies

PAULINE KAEL

Sometime during the last year, a number of the most devoted moviegoers stopped going to the movies. I say "a number" because I have no idea how many are actually involved, but I keep meeting people—typically, men in their late twenties and early thirties—who say, "You know, I just don't have the impulse to go to a movie anymore," or "There aren't any movies anymore, are there?" The interest in pictures has left these people almost overnight; they turned off as suddenly as they'd turned on, and, since they no longer care to go, they feel that there's nothing to see. It was no accident that the Americans walked off with most of the top awards at Cannes this year. Right now, American movies—not the big hits but many of the movies that Hollywood considers failures—are probably the best in the world. No country rivals us in the diversity of skilled, talented filmmakers, but there are few lines for the sorts of films that young audiences were queuing up for a couple of years ago. They talked fervently then about how they loved movies; now they feel there can't be anything good going on, even at the movies.

Whatever their individual qualities, such films as "Bonnie and Clyde," "The Graduate," "Easy Rider," "Five Easy Pieces," "Joe," "M*A*S*H," "Little Big Man," "Midnight Cowboy," and "They Shoot Horses, Don't They?" all helped to form the counterculture. The young, anti-draft, anti-Vietnam audiences that were "the film generation" might go to some of the same pictures that the older audience did, but not to those only. They were willing to give something fresh a chance, and they went to movies that weren't

Reprinted by permission; © 1974 The New Yorker Magazine, Inc.

certified hits. They made modest—sometimes large—successes of pictures that had new, different perceptions. A movie like the tentative, fumbling "Alice's Restaurant" would probably be a flop now, because student audiences are no longer willing to look for feelings, to accept something suggestive and elliptical and go with the mood. Students accept the elliptical on records—the Joni Mitchell "Court and Spark," say, and some of the more offbeat Carly Simon cuts—but not in movies. The subdued, fine-drawn "McCabe & Mrs. Miller," which came out in 1971, managed to break even, but the soft-colored "Thieves Like Us," the latest film by the same director, Robert Altman, has been seen by almost nobody. Those who might be expected to identify with Jeff Bridges in "The Last American Hero" are going to see Clint Eastwood in "Magnum Force" instead. They're going to the kind of slam-bang pictures that succeed with illiterate audiences in "underdeveloped" countries who are starved for entertainment. The almost voluptuously obsessive "Mean Streets"—a film that one might have thought would be talked about endlessly—passed through college towns without causing a stir. The new generations of high-school and college students are going to movies that you can't talk about afterward—movies that are completely consumed in the theatre.

There is no way to estimate the full effect of Vietnam and Watergate on popular culture, but earlier films were predicated on an implied system of values which is gone now, except in the corrupt, vigilante form of a "Dirty Harry" or a "Walking Tall." Almost all the current hits are jokes on the past, and especially on old films—a mixture of nostalgia and parody, laid on with a trowel. The pictures reach back in time, spoofing the past, jabbing at it. Nobody understands what contemporary heroes or heroines should be, or how they should relate to each other, and it's safer not to risk the box-office embarrassment of seriousness.

For many years, some of us alarmists have been saying things like "Suppose people get used to constant visceral excitement—will they still respond to the work of artists?" Maybe, owing partly to the national self-devaluation and partly to the stepped-up power of advertising, what we feared has come about. It's hardly surprising: how can people who have just been pummelled and deafened by "The French Connection" be expected to respond to a quiet picture? If, still groggy, they should stumble in to see George Segal in Irvin Kershner's "Loving" the next night, they'd think there was nothing going on in it, because it didn't tighten the screws on them. "The Rules of the Game" might seem like a hole in the screen. When "The Getaway" is double-billed with "Mean Streets," it's no wonder that some people walk out on "Mean Streets." Audiences like movies that do all the work for them—just as in the old days, and with an arm-twisting rubdown besides. College students don't appear to feel insulted (what's left to insult us?); they don't mind being banged over the head—the louder the better. They seem to enjoy seeing the performers whacked around, too; sloppy knockabout farce is the newest smash, and knockabout horror isn't far behind. People go for the obvious, the broad, the movies that don't ask them to feel anything. If a movie is a hit, that means practically guaranteed sensations—and sensations without feeling.

I often come out of a movie now feeling wiped out, desolate—and often it's a movie that the audience around me has reacted to noisily, as if it were having a high, great time—and I think I feel that way because of the nihilism in the atmosphere. It isn't intentional or philosophical nihilism; it's the kind one sometimes feels at a porn show—the way everything is turned to dung, oneself included. A couple of years ago, I went with another film critic, a young man, to see a hard-core movie in the Broadway area, and there was a live stage show with it. A young black girl—she looked about seventeen but must have been older—did a strip and then danced naked. The theatre was small, and the girl's eyes, full of hatred, kept raking the customers' faces. I was the only other woman there, and each time her eyes came toward me, I had to look down; finally, I couldn't look up at all. The young critic and I sat in misery, unable to leave, since that would look like a put-down of her performance. We had to take the contempt with which she hid her sense of being degraded, and we shared in her degradation, too. Hits like "The Exorcist" give most of the audience just what it wants and expects, the way hard-core porn does. The hits have something in common: blatancy. They are films that *deliver*. They're debauches—their subject might almost be mindlessness and futurelessness. People in the audience want to laugh, and at pictures like "Enter the Dragon" and "Andy Warhol's Frankenstein" and "The Three Musketeers" and "Blazing Saddles" they're laughing at pandemonium and accepting it as the comic truth.

The counterculture films made corruption seem inevitable and hence something you learn to live with; the next step was seeing it as slapstick comedy and learning to enjoy it. For the fatalistic, case-hardened audience, absurdism has become the only acceptable point of view—a new complacency. In "The Three Musketeers," Richard Lester keeps his actors at a distance and scales the characters down to subnormal size; they're letching, carousing buffoons who don't care about anything but blood sport. The film isn't politically or socially abrasive; it's just "for fun." At showings of "Chinatown," the audience squeals with pleasure when Faye Dunaway reveals her incest. The success of "Chinatown"—with its beautifully structured script and draggy, overdeliberate direction—represents something dialectically new: nostalgia (for the thirties) openly turned to rot, and the *celebration* of rot. Robert Towne's script had ended with the detective (Jack Nicholson) realizing what horrors the Dunaway character had been through, and, after she killed her incestuous father, helping her daughter get to Mexico. But Roman Polanski seals the picture with his gargoyle grin; now evil runs rampant. The picture is compelling, but coldly, suffocatingly compelling. Polanski keeps so much of it in closeup that there's no air, no freedom to breath; you don't care who is hurt, since everything is blighted. Life is a blood-red maze. Polanski may leave the story muddy and opaque, but he shoves the rot at you, and large numbers of people seem to find it juicy. Audiences now appear to accept as a view of themselves what in the movies of the past six or seven years counterculture audiences jeered at Americans for being—cynical materialists who cared for nothing but their own greed and lust. The nihilistic, coarse-grained movies are telling us that nothing matters to us, that we're all a bad joke.

It's becoming tough for a movie that isn't a big media-created event to find an audience, no matter how good it is. And if a movie has been turned into an event, it doesn't have to be good; an event—such as "Papillon"—draws an audience simply because it's an event. You don't expect Mount Rushmore to be a work of art, but if you're anywhere near it you have to go; "Papillon" is a movie Mount Rushmore, though it features only two heads. People no longer go to a picture just for itself, and ticket-buyers certainly aren't looking for the movie equivalent of "a good read." They want to be battered, to be knocked out—they want to get wrecked. They want what "everybody's talking about," and even if they don't like the picture—and some people didn't really care for "A Touch of Class," and some detested "The Three Musketeers," and many don't like "Blazing Saddles," either—they don't feel out of it. Increasingly, though, I've noticed that those who don't enjoy a big event-film feel out of it in another way. They wonder if there's something they're not getting—if the fault is theirs.

The public can't really be said to have rejected a film like "Payday," since the public never heard of it. If you don't know what a movie is and it plays at a theatre near you, you barely register it. "Payday" may not come at all; when the event strategy really works, as it has of late, the hits and the routine action films and horror films are all that get to most towns. And if a film turns up that hasn't had a big campaign, people assume it's a dog; you risk associating yourself with failure if you go to see Jon Voight in "Conrack" or Blythe Danner in the messed-up but still affecting "Lovin' Molly." When other values are rickety, the fact that something is selling gives it a primacy, and its detractors seem like spoilsports. The person who holds out against an event looks a loser: the minority is a fool. People are cynical about advertising, of course, but their cynicism is so all-inclusive now that they're indifferent, and so they're more susceptible to advertising than ever. If nothing matters anyway, why not just go where the crowd goes? That's a high in itself.

There are a few exceptions, but in general it can be said that the public no longer discovers movies, the public no longer makes a picture a hit. If the advertising for a movie doesn't build up an overwhelming desire to be part of the event, people just don't go. They don't listen to their own instincts, they don't listen to the critics—they listen to the advertising. Or, to put it more precisely, they do listen to their instincts, but their instincts are now controlled by advertising. It seeps through everything—talk shows, game shows, magazine and newspaper stories. Museums organize retrospectives of a movie director's work to coördinate with the opening of his latest film, and publish monographs paid for by the movie companies. College editors travel at a movie company's expense to see its big new film and to meet the director, and directors preview their new pictures at colleges. The public-relations event becomes part of the national consciousness. You don't hear anybody say, "I saw the most wonderful movie you never heard of;" when you hear people talking, it's about the same blasted movie that everybody's going to—the one that's flooding the media. Yet even the worst cynics still like to think that "word of mouth" makes hits. And the executives who set up the machinery of manipulation love to believe that the public—the public that's sitting stone-dead in front of its TV sets—spontaneously discovered their wonderful movie. If it's a winner, they say it's the people's choice. But, in the TV age, when people say they're going to see "Walking Tall" because they've "heard" it's terrific, that rarely means a friend has told them; it means they've picked up signals from the atmosphere. It means "Walking Tall" has been plugged so much that every cell in a person's body tells him he's got to see it. Nobody ever says that it was the advertising that made him vote for a particular candidate, yet there is considerable evidence that in recent decades the Presidential candidates who spent the most money always won. They were the people's choice. Advertising is a form of psychological warfare that in popular culture, as in politics, is becoming harder to fight with aboveboard weapons. It's becoming damned near invincible.

The ludicrous "Mame" or the limp, benumbed "The Great Gatsby" may not make as much money as the producing companies hoped for, but these pictures don't fail abjectly, either. They're hits. If Hollywood executives still believe in word of mouth, it's because the words come out of their own mouths.

The businessmen have always been in control of film production; now advertising puts them, finally, on top of public reaction as well. They can transcend the content and the quality of a film by advertising. The new blatancy represents the triumph—for the moment, at least—of the businessmen's taste and the businessmen's ethic. Traditionally, movies were thought linked to dreams and illusions, and to pleasures that went way beyond satisfaction. Now the big ones are stridently illusionless, for a public determined not to be taken in. Audiences have become "realists" in the manner of businessmen who congratulate themselves for being realists: they believe only in what gives immediate gratification. It's got to be right there—tangible, direct, basic, in their laps. The movie executives were shaken for a few years; they didn't understand what made a film a counterculture hit. They're happy to be back on firm ground with "The Sting." Harmless, inoffensive. Plenty of plot but no meanings. Not even any sex to worry about.

Much—perhaps most—of the students' and educated moviegoers' unresponsiveness to recent fine work can be traced to the decisions of the movie companies about what will sell and what won't. With their overweening campaign budgets for "The Great Gatsby" and "Chinatown," the Paramount executives didn't even take a full-page ad in the *Times* to announce that "The Conversation" had won the Grand Prize at Cannes. They didn't *plan* on "The Conversation" being a success, and nothing now is going to make them help it become one. "Gatsby" and "Chinatown" were their pictures, but "The Conversation" was Francis Ford Coppola's, and they're incensed at his being in a position (after directing "The Godfather") to do what he wanted to do; they're *hurt* that he flouts their authority, working out of San Francisco instead of Los Angeles. And they don't really have any respect for "The Conversation," because it's an idea film. It's the story of a compulsive loner (Gene Hackman), a wizard at electronic surveillance who is so afraid others will spy on him that he empties his life; he's a cipher—a cipher in torment. There's nothing to discover about him, and *still* he's in terror of being bugged. (Hackman is a superlative actor, but his peculiarity, his limitation, like Ralph Richardson's when he was younger, is his quality of anonymity: just what is right for this role.) "The Conver-

> I never saw ROBIN HOOD when it came out. . . . at that time I was sort of afraid to see it. You know, you are always afraid of not being any good, terrified of it, and not being any good, publicly. It hurts, distressingly. So I hadn't seen that film and in 1950 something—it was playing on the Champs Elysees and my son was ten years old and he wanted to see it. . . . The main thing is this; I thought the film was adorable. I had no idea it was so good. It was enchanting and I thought, good gracious, it's a classic, it really is a classic! When we made those films we had no idea what we were making, that we were making the best of their kind. We were, and that was marvelous.
>
> —Olivia de Havilland

sation" is driven by an inner logic. It's a little thin, because the logic is the working out of one character's obsession, but it's a buggy movie that can get to you so that when it's over you really feel you're being bugged. Maybe the reason the promotion people didn't try to exploit the Watergate tie-in was that they suspected the picture might also be saying something about movie companies. If a film isn't promoted, it's often because something about it—the idea itself, or the director's obstinate determination to make it—needles the bosses.

Executives show a gambler's ardor in arranging the financing of a picture. Sometimes they buy into one when it's finished or almost finished, in what appears to be the absolute conviction that it's a winner. But almost any straw in the wind can make them lose confidence. They'll try out a tricky, subtle movie on a Friday-night preview audience that has come to see "Walking Tall" or John Wayne in "McQ," and decide that the movie has no public appeal. They pull away from what they fear will be a failure; within the fiefdom of their company they don't want to be associated with a risky venture. They all snuggle deep into the company's hits; a picture like "The Sting" becomes a soft fur collar that they caress themselves with. The company that has "The Sting" doesn't worry about a real sendoff for "The Sugarland Express": where are the big stars? The company with "The Exorcist" doesn't give much thought to a campaign for "Mean Streets": some of the executives don't find it "satisfying," so they're sure the public won't. The movie companies used to give all their pictures a chance, but now they'll put two or three million, or even five, into selling something they consider surefire, and a token—a pittance—into the others. And when an unpublicized picture fails they can always cover their tracks by blaming the director. "There was nothing we could do for it," the executives in charge of advertising always say, and once they have doomed a picture, who can prove them wrong?

What isn't generally understood is that the top men don't want to be proved wrong and the lower-echelon executives have a jobholder's interest in proving their bosses right. For all the publicity the companies get from giving a picture "a second chance"—never really having given it a first—I can think of only one or two cases when they honestly did provide a fresh chance, and there's a whole morgueful of movies that were killed despite indications of public response; for example, Gillo Pontecorvo's only picture after "The Battle of Algiers"—"Burn!," starring Marlon Brando, which came and went so fast that hardly anybody knows it exists.

If the company men don't like a picture, or are nervous about its chances, or just resent the director's wanting to do something he cares about (instead of taking the big assignments they believe in), they do minimal advertising, telling him, "Let's wait for the reviews," or "We'll see how the reviewers like it," and then, even if the reviews are great, they say, "But the picture isn't doing business. Why should we throw away money on it?" And if he mentions the reviews, they say, "Listen, the critics have never meant anything. You know that. Why waste money? If people don't want to go, you can't force them to buy tickets."

There's a natural war in Hollywood between the businessmen and the artists. It's based on drives that may go deeper than politics or religion: on the need for status, and warring dreams. The entrepreneur class in the arts is a relatively late social development; there were impresarios earlier, but it was roughly a hundred years ago, when the arts began to be commercialized for a large audience, that the mass-culture middleman was born. He functions as a book publisher, as a theatrical producer, as a concert manager, as a rock promoter, but the middleman in the movie world is probably more filled with hatred for the artists he traffics in than the middleman in any other area. The movie entrepreneur is even more of a self-made man than the others; he came out of nowhere. He has to raise—and risk—more money, and he stands to gain more. In a field with no traditions, he is more of a gambler and less of an aesthete than entrepreneurs in the other arts. He's a street fighter, his specialty low cunning. Even if he's a second- or third-generation movie executive with a college education, or a Harvard-educated lawyer turned agent turned producer, he's learned to be a street fighter if he wasn't born to it, and he has the same hatred of the artist. The artist, with his expressive needs—the artist, who, by definition, cares about something besides money—denigrates the only talent that the entrepreneur has: raising money. Nobody respects the entrepreneur's dream of glory, and nobody respects his singular talent—least of all the artist who needs him, and is often at his mercy.

The entrepreneur has no class, no status; and, whether he was a scrambling junk dealer or a scheming agent or a poor little rich boy who managed to survive his mogul father's ruthless bullying, he knows that. A director or an actor doesn't even have to be an artist—only to identify himself as an artist—to get the cachet, while the moneyman is likely to be treated as a moneygrubbing clown. Some few—Joe Levine, and Sam Goldwyn before him—have been able to make celebrities of themselves by acquiring a comic status, the status of a shrewd, amusing vulgarian. In no other field is the entrepreneur so naked a status-seeker. Underlings are kept busy arranging awards and medals and honorary degrees for the producer, whose name looms so large in the ads that the public—and often the producer himself—comes to think he actually made the pictures. Ross Hunter, Robert Radnitz, even Hal Wallis in recent years hardly have room in their advertising for the writers' and directors' names. The packagers offer themselves as the stars, and in many cases their pictures fail because they insist on employing non-entity directors who don't assert any authority. . . .

The Docudramatelementary

NORMAN CORWIN

The documentary film—the agreed-upon name for a unique blending of art and journalism—is meeting new demands of specific as well as mass audiences. As Norman Corwin explains, this film form is becoming a staple for television, but as today's students will point out, it is also a welcome addition to the classroom.

Whenever a vast occasion comes along—the death of a president, the visit of a pope, a round trip to the moon, an East-West detente garnished with honor guards, a national election, the Watergate hearings—then the same medium which brings us so many hours of who-dunits, private eyes, game shows, old movies, reruns, trivia and recycled slop becomes vital, dynamic, resourceful, imaginative and sporadically magnificent. These finest hours are all documentary. They are not called such, but that is what they are.

It happens that TV and the documentary have a special affinity. Whereas the big eye has crippled or destroyed whole entities like radio drama, periodicals (*Look, Life, Collier's*), B-pictures, newspapers and living room conversation, and has affected God knows what else that is not measurable by any economic index, at the same time it has been the documentary's best friend.

Before television, the documentary film had been, relatively speaking, an esoteric branch of an otherwise popular medium. One proof of the rare-bird nature of the early documentary is to ask yourself how many of the following names you recognize: Anstey, Cavalcanti, Flaherty, Grierson, Ivens, Leacock, Legg, Lorentz, Rotha, Ruttman, Strand, Wright. Beyond Grierson and Flaherty, who are at least known to students of film, the rest mean nothing to most of us. Yet every one was important to the history of the documentary.

It was not our fault that these people were not part of our experience, as were Griffith, Chaplin, DeMille, Lubitsch and a hundred other film familiars that we grew up on. The fault, if it can be called a fault, lay in the disinterest of motion picture exhibitors; there was no chance for documentaries to get a big audience so long as audiences were not exposed to them in any form. And without big audiences, there was no big money to produce them; and so the cycle was closed.

A generation ago, the term documentary was seldom heard. Movie people and exhibitors referred to documentaries by length, not character; they were shorts. Just shorts. If a feature-length documentary was made, they didn't know what to call it, and, worse, they didn't know where to put it. Mostly they just ignored it, and let it die.

But TV soon discovered that the documentary was not a luxury, not a freak, not an ary vehicle, but a necessity. Because the medium is immediate, simultaneous and widespread, it shares certain characteristics with newspapers and radio—the need, indeed the compulsion, to gather and disseminate news, and to deal with information and public opinion as vital commodities.

The term documentary itself has ceased to frighten people. For a while the television industry searched desperately for a viable synonym, to get away from the fancied or actual stigma of the term. They came up with "telementaries," "docudramas" and "fact-dramas." All uniformly starchy and self-conscious names, all happily stillborn.

The news documentary came naturally to TV; the theme documentary followed after a while, and quickly became sophisticated. Basic reportage was outfitted with skills that had not been considered necessary or important to factual content: music, planned photography (as against candid or spontaneous), carefully structured writing. The documentary began to make larger and larger statements, as in the case of Edward R. Murrow's disposal of Senator Joseph McCarthy, the controversial *The Selling of the*

Reprinted by permission of Norman Corwin from *The Journal of the Producers Guild of America.*

Pentagon, Pont of Order, Titticut Follies, the barrage of films on our unhappy adventure in Vietnam, ringing tocsins on ecology, prison reform, the population explosion, our shrinking resources, and so on into the awards season.

A measure of the effectiveness of documentaries on political or social subjects, especially when they concerned military, economic or administrative issues, was the uproar they created. Instead of being damned with faint praise, they were praised with loud damns. Denials, assertions, accusations, angry charges, subpoenas. Whether or not these pictures cast much light, they generated a good deal of heat. To their credit, let it be said; for a supine medium, stereotyped forms, a play-it-safe attitude and an unbalanced diet of medics, spies, cowboys, sitcoms and give-aways, is of small value to the public, the country, or our time. Even as entertainment, a tenth rerun of *Hogan's Heroes* or *I Love Lucy* would appear to stand on the threshold of diminishing returns.

As archive, the documentary flourished. Television opened vaults that seemed as sealed as Tut's tomb. Old series like *Victory at Sea, The Churchill Years, the FDR Series*, would run for twenty-six weeks, sometimes longer. To feed them, research teams scoured private and government film libraries, and turned up what in film was the equivalent of ancient scrolls, artifacts, potsherds and gemstones. It is conceivable that the film depositories will be all mined out some day, like coal reserves, but there is no sign of that being imminent. New series, like *The Second World War*, keep coming along, and manage to satisfy the standards of both good documentary-making and good history. Esthetic trips like Sir Kenneth Clark's *Civilization* series put in a good word for the abiding values of culture; David Wolper's excursions into recent and current history (*The Rise and Fall of the Third Reich, Wattstax, Visions of Eight*) are vivid chronicles that should endure on the permanent shelf.

The compilation documentary is not necessarily sober, relevant, foreboding or rhetorical. A recent Academy nomination, *Legendary Heroes*, had to do with heavyweight boxing champions of the past. It has incredible footage, some of which must have been found in attics and rummage sales from Finland to Australia. Every so often somebody puts together an anthology of comedy scenes, or dance numbers, or great moments in football or aviation. This is mostly scissors-and-cement stuff, but even at its least imaginative it is instructive, like an illustrated article in an encyclopedia, or a book on succulents.

The creative documentary grows in all directions. If you like animals, there are Irwin Rostein's fine works on the grizzly bear and the maligned wolf, Paul Radin's classic reenactment, *Born Free* (lions), and dozens of pictures on apes, penguins, white sharks, even one on a rare snail. If you like the taste of salt, there are the Cousteau specials and Bruno Vailati's *The Seven Seas*. If you are concerned with being overweight, then you must—repeat, must see *A Matter of Fat*, produced with its usual fine hand by the National Film Board of Canada. If only you can find the picture in a theatre, that is.

We are accustomed to great changes taking place periodically in stage and film drama, and these changes are marked off by such familiar terms as neo-realist, avant garde, new wave, theatre of the absurd. The changes in the documentary film have been as many if not more, but they are not as well known or codified, because until recently the documentary itself was not well known. That has been altered, thanks largely to the tube, not the movie houses. For where, in any big city, on any weekend, can a man take his children, his Ms., or just himself, to see a picture that comments directly, informationally, factually, upon the world around us, be it a film on volcanoes or whales or obesity or Jack Johnson or autistic children or Beethoven or Soutine or future shock? Not many outlets. Maybe an art house or two.

Fortunately, though, one can stay at home and see grizzlies and sharks and old-time heavyweights at odd hours. Whatever TV's sins, and they are many, it did bring the documentary in from Siberia and gave it a warm home just across the tracks from the mansions of Lucy, Hogan, Gilligan, Welby and M. Tyler Moore. Be grateful for big-sized favors.

Film, Movies, and Audiences

PENELOPE HOUSTON

In this introduction to her book, **Contemporary Cinema**, Penelop Houston offers a look at contemporary film in an era which marks both the maturity and the decline of the movies. No longer is cinema actually a mass medium, yet in its own way it represents a force within society that far eclipses its declining distribution. Cinema as an art form is still unique, seeking traditions which reflect national origins and responding to events as a social historian.

The past changes and developing trends observed by this British film critic are valid for the American film as well as for the British cinema.

Films or movies, the pictures or motion pictures: even the choice of word reaches out tentatively towards the definition of an attitude. "Film" is neutral; "movies" ought to be fun; "the pictures" means a double-feature and a choc-ice; "motion picture" is American and assertive, suggesting an Academy Awards ceremony or a graduate thesis on "the medium." Entertainment, art, mass communication; industry, private experiment, public service; the most important of the arts, in terms of twentieth-century society, or an art only on sufferance; the one art whose production can take place in factory conditions, or an industry with an art locked within it, perpetually struggling to break free. The sweeping definitions could be almost indefinitely extended: "seventh art," "tenth muse," "opium for the masses." Call it all these, and then come back again to the cinema. And "that which makes the cinema," said René Clair forty years or so ago, "is not to be discussed."

It is only during the last few years, however, that a new definition has crept into the list: the mass medium in danger of losing its mass audi-

---

Reprinted from *The Contemporary Cinema* by Penelope Houston, © 1963. Used by permission of Penguin Books Ltd.

---

ence. To look back to 1946, in Britain, is to remember a popular cinema which is never likely to come again. Over thirty million cinema tickets were sold each week. At the roundabouts on the arterial roads leading out of London the big grey Odeons stood guard, forbidding blockhouses in the heavy thirties style. Andy Hardy and Old Mother Riley, Abbott and Costello and the Bowery Boys, Tarzan and Blondie kept "the pictures" turning over. Now only the indestructible Tarzan remains, the last survivor from the age of innocence.

Over the intervening years, "the pictures" have been losing ground steadily to "film," and the Odeons have become filling stations or factories or dance-halls. A habit has disintegrated, for the most part unregretted, and if the sociologists' interest has appeared only mildly aroused it is probably because the shift has been one of emphasis and situation rather than more fundamentally of public taste. *Coronation Street* now nets in two evenings two-thirds or more of that weekly thirty million; even *Tonight* collects about a quarter of it. Television has become the routine, borrowing wholesale from the cinema the comedy series and Westerns and thrillers, the habit-forming programmes. The new habit has attracted all the sociological attention, while the old one has been allowed quietly to decline. And decline it has. By 1962, according to a Board of Trade estimate, the cinema audience in Britain was down to about eight million a week, while six years had seen the closing down of more than a third of the nation's cinemas.

The pattern has been found to repeat itself in almost every country with an expanding television service. And, as each cinema industry in turn laboriously discovers for itself, there are other counterattractions. Cinema managers in America, then in Britain, more recently in France, have voiced their complaints in almost identical terms: too many cars (*la motorisation*, say the French, will be the death of the cinema); too many other things for people to do with their time. An industry which had encouraged its audience to regard it as a habit, to queue at the same time each week for a film as much like last week's as possible, to buy cinema as unthinkingly as it bought toothpaste or cigarettes, discovered with a deep sense of shock and affront that the wares it had been selling for so long as necessities were suddenly being treated as luxuries. The nightly switch-on replaces the weekly visit to the pictures: only the cinema manager can be said really to regret it.

But, of course—and it is by no means a paradox—a declining audience need not also mean a less enthusiastic one. The Pilkington Report, in another context, has nailed the fallacy of claiming to gauge public taste on a purely statistical basis. People watch television, as they used to go to the movies, not to see *something*, but to see *anything*. A mass audience brings its own apathy, and the fact that a vast number of people are watching the same thing does not prove that they are enjoying themselves, merely that they are there. The rebellion of the docile and tractable audience of fifteen years ago forced the entertainment cinema to change its strategy. It has discovered that any picture aimed purposefully enough at the big commercial market (a *Ben-Hur* or a *South Pacific*, a *Longest Day* or a *Dr No*) will make at least as much money as it would have done fifteen years ago, and probably a good deal more. Movies must emphasize their difference from each other, not their similarities; selling becomes a series of shrill demands for public attention. But if the selling is right, then, unmistakably and even enthusiastically, the audience is there. And, at the same time, there has never been a larger, more wide-awake, or more interested public for the kind of film which only a few years ago would have seemed desperately specialized. The distributors who acquired *L'Avventura* or *L'Année dernière à Marienbad* or *Shadows* knew what they were about: yesterday's defiant risk becomes today's cocktail-party talking point.

This cinema has become fashionable—sometimes to an extent dangerous for its own good. Directors' reputations go up and down as rapidly as speculative shares. Buy blue-chip Bergmans in 1959 and Antonionis in 1961; watch the continental festivals for the next hot tip, the next director whose work will be talked up, written up, photographed for the glossies, before most people have even got around to seeing it for themselves. Film magazines all over the world weigh in with articles which uncover the same new trends at the same time: when the trends

> A nation's films reflect a nation's thoughts.
> —Penelope Houston

turn out to be not quite what was expected, the disillusionment comes as abruptly as the discovery. New directors are continually being told that they are betraying a promise they never knew they had shown: behind them, the next new wave is already thundering up the beach. In this atmosphere, which makes for liveliness if not for stability, the queues swing over from the Odeons to the specialized cinemas, the Hollywood talents are scattered to the winds of Europe, and Hollywood itself no longer looks like the capital of the cinema, but the Park Avenue of the American television industry.

In the immediate post-war years, specialized cinemas were few in number and relatively regular in their clientele. Now they are all over the place, and the number of people who would never think of going to see a film in a foreign language falls away every year. The reason, perhaps, is not only that the specialized film is more readily accessible than it ever used to be, but also that the cinema has found its responsive public because it can be taken so thoroughly for granted. A generation has grown up with the sound film, with colour, with the whole vocabulary of the screen. The old critical battlefields —Can movies properly be called an art at all? Are silent films intrinsically better than the talkies? Are big screens a dead loss creatively? —are deserted. No one any longer has to have close-ups and flashbacks defined for them, to be told in basic terms how the movies work. The syntax of the moving image (film *or* television) has become one of the integral, unquestioned things in everyone's experience.

So experiment becomes that much easier. And this whole atmosphere, with its hints of creative possibility, has made the cinema—or at any rate the European cinema—a more stimulating place to work in. But there have also been heavy casualties, most obviously in the decline of the Hollywood empires, those power symbols of the international cinema. Hollywood domination at its worst may have seemed brutalized, a bronze idol which took out its human sacrifice in talent; but at its best, it afforded its own kind of stability. There was confidence, because there was continuity. A studio could take the time to let young artists and actors develop, sure that it would still be there when the time came round to get the best out of them. Orson Welles spent the better part of his first year at R.K.O. watching films, and then emerged to direct *Citizen Kane*. This could hardly happen now: the ballast that kept the whole thing afloat has gone, along with all the average, unpretentious, easy-going movies which were never intended to do more than provide the audience with a way of passing the time, the studios which promoted them with a steady income, and the people who made them with a means of exercising their craft.

Production investment touches fantastic levels. Even the rights to *My Fair Lady* change hands at more than $5,000,000, while every news bulletin on *Cleopatra* quoted a slightly higher figure, a few more millions on a production budget which has been estimated at anything between $30,000,000 and $40,000,000. To get back the kind of money that is being spent on them, some of these films have not only to be best sellers in the normal sense but to join the ten or twenty top sellers in the whole of cinema history. So the production investment is hedged around with safeguards, in the form of the right cast, the right big-screen system, the right sales campaign. It is all a good deal more like launching a battleship, one director has said, than making a film. It has to be.

Only the American industry, with its world market, internationally known stars, and long-term experience, can readily afford the kind of investment involved in one of the super-spectacles. For Europe and the Eastern cinemas the best chances lie in films of moderate cost which can get back their expenses within a limited market, and in productions whose quality breaks down the international barriers. So the cinema of the sixties presents its own form of split personality: the big and the small; the expensive and the cheap; the very safe and the very daring—success can lie at either end of the scale, but is unlikely to be found too near the middle.

Trash sells faster than ever, but it has to be exploitable, sensational trash. So the nudist films, the cut-price horror films, the censor-free club cinemas trading on the dismal delights of the supposedly illicit, come and go. *My Bare Lady* and *Some Like It Nude* compete with *The White Slavers* and *Juvenile Passion*. At a rather higher level, fashion goes in waves and extremism flourishes. Uncertain of its public, the film industry will try anything once and most things more than once. And the cinema, consequently, becomes more tense and nervous, an excitable industry which has not quite come to terms with its own reduced circumstances. But if this applies, in general terms, to America and Western Europe, on the other side of the world newer industries are still developing, still unassailed by television and the other competitors, still able to find audiences open to experience at a simpler level.

This is just a part of the pattern of contemporary cinema, that relation of the audience to the industry which determines so much of what we see on the screen. It is a strikingly different picture from the one confronting Roger Manvell when, during the war, he wrote his famous Pelican *Film*, the book which must have started so many of his juniors along the road to the cinema. Then Hollywood still dominated, the Italian cinema had hardly begun to shake off the deadening weight of Fascism, the Indian and Japanese industries remained more or less unknown quantities, and the cinemas of the West had no problems about where to look for an audience. Although the cinema already had more than forty years of history behind it, its critical literature was not much more than twenty years old and its historians had formed their theories in the days before sound. The last two decades have seen an enormous accumulation of experience, with ideas about the cinema shifting and expanding to match what the screen shows us. The cinema of Antonioni, Resnais, Godard, Mizoguchi, Welles influences our ideas about the past as well as the future.

Too young to have acquired its academic traditions, old enough to feel the need for them, the cinema remains an art in search of a history. The popular art lives in the present; and the cinema, which has been above all a means of expression for the myths and dreams of this century, has also been the art of the present tense, of images which on the screen are always happening *now*, as we watch. For this reason among others, the film critic is perhaps especially susceptible to the influence of the climate in which he is writing. Our feelings about what the screen can do alter as we see what it is doing.

At the moment, for instance, the Western cinema looks a great deal less like a mass medium than it did twenty years ago. Does this mean, in effect, that television has assumed some of its duties? In the thirties, Arthur Elton and Edgar Anstey made a celebrated documentary called *Housing Problems*, an exposé of living conditions in the slums of Britain. Now, if only in terms of the audience reached and the impact made, a single item in *Panorama* would do an infinitely more effective propaganda job than a film, and give as well that absolute conviction of here and now which is television's special advantage over the cinema.

Since cinema is no longer *the* mass medium —and at some moments looks a little shaky about its own future as *a* mass medium—the attitudes of the artists who work in it and the critics who write about it are bound, directly or indirectly, consciously or unconsciously, to be affected. One of the more widespread tenets of film criticism, recently restated by Siegfried Kracauer in his book *Nature of Film* (1961), is that realist cinema is the best and truest cinema: "Films are true to the medium to the extent that they penetrate the world before our eyes." Cinema began in observation, with Lumiére's train pulling into that distant station, yet within a few years Georges Méliès was demonstrating where fantasy might take it. The cinema of fact and that of fancy, the cinema which observes and the cinema which imagines, continually coexist and overlap. There is no morality of art which can validly determine that one type of film has more "right" on its side than another.

There is, of course, a strong pull towards realism, to the use of the camera as a recording instrument, as there is a continual impulse towards the role of social historian. And through the post-war history of the Italian cinema, more distinctly than any other country's, comes the transition from one way of thinking to another, one form of realism to another. Neorealism, that great aspiration of the late forties, influenced everyone who thought about films. The movement, considered collectively, probably remains the most influential single force in post-war cinema. But it belonged very specifically to its time, just as the Italian cinema of recent years is demonstratively contempory. If *L'Avventura* now seems more relevant, more of our time, even more *real* than *Bicycle Thieves*, this is partly because a decade or so of film-making has changed some ideas about screen realism, as about the cinema itself. The cinema advances through the questions its artists put to themselves; and the Italians, in the late forties and again in the early sixties, have been asking many of the right questions.

QUESTIONS FOR DISCUSSION

1 Describe the view of contemporary films presented by Pauline Kael. Is that view accurate, incomplete, too negative? Use specific examples to support your position.

2 Fewer films are now produced in Hollywood by the major studios than in past decades. Why?

PROJECTS

1 Invite to class the manager of a local movie theater and interview him/her to determine:
   (a) how movies are booked
   (b) the theater's policy regarding film ratings
   (c) how the theater's location affects the film selection.

2 See a first-run feature film at a local movie theater. Analyze it to determine the following:
   (a) purpose
   (b) special techniques
   (c) quality of performance
   (d) overall merit
   (e) probable intended audience

MUSIC

ROCK ON THE ROCKS OR BUBBLEGUM ANYBODY?

IRVING LOUIS HOROWITZ

A year ago there were three AM radio stations in New York City that played only rock music. Now there is one. Four years ago dozens of discotheques and clubs featured rock music in New York. Now most of them are out of business.

Rock 'n' roll is dying. It is now going through the terminal symptoms that jazz went through in the forties and early fifties. And it will die the same way jazz did—by growing up, by being transformed.

Jazz picked up most of its fans during its dance stage. Post-World-War-II beboppers crowded into ballrooms across the country to hear the new music and dance the night away to toe-tapping rhythms.

It's got a good beat. You can dance to it.

Rapport. For many years there was a close mutual appreciation between performer and audience. But as the art form matured, so did the musicians. They came to know much more about jazz than their audiences did. The fans knew nothing of the notation system, complex rhythms, time signatures. They just wanted to hear *Caravan* or *One O'Clock Jump*. A professional distance began to develop between artist and listener—some musicians looked on their audiences with contempt and took few pains to conceal it.

Distance from the general audience was reinforced by the appearance in the late thirties of a new type of fan. In the slang of the day these jazz followers were known as alligators. Like the groupies of the late sixties, they didn't dance —they stood in front of the bandstand all night and listened. Alligators understood. They knew the music. They knew the instruments and the soloists and they appreciated what they heard.

In this context many musicians came to define their own worth not in terms of the mass audience and the hit record, but in terms of peer approval. If the guys in the band and a few sophisticated fans appreciated what one was doing musically, then he was a success—and the rest of the audience be damned. Before they would play, the Modern Jazz Quartet and the Charlie Mingus Quartet often made outrageous demands for concert-hall levels of silence in their audiences. The jazz musician came to expect a nonemotional response to emotion. In some sense this is what the rock culture was originally in rebellion against.

The transition from get-up-and-dance music to sit-down-and-listen music took several years, but it was discernible in many later jazz bands —Cab Calloway's and Duke Ellington's, for example—and in the swing orchestras of Harry James and Benny Goodman.

Package. Finally, jazz moved from the dance floor to the concert hall. Norman Granz, the Bill Graham of his day, collected the biggest stars into one-nighter packages—Jazz at the Philharmonic—that toured the largest auditoriums in the country. These packaged performances stifled the creativity of many brilliant musicians, but there was big money in them. As Granz's malignant concerts spread through the land, jazz began to die.

The big bands acknowledged their mass audiences and, when pressed, they would play their familiar, danceable hits. But to maintain their self-esteem and professional integrity many artists sought other outlets. Small groups began to develop within the larger bands. The big band was for mass appeal—the small group was for displaying musical expertise and for building personal satisfaction. From Artie Shaw's orchestra came the Grammercy Five, and from Benny Goodman's big outfit came the Benny Goodman Trio. Instead of dancing, audiences were expected to sit and listen to Teddy Wilson's educated piano or to the cascading vibes of Lional Hampton.

"Rocks on the Rocks or Bubblegum Anybody?" by Irving L. Horowitz. Reprinted from *Psychology Today* Magazine, January 1971. Copyright © Communications/Research/Machines, Inc.

Thelonious Monk and Dizzy Gillespie achieved results similar to those of Bartok and Stravinsky—by innovating and creatively extending their traditions. The soloist became king, and Charlie Parker and, later, John Coltrane were canonized.

As the musicians grew older, so did their fans. Young, unsophisticated ears didn't know enough about the music to appreciate a good tenor-sax solo by Lester Young or Ben Webster. Artists became intraprofessional. Financial success ceased to be a criterion for musical esteem. The musicians who did reach mass audiences had by definition "sold out," and their sounds were disdained—they were "commercial" and "Tin Pan Alley."

And then came rock 'n' roll.

It's got a good beat. You can dance to it.

The emphasis again was mass appeal. There were few intraprofessional standards, so an artist's worth was defined in the simplest, most obvious way—in terms of how many records he could sell. The focus was on the 45 r.p.m. single, and the Top 40 list was updated every week.

Every music reflects the society in which it flourished. In the Renaissance new needs for humanistic expression gave birth to tonal music which rejected the previous ecclesiastical doxology of the Medieval period. The ideals of freedom in the French Revolution gave rise to the chromatics and the gradual development from the sonata to the cyclical form of the Romantic Movement. Jazz itself, inherently an interracial music, represented a mixture of polyphonic African rhythms and modes with the tonal homophony of the European colonizers.

And rock music, a child of the technological age, reflects its parentage in every aspect. Each year amplifiers and preamplifiers get more sophisticated and more powerful, speaker systems get larger and louder, and new electronic gimmicks alter the sound or become part of it (feedback, cross-phasing, fuzz tones, wah-wah).

The contemporary recording process is so complex that a new group cannot make an album without sophisticated knowledge of electronics—mikeing, mixing and mastering. Since *Sergeant Pepper*, the multi-track tape recorder has taken over. Voices and instruments are cut onto separate tracks so that the producer can make the piano louder than the bass on one chorus, or add echo to one voice but not another. Six months later, if he feels like it, he can add a background of violins or cricket chirps.

Electronic experimentation has taken rock artists away from their roots—the song and the beat. To hear the Beatles as a group one must return to *Revolver*, vintage 1966.

Today's young take all the gadgetry for granted—they are not alienated by technological innovation, nor are they particularly impressed. Jazz musicians, on the other hand—especially followers of Gillespie and Monk—tend to resist technological innovation. Some, like Freddie Hubbard and Ornette Coleman, openly state their opposition to electronic music. They tend to think that any device not to be found in a nineteenth-century symphony orchestra is by definition not a musical instrument.

Hit. As rock has matured it has gone through many of the self-conscious changes that marked the rise and fall of jazz. In the first place musicians have changed their definition of success. The hit single is no longer necessary. A group can have a successful album without the support of a Top 40 single (for example, Jefferson Airplane, Jimi Hendrix, Country Joe and the Fish). And if an artist is respected by his fellow musicians, finds approval from a devoted circle of sophisticated fans, and is certified by a semiprofessional publication like *Rolling Stone*, he can maintain high self-esteem even while remaining relatively unknown (for example, Van Dyke Parks, Randy Newman, Captain Beefheart). Some artists at their pinnacles—Bob

> The jazz musician came to expect a nonemotional response to emotion. In some sense this is what the rock culture was originally in rebellion against.
> —Irving Louis Horowitz

Music 79

Dylan, for example—have turned their backs on their audiences and retreated into seclusion. They may need to do this to preserve their sanity, but the effect is to increase the separation between artist and audience. The Beatles swore off personal appearances in 1966. Dylan retired to his Woodstock home after his motorcycle accident in 1966 and has made few public appearances since then; Elvis retreated from public appearances and holed up in his Tennessee mansion for nine years before his recent comeback at the International Hotel in Las Vegas.

Rock music has just entered the sit-and-listen stage. Even five years ago one could see the young dancing wildly to the omnipresent beat at San Francisco's Fillmore Auditorium. Now the fans don't dance—they sit, they concentrate, they get close to the stage so they can watch the guitarist move his fingers. They know rock music; they know the electric guitar; and they can tell immediately whether their favorite soloist is in peak improvisational form.

Super-groups. Just as the stars of yesterday's big bands sought professional recognition and creative opportunities by splitting off to form their own trios and quartets, the most talented musicians today look to each other for support in super groups.

Many rock musicians have begun to look down on the mass audience. The leader of a top English group said after a recent U.S. tour that American audiences are indiscriminately appreciative—they applaud and yell for more, whether the performance is inspired or inept. This instills in the rock artist the same disrespect and contempt for the audience that the jazz musician felt when he finally gave in to a half-dozen requests for *Tico Tico*. Frank Zappa, on the first dissolution of the Mothers of Invention, complained that most audiences "wouldn't know music if it came up and bit 'em on the ass."

Rock is dying because it has matured and its fans have become self-selective. They sit intently and listen to complex guitar arrangements and improvisations. Eric Clapton, Mike Bloomfield and Frank Zappa are being hailed as the greatest guitarists and rock musicians of our age. Their fans are devoted, musically sophisticated, and old. Young teenagers find it very difficult to follow the improvisational music because they do not have background experience with rock. Their ears are not yet equipped to understand or appreciate complexity and innovation. Innovation is a break with tradition, and a thirteen-year-old has no tradition by which he can judge the improvisational forms being explored by many rock musicians.

Bubblegum. Young teenagers don't like to sit and listen anyway. They want to move. And so they turn to the simpler, more danceable music that has come to be known as *bubblegum. It's got a good beat. You can dance to it.*

To the disbelief and dismay of rock fans, bubblegum music has scored tremendous financial successes. *Sugar, Sugar* sold six million copies, making it the fifth largest-selling record in history. It is the Archies, Tommy Roe and Bobby Sherman who get the golden records—not Traffic, not Leon Russell, and not Delaney and Bonnie.

Rock fans speak of bubblegum in a tone usually reserved for words like *excreta*. They look down on the 1910 Fruitgum Company with the same distaste that their parents reserved for Chuck Berry and Danny and the Juniors: *How can you listen to that garbage over and over? It's so simple, so repetitious, so childish.* Is this observation any more true of *Sugar, Sugar* than it was of *At the Hop*?

Different types of music appeal to different types of persons, yet there are always artists at the interface who want to reconcile the generations. Thus, in the mid-fifties white artists came out with cover versions of black rhythm-and-blues songs. In the early sixties rock songs became legitimate when they were set to the schmaltzy arrangements of Percy Faith, Ray Conniff, and the Hollyridge Strings. These albums catered to the older audience. The younger generation snickered as they would at a fifty-year-old housewife who wore a miniskirt and headband. Staying young beyond one's chronology is a complex and often painful undertaking. As Jefferson Airplane explains: "One generation got old/One generation got soul."

Today there are fewer gap-bridging acts. This is partly because groups are providing their own nostalgic ties with older musical styles. A Mantovani version isn't needed any more—one can get lush, syrupy strings on the Beatles' last album, *Let It Be;* and on *Self Portrait,* Bob Dylan provides his own undercover versions of *Blue Moon* and *I Forgot More Than You'll Ever Know About Love.*

Voltage. In the search for new identity and innovation it was inevitable that rock would reiterate jazz. New bands don't feature just the electric guitar—trumpets, flutes, violins and other traditional instruments are accepted in the contemporary rock band, as long as they are electric. Many recent bands (Blood, Sweat and Tears, Chicago, and Cold Blood, for example) are highly reminiscent in their instrumentation of such earlier groups as Miles Davis' Tentet in the late forties. And the loud, brassy arrangements are direct descendants of Count Basie. A promising new group, Ten Wheel Drive, provides a mixture of Big Mama Thornton blues and a tenor sax reminiscent of Coltrane, all set to tight arrangements that remind one of The Jazz-Messengers with Art Blakey and Horace Silver.

Other rock artists are reviving traditional jazz forms—on piano, Leon Russell sounds like Jelly Roll Morton, and Janis Joplin was certainly the best jazz singer since Ma Rainey and Bessie Smith.

With other artists—Miles Davis, Don Ellis and Gary Burton, for example—the cross-fertilization between musical forms is so complete that classification becomes meaningless, or at least tedious.

Tracks. Other events in the evolution of jazz give hints of the future development of rock. For a brief period jazz found acceptance as background music in movies (*East of Eden, The Man With The Golden Arm*), and later served a similar function on action TV shows (*Peter Gunn, Richard Diamond*). Similarly, rock has recently found its way onto the sound tracks of dramatic movies (*Easy Rider, Zabriskie Point*), and we can expect that soon TV shows will feature rock 'n' roll theme music. After the extended stay of The Who at the Metropolitan Opera, anything can happen.

The musical statements that rock will make in its final years can only be guessed at. Innovation in style and song is essential in recent rock

> Every music reflects the society in which it flourished. ... And rock music, a child of the technological age, reflects its parentage in every aspect.
> —Irving Louis Horowitz

music—any group that fails to innovate does not attract a mass audience. No modern artist becomes popular on someone else's songs, unless he has arranged unique interpretations (e.g., Janis Joplin, Joe Cocker).

When any music reaches the sit-and-listen phase, it becomes a different music—jazz becomes modern jazz, rock becomes *hard* or *acid* rock. The music fails to pick up a new, young audience and it begins to die. Perhaps twenty years from now we will look back on Woodstock as the beginning of the end—similar to Benny Goodman's famous Paramount Theater and Carnegie Hall engagements of 1938. It may have marked the crystallization of the sit-and-listen phase, and therefore the imminent death of rock 'n' roll.

Perhaps fifteen years from now there will be a bubblegum revival, the Archies will be likened to Bill Haley and the Comets, and Bobby Sherman will be called the musical genius of his time who broke away from tradition and forged the new music.

Sociological speculations are many and fascinating. But when some new musical form sweeps the mass audience out from under the aging bubblegum musicians, the young fans will have a clear and classic reason for liking the new music: *It's got a good beat. You can dance to it.*

IT'S A FAMILY AFFAIR (PARTS 1 AND 3)

MICHAEL SHAIN

Michael Shain has managed to pin down the amorphous music industry in this penetrating view of popular music's impact on our culture. In an almost historic analysis of popular music, Shain traces the development of bubblegum music for sub-teens, pop hits, soul music, and underground protest music from counterculture artists. Shain argues rather convincingly that the pop music medium has been and continues to be a central force in shaping the attitudes, values, and life-styles of college students and other young people.

PART 1

As a purveyor of popular culture, the music industry has challenged television, movies, radio and print in terms of impact, especially on the young. It was a central force in shaping the generation that grew up in the sixties; its influence may be as pervasive on the one growing up in the seventies. Unburdened by government regulation, the music industry has been freer than broadcasting to adventure creatively and, consequently, to keep up with and at times ahead of the changing life-styles of its audience.

Jac Holzman, president of Elektra Records: "The music business is far less restrictive than any of the other communications media. That's why it has been so successful. Because the music business responded to an audience—swiftly and reasonably accurately—it encouraged in its artists a high degree of artistic freedom."

That freedom has been exercised in the form

Reprinted from "It's a Family Affair" by Michael Shain in *Broadcasting Magazine*, December 27, 1971. Used by permission of Broadcasting Magazine.

of rock and roll and its evolution from *Rock Around the Clock* to *Sgt. Pepper's* to *Sweet Baby James*. Most rock and roll was never "good music." It had very little to do with music actually: Music was only its vehicle. When it can be looked back on from a clearer vantage, say twenty years from now, its sociological impact may far outweigh any innovations it may have made in music.

The rock phenomenon of the sixties can most simply be defined as self-conscious rock and roll, a musical form finally recognized as a strong communicator and used as such. Musical content has gained a greater importance of late, but rock and roll has proved itself to be intelligent music for reasons other than musical. It is able to speak to the conditions.

The history of early rock and roll is basically a history of white artists "covering" hits by black artists, refining the blacks' rhythm and blues. In 1955 Bill Haley and the Comets recorded *Shake, Rattle and Roll*—an R&B release on Atlantic by "Big" Joe Turner in 1949—with the lyrics cleaned up a bit. It became what is considered the first rock-and-roll hit. At the same time, Sam Phillips was recording a group of country singers who were doing some very different things with what was then termed "hillbilly music." On his Sun label, he had Jerry Lee Lewis, Johnny Cash, Roy Orbison and Elvis Presley, a skinny kid with slicked-back hair from Tennessee. Mr. Phillips cashed in on his farsightedness when he sold the Presley contract and tapes to RCA for $40,000 in 1955—which turned out to be the cheapest $40,000 RCA ever spent. RCA and Presley's manager, Colonel Tom Parker, toned Elvis down a bit musically (a little less raunch, a lot more crooning), told him to wiggle his hips, and gave him a song originally recorded by Big Mama Thornton, a large, black woman with a gravelly voice. The song was *Hound Dog*.

If America was not ready for the originals by black artists—who were admittedly less polished, if perhaps more authentic—by the end of the fifties, genuine black music had its foot in the door of public acceptance in the person of Little Richard Penniman. Little Richard was, and still is, a screamer and a stomper. A former gospel singer, he wrote and performed songs that were so energetic, so infectious, so individual in style that he could neither be covered nor ignored. Chuck Berry, another giant of the fifties, is also black, but unlike Little Richard or Ray Charles, his roots are not in blues, but in country music, and his appeal is to white audiences. Chuck Berry's contributions to the development of rock and roll are many. The most important is that he was the first rock-and-roll poet; i.e., he put a message in his lyrics. The message he repeated over and over—in those lyrics and in countless hits—was that rock and roll was good, and it was here to stay.

Just as these men meteored into prominence and wealth during the last half of the fifties, by the beginning of the sixties they were all off the scene. Elvis was drafted, Buddy Holly and Richie Valens were killed in a plane crash, Chuck Berry was in jail, Little Richard—after what he considered a close brush with death on a flight—disappeared into the ministry, Jerry Lee Lewis was in disfavor and seclusion after marrying his thirteen-year-old cousin. The vacuum was filled with white artists who were so pallid (Annette Funicello, Paul Anka, Connie Francis) that music-with-a-backbone became the exclusive domain of the black artist. Phil Spector, "the first teen-age tycoon," was making records with the Crystals and Darlene Love that were to lay the groundwork for the records Berry Gordy and Motown would make all through the sixties and that we now call "soul." Ray Charles was also at his peak during this time while he was working for Jerry Wexler at Atlantic. Two exceptions, white acts who were making formative music with spunk and popularity during this transition period, were Dion and the Belmonts and, especially, the Beach Boys.

In November of 1963, a group from Liverpool changed the entire face of pop music with a song called *I Want to Hold Your Hand*.

Jerry Moss, president of A&M Records: "One thing you have to congratulate the Beatles for, I mean besides selling records, is that the Beatles sold a lot of record players. They opened up an entire new generation of people who were listening to records. And more people are growing up, thanks to the Beatles, with record players since they were eight and nine. And continuing to buy other records when they're ten, eleven, twelve. I think it's also the reason you have such long-term successes now. The Rolling Stones have been selling records for eight years. Used to be an artist had two or three hot years. That's not the situation any more. His audience is starting at an earlier age. That artist is growing right along with the people who are buying his records."

The British pop explosion, by hindsight, was almost inevitable. For many years, and to this day, the young people of Britain devoured all the music that America had sent them. Artists who had long fizzled out in the States played to packed houses in Europe. It was only natural that the younger musicians in England would absorb the music and begin to produce their own.

Exactly what it was that the British, and the Beatles especially, added to what was unabashedly American is hard to say. Between 1964 and 1966, the years of the British invasion of the U.S. music industry, record sales jumped 34%. The Liverpool bands—Freddie and the Dreamers, the Dave Clark Five, Gerry and the Pacemakers—made happy, good-time music to contrast with the darker, slicker records out of Detroit and South Philadelphia that still gripped America. The other half of the British explosion,

> The impact of the Beatles cannot be waved away. They changed what we listened to and how we listened to it; they helped make rock music a battering ram for the youth culture's assault on the mainstream; and that assault in turn changed our culture permanently. And if the "dream" the Beatles helped create could not sustain itself in the real world, that speaks more to our false hopes than to their promises. They wrote and sang songs. We turned it into politics and philosophy and a road map to another way of life.
> —Jeffrey Greenfield

led by the Rolling Stones along with The Animals and the Yardbird, was rooted in American blues. Mick Jagger of the Stones and Jimmy Paige, then of the Yardbirds and now with Led Zeppelin, grew up with the vintage delta blues of Leadbelly and Robert Johnson and the newer Chicago electric blues of Big Bill Broonzy, John Lee Hooker and Muddy Waters. In the late sixties, the indigenous American blues came back across the ocean, and on a wave of tremendous record sales, in the form of bands like Cream and Led Zeppelin, while the black originators of this wildly successful music form worked for subsistence pay in the clubs of the big-city ghettos.

The phenomenon of rock had its beginnings in late 1966. Despite widespread opinion that places all of the credit for the development of this popular music form squarely on the Beatles, there was an uncommon fusion of several different influences that brought rock to its current dominance. Put simplistically, half the revolution came about when the Beatles began to expand their music in terms of lyrics and instrumentation (George Harrison's addition of the sitar, Paul McCartney's infatuation with full orchestras, John Lennon's increasingly complex and mature lyrics). The other half fit into place when a Los Angeles group, the Byrds, recorded a folk, acoustical song, *Mr. Tambourine Man*, with electric guitars and whining harmonies and made it a hit. It was one of the first times that sophisticated—even literate, if you will—lyrics were applied to a rock-and-roll song.

Within a year, the San Francisco sound of the Jefferson Airplane, The Grateful Dead, and Country Joe and the Fish helped bring some of the creative energy and record sales back to America. They rode the flowering hippie movement out of the Bay Area until the themes of love, communal living, protest and drugs had spread to every corner of the country. California became the warm, cozy womb where most of the rock we still hear today was conceived, nurtured and bloomed.

Many theories have come forward on the reasons why California supplied so many good bands. Some credence must be given to the fact that Los Angeles and the Bay Area (and some of the larger cities and towns between) have been able to support small clubs and dance halls during the years when similar spots were folding in the East. In a record market that is glutted with more new talent every year (although the number of new acts has recently declined somewhat), these training grounds where musicians can "pay their dues" are of integral importance.

California is *the* the youth state of the union. More than half the people in it are under thirty and three-quarters of those are under twenty. California experienced its great population jump after the second World War. And as all those post-war babies got into their teens, they told the rest of the world about the joys of youth in California, via the Beach Boys. It's no coincidence that a generation of political radicals and the group of musicians that pioneered American rock came from the same place.

Very little can be said about *Sgt. Pepper's Lonely Hearts Club Band* that has not been said before. Not since Lexington has there been a shot like that one. Sgt. Pepper's ushered in the concepts on which most of popular music is still based. The idea of an integrated package for an LP began with this album. Today, it has become so important that artists now have standard clauses in their contracts that give them control over cover art, album stuffings, etc., as well as creative control over the music. The whole idea of a "concept" pop album began here. That is, an album should not be just twelve to fourteen singles put together on a bigger piece of vinyl. It should be an entity unto itself, and its contents should be integral. Most important, Sgt. Pepper's blew the walls out of popular music. Never again would pop have to fit into a mold or subjugate itself to a formula. The entire world of music—anything that was sound, really—could be used to communicate ideas that were not being said anywhere else. That eclecticism has characterized rock ever since the summer of 1967.

The doors were opened to the minds of millions of young people—a huge aperture indeed. Through those doors rushed groups like the Mothers of Invention, the Doors, Jimi Hendrix, The Band, The Who and the Buffalo Springfield, perhaps the most respected American rock band ever. Their music expanded consciousnesses, protested societal inequities, reinforced peer group values and sometimes just made kids happy.

Right now rock is in a singer-song-writer period, with some major exceptions and startling dichotomies. Carole King has sold (by A&M's count) 3.7 million albums and 1.6 million tapes of her *Tapestry* album, for a combined dollar volume (in distributor sales) of $15 million. James Taylor has sold nearly as many of his *Sweet Baby James*. Still, the best of this new genre remain cult tastes: Neil Young, Laura Nyro, Randy Newman.

At the other end of the spectrum of this third generational group of musicians is Grand Funk Railroad, a band which got very little airplay on major stations but made it to the top on the basis of live performance—a very loud, very exciting experience. And it has prospered phenomenally. Funk's six albums have sold over 20 million copies (records and tapes) in their two-and-a-half years on the scene, for a retail value close to $120 million.

But the loud sound is not really outselling the soft as it did several years ago. Both now coexist in a period of pop music not noted, as were earlier ones, for the dominance of heraldic superstars, but for a diversification in tastes. Nevertheless, rock still speaks to conditions....

PART 3

Stan Kaplan has a reputation as an outspoken broadcaster, often critical of his colleagues in radio. With his wife he owns and runs two contemporary stations, WAYS(AM) Charlotte, N.C. and WAPE(AM) Jacksonville, Fla. They recently contracted to purchase an FM in Charlotte, WRNA, subject to FCC approval.

Stan Kaplan: "The record business, like Gaul, is divided—but into four parts. The first part is the music for subteens—Donny Osmond and the Partridge Family. The second is the pop hit that goes beyond the sub-teen market—*American Pie* [by Don McLean] is an example of that type of music. Then there's soul. And then there's the underground stuff, music that is primarily on albums. Now, I'm not talking about country or novelty-type music here, just popular music. The contemporary stations are the only people who will program a little bit from all those types of music. The MOR station may program the pop or sub-teen hit, but it certainly won't go near the soul or underground things. And the black stations won't touch the sub-teen stuff. And because we take a little bit from each, we have the greatest effect on record sales. That's why I find a record man every time I open a drawer.

"The first conflict between the record business and radio is that they want us to play new products while we want to play established hits," Mr. Kaplan says. "And if there's been any change in promotion men in the last half-dozen years, it has been that a promotion man would rather have me play a new song on any other label than play an established hit, even if it's on his. The second conflict arises over the length of the playlist—they, for the most part want them longer; we, for the most part, want them shorter."

KDAY(AM) Santa Monica [Calif.] is one of the few stations in the U.S. that programs progressive rock on the AM side of the dial. KDAY doesn't have Top 20 or Top 30 lists of the week, and limits its commercials to eight minutes an hour. And although its DJ's have large followings, they're not the usual "jivers" of AM radio. The approach proved so prosperous that other stations in the market are beginning to adopt similar sounds. Bob Wilson is the program director, and principally responsible for leading the way to album cuts and longer playlists on AM radio in Los Angeles.

Bob Wilson: "A lot of the problems that the record business has had with radio have been of its own making. There is simply too much product. For years, the record companies have been throwing blind records off the wall and hoping that one of them will fall on the turntable. I have a thousand and twelve cuts to listen to each week. I can't possibly listen to them all. But I think the record industry has learned that they really can't do that any more. And the product level has gone way down.

"But our differences have lessened in the last year or eighteen months—mainly because we have expanded our playlists and [Bill] Drake [the program consultant] and KHJ [(AM) Los Angeles] are playing more album cuts and the like."

One of the more heartening developments of the last several years, Messrs. Kaplan and Wilson agree, is the increase in the number of commercials that record companies are buying. "It's something they should have done a long time ago," Mr. Kaplan says vigorously. "Instead of wasting all that time and money on a promotion man, they now buy more spots to give the audience a little taste of it. And once they get them into the stores, they can do something."

If there is one point of contention between

radio and the manufacturers, it is the misrepresentation of sales figures. "A promotion man will come in here and rave and tell me that he sold 32,000 copies of some record in L.A. What he won't tell me is that he got 22,000 back," Bob Wilson complains.

Stan Kaplan simply says, "They lie. There's no way that either you or I are going to get any truthful figures out of the record companies. They just won't tell you."

WABC(AM) New York is the highest-rated rocker in the largest market in the country. Rick Sklar has been programing the station for seven years now, although he likes to say, "They [the audience] program the station; I'm just a researcher, statistician." Forgetting what the Pulse books say, WABC has made its success based on a format of "much more music," a Drake phrase. At WABC the phrase is "music is our message," but either way it means the same thing. People who tune that kind of station want music, not talk or jingles or even commercials, just music. And WABC gives it to them.

The controls and systems that Mr. Sklar uses to determine playlists are always changing, evolving into better barometers and "trying to keep the record companies off guard," Mr. Sklar says.

"Pretty soon the record companies figure out your system and try to throw it off. A prime example is the free records that they give to stores in hopes that when a station calls, they'll tell us that it's selling. They do themselves a disservice and us a disservice when they try to misrepresent sales."

Mr. Sklar explains that "we have custom controls because they help us get to where we want to go. Not where *we* want to go, really, but just to get to our target audience." He adds: "The day you think you know anything in this business, you're lost. You can't think you know more than anybody else out there. The program director is only the interpreter between the audience and the station. But it gets difficult when the record people begin to foul up those lines."

Bob Wilson: "Unfortunately, though, I find the promotion men in general are less knowledgeable than they were five years ago. By less knowledgeable, I mean about the business *in toto*. It's true that there is a little less hype, but that's only because they don't really know enough to be able to hype you."

Rick Sklar: "There hasn't really been that much change in promotion or techniques that I can see. There are still only two types of guy that come in here. (1) The old timer who does shoot straight with you and gives you factual information, or the old-timer who's learned every trick there is. (2) And the younger ones who give you facts or the ones who try to hype us. The ones who really don't know what they're doing and try to hype us usually don't stay around very long. The promotion man who calls every three months or so and says 'This is a good record and you're not on and you should be' is of much greater service than the guy who comes around every week and tries to push his stiffs on us."

Stan Kaplan: "No matter what the record companies say about their supposed honesty now, I've never had anyone come into my office and tell me, 'This record's a stiff.' "

Bob Wilson: "Stations must find their popularity in some kind of music, and have standards that they can apply to it, a measuring stick. Slowly but surely, I think the record people have begun to understand this and are beginning to act a bit differently."

Stan Kaplan: "What the record companies don't understand about that great, unwashed audience out there is that they have a choice. They can turn that dial and tune you out. And I'm not about to take that chance."

One of those who has tried to bring the radio and record industries closer over the last fifteen years is Erny Tannen, owner of five AM outlets in Pennsylvania, Rhode Island and Maryland. Three years ago, when the National Association of Broadcasters approached him to join, Mr. Tannen told its representatives he felt the association should be doing more to foster a better relationship with record manufacturers. As a result, the NAB-RIAA (Recording Industry Association of America) liaison committee was established in 1969. Unfortunately, the committee has not yet proved a viable organ and has met only twice in the last two years.

Erny Tannen: "I can't see how two huge industries, so dependent one on the other, can have so little dialogue, except at the least meaningful level." Recalling the time he ran a station in Pittsburgh about fifteen years ago, during the payola scandals: "I wrote a series of letters to *Billboard* that they used as the basis of several editorials on the subject. And what I said was that there was no relationship between radio and the record industry on an executive level, and that situation's still true today.

Not enough has been done on a management level to iron out our differences. Someone has to explain to the record industry the economics of running a radio station. All the successful radio stations are formatted. Even the progressive stations without formats are, if you know what I mean. Running a station necessitates having a specific programing scheme in order to maximize a significant share of a market. It's just not possible to get everything played."

Despite its infrequent meetings, the committee did conduct a survey to determine what kind of music stations were playing, simply to let the manufacturers know. It also has been active on the matter of drug lyrics. At its January 1971 meeting, the NAB board adopted a proposal which requested record manufacturer to supply printed copies of lyrics along with the records they send to stations. Several months later the FCC's drug-lyric policy statement was released. Members of the liaison committee were disturbed that the board did not consult them before issuing its resolution.

Mr. Tannen: "Not only did it seem to me that this was an implied infringement of First Amendment rights but they did not even talk to the committee whose function it was to discuss this. The record people on the committee pointed that the lyrics are really owned by the publishers, not the record companies, and in order for them to provide lyrics with the records, it would involve complications with the publishers."

At the June 1971 board meeting, members of the liaison committee presented their exceptions to the policy, which subsequently was tempered. The music publishers association offered its cooperation to the NAB and that board set up consulting services among the NAB, RIAA and MPA to which broadcasters may refer questions arising out of lyrics with drug-oriented content.

THE STRANGE DEATH OF ROCK AND ROLL

LANGDON WINNER

"All around the world, rock and roll is here to stay. You can hear that juke box jumpin', all night and all through the day." These words of a song by Little Richard, inaccurate when he first sang them in 1958, are entirely correct now, ten years later. They point to a phenomenon which deserves considerably more attention than it has so far received. For the closest that Western civilization has come to unity since the Congress of Vienna in 1815 was the week that the *Sergeant Pepper* album was released. In every city in Europe and America the stereo systems and radios played, "What would you think if I sang out of tune ... Woke up, got out of bed ... looked much older, And the bag across her shoulder ... in the Sky with diamonds, Lucy in the ...," and everyone listened. At the time I happened to be driving across country on Interstate 80. In each city where I stopped for gas or food—Laramie, Ogallala, Moline, South Bend —the melodies wafted in from some far off transistor radio or portable hi-fi. It was the most amazing thing I've ever heard. For a brief while the irreparably fragmented consciousness of the West was reunified, at least in the minds of the young. Every person listened to the record, pondered it and discussed it with friends. While it is no doubt true that I have little in common with the gas station attendant in Cheyenne, Wyoming, we were able to come together to talk about the meaning of *A Day in the Life* during those few moments in which the oil in my VW was being changed. Perhaps the only thing which is certain to be shared by the young of America (or more significantly, the young of the whole world) in this age of violence and extreme divisions is an uncomplicated knowledge of the songs of rock.

From *Rock and Roll Will Stand*, edited by Greil Marcus. Copyright © 1969 by Greil Marcus. Reprinted by permission of Beacon Press.

Music 87

RETURN TO GOOD-TIMES ROCK

TIME

The conga line forms midway through the Beach Boys' second encore, a lilting paean to puberty called California Girls. *By the time the song ends, the line has grown to 5,000 teenagers and is snaking all over Kansas City, Mo.'s Arrowhead Stadium. Turning toward the stage, the churning serpent finds a lion's voice: "Chicago, Chicago!" As 35,000 spectators pick up the chant, seven young men amble onstage to join the Beach Boys for a socko finale. They are the group known as Chicago. With five guitarists, two drummers and a three-piece brass section wailing, the combined bands form a rock juggernaut that quickly transforms the stadium into an enormous, throbbing, outdoor discothèque. The crowd has been on its feet for most of the six-hour concert.*

In the entire history of rock, there have been few groups as popular or durable as the Beach Boys and Chicago. Between them they have sold over 65 million records and survived the popularity of scores of psychedelic, protest and glitter groups. For more than a decade, the anthem of the Beach Boys has been sweet, close harmony, and its gospel essentially nothing more profound than the joys of teen-age love, uncluttered California freeways and the eternal search for the perfect wave. As for Chicago, they are hard-jazz rockers whose first album in 1969 included a taped replay of some of the street violence at the Democratic Convention the year before.

The joining of the Beach Boys and Chicago has turned out to be the event of the burgeoning outdoor rock season. By the end of their twelve-city trek, the double bill will have played to a total audience of 700,000 and grossed an estimated $7.5 million. Though allowances may be recession-tight, and the price of gas high enough to make cruising prohibitive, the kids have poured into town just as though the music were an old-time religion.

Unaffected by the anguish of the recent past, they are waving off hard drugs and hard political lines in favor of good-time music and that oldest of adolescent verities: fun. Gone are the trademarks of yesteryear: denim fatigues, dove-crowned peace flags, bottles of Ripple wine. In their place can be found pastel tennis shoes, American flags and Tab. Many fans come in halter tops for a suntan and to be part of the carnival scene. They just want to dance boogie and sing along. Says Chicago Lyricist Robert Lamm, 30: "These days nobody wants to hear songs that have a message."

AMERICAN CONTEXT

One of the first to detect the trend to conservatism was James William Guercio, 29, a former Mothers of Invention guitarist turned millionaire moviemaker (*Electra Glide in Blue*). He manages Chicago and occasionally sits in on bass with the Beach Boys. Guercio brought the groups together. Garbed in a baggy football jersey bearing his last name and the numeral 1 and sitting in the living room of his $30,000 mobile home, Guercio tries to explain it all: "The American experience is found in Southern California and the streets of Chicago. These bands sing about youth, love and marriage in an American context. America—it's the common denominator."

Inside the Kansas City stadium where *Time* Correspondent David DeVoss caught the show, three acrobats and a high-wire aerialist warmed up the audience. Vaudeville too is a common denominator. The Beach Boys came out first and launched into *Sloop John B*. Later came *Sail On Sailor* and *Surfer Girl*, all close-harmony classics. The Boys broke the aquatic mood by asking the kids to sit down during a reverent *a cappella* version of *Their Hearts Were Full of Spring*. Obviously, the avoidance of message was no sweat for the Beach Boys. At their peak, in the early and middle 1960s, it was not necessary to live in California to understand them. Everyone

---

Reprinted by permission from TIME, The Weekly Newsmagazine; Copyright Time Inc.

knew what it meant to *Be True to Your School*, and there was room in every male imagination for a *Surfer Girl*. The only time the Beach Boys ever took up political topics was in their 1971 album *Surf's Up*, in which they dabbled in ecology (*Don't Go Near the Water*) and warned their followers of the perils of mob action (*Student Demonstration Time*).

TURNABOUT PLAY

Chicago invested more in protest. In early songs they sang out against police brutality, linked Viet Nam and the riot in Watts and protested the student apathy that followed the Kent State killings. Their 1971 album, *Chicago III*, contained a war-casualty poster. *Chicago Live at Carnegie Hall* came with a chart explaining voter-registration procedures. But the group's message songs have regularly been outnumbered by pulsating instrumentals. Four of Chicago's seven members studied at music schools, and the group's glory has been a classically constructed mix of jazz-rock, rhythm and blues, calypso and country. So it was last week. There was no sitting down while Chicago blasted out such ballads as *Saturday in the Park* and their new Top 20 record, *Old Days*.

Rock as a social force may well be dead, but the music itself is getting more varied and lively all the time. Jazz and country, for example, now play as important a part in rock as blues and folk. Anyway, says Lamm, "we always considered ourselves professional musicians, not pop stars or politicans. The world in the past two years has done a 180° turn in terms of political expression." Turnabout can be fair play for both performer and listener. Says Beach Boy Mike Love, 34: "We're giving the kids something positive for their money, and it appears that it is working in our favor." As a way of savoring the favor, the Beach Boys will include their own version of *Battle Hymn of the Republic* on their next album.

QUESTIONS FOR DISCUSSION

1. Describe the relationship among radio, the recording industry, and the audience. How are these entities separate in function yet dependent on each other? Who is the final arbiter in determining what music becomes popular?

2. In what ways has the "music revolution" of the sixties altered the role of radio?

3. Contrast the lyrics from Rogers and Hammerstein's musical **Carousel**, or a similar musical, with those of the Beatles' **Sergeant Pepper** album. In what ways do they reflect different social values and perceptions of reality?

PROJECTS

1. Analyze the number one song in each category listed in a current issue of **Variety** or **Billboard** to discover the meanings or messages found or implied in the lyrics. Cite appropriate passages.

2. Identify the types of music each member of your family prefers. What do you think accounts for the differences or similarities in taste?

Music

COMICS, GRAFFITI, AND CLOTHING

The Comics on the Couch

TIME

He was someone you could always count on, the savior of the helpless and oppressed, society's sword against the forces of evil and injustice. He could, among other things, "hurdle skyscrapers, leap an eighth of a mile, run faster than a streamline train—and nothing less than a bursting shell could penetrate his skin." He was, in short, a good buy for a dime. Even by today's hyped-up standards, Superman was quite a guy.

Yes, was. The man of steel that many Americans grew up with is not what he used to be. For one thing, his alter ego, Clark Kent, has given up the *Daily Planet* to become a newscaster for the Galaxy Broadcasting System, getting in and out of blue tights and red cape during commercial breaks. ("Personally, I still prefer Walter Cronkite," a mini-skirted Lois tells him. She, at least is unchanged—as obnoxious as ever.) For another, Superman has succumbed to urban jitters; he obviously needs to spend some time on the couch. Just listen to some of his recent complaints: "I'm finished being anybody's Superman! ... For years I've been dreaming of working and living as a plain man—without the responsibilities, the loneliness of Superman ... I've a right to bitterness. No man has a better right. I've denied myself the comforts of home and family to continue helping these ingrates. I thought they admired me—for myself! I've lived in a fool's paradise!"

Superhangups for a superhero, but Superman is not the only hero hanging his cape outside Dr. Feelgood's door. Today almost all comic-book characters have problems. As in many fields, the word is relevance. The trend may have begun

---

Reprinted by permission from *Time*. The Weekly Newsmagazine; © Time Inc.

a decade ago, but in the socially aware seventies it has reached full blossom. The comics' caped crusaders have become as outraged about racial injustice as the congressional Black Caucus and as worried about pollution as the Sierra Club. Archfiends with memorable names like the Hulk and Dr. Doom are still around, but they are often pushed off the page by such new villains as air pollution and social injustice. Sometimes, indeed, the comics read like a *New York Times Illustrated*.

Recently the comics have discovered yet another field—a mixture of science fiction and the occult that lies somewhere beyond Consciousness III. In a comic book called *The New Gods*, for example, the forces of the good, the beautiful, under-thirties, battle the forces of evil, the ugly militarists of Apokolips, in weird sequences that look and read like nightmares. Whatever they are doing, American comics, both the books and the strips, are full of life. In their seventy-fifth year, they are bursting—wump, bomp, oof! and zap!—from the page in a dozen new directions.

Along with responsibility has come respectability. One of the newest things about the new comics is that more than ever before they are being taken seriously as an art form by critics and as an authentic cultural expression by sociologists. Half a dozen or so learned histories have been written about them, and art galleries give them serious exhibitions. The comics have been included in courses at Brown University, and the creators of the new styles, particularly Marvel Comics' Stan Lee, who invented the idiom, are mobbed like rock stars on the campuses. So popular is Lee, in fact, that he gave a kind of sound and light show at Carnegie Hall.

Not all of the comics are trying to be with it, of course. *Blondie*, a strip that is syndicated in 1,164 newspapers and is one of the most widely read series in the world, still exists in a timeless never-never land of middle class clichés where only Daisy the dog seems to have a spark of intelligence. Despite wrist TVs and spaceships, Dick Tracy continues to chase odd-looking crooks like Retsen Nester, a bald-domed, bespectacled type who hides heroin in volumes of Mother Goose. In the same old way, Little Orphan Annie and Sandy still fight the Red Menace and bleeding-heart liberals, and will probably continue to do

Comics, Graffiti, and Clothing   91

so well into the twenty-first century. In a recent episode Annie was trying to find a poor but honest person who needed only Daddy Warbucks' "survival kit," $11,000, to make good. Daddy, a billionaire, is convinced that the "good old-fashioned pioneer spirit that made this country great is not dead" but "just kinda takin' a nap."

Many of the other oldtimers, however, have changed just about everything but their costumes. Evil, they are discovering, was much easier to spot when it had a funny name and wore an ugly mask. In a recent comic book adventure, the Green Lantern collars a kid who has been beating up a fat man. But after being bombarded with garbage by the kid's ghetto neighbors, the Emerald Crusader learns that the man he has saved is a corrupt slumlord who is about to tear down the block for a parking lot. "I been readin' about you," says an old black who is soon to be evicted. "How you work for the blue skins and how on a planet someplace you helped out the orange skins, and you done considerable for the purple skins. Only there's skins you never bothered with—the black skins! I want to know: How come? Answer me that, Mr. Green Lantern!"

Now it's no good just to zap a few uglies either, as of yore. The Green Lantern and his superhero colleagues are constantly being reminded these days that the funny fiends are just front men for some very unfunny social ills. The Green Lantern and his chum, the Green Arrow, are lectured by a youthful victim: "Drugs are a symptom, and you, like the rest of society, attack the symptom, not the disease." Another big change has been the introduction of black characters, who now appear in such strips as *Peanuts, Archie, Li'l Abner* and *Beetle Bailey; Friday Foster*, a swinging soul sister from Harlem, has a strip all her own. Until a few years ago, the color barrier blocked all but a few Negro caricatures from the comics.

When it comes to politics, *Li'l Abner* and *Pogo*, which have satirized it for years, are at least as up to date as the men in Washington. Two characters that bear a remarkable resemblance to Senators Hubert Humphrey and Hugh Scott were recently dispatched to Li'l Abner's Dogpatch to learn why it is the one pollution-free spot in the U.S. Reason: the Gobbleglops, which look like pigs with bunny tails, gobble up, in the words of Mammy Yokum, "all glop, irregardless ... They's natcheral-born incinerators. Thass why glop goes in 'em an' none comes out!!" *Pogo* has been invaded by an odd beast, half Great Dane and half hyena, that looks and alliterates like Spiro T. Agnew, by a bulldog that might be taken for J. Edgar Hoover, and by a pipe-smoking, improbable baby eagle that might fool even Martha Mitchell into thinking she had seen John. This trio of animal crackers spends most of its time trying to decipher messages from an unseen chief who chooses to communicate by means of undecipherable paper dolls. "Dashing deep-digging thought dominates his delectable display," asserts the Spiroesque Great Dane-hyena, who wears the uniform—or half the uniform—of a Greek colonel.

While the political spectrum of the regular comic strips ranges from the moderately liberal (*Pogo*) to the archconservative (*Little Orphan Annie*), a relatively new phenomenon, underground comics, is pursuing radical political and sexual themes that their aboveground brothers would never dare to touch. Begun in the mid-sixties, the undergrounds, or head comic books, such as *Zap* and *Despair* and strips in papers like the *Berkeley Barb* and Manhattan's *East Village Other*, speak for the counterculture in a zany, raunchy and often obscene idiom. In one issue of the *East Village Other*, a strip depicts an Army company in Viet Nam. The sergeant's command "Present arms!" literally brings out the arms of the men in his company, heroin addicts all. Later, when all of the men are dead of overdoses—including the sergeant, whose name is, of course, Smack—it turns out that the CIA is the ultimate pusher. "Put it this way," says the agency's spook in charge, "we consider this something of an investment."

Like the movies, comics are in many ways a now art form. Perhaps because they grew up together, they have certain styles and techniques in common. Cinematic techniques like montage, the dissolve of one scene into another, appeared in the comics well before they were seen on the screen or perfected by Eisenstein. At the same time, the movies were ahead of the comics in developing the continuing adventure serial. Any influence that one form may have had on the other should not be exaggerated. Some directors insist, however, that there was a certain amount of give and take. "There was a connection between Happy Hooligan and Chaplin," says Italian Director Federico Fellini, "and there were aspects of Popeye and Wimpy in Buster Keaton." Fellini, who began his career in the thirties as a writer of adventure and science-fiction comics, has been an *appassionato* of the *fumetti*,* Italy's comic books, ever since he was a *ragazzino*, and admits that the comics probably gave something to his own moviemaking. Says he: "A sense of the comic and the humorous in my films, wonder, and a feeling for the fantastic—maybe these came from the comics I read as a little boy."

With a few exceptions—*Wonder Woman* was into Women's Lib twenty years before Betty Friedan—the comics have always appealed to men more than women, to little boys more than little girls. One reason is the inevitable boy companion that the ten-year-old could identify with—*Batman's* Boy Wonder Robin, the Sandman's Sandy, the Shield's Rusty, to name only a few. Even when the ten-year-old identified too closely with that clever brat on paper as a rival, it was good for sales. Cartoonist Jules Feiffer, who has lately turned to writing for the theater

---

* Literally "little smokes," a reference to the word balloons that show what the characters are saying.

and the movies (*Carnal Knowledge*), was both repelled and drawn to the Boy Wonder. "One need only look at him," Feiffer writes, "to see he could fight better, swing from a rope better, play ball better, eat better, and live better. For while I lived in the East Bronx, Robin lived in a mansion, and while I was trying somehow to please my mother—and getting it all wrong —Robin was rescuing Batman and getting the gold medals. You can imagine how pleased I was when, years later, I heard he was a fag."

Feiffer's was a love-hate relationship that the comic books lost for a while in the fifties and early sixties, when sales dropped and the industry appeared headed for extinction. In a world where almost anything was possible and usually visible on a 21-inch screen, outracing a locomotive or buzzing around like an ugly bug in drag seemed somehow tame and tedious. Young readers today, the comic men soon discovered, are more interested in their own problems and the problems they see around them. It is possible, indeed, to see the comics as an art of the people, offering clues to the national unconscious. Superman's enormous popularity might be looked upon as signaling the beginning of the end for the Horatio Alger myth of the self-made man. In the modern world, he seems to say, only the man with superpowers can survive and prosper. Still, though comics are indeed a popular art form, it is going a bit far to compare, as Critic Maurice Horn does, *Gasoline Alley* to Goethe's *Wilhelm Meister* and *Little Orphan Annie* to the works of Charles Dickens and Victor Hugo. As Mammy Yokum might say: "Some folks don't know when to stop."

Walt Kelly, still one of the best cartoonists, is a more solid expert on the genre. "A comic strip is like a dream," Turtle tells Bear in *Pogo*. "A tissue of paper reveries. It gloms an' glimmers its way thru unreality, fancy an' fantasy." To which Bear naturally responds: "Sho' 'nuff?" Sho' 'nuff.

Comix

CHARLES-GENE MC DANIEL

The comix are trying to tell us something, something we do not read in the comics—or anywhere else in most newspapers. Physically patterned after comics, the comix are the counterculture's alternative to comics and, like much else associated with antiestablishment phenomena, they have been an underground development. At least until lately. They have grown in popularity, perhaps because of the urgency of some of their messages, perhaps because of the countercultural tendencies of some of those who are part of the establishment and are bringing comix to the surface and to a wider audience.

The first museum exhibition surveying comix was staged this year by the Museum of Contemporary Art in Chicago. This is an appropriate setting for showing these irreverent expressions, for this brash little museum is something of an anti-museum, having no permanent collections and staging exhibitions of some of the avantist of the avant garde work of contemporary artists.

I went to see the show with some reservations, expecting not to like it. How could comix, by any stretch of the imagination, be called art? If only the graphic aspects are considered, the comix generally do fail to meet the standard criteria of pictorial excellence. Viewed in their gestalt, however, they are artful indeed. The social and political satire is biting. The literary contents as well as the drawing are often spontaneous and fresh.

In short, my predilections were wrong. I liked the show. I went back to see it again. Not only did I like the show, I am now a comix fan, apparently a member of a growing club. Comix have surfaced slowly, since they first appeared in 1968, perhaps boding a longer life than some flashy fads have had. Other than the museum

Reprinted from *The Progressive* magazine. © by the Progressive, Inc.

exhibition, they have received little visible public attention. One essay appeared in a now-defunct art magazine. *Playboy* ran an article about comix in December, 1970. And there may have been another magazine article or two. An X-rated feature-length movie cartoon, *Fritz the Cat*, based on Robert Crumb's comix character, has received wider attention than the comix on which it is based.

The youthful artists who create comix are concentrated around San Francisco, breeding ground for many contemporary subterranean cultural developments. While it takes a while to recognize their genius, their artistic ancestors who, in their own unique ways, were as brash and nearly as bawdy as they, also received belated and reluctant—often posthumous— recognition. Daumier spent six months in a French prison for a cartoon aimed at Louis Philippe in the nineteenth century. Hogarth in the eighteenth century portrayed the foibles of the England of his time. And an embittered Goya in eighteenth century Spain made pointed social criticisms with his etchings. Georg Grosz and Toulouse-Lautrec dipped their pens in the same acerbic well; and Thomas Nast and Herblock and Bill Mauldin as single-panel cartoonists have held an unflattering mirror before the face of American society.

While the comix creators have avoided prison, their creations have encountered legal problems. A number of bookstores, including Ferlinghetti's famed City Lights, were raided in November, 1969, for selling comix books. Since then, the arm of the law has relaxed while the eye of the law has blinked. Or, more importantly, the courts have held that the social order will not crumble or the nation's moral fiber be weakened by explicit depiction of genitalia or sexual acts, no matter how unorthodox.

Mad was the progenitor in the 1950s of the comix developments, although the comic strip lineage in the United States dates from the 1890s. From *Mad* the comix inherited an irreverence for social taboos, but comix have gone beyond *Mad*. While *Mad* is suggestive, it is not explicit. And its language is not spiced with the tabooed words the disrespectful young use so consistently. Comix also have a kissing kinship with the sexually explicit "eight-pagers" which depicted comics characters in pornographic situations. These naughty little books of four and five decades past gave men their jollies in days before books of photographed sex became so freely available.

What the comix artists do is quite different from the utilization of comix by Pop artists, notably Andy Warhol and Roy Lichtenstein, who seek to elevate the vulgar (in its basic meaning) to fine art by enlarging comic panels and painting them on canvas. The comix creators use a popular cultural art form to perpetuate unpopular insights in a form likely to be understood by the lowest common denominator.

Comics often have done subtly and surreptitiously what the comix do boldly and forthrightly. "The funnies" are hardly that, with their shoot-and-ask-questions-later justice, their immediate retribution against antisocial acts without benefit of a trial. Evil has been depicted in such strips as *Dick Tracy* with no attempt to understand the evil-doer. *Little Orphan Annie* has promoted simplistic right-wing views, and Al Capp has used *Dogpatch* as a forum to denounce anti-war activists. Among the widely read comic strips, Walt Kelly's *Pogo* alone has shown a liberal bent. For several decades the comics themselves have received considerable attention as cultural phenomena and an influence on the young.

The proliferation of comix dates from the appearance of Crumb's *All New Zap Comix* in the spring of 1968. Crumb drew and published the comix and hawked them on San Francisco street corners. Although it seems incongruous, two comix had preceded *Zap* in the mid-sixties in Austin, Texas—*The Adventures of Jesus* by a pseudonymous "Foolbert Sturgeon" (now a university professor) and *God Nose* by Jack Jaxon.

It was, however, Crumb's efforts—and perhaps his geography as well—which gave impetus to the growth of comix. Crumb, too, remains the "old master" of the genre. The *Zap* series which originated with him remains the best known. Other comix compilations bear such titles, singly or in series, as *Toony Loons, Yellow Dog, Capt. Guts, Greaser Comics, Legion of the Charlies, Air Pirates, Slow Death, Skull, Coochie Cootie Men's Comics, Believe It or Leave It, Subvert, Mother's Oats, Hungry Chuck Biscuits, Hydrogen Bomb Funnies,*

Mom's Homemade Comics, and *Jesus Meets the Armed Services.* The targets of some of the artists' barbs are found in the very titles.

Although San Francisco is unquestionably the comix capital, the books have been published also in Chicago, Madison, Milwaukee, Detroit, Washington, and Providence, as well as Austin and elsewhere. Comix strips are seen in such underground newspapers as the *East Village Other,* the *Berkeley Barb,* and *Good Times.*

To the names of comix creators Crumb and Jaxon, add (among the better known ones): Gilbert Shelton, who worked in Austin; "Spain" Rodriguez, a native of Buffalo; S. Clay Wilson, from Kansas; Robert Williams, Rand Holmes, Rick Griffin, Victor Moscoco; Dave Sheridan and Fred Schrier, former students at the Cleveland Institute of Art; and Yossarian.

Not all of the comix efforts are deliberate put-downs of establishmentarian values. Many simply are entertainment featuring the values of a generation whose values are disdained by the older generation, just as the younger generation disdains the hypocritical values of the older. By this token, even the "entertaining" comix can be viewed as undermining the dominant culture, but the criticism is secondary.

Some of the work smacks of mere undergraduate impudence and often seems, to one of another generation, somewhat juvenile. Some of it is obsessively scatological, with language expletives which violate the pronounced moral code. Taken as a whole, however, the work represents an important critique of national values.

Shelton's work is the most pointedly political. His *Believe It or Leave It* series is brilliant satire. He uses irony to make telling points about the social order. The series begins, "You don't know how good you got it here in America, Bub. For example ... " Then follow panels ostensibly depicting situations in other countries, such as: "In some foreign countries government spies 'tap' private telephones and open other people's mail without even asking their permission." Another panel shows a jowly man speaking Greek standing behind a news commentator and the caption reads, "Some governments intimidate the mass media into agreeing with the rulers' political dogma."

Shelton's parody of *Dick Tracy* begins with a memorandum to police: "Rookies: When dealing with hippies, radicals, and niggers, shoot first and ask questions later. Above all, don't let them get to their Jewish lawyers."

Yossarian's *An' Das a Fact* in *Good Times* is more iconoclastically amusing than critical; such as, "Virginity is not only antisocial. Actually it's an elitist crime which will be dealt with unmercifully after the revolution." Or, "The average 125 lb. New York City junkie can run the 100 yd. dash in 4.3 sec., while carrying two televisions and an air conditioner." Many—indeed, most—of the strips are replete with sex and violence in juxtaposition. The sex is preposterously exaggerated, and the violence has been considered to be similarly overstated. Maybe it is in its raw form; but in view of the statistics relating "legitimate" (government-sanctioned) and "illegitimate" acts of violence, it seems hardly exaggerated in degree.

Patricia Stewart, curator at the Museum of Contemporary Art, in a catalogue essay for the comix exhibition, summarized the thrust of what the comix are saying: "The technical and conceptual sophistication of these works ruthlessly reveals the inherent perversion of a culture where sex is rated X while violence is GP."

Is anybody listening?

Graffiti Lives

BONNIE O'BOYLE

The time is coming when maintenance men and cleaning women may be branded as book burners. Every day they go about their work scrubbing, mopping and obliterating the real nitty-gritty pop literature of the sixties: graffiti, the writing on the walls. The janitors of the world don't think of that as literature, but Edward Albee paid tribute to a question scribbled on a wall by using it as a play title: "Who's Afraid of Virginia Woolf?" And "Stop the World, I Want To Get Off" was a popular London graffito (singular of graffiti) long before it went up in lights advertising Anthony Newley's musical.

As literature, graffiti's conceits, ideas, splendid suspensions of logic and twisted aphorisms have turned up in the popular language of the people. Some graffiti properly belong in Bartlett's *Familiar Quotations*, like "God isn't dead; He's living in Argentina under an assumed name"; "Yankee, go home! And take me with you"; "Stamp out mental health"; "Draft beer, not men." And if "Burn, baby, burn" didn't begin as a graffito, it had most of its exposure on walls.

A good graffito has all the qualities of an old saying or adage—it's short, memorable and has low-voltage shock quality. It often has humor, sometimes black humor with an unpleasant bite: "Ban the bomb, save the world for conventional warfare" is a famous New York underground statement that destroys some of your complacency. Other graffiti hark back to the Keystone cops type of slapstick, shriveling a person or point with an absurd kind of ridicule bordering on the burlesque: "J. Edgar Hoover sleeps with a night lite." The best humorous graffiti take a droll look at modern society and its hang-ups. An urban pessimist wrote "Chicken Little was right" on a pillar of New York's Lexington Avenue subway, for example. "Sacred cows make great hamburger" is not only a prime slice of wall writing, it's a kind of manifesto of graffito-dom. When the mammoth glass expanse of the Lever Building went up in New York, one anonymous person crouched ant-like in its shadow and chalked on the sidewalk, "In case of emergency, break glass and pull down lever." Everyone who feels like a pygmy in the cavernous American cities can appreciate the sentiment. On occasion, graffiti attack society—indirectly. For instance, couldn't "Mary Poppins is a junkie" be an admission that the world we live in isn't Disneyland after all?

Because wall writing makes social comment and because it is spontaneous (or should be), sociologists, psychologists and historians are studying it seriously. This is a logical development. For some time, social scientists have been popularizing their disciplines by delving into studies of comic books, daytime serials and even motion picture fan clubs. Any contemporary development, they reason, fills a human need and therefore is a potential source of information about the humans involved. Wall writing has even gone into the university classroom via a course taught at the New School for Social Research in New York by Robert Reisner, a jazz critic and humorist turned graffiti scholar (*Great Wall Writing* is one of his books). He doesn't consider it unusual that academicians are starting to analyze graffiti: "The question isn't why they're doing it now, but why people didn't notice wall writing hundreds of years ago. Sometimes the humblest remains—like graffiti—are evidence of symptoms of society, but they're so apparent that people ignore them. Instead studies were made about why gray-eyed people ate ham on Wednesdays. The historical graffiti tell us how common people lived, something you don't always find in history which comes down to us from the nobles' point of view. Today, too, the walls reflect what's happening. They show us that people are informed and that this is a sophisticated, cultured society."

The civil rights movement, for instance, is documented by graffiti. There are the scrawled slogans of the ghettos, from Watts to Harlem: "Black Power now" and "Burn, baby, burn." There are also the racist responses, like this one which cropped up on a New York campus: "All Negroes get out of City College." Reisner believes such remarks are valuable because they publicize issues that aren't honestly debated in

---

Reprinted from *Seventeen*®. Copyright © 1969 by Triangle Publications. Inc. Used by permission of Bonnie O'Boyle.

the mass media, where they're written about in polite euphemisms. "A hate message doesn't mean that the whole country hates something," he says, "but just seeing such a statement is beneficial because otherwise we would feel that everything is rosey." A near classic debate took place at Northwestern University after an Afro-American newspaper had been mutilated Someone retaliated by writing "Black is beautiful" on a wall. That was scratched out and replaced with "White ain't so bad." Final word came the next night. "Black is *still* beautiful."

Graffiti dialogues are a form of free communication. The public writing place is an open forum for the writer and his critics to carry on comparison and refutation. One of the classic graffiti sequences, a delightful exchange, started with the comment: "I like Grils." Underneath, a second person wrote: "It's girls, stupid, G-I-R-L-S." And a third passerby added the punch line: "What about us Grils?"

On the other hand, national causes can provoke real graffiti wars. Not long ago the perennial border dispute between the Irish Republic and Northern Ireland (still under the English crown) broke out again. Both sides made their positions clear on the walls of Belfast. The Northerners wrote "Up the Queen" and "No Pope here," while the Catholic Republicans scribbled back "No Queen here" and "Up the Pope," adding for good measure "Up Celtic" (the name of a Catholic Scottish soccer team).

The most ancient examples of graffiti are probably the scratchings found on early Egyptian monuments. Hieroglyphs also jump to mind as wall writings, but these aren't true graffiti because they represent systematic accounts or stories rather than single statements. Graffiti, instead, are just what their name indicates—"scratches" or "scribbles" from the Italian verb *graffiare*.

In 1868, archeologists uncovered barracks used by the Seventh Battalion of the Roman police, and scratched on the walls were graffiti nearly two thousand years old, giving some very blunt, funny (sometimes obscene) views of the officers and the Roman emperors. Wall writing must have been a widespread problem in ancient Rome. We know property owners near the Porta Portuensis had to put out a sign asking people not to scribble on their walls. The medieval knights had their coats of arms carved on churches to indicate their attendance for a ceremony or the end of a pilgrimage, and it isn't hard to see in these the forerunners of the initials carved in the old oak tree. Other ancient graffiti are less pleasant, like the words carved in the wall of Ashwell Church just as the Black Death was sweeping England in the fourteenth century: "The beginning of the plague was in 1350 minus one... wretched, fierce, violent." This staccato message conveys the atmosphere of the times in a flash.

Most graffiti are anonymous, but we know that sharp-tongued Jonathan Swift wrote this one on the window of an English inn called The Three Crosses: "There are three crosses at your door; hang up your wife and you'll count four." Public inns and houses provided most of the graffiti put into what was possibly the first collection ever made, a book called *The Merry-Thought; or, the Glass-window and Bog-House Miscellany* which was published in England in 1731 by a man with the droll name of Hurlo Thrumbo. In his introduction, Thrumbo decried the careless destruction of casual scribblings, especially by the innkeeper, "his rooms new-painted and white-wash'd every now and then, without regarding in the least the Wit and Learning he is obliterating, or the Worthy Authors, any more than when he shall have their Company."

Why do people write on walls? To deface the property of an enemy, to shock passersby with obscenities, to express opinions and emotions, to pass the time? There are a lot of reasons. This was discovered by psychiatrist Harvey Lomas and his assistant Gershen Weltman when they scoured bars, hospitals, gas stations and schools in the Los Angeles area to prepare a recent graffiti report for the American Psychiatric Association. They found that some people even use graffiti as a way of roping off territory or proving themselves, like the boy who wrote "This is Tony's turf" on a wall. People carve their initials on walls, tables and telephone booths for the same reason—they want to put their names on something for posterity. Sometimes it's the only kind of possession an underprivileged person can have.

Initialing is also a traditional custom in certain spots, especially in favorite college social hubs, like Morey's at Yale, where undergraduates have been carving their initials on the tables for decades. Morey's has turned up in songs, poems and stories; it's even in *Frank Merriwell at Yale*, where a rival of Frank's is touted as "the most influential soph in college" because his initials were on a round table down at Morey's.

Psychiatry and tradition aside, there is one simple explanation for our walls being covered with graffiti—people want an audience for their wit, their frustrations, even their hates. Graffiti are free in every sense. There are no editors, proofreaders, publishers or typesetters to wade through, not even a censor until the janitor comes along. And if your graffito is in a subway or railroad station, it can stay up until the next paint job. Certainly there is a disproportionate amount of egotism involved in marking up somebody else's property with personal initials and sentiments like "I hate cops," "John [I the writer] loves Mary," and "Clancy [that I again] was here." Travelers on the London underground were mystified by a graffito in exotic script until it was identified by a scholar as Osmania (a written version of the Somali language) and translated: "I hate English pudding!"

Even the intellectual graffiti are at bottom hubris-ridden, a kind of showing off on a sophisticated level, but the results are so entertaining that it doesn't matter. One of the best thinking-man's graffiti was discovered in New York. The first line was: "Shakespeare eats Bacon" followed by: "It can't be Donne."

All meaningless unless you remember your English literature. The Ivy League colleges are noted for intellectual gamesmanship on their walls. The nerve center is Harvard's Lamont Library, which displays such classics as "Reality is a crutch," "War is good business. Invest your sons," and "God isn't dead; He just doesn't want to get involved." But the prize for inscrutability should go to Yale, where a student wrote in Japanese his opinion of a prominent architect: "Yamasaki is strictly Shinto Gothic." Yale also indirectly inspired a graffito that made the pages of the *New York Times*. After the University had released its map indicating that Leif Ericson, not Columbus, had discovered America, the *Times* ran (as its "Quotation of the Day") an opinion from Boston's Italian district: "Leif Ericson is a fink."

Anyone can write graffiti, but most come from the poor, who cover their neighborhoods, tunnels and underpasses with names, four-letter words and revolutionary slogans. Other great sources are the intellectual communities of Greenwich Village and Haight-Ashbury, who register their comments on the walls of coffeehouses. The middle class masses probably make some contribution although Lomas and Weltman say they use "commercial graffiti" instead. Surprisingly, businessmen pick up cultural trends faster than sociologists at times. The commercial graffiti are the buttons and bumper stickers in neon colors that take their messages from the walls and are sold in book and card shops. All the great graffiti like "Frodo lives" and "Help retard children—Support our schools" have ended up on buttons. Reisner calls the button phenomenon "walking graffiti": "They're used by people who are expressing a sentiment openly, not anonymously on the walls, but of course, it's not original. A lot of the people who buy those buttons don't even believe in what the message is—they just think it's a smart thing to do. Sometimes they even hide them under their lapels and flash them to friends that way."

Commercialization is one of the great compliments paid to contemporary graffiti. You can't market "Foxie was here" to the general public, but you can market today's imaginative mural output without worrying about authors' rights. Graffiti have never been better. Take the classic graffito of the World War II period, the ubiquitious "Kilroy was here," which isn't especially interesting and was drained of humor long ago. Today Kilroy has been replaced by a mysterious being called Overby who appears in what might be called metaphysical statements like "Overby lives" or "Overby rules." What is Overby? The Establishment perhaps, or even that other great enemy of American youth: "Down with the draft; Overby strikes every seven hours." Like much good literature, a graffito lends itself to interpretation.

Thrumbo's complaint is still unheeded after 238 years: landlords and keepers of public houses continue to whitewash graffiti. Yet no one has succeeded in stemming the flow. Certainly signs such as "Do not write on the walls" have no effect, except as inspiration for retorts like "Maybe we should type?" Which is just as well.

Clothing: Our Extended Skin

MARSHALL MC LUHAN

Economists have estimated that an unclad society eats forty percent more than one in Western attire. Clothing as an extension of our skin helps to store and to channel energy, so that if the Westerner needs less food, he may also demand more sex. Yet neither clothing nor sex can be understood as separate isolated factors, and many sociologists have noted that sex can become a compensation for crowded living. Privacy, like individualism, is unknown in tribal societies, a fact that Westerners need to keep in mind when estimating the attractions of our way of life to nonliterate peoples.

Clothing, as an extension of the skin, can be seen both as a heat-control mechanism and as a means of defining the self socially. In these respects, clothing and housing are near twins, though clothing is both nearer and elder; for housing extends the inner heat-control mechanisms of our organism, while clothing is a more direct extension of the outer surface of the body. Today Europeans have begun to dress for the eye, American-style, just at the moment when Americans have begun to abandon their traditional visual style. The media analyst knows why these opposite styles suddenly transfer their locations. The European, since the Second War, has begun to stress visual values; his economy, not coincidentally, now supports a large amount of uniform consumer goods. Americans, on the other hand, have begun to rebel against uniform consumer values for the first time. In cars, in clothes, in paperback books; in beards, babies, and beehive hairdos, the American has declared for stress on touch, on participation, involvement, and sculptural values. America, once the land of an abstractly visual order, is profoundly "in touch" again with European traditions of food and life and art. What was an *avant-garde* program for the 1920 expatriates is now the teenagers' norm.

The Europeans, however, underwent a sort of consumer revolution at the end of the eighteenth century. When industrialism was a novelty, it became fashionable among the upper classes to abandon rich, courtly attire in favor of simpler materials. That was the time when men first donned the trousers of the common foot soldier (or *pioneer*, the original French usage), but it was done at that time as a kind of brash gesture of social "integration." Up until then, the feudal system had inclined the upper classes to dress as they spoke, in a courtly style quite removed from that of ordinary people. Dress and speech were accorded a degree of splendor and richness of texture that universal literacy and mass production were eventually to eliminate completely. The sewing machine, for example created the long straight line in clothes, as much as the linotype flattened the human vocal style.

A recent ad for C-E-I-R Computer Services pictured a plain cotton dress and the headline: "Why does Mrs. 'K' dress that way?"—referring to the wife of Nikita Krushchev. Some of the copy of this very ingenious ad continued: "It is an icon. To its own underprivileged population and to the uncommitted of the East and South, it says: 'We are thrif-ty, simple, hon-est; peace-ful, home-y, go-od.' To the free nations of the West it says: 'We will bury you.'"

This is precisely the message that the new simple clothing of our forefathers had for the feudal classes at the time of the French Revolution. Clothing was then a nonverbal manifesto of political upset.

Today in America there is a revolutionary attitude expressed as much in our attire as in our patios and small cars. For a decade and more, women's dress and hair styles have abandoned visual for iconic—or sculptural and tactual—stress. Like toreador pants and gaiter stockings, the beehive hairdo is also iconic and sensuously inclusive, rather than abstractly visual. In a word, the American woman for the first time presents herself as a person to be touched and handled, not just to be looked at. While the Russians are groping vaguely toward visual consumer values, North Americans are frolicking amidst newly discovered tactile, sculptural spaces in cars, clothes, and housing. For this

---

From *Understanding Media: The Extensions of Man* by Marshall McLuhan. Copyright © 1964 by Marshall McLuhan. Used with permission of McGraw-Hill Book Company.

reason, it is relatively easy for us now to recognize clothing as an extension of the skin. In the age of the bikini and of skin-diving, we begin to understand "the castle of our skin" as a space and world of its own. Gone are the thrills of strip-tease. Nudity could be naughty excitement only for a visual culture that had divorced itself from the audile-tactile values of less abstract societies. As late as 1930, four-letter words made visual on the printed page seemed portentous. Words that most people used every hour of the day became as frantic as nudity, when printed. Most "four-letter words" are heavy with tactile-involving stress. For this reason they seem earthy and vigorous to visual man. So it is with nudity. To backward cultures still embedded in the full gamut of sense-life, not yet abstracted by literacy and industrial visual order, nudity is merely pathetic. The Kinsey Report on the sex life of the male expressed bafflement that peasants and backward peoples did not relish marital or boudoir nudity. Khrushchev did not enjoy the can-can dance provided for his entertainment in Hollywood. Naturally not. That sort of mime of sense involvement is meaningful only to long-literate societies. Backward peoples approach nudity, if at all, with the attitude we have come to expect from our painters and sculptors—the attitude made up of all the senses at once. To a person using the whole sensorium, nudity is the richest possible expression of structural form. But to the highly visual and lopsided sensibility of industrial societies, the sudden confrontation with tactile flesh is heady music, indeed.

There is a movement toward a new equilibrium today, as we become aware of the preference for coarse, heavy textures and sculptural shapes in dress. There is, also, the ritualistic exposure of the body indoors and out-of-doors. Psychologists have long taught us that much of our hearing takes place through the skin itself. After centuries of being fully clad and of being contained in uniform visual space, the electric age ushers us into a world in which we live and breathe and listen with the entire epidermis. Of course, there is much zest of novelty in this cult, and the eventual equilibrium among the senses will slough off a good deal of the new ritual, both in clothing and in housing. Meantime, in both new attire and new dwellings, our unified sensibility cavorts amidst a wide range of awareness of materials and colors which makes ours one of the greatest ages of music, poetry, painting, and architecture alike.

QUESTIONS FOR DISCUSSION

1. How do comics, graffiti, and clothing each function as a mass medium?
2. What themes recur in contemporary comics and graffiti?
3. What kinds of information does clothing communicate about people?

PROJECTS

1. Prepare a content analysis of three consecutive issues of **Mad** magazine or a comic book of your choice. Consider:
   (a) view of the establishment
   (b) view of authority figures
   (c) type of humor
   (d) most popular topics

2. Decide on a social comment you wish to make, such as antiwar, personal independence, or a similar topic. Select the medium which best makes your statement—comic strip, graffiti, or clothing—and either make the statement or describe in detail how you would do it.

MEDIA FORMS PROJECT

1. A story, essay, or play can be transmitted for popular consumption through many media forms. Well-known examples include **Gone With the Wind** and **The Godfather** (or select your own example), both of which have been presented in book, movie, and television forms. In what ways did shifting from one form to another (from book to movie to television script) alter the work's content in relationship to:
   (a) fidelity to original story or intent
   (b) time/space relationships
   (c) censorship/editing
   (d) portrayal of character
   Which form(s) do you prefer and why?

2. Select a theme or topic such as the Viet Nam war, images of women, or other area of interest. Collect examples that illustrate the treatment of this topic in various media forms, such as:
   (a) TV
   (b) radio
   (c) film—documentary and fiction
   (d) comics
   (e) music

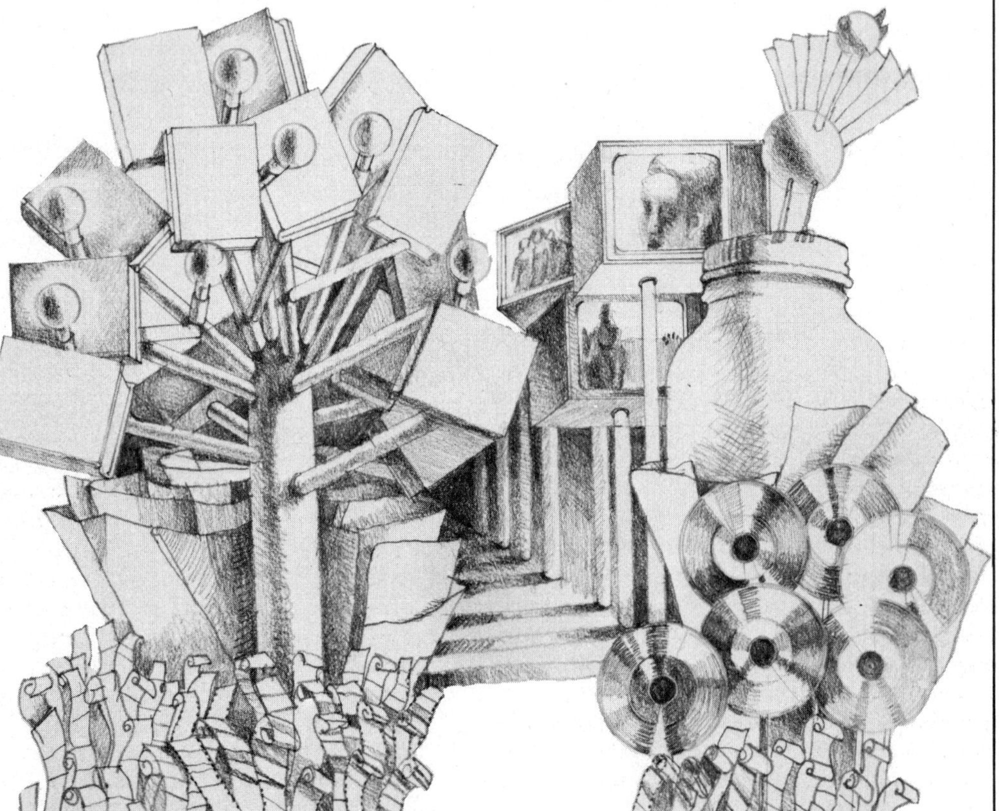

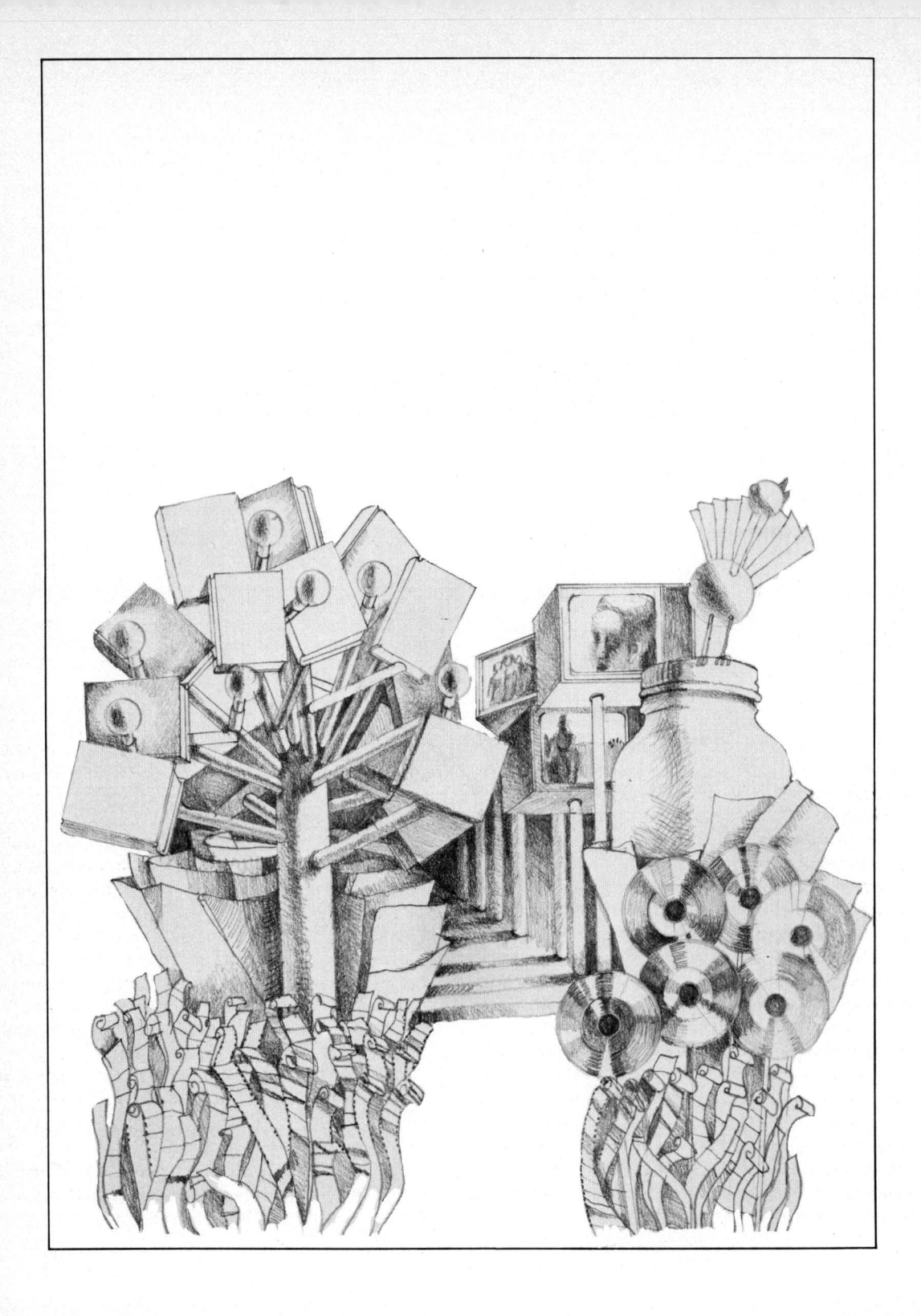

MEDIA CONTENT

When Marshall McLuhan argues that the medium is the message, he suggests that the message becomes subordinate to the medium's effect on its audience. The message is, however, no less important to the medium than the automobile is to the highway system.

The messages of modern media include a wide range of program types and formats, each trying to attract the largest audience. The message that people seem to desire most is that which entertains, providing a respite from the reality of daily living. Increasingly the most serious and sophisticated media content is churned through a system that serves a finished product in the most palatable (entertaining) manner possible. The greatest effort, even in simply providing information, often goes into shaping the material to make it easy to relate to. Consequently, news tends to be selected for people who relate well to Walter Cronkite, and vast numbers of minority group members are deprived of information essential to them.

A primary motive in content selection is to deliver an audience to an advertiser—usually for a fee. Advertising is the support system for commercial media and constitutes a unique content form of its own. Over the past decade subtle but significant shifts in news presentation have emerged. A prime example is the new personal journalism, that describes everyday gestures and modes of behavior toward peers, superiors, and inferiors, in addition to various other symbolic details within a given reporting scene. Other examples include a new emphasis on equality for women and minorities. We can also see how the televising of national sporting events alters the way those events are conducted.

This section is a journey through most of the significant content areas of mass communication. Discriminate and be selective as you read through these areas. Select the best content for you. Read critically and consider how media content—including this book—is shaped and how it in turn affects your own perceptions and attitudes.

THE NEWS AND NEWSPERSONS

Versions of National News

EDWARD JAY EPSTEIN

News is essentially protean in character. Any happening can be reported in a multitude of different forms and takes on radically different appearances in different news media. Nor is there necessarily one correct way of reporting an event. Alternative ways always exist for organizing information, and events themselves do not ineluctably determine the forms in which they are reported. Yet in examining the product of a news organization, one may find striking similarities in the ways in which the news is presented and the direction it takes. What accounts for these consistent directions and news forms is the central question that this study attempts to answer, or at least to clarify in the case of network news organizations.

The main finding of this study is that the pictures of society that are shown on television as national news are largely—though not entirely—performed and shaped by organizational considerations. To maintain themselves in a competitive world, the networks impose a set of prior restraints, rules and conditions on the operations of their news divisions. Budgets are set for the production of news, time is scheduled for its presentation, and general policies are laid down concerning its content. To satisfy these requirements—and keep their jobs—news executives and producers formulate procedures, systems and policies intended to reduce the uncertainties of news to manageable proportions. The timing, length, content and cost of news thereby becomes predictable. Since all the networks are in essentially the same business and compete for the same or similar advertisers, affiliates and audiences, under a single set of ground rules laid down by the government, the news product at each network is shaped by very similar requisites. The basic contours of network news can thus be at least partly explained in terms of the demands which the news organizations must meet in order to continue operating without crises or intervention from network executives. In this respect, four critical demands structure the scope and form of network news.

First, there is the budgetary requisite set by the economic logic of network television. The prevailing assumption among network executives . . . is that increasing the budget of a news program for news gathering or production past a certain point will not bring about a commensurate increase in advertising revenues, and that the point at which these diminishing returns set in is located immediately beyond the budget necessary to produce the minimum amount of news programming of adequate technical quality to fill the news schedule. These assumptions proceed from the audience-flow theory that network news programs, unlike entertainment or local news programs, inherit most of their audience from the preceding programs. In other words, national news does not attract its own audience to any significant extent. Therefore, the logic goes, increased expenditures for the scope and quality of the news effort will not necessarily increase the size of the audience—or of the advertising revenues, which are dependent on the size of the audience.

Whatever the merits of this theory, the fact that network executives commonly accept its implications profoundly limits the news operation. Because budget levels are fixed with an eye toward filling a specific number of minutes of news programming a week, the allocation of funds for the unseen parts of news gathering tends to be held to a minimum. For one thing, there is no economic incentive to spend money on searches for original information, or intelligence gathering, since it is not presumed that scoops, exclusives or original reporting significantly increase the audience, and hence the revenue, for network news. Instead, for advance notice of news events, the networks rely heavily on the wire services, the *New York Times* and other secondary sources. Similarly, investigative reports requiring a large amount of field

From *News From Nowhere: Television and The News*, by Edward Jay Epstein. Copyright © 1973 by Edward Jay Epstein. Reprinted by permission of Random House, Inc. Most of the material in this book originally appeared in *The New Yorker*.

> During most of the quarter century I've been a reporter—or whatever you want to call it—I've been out dealing with primary news sources. It's hard, to give that up; some day I'd like to go back to that. When, I have absolutely no idea. . . .
>
> Anchorman is a word we have to live with, I suppose. It's not such a bad word, and it's better than some.
>
> —John Chancellor

work and research are a luxury which cannot be justified in terms of economic returns. Networks therefore simply do not maintain the research facilities and staff which would be necessary to support investigative reporting on a regular basis; instead, select subjects are occasionally explored in depth by a documentary or special-events unit, which also must meet network requisites.

Further, since there is no economic reason regularly to employ more film crews than is necessary to produce the daily quota, coverage is generally limited to a dozen or so selected events. This, in turn, requires that the events which are selected for coverage are highly predictable and almost certain to produce a usable news story. Though they would extend the range of coverage to less definite and more risky events, additional crews would not be economically justifiable under the assumptions of this theory. Also, because direct information is not always available about the precise news content of planned events—what will emerge, for example, in a scheduled hearing or speech—producers and assignment editors must rely routinely on certain broad-gauged criteria to narrow down the field of possibilities. Consequently, there tends to be a repetition of certain types of story situations and newsmakers over long periods of time, or what Walter Lippmann would have called a "repertory of stereotypes."

Moreover, since it is less expensive to take a film story from some cities than from others, according to the budgetary accounting practices of the networks, the filmed news tends to be skewed toward certain geographic areas of the country—specifically, New York, Washington and, to a lesser extent, Chicago. The societal themes depicted on network news thus tend to be illustrated with a disproportionate number of visual examples taken from a few cosmopolitan centers with special problems.

Finally, the economic logic tends to focus attention on a relatively small group of newsmakers who are actively engaged in conflicts or contests for office. Since there is no economic justification in overcoverage, according to the accepted rationale, assignment editors tend to ration the camera crews among newsmakers that can be relied on with a fair degree of certainty to produce usable happenings. For this purpose, it is generally assumed that high-ranking figures of authority involved in heated conflicts or challenges to their authority are more likely to produce news than newsmakers who are explicating developments or policies in a complex world. The more heated the dispute or challenge, the more certain the news story.

A second basic requisite that network news divisions are expected to meet is that their program maintain—or at least not significantly diminish—the networks' "audience flows." While it is presumed that network news cannot *attract* large numbers of new viewers to a channel, no matter how high the quality of its coverage, executives also generally believe that "visually unsatisfactory" news, as one NBC vice-president put it, can cause a significant number of viewers to change channels. Since any noticeable reduction in a network's audience flow during the dinnertime news seriously affects the ratings of the entire prime-time schedule—programs begin with a smaller "base" audience—network executives insist that the news be presented in its most visually satisfactory form, no matter how complex or difficult to comprehend the subject is. The effectiveness of the visual presentation is measured by a low "turn-off" rate among viewers. The logic of audience maintenance can thus be extrapolated from analyses of audience studies.

The first assumption made by news executives and producers is that viewers' interest is most likely to be maintained through easily recognizable and palpable images, and conversely, most likely to be distracted by unfamiliar or confusing images. This has special force in the case of the dinnertime news, when, according to studies, the audience has fewer years of formal education than the population at large—and a large proportion of viewers are children. In practice, therefore, cameramen, correspondents and editors are instructed to seek out and select pictures that have an almost universal meaning. Hence, stories tend to fit into a limited repertory of images, which explains why so often shabbily dressed children symbolically stand for poverty; uniformed police symbolically stand for authority; fire symbolically stands for destruction, and so forth. Since television is regarded as a medium for the "transmission of experience" rather than "information," complex issues are represented in terms of human experience; inflation, for example, is pictured as a man unable to afford dinner in a restaurant. Of course, the repertory changes, but at any given times, images, especially emotional ones, which are presumed to have the broadest possible recognition, are used to illustrate news events.

A second assumption in this logic of audience maintenance is that scenes of potential conflict are more interesting to the audience than scenes of placidity. Virtually all executives and producers share this view. Situations are thus sought out in network news in which there is a high potential for violence, but a low potential for audience confusion. News events showing a violent confrontation between two easily recognizable sides in conflict—for example, blacks versus whites, uniformed police versus demonstrators, or military versus civilians—are preferable to ones in which the issues are less easily identifiable. However, even when the conflict involves confusing elements, it usually can be reconstructed in the form of a two-sided conflict. Therefore network news tends to present the news in terms of highly dramatic conflicts between clearly defined sides.

A third closely related assumption is that the viewer's span of attention—which is presumed to be limited—is prolonged by action, or subjects in motion, and sharply reduced by static subjects, such as "talking heads." As has been previously discussed, the high value placed on action footage by executives leads to a three-step distillation of news happenings by correspondents, cameramen and editors, all of whom seek the moment of highest action. Through this process, the action in a news event, which in fact may account for only a fraction of the time, is concentrated together and becomes the central feature of the happening. This helps explain why news on television tends willy-nilly to focus on activity.

It is further assumed in this logic that news reports are more likely to hold viewers' attention if they are cast in the form of the fictive story, with narrative closure. For this purpose, it will be recalled, stories are generally edited so that there is a discernible beginning, middle and end; rising action, a climax, then falling action; conflict and then apparent resolution. This self-contained form tends to "lock" an audience into a news story, an NBC vice-president for audience research suggested. The net effect is that most events on network news are presented as miniature documentaries with similar plots: two opposing sides confront each other, the tension builds to a climax, and then there is an apparent denouement. As Reuven Frank instructed, news is thus given "all the attributes of fiction."

Affiliates place a third basic requisite on network news in requiring that it be *national* news. The stations affiliated with a network, it will be recalled, substitute the half-hour network news for their own local programing, which is generally highly profitable, because they are expected by the FCC to provide some coverage of national as well as local issues. To meet this expectation, producers must solve the problem of converting local happenings—since all news happens in *some* locality—into national stories. The "nationalization of news," which is commonly regarded by network producers as the crux of their operation, is accomplished by using reports about particular events as illustrations of national themes. Almost any event can be subsumed under a universal category. The opening of a municipal heating plant in a single city was, for example, utilized by CBS to illustrate its ongoing "Can the World Survive?" theme. Since producers can easily "commission" stories about happenings which illustrate themes that are presumed to be of national interest or simply concentrate their coverage on newsmakers associated with national causes, the precommitment of network news to an agenda of national themes and causes is virtually assured.

Finally, government regulation of television sets a fourth basic requirement for network news: it must conform to certain outside standards of fairness in the presentation of controversial issues. Since the Federal Communication Commission defines fairness simply as the presentation of opposing views on an issue, network news commonly has satisfied this requisite by soliciting views from spokesmen of two opposing sides in a controversy—and then editing the opposing views together as a "dialogue." To avoid any apparent disparities in the presentations, equally articulate spokesmen are usually selected to present the arguments on each side. Complicated issues thus appear to be merely a point-counterpoint debate between equally matched opponents.

Nor is this framework of fairness conducive to questioning the arguments presented, or exposing the weakness or superiority of one or another side in a controversy. For even to appear to favor one side might be construed as an unfair presentation by network executives who closely monitor the news. Quite inadvertently, the fairness standards encourage rhetoric and even demagoguery, at least to the degree that spokesmen in a controversy are aware that their arguments are not likely to be questioned. Moreover, the networks' vulnerability to government regulation—which includes antitrust action as well as the FCC—requires a firm policy of neutrality in the view of key network executives. This entails recruiting correspondents

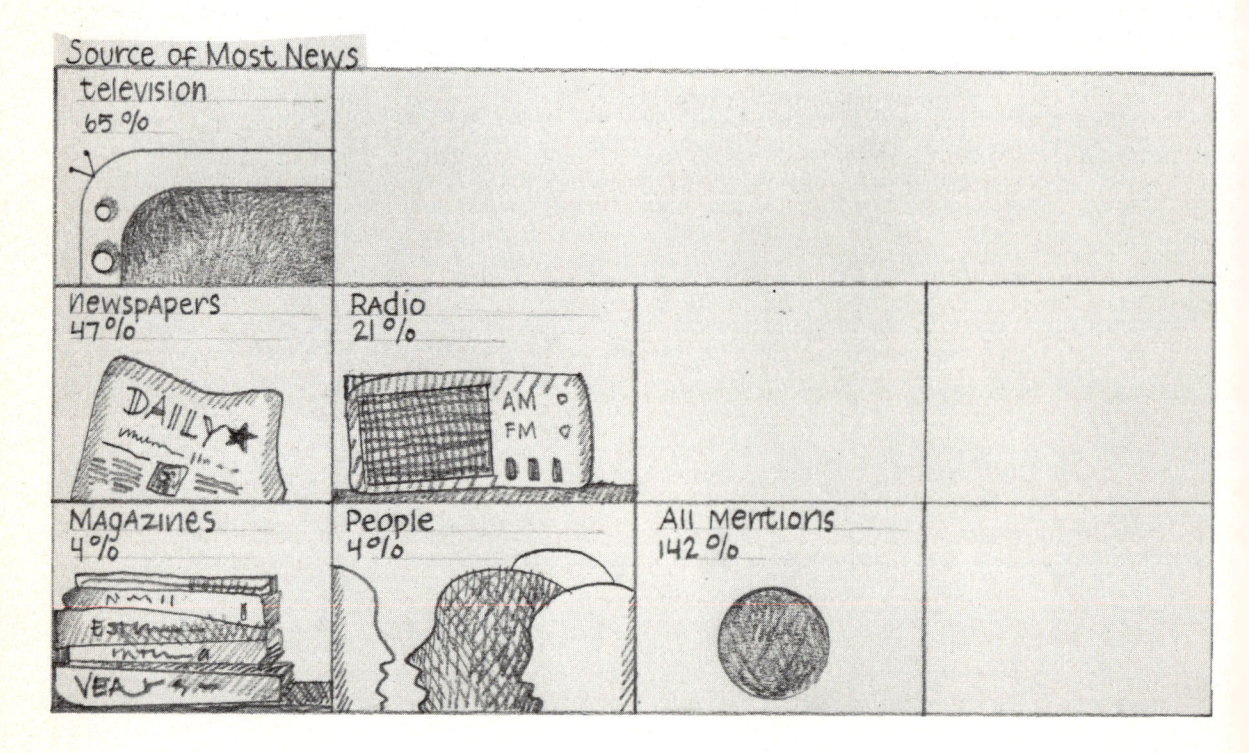

Source of Most News

television 65%

newspapers 47%

Radio 21%

Magazines 4%

People 4%

All Mentions 142%

without fixed views on political subjects, frequently rotating those who cover sensitive subjects, and not encouraging them—if only by not making sufficient time or resources available—to attempt to resolve controversial issues in favor of one side or another by conducting their own investigations. In a very real sense, then, the network policies of fairness and neutrality limit, if not define, the style of journalism on network news.

To be sure, network news cannot be entirely explained in terms of organizational requisites. The personal opinions of newsmen color newscasts to some degree, no matter how stringent a network's controls; also, reporting and editorials in other news media, especially the *New York Times* and *Time* magazine, help crystallize issues and heavily influence the producers in their selection of news. Nonetheless, the organizational imperatives of network news, and the logics that proceed from these demands, irresistibly shape the pictures of society in consistent directions, and therefore produce a very particular, perhaps unique, version of national news. In this version, all local events tend to be transmuted to great national themes, with the inevitable loss of their local and specific character. Since the events that are used to illustrate the national themes tend to be taken from large cosmopolitan centers, which are economically and geographically the most convenient sources of news, the themes tend to follow the line of conflict in such cities as New York, Washington and Chicago. To maintain the interest of the audience, happenings involving visual conflict are routinely selected over less violent ones, and ones involving recognizable figures of authority are selected over less identifiable images. . . .

This version of the news is not the product of a group of willful or biased or political men, but of an organization striving to meet the requisites needed to survive in a competitive world. While other critiques, starting from very different premises about news, have reached similar conclusions about the version of the news that television presents, the organizational approach produces a different set of causes and implications. For example, perhaps the most common critique made of television news by other journalists—and faculty members of journalism schools—is that it is superficial in the sense that it affords only scant coverage of news events, lacks depth or sufficient analysis of events, and engages in only a minimum amount of investigative reporting. The main thrusts of such criticism are that television newsmen lack journalistic credentials, and that producers and executives are lax or indifferent toward their responsibilities—or else lack public spirit. For example, in examining the deficiencies of television news, the Alfred I. Dupont-Columbia University *Survey of Broadcast Journalism* suggested:

> This might give the impression that all broadcasters are assumed to be evil men. This is obviously far from true. There are in broadcasting as elsewhere in our society the public-spirited along with the mean. At the moment, unfortunately, the latter seem to prevail.

The implication that runs through this type of critique is that the level of journalism is set by the magnanimity of broadcasters, and that more enlightened or public-spirited broadcasters can remedy the insufficiencies in network news. It then follows that changing or educating the broadcasters will improve the news product. The organizational approach suggests, however, that the level of journalism in network news is more or less fixed by the time, money and manpower that can be allocated to it, and that these resources are ultimately determined not by "mean" or public-spirited broadcasters, but by the requisites which the news divisions must meet in order to maintain their operations. And these requirements imposed on the news divisions are not arbitrary; they flow from the logic and structure of network television. As the previously discussed case of Fred W. Friendly illustrated, an executive, no matter how public-spirited, who over time fails to meet these requirements will be replaced, or his responsibilities in the organization will be changed. Any substantial improvement in the level of network journalism, such as expanding coverage of events to a truly nationwide scale, would therefore require a structural change in network television which would effectively reorder the economic and political incentives, rather than merely a change of personnel.

Post-Watergate Reconstruction—Media (from *Commonweal*)

SISYPHUS

The press functions like one continuous unfulfilled New Year's resolution.

Its performance during the corrupt Nixon Presidency suggests the press should either claim less or perform better. Otherwise, it will suffer additional distrust, even disrepute, on the part of Americans.

Prospects for improvement are discouraging, because, if for no other reason, editors are more snarlingly sensitive to criticism than those in any other occupation—except, perhaps, bankers. Yet, its freedom is as bountiful as its sense of responsibility is in short supply. Pre-publication censorship was quite properly demolished two centuries ago; post-publication censorship has dissolved as a result of the Sullivan and Pentagon Papers cases involving the good, grey *New York Times*. However, the press seeks additional protection from Congress in the form of a so-called "press-shield" law. What Congress giveth, it can taketh away, the press lords should keep in mind, afflicted as they are by delusions of moral grandeur.

We can let those who delight in profound philosophical debates wrestle about where to draw the line between freedom and responsibility, liberty and license. The practical problem, considering the foul mood of Americans toward newspapers, radio and television, is simply to promptly reform their technical operations and format coverage. The difference in approach is, as in reasoning, inductive rather than deductive.

Television and radio performance is dismal.

Reprinted from *Commonweal* Magazine, by permission of Commonweal Publishing Co.

Their "news" programs, from which most Americans obtain their knowledge about current events, mostly consist of a pretty voice reading stories provided for a fee by the two major national news-gathering associations, the Associated Press (AP) and United Press International (UPI). Program directors try to disguise the reading-by-rote. At least, Frank Blair of the NBC "Today" show is honest about it—he openly reads the news dispatches on camera. But there is one excuse for radio and TV—each is primarily designed to entertain, not inform.

Newspapers have no such excuse. Editors, amid drinks and smoke of their annual self-congratulatory conventions, insist their job historically has been to "afflict the comfortable and comfort the afflicted." The reverse is, in fact, the rule.

With few exceptions, newspapers are community bulletin boards for the middle-class—or, more precisely, for the orthodoxy of their middle-class readers.

The press peddles crime and catastrophe—padded with good-will editorials, sometimes simply rewrites of editorials originally appearing in the *New York Times*.

Journalism schools emphasize irrelevant accuracies—how high is the steeple? The schools have all the intellectual content of "a training school for A&P clerks," as A. J. Liebling once wrote about the one he attended, perhaps the most prestigious, the Columbia University Graduate School of Journalism.

The press, until the ghettos erupted and the traffic jams worsened, ignored among other major stories:

- Migration of an estimated three million Americans from farm to city between 1957 and 1964.
- Creation of slovenly white suburbs by means of federally-funded housing and interstate highway programs designed by Congress to favor private interests.

Newspapers are shot through with contradictions. They laud "Brotherhood Week" each year on the editorial pages, while employing no black reporters in the newsrooms. They bleed editorially from time to time for the poor, while accepting deceptive advertising placed by food and furniture stores and running color-photos of baked Alaska and other expensive recipes on their "women's pages." Even the best of the newspapers, the *Washington Post* and *The New York Times* among others, run weekly financial and real-estate sections that are straight shills for the most base motivations in those economic sectors.

Unfortunately, the fabled critics of the press are dead or retired—Liebling, Seldes, and Hollenbeck. The 1947 Hutchins Commission's report on freedom of the (American) press is a dusty curiosity in libraries. At present, a monthly tabloid-sized publication, [*More*], seeks to monitor the media, but, instead, tangles itself up in intramuralisms that interest press people, but are unfathomable to laymen who wish to know what's wrong.

There have been tons of newsprint spent over what's wrong. Contrary to George Seldes, it's not that advertisers control news-columns, although their footprints are not uncommon in newsrooms. It's not so simple as a conspiracy of economic interests. In fact, there's less "cooking" of the news these days.

Nor is it another favorite bête-noire of critics—the prevalence of communities in which the only newspaper(s) is owned by one publisher. Responsible publishers in Providence, Louisville, Atlanta and Eugene (Ore.) have demonstrated that pretty good newspapers—fair and comprehensive—can be produced without competition. However, the prevailing pattern may be typified by the one-ownership morning and afternoon newspapers in Worcester, Mass., either of which may be thoroughly read in about seven minutes—even if the lighting's bad.

No, a major problem, perhaps *the* major problem, is more elusive. It might be termed a consensus approach to the news—after all, the *original* Section 2 of Article I of the Constitution stated a consensus attitude—that a Negro was three-fifths of a white person for purposes of allocation of seats to states in the House of Representatives. A consensus approach, reflecting one or more major orthodoxies among readers, is reinforced by ill-informed editors, lazy reporters paid low salaries and standard news-coverage techniques that shape the content of the news itself.

Readers of the "better papers" and viewers watching only educational TV and/or radio don't comprehend the shoddiness of most newspapers, north, south, east and west—although the opinion-ridden, columnist-laden *New York Post* does provide for interested New Yorkers an example of the severe shortcomings of papers elsewhere.

A David Broder may stumble, a Mary McGrory may mislead because of a journalistic "love-affair" with a public personality, or a James Reston may go stale. But such drawbacks are minor compared to the faults of most reporting. In fact, relatively few readers are aware these three talents even exist. And this brings us to the press associations, AP and UPI, the so-called "wire services."

The AP boasts that three million words of copy move each day through its vast automatic teletype circuits to more than 1260 dailies and 3350 radio and TV stations in the United States. Days go by without either the *Washington Post* or the *New York Times* printing an AP (or UPI) story on page one. But for all but a handful of newspapers the wire services are the only source for news beyond their immediate circulation "by-lines"; they can cite that of Walter Mears, the AP political reporter, not Broder or McGrory or Reston. More people read his dispatches than any other reporter's. Mears is a good reporter. So are other wire service reporters covering national news such as Walter Leubsdorf and Steve Gerstel. UPI's Frank Eleazar knew more about the House of Representatives than the combined staffs of the *Washington Post* and the *New York Times'* Washington bureau.

But as Timothy Crouse points out in his book

The News and Newspersons 111

about the 1972 Presidential campaign reportage, *Boys on the Bus*, the AP and UPI stories on major matters—politics, civil rights, labor disputes, etc.—are overly cautious: "There is an inverse proportion between the number of persons a reporter reaches and the amount he can say. The larger the audience, the more inoffensive and inconclusive the article must be. Many of the wire men are repositories of information they can never convey."

> "I never go home without feeling we've done an inadequate job. I guess we can't do everything; but the things that get left on the cutting room floor, on my desk, that ought to have been broadcast that day appall me."
>
> —Walter Cronkite

Wire-service dispatches are the staple of American newspapers. A news editor often will prefer a wire-service story over that of his newspaper's own reporter's coverage of the same event if the latter's is not in conformity with the wire-service story. And wire-service reporters emphasize superficial conflicts. After all, they are weaned on fires and accidents. "If you don't learn how to write an eight-car fatal on Route 128 (Boston), you're gonna be in big trouble," Mears says. The deeper controversies become slighted because they violate the consensus-syndrome.

Moreover, the wire-services' coverage of Congress, for example, is deficient. A reporter finds himself covering more than one Congressional hearing. Consequently, he attends one where he finds a witness' press-release, incorporating his testimony. He scurries off to his other assigned hearing, unable to stay for the more productive questioning of the witness. It's happened that a wire-service reporter has covered four hearings in one morning. His stories become coverage by press-release, plus a snippet of testimony shared by an understanding reporter able to remain throughout hearings. The AP reports that 25 to 30 percent of its domestic news each day carries Washington date-lines. At the same time, the wire-service reporter is drilled to remember that at any minute of his working day there's a client newspaper going to press. Inadequate staffing is, then, aggravated by time pressures.

Another deficiency, seldom analyzed, is the role of the "rewrite" reporter. He, or she, sits in a newsroom, accepts notes over the telephone from a reporter and then, without first-hand knowledge, rewrites the notes into a story for publication. The failings of this technique often overcome the advantage—the technical one of speeding coverage of an event into print. The failing is tremendous as practiced by the weekly newsmagazines. Tens of thousands of words conveyed from their Washington bureaus to the home-office in Manhattan where unknowing editors select those stories to be included in the next issue and turn morasses of words over to rewrite men to be reworked into easy-flowing narratives. The product is notoriously unreliable. The editors in New York have reworked Woodrow Wilson's definition of news as "the atmosphere of events" into a formula: news is what the editor says it is.

Another deficient news-gathering method is that of the news-conference. The Presidential is the most widely known.

In December, 1929, with the stunning October stock-market crash reverberating throughout the country, President Hoover held a press conference. In response to one question, he reported that Christmas retail purchases were running at a volume comparable to the previous Christmas season's level. There was apparently only one other question from reporters—as to whether the newly-elected President of Mexico would sleep at the White House during his forthcoming visit. President Hoover replied that he didn't expect that to happen.

But that occurred 45 years ago, comes the challenge. But in 1974, a recent televised press conference of President Ford's shows a worsening of the format—individual reporters strutting on camera as they asked questions . . . disjointed questions about the Nixon pardon . . . no informed questioning about the dolorous economic condition.

Additional practices compound inadequate news coverage—reporters who collect news-sources as lawyers collect clients, reporters huddling after joint interviews to make certain they all agree on the "lead" of the story each will write (comparable to price-fixing among corporations), and editors who lurch from issue to issue for prime coverage, a sort of interest-spasm of the day approach. There are other flawed practices, one of which is the ground-rules reporters, individually or collectively, accept as a basis for interviewing a political personnage in Washington:

1. God's in his Heaven, Rev. Billy Graham said today (on-the-record).
2. God's in his Heaven, an authoritative source said today (not for attribution).
3. God's in his Heaven, it can be reliably reported (an extreme form of the back-grounder without attribution).
4. Off-the-record rule under which the Rev. Graham tells reporters that God's in his Heaven, but reporters can't print it in any form or shape.

Occasionally, reporters refuse to be bound by such rules originally designed to oblige the reporter without embarrassing his source. Occasionally, there is mentioned a need to reevaluate the whole constellation of news-coverage in Washington, whether by wire-services, the *Post*, the *Times* or the Washington bureaus of daily newspapers.

Competent news-coverage is in a class with Samuel Johnson's observation when told about there being a woman minister in the neighborhood: the wonder, he said, like that of a dog walking on hind-legs, is not that it's done well, but that it's done at all.

The press is misleading itself in the wake of Watergate. The persistence of two *Washington Post* reporters, Woodward and Bernstein, is not to be undervalued; nor is it to be overlooked that both were inexperienced reporters who uncovered pieces of the scandal, while for month-after-month big-shot newspapermen in Washington scoffed or ignored them. But primarily it was the persistence of Congressional committees and federal judges and juries that exposed the corruption of the Nixon Presidency.

The downfall of Nixon isn't being greeted joyously everywhere. Alan Otten of *The Wall Street Journal* recently wrote: "While the press is on a jag of self-satisfaction and self-congratulations, there is an unhappily large number of Americans who aren't overjoyed by the Watergate exposures—in fact, they're annoyed, angry and hostile." They are joined on the left by those who recall the press's glamorization of Presidents, the press's self-censorship of our bombing of Cambodia and more than faint indications that working reporters voluntarily, and sometimes for pay, help the CIA and other intelligence agencies. Blacks share the distrustful mood. The *Washington Post*, in a recent series, noted that during the first 19 weeks of this year, nearly 1500 news-items were broadcast on the CBS Evening News, but of these only 20 focused on black problems. And, of the 20, nine dealt with the so-called "Zebra killings" in San Francisco and two about Hank Aaron's home-run achievements.

> Every reporter knows that when you write the first word you make an editorial judgment.
> —Robert Kintner

Customarily, Presidents and their assistants and the reporters assigned to the White House are locked in fond, not deadly embrace. The role is mistakenly symbiotic, not adversary as it should be. Washington correspondents, assuming even the best of intentions by officers of government, should remember an observatin of a British government official to reporters: "You think we lie to you. But we don't lie, really we don't. However, when you discover that, you make even a greater error. You think we tell you the truth."

The news media are in trouble; only a few of their practitioners understand this.

"A popular government without popular information or the means of acquiring it," James Madison remarked, "is but a prologue to a farce or tragedy or perhaps both."

We shall see if press people turn away from divvying up with politicians free news and free publicity in time to reform formats of coverage before public opinion unfairly shackles them with restraints believed permanently long ago cast off.

from All the President's Men

CARL BERNSTEIN and BOB WOODWARD

This short excerpt from the historic journalistic account of one newspaper's monumental role in exposing government corruption is an example of how an effective newsroom team functions. The relationship between the reporter and the editor and a supportive publisher is a story of journalistic competitiveness and cooperation.

Gradually Bernstein's and Woodward's mutual distrust and suspicions diminished. They realized the advantages of working together, particularly because their temperaments were so dissimilar. The breadth of the story, the inherent risks and the need for caution all argued for at least two reporters working on it. By dividing the work and pooling their information, they increased their contacts.

Each kept a separate master list of telephone numbers. The numbers were called at least twice a week. (Just the fact that a certain source wouldn't come to the phone or return calls often signaled something important.) Eventually, the combined total of names on their lists swelled to several hundred, yet fewer than 50 were duplicated. Inevitably, they crossed each other's tracks. "Don't you guys work together?" a lawyer once asked Woodward. "I just this minute hung up on Carl." On another occasion, a White House aide said, "We've been trying to figure out why some of us get calls from Bernstein and others seem to be on Woodward's list." There was no reason. The reporters wanted to avoid tripping over each other's work as much as possible. In general, they preferred to keep their contacts divided because confidential sources would feel more comfortable that way: more time could be invested in developing a personal relationship.

To those who sat nearby in the newsroom, it was obvious that Woodstein was not always a smoothly operating piece of journalistic machinery. The two fought, often openly. Sometimes they battled for fifteen minutes over a single word or sentence. Nuances were critically important; the emphasis had to be just right. The search for the journalistic mean was frequently conducted at full volume, and it was not uncommon to see one stalk away from the other's desk. Sooner or later, however (usually later), the story was hammered out.

Each developed his own filing system; oddly, it was Bernstein, by far the less organized of the two, who kept records neatly arranged in manila folders labeled with the names of virtually everyone they encountered. Subject files were kept as well. Woodward's record-keeping was more informal, but they both adhered to one inviolate rule: they threw nothing out and kept all their notes and the early drafts of stories. Soon they had filled four filing cabinets.

Usually, Woodward, the faster writer, would do a first draft, then Bernstein would rewrite. Often, Bernstein would have time to rewrite only the first half of a story, leaving Woodward's second half hanging like a shirttail. The process often consumed most of the night.

As the number of leads and components in the Watergate story increased, the reporters became almost possessed by it. And, tentatively at first, they became friends. Neither had many demands on his time. Woodward was divorced; Bernstein separated. They often remained in the newsroom until late at night, making checks, reading clippings, outlining their next steps, trading theories. Sometimes they were joined by Barry Sussman, who ultimately was detached from his regular duties as city editor and given prime responsibility for directing the *Post*'s Watergate coverage.

Sussman was 38, gentle in his manner, slightly overweight, curly-haired, scholarly in demeanor. He had been a desk man on a small-town newspaper near the Virginia-Tennessee line, a speed-reading instructor at New York University, a society editor, and then suburban editor for the *Post*—a vagabond journalist who had left Brooklyn odd-jobbing his way to Washington.

© 1974 by Carl Bernstein and Bob Woodward; reprinted by permission of Simon & Schuster, Inc.

Sussman had the ability to seize facts and lock them in his memory, where they remained poised for instant recall. More than any other editor at the *Post*, or Bernstein and Woodward, Sussman became a walking compendium of Watergate knowledge, a reference source to be summoned when even the library failed. On deadline, he would pump these facts into a story in a constant infusion, working up a body of significant information to support what otherwise seemed like the weakest of revelations. In Sussman's mind, everything fitted. Watergate was a puzzle and he was a collector of the pieces.

At heart, Sussman was a theoretician. In another age, he might have been a Talmudic scholar. He had cultivated a Socratic method, zinging question after question at the reporters: Who moved over from Commerce to CRP with Stans? What about Mitchell's secretary? Why won't anybody say when Liddy went to the White House or who worked with him there? Mitchell and Stans both ran the budget committee, right? What does that tell you? Then Sussman would puff on his pipe, a satisfied grin on his face.

Sussman's passions are history and polling. His hero is Jefferson, but the reporters always imagined that George Gallup ran a close second. Almost every time there had been a big demonstration in town during the height of the anti-war movement, Sussman had sent out teams of reporters to ask demonstrators their age, politics, home towns and how many previous demonstrations they had been in. Each time, he came up with the same conclusion almost every reporter on the street had already reached—the anti-war movement had become more broad-based and less radical. Since the break-in at Democratic headquarters, Sussman had been studying the Teapot Dome scandal of the Harding administration. He had a theory about Watergate that Bernstein and Woodward did not quite understand—it had to do with historic inevitability, post-war American ethics, merchandising and Richard Nixon.

Sussman and the other editors at the Post were by temperament informal. The reporters were never formally assigned to work on Watergate full time. They sensed that as long as the stories continued to come, there would be no problem. If they failed to produce, anything might happen in the competitive atmosphere of the *Post* newsroom. In the weeks after the story on the Dahlberg check, Rosenfeld became noticeably nervous as Simons and Bradlee showed an increasing interest in the Watergate affair. The invariable question, asked only half-mockingly of reporters by editors at the *Post* (and then up the hierarchal line of editors) was "What have you done for me today?" Yesterday was for the history books, not newspapers.

> I believe it was Thoreau who said something on the order of 'You can't ignore a trout in the milk.' We're seeing a lot of trouts in the milk these days. You can't ignore what's happened to the stock market, to food prices. If reporting these facts produces an increase of economic worries, then we have to live with that. What we are reporting now is much easier for the people to understand than, say, the reporting on Dick Nixon, because the people can go to the supermarket and see the prices on the shelves. I don't think they tend to blame the carrier of the message in this instance.
> —John Chancellor

That had been the working ethic of the *Post* since Ben Bradlee took command in 1965, first as managing editor and, in 1967, as executive editor. Bradlee had been recruited with the idea that the *New York Times* need not exercise absolute preeminence in American journalism.

That vision had suffered a setback in 1971 when the *Times* published the Pentagon Papers. Though the *Post* was the second news organization to obtain a copy of the secret study of the Vietnam war, Bradlee noted that "there was blood on every word" of the *Times*' initial stories. Bradlee could convey his opinions with a single disgusted glance at an indolent reporter or editor.

from The New Journalism

TOM WOLFE

In the following segment from Tom Wolfe's collection **The New Journalism**, *the author provides guidelines for the new reporting form. Many people argue about how objective the new journalism is, but Wolfe points out that this new form of reporting best reflects "the way people are living today."*

And so all of a sudden, in the mid-Sixties, here comes a bunch of these lumpenproles, no less, a bunch of slick-magazine and Sunday-supplement writers with no literary credentials whatsoever in most cases—only they're using all the techniques of the novelists, even the most sophisticated ones—and on top of that they're helping themselves to the insights of the men of letters while they're at it—and at the same time they're still doing their low-life legwork, their "digging," their hustling, their damnable Locker Room Genre reporting—they're taking on *all* of these roles at the same time—in other words, they're ignoring literary class lines that have been almost a century in the making.

The panic hit the men of letters first. If the lumpenproles won their point, if their new form achieved any sort of literary respectability, if it were somehow accepted as "creative," the men of letters stood to lose even their positions as the reigning practitioners of nonfiction. They would get bumped down to Lower Middle Class. (Appendix IV.) This was already beginning to happen. The first indication I had came in an article in the June, 1966, *Atlantic* by Dan Wakefield, entitled "The Personal Voice and the Impersonal Eye." The gist of the piece was that this was the first period in anybody's memory when people in the literary world were beginning to talk about nonfiction as a serious artistic form. Norman Podhoretz had written a piece in *Harper's* in 1958 claiming a similar status for the "discursive prose" of the late Fifties, essays by people like James Baldwin and Isaac Rosenfeld. But the excitement Wakefield was talking about had nothing to do with essays or any other traditional nonfiction. Quite the contrary; Wakefield attributed the new prestige of nonfiction to two books of an entirely different sort: *In Cold Blood*, by Truman Capote, and a collection of magazine articles with a title in alliterative trochaic pentameter that I am sure would come to me if I dwelled upon it.

Capote's story of the life and death of two drifters who blew the heads off a wealthy farm family in Kansas ran as a serial in *The New Yorker* in the Fall of 1965 and came out in book form in February of 1966. It was a sensation—and a terrible jolt to all who expected the accursed New Journalism or Parajournalism to spin itself out like a fad. Here, after all, was not some obscure journalist, some free-lance writer, but a novelist of long standing . . . whose career had been in the doldrums . . . and who suddenly, with this one stroke, with this turn to the damnable new form of journalism, not only resuscitated his reputation but elevated it higher than ever before . . . and became a celebrity of the most amazing magnitude in the bargain. People of all sorts read *In Cold Blood*, people at every level of taste. Everybody was absorbed in it. Capote himself didn't call it journalism; far from it; he said he had invented a new literary genre, "the nonfiction novel." Nevertheless, his success gave the New Journalism, as it would soon be called, an overwhelming momentum.

Capote had spent five years researching his story and interviewing the killers in prison, and so on, a very meticulous and impressive job. But in 1966 you started seeing feats of reporting that were extraordinary, spectacular, (Appendix VI). Here came a breed of journalists who somehow had the moxie to talk their way inside of any milieu, even closed societies, and hang on for dear life. A marvelous maniac named John Sack talked the Army into letting him join an infantry company at Fort Dix, M Company, 1st Advanced Infantry Training Brigade—not as a recruit but as a reporter—and go through training with them and then to Vietnam and into battle. The result was a book called *M* (appearing first in *Esquire*), a nonfiction *Catch*-22 and, for my money, still the finest book in any genre published about the war. George Plimpton went into training with a professional football team, the

From pp. 25–28 "And so all . . . Take a look!" by Tom Wolfe in *The New Journalism* by Tom Wolfe. Copyright © 1973 by Tom Wolfe and E. W. Johnson. By permission of Harper & Row, Publishers.

Detroit Lions, in the role of reporter playing rookie quarterback, rooming with the players, going through their workouts and finally playing quarterback for them in a preseason game—in order to write *Paper Lion*. Like Capote's book, *Paper Lion* was read by people at every level of taste and had perhaps the greatest literary impact of any writing about sports since Ring Lardner's short stories. But the all-time freelance writer's Brass Stud Award went that year to an obscure California journalist named Hunter Thompson who "ran" with the Hell's Angels for eighteen months—as a reporter and not a member, which might have been safer—in order to write *Hell's Angels: The Strange and Terrible Saga of the Outlaw Motorcycle Gang*. The Angels wrote his last chapter for him by stomping him half to death in a roadhouse fifty miles from Santa Rosa. All through the book Thompson had been searching for the single psychological or sociological insight that would sum up all he had seen, the single golden *aperçu*; and as he lay sprawled there on the floor coughing up blood and teeth, the line he had been looking for came to him in a brilliant flash from out of the heart of darkness: "Exterminate all the brutes!"

At about the same time, 1966 or 1967, Joan Didion was writing those strange Gothic articles of hers about California that were eventually collected in *Slouching Towards Bethlehem*. Rex Reed was writing his celebrity interviews—this was an old journalistic exercise, of course, but no one had ever quite so diligently addressed himself to the question of, "What is So-and-so *really* like?" (Simone Signoret, as I recall, turned out to have the neck, shoulders and upper back of a middle linebacker.) James Mills was pulling off some amazing reporting feats of his own for *Life* in pieces such as "The Panic in Needle Park," "The Detective," and "The Prosecutor." The writer-reporter team of Garry Wills and Ovid Demaris was doing a series of brilliant pieces for *Esquire*, culminating in "You All Know Me—I'm Jack Ruby!"

And then, early in 1968, another novelist turned to nonfiction, and with a success that in its own way was as spectacular as Capote's two years before. This was Norman Mailer writing a memoir about an anti-war demonstration he had become involved in, "The Steps of the Pentagon." The memoir, or autobiography (Appendix III), is an old genre of nonfiction, of course, but this piece was written soon enough after the event to have a journalistic impact. It took up an entire issue of *Harper's Magazine* and came out a few months later under the title of *The Armies of the Night*. Unlike Capote's book, Mailer's was not a popular success; but within the literary community and among intellectuals generally it couldn't have been a more tremendous *succès d'estime*. At the time Mailer's reputation had been deteriorating in the wake of two inept novels called *An American Dream* (1965) and *Why Are We In Vietnam?* (1967). He was being categorized somewhat condescendingly as a journalist, because his nonfiction, chiefly in *Esquire*, was obviously his better work. *The Armies of the Night* changed all that in a flash. Like Capote, Mailer had a dread of the tag that had been put on him—"journalist"—and had subtitled his book "The Novel as History; History as the Novel." But the lesson was one that nobody in the literary world could miss. Here was another novelist who had turned to some form of accursed journalism, no matter what name you gave it, and had not only revived his reputation but raised it to a point higher than it had ever been in his life.

By 1969 no one in the literary world could simply dismiss this new journalism as an inferior genre. The situation was somewhat similar to the situation of the novel in England in the 1850's. It was yet to be canonized, sanctified and given a theology, but writers themselves could already feel the new Power flowing.

The similarity between the early days of the novel and the early days of the New Journalism is not merely coincidental. (Appendix I.) In both cases we are watching the same process. We are watching a group of writers coming along, working in a genre regarded as Lower Class (the novel before the 1850's, slick-magazine journalism before the 1960's), who discover the joys of detailed realism and its strange powers. Many of them seem to be in love with realism for its own sake; and never mind the "sacred callings" of literature. They seem to be saying: "Hey! Come here! This is the way people are living now—just the way I'm going to show you! It may astound you, disgust you, delight you or arouse your contempt or make you laugh. . . .Neverless, this is what it's like! It's *all* right here! You won't be bored! Take a look!"

Bad News (Judgement?) Drives Out the Good

RAY McHUGH

Both Ray McHugh in this article and Marty Glass in the following one touch vulnerable points in today's news systems. Audiences receive news geared to mass interests and consumption—due in large part to time and space limitations of the various media. Both writers point out that news gathering is, in part, a process of abstracting and leaving out, often at the expense of unique or unpopular perceptions and issues.

Why don't you report the good things?

Why don't you write about all the fine young people in America who are trying to do something for their country?

These questions have been fired with increasing regularity at newsmen across the United States, not only by Vice President Spiro Agnew, but by churchmen, civic leaders, just plain parents and by some of our colleagues.

The other night in Washington, fifty-five of those fine young people met the President of the United States and the leaders of Congress. They were the state finalists in the Veterans of Foreign Wars *Voice of Democracy* contest and guests of honor at the annual VFW congressional dinner that saw President Nixon present the veterans' 1970 award to Senator Henry Jackson, Democrat of Washington. More than 400,000 students had entered the competition.

As the President arrived in the huge banquet room, the U. S. Marine Corps Band struck up *Hail to the Chief* and some 2,000 veterans and congressmen from every corner of the country stood and cheered. The high school students, boys and girls, stood in awe, almost disbelief.

Abruptly, the President interrupted the program scheduled. He walked to the long table where the winners were arranged and, one by one, he shook their hands and offered his personal congratulations.

The boys shifted self-consciously from one foot to another and stammered their thanks. The girls wept with emotion and one little high school junior from Nebraska threw her arms around Mr. Nixon's neck and kissed him on the cheek.

The President loved it. The veterans loved it.

But the next day, as the departing VFW commanders scanned the three Washington daily newspapers for an account of their evening, they were disappointed and angry. Two had ignored it. The third accorded it two grudging inches in the third section.

But there was a picture of three hippie students being arrested at San Francisco State. There was a picture of another group of young radicals giving the "Black Power" salute outside the Bel Air, Md., trial of H. Rap Brown. There was a picture of girls involved in the Women's Liberation Movement.

But there was no picture of a fifteen-year-old girl kissing her president, no picture of three boys and two girls who shared $13,500 in VFW college scholarships for their scripts on *Freedom's Challenge*. There wasn't even a story.

The veterans were angry at the newspapers in Washington. Perhaps it's time that all of us in the press took another look at "what's news."

Reprinted from *Seminar*, a Quarterly Review for Journalists by Copley Newspapers, June 1970. Mr. McHugh is Chief, Copley Newspapers Washington Bureau.

What's News

MARTY GLASS

There's been a lot of murder and rape in the Bay Area during the past few weeks. [August, 1969]

A pregnant woman was raped and stabbed in the throat with a butcher knife by two men in the Haight. Two San Jose girls, 14 and 15, were discovered with hundreds of stab wounds in their bodies. A seventeen-year old girl from Salinas found strangled with a red belt; police suspect this job was linked with the murder of eight girls in Ann Arbor, Michigan. A gang attack in the Hunter's Point section of San Francisco led to one man murdered, his girl raped, and his father slashed. And then there's the weird L.A. movie star murders of Sharon Tate, the pregnant wife of Roman Polanski, and three friends in their secluded Bel Air mansion.

There have been ninty-six murders so far this year in the Bay Area, just six less than the total for 1968.

The Bay Area newspapers blazed out the news in giant headlines. "Savage Slaying Mystery," "Shocking Murder," "A Story of Savagery," "Big Search for Knife Killer of Two San Jose Girls," "Big Hunt for Picnic Killer," and so on.

There's a big lie behind all this. The stories are more or less true; the accounts bear some police-filtered relation to the truth, but there's still a big lie behind the grisly intimate details of bloody mayhem and brutal sexual assault.

The lie is linked to the idea of "news" in the daily papers. What does "news" mean? "News" is what stands out on the vast, flat and presumably irrelevant plain of mundane events, "news" is what deviates from the ordinary and the normal, "news" is what someone else decides is important.

Supposedly, everything which isn't worth knowing about isn't of public concern. The daily papers convey a very strong and very indirect message; there's a normal, everyday life which is OK and unexceptional—not worth talking about. And then there's "news": anything which stands out, anything that doesn't happen all the time and is, therefore, of interest.

Life is good. That's the realm where things are taken care of. "News" is when something goes wrong.

This is pure bullshit. The real news isn't in distinct, bizarre events. The real news is what happens twenty-four hours a day all day long everywhere. This is the news we don't read about in the daily papers because the people who control those papers don't want us to know about it and do everything they can to distract out attention from it.

Fortunately, they can't succeed. We don't need their papers to tell us about the real news. All we have to do is open our eyes.

The real news is the expression on the faces of children sitting in tenement doorways with nothing to do. The real news is the tenement itself.

The real news is the despair and humiliation on the faces of people waiting for hours for a lousy check in the welfare or unemployment offices. And it's also on the emptied faces of people who have jobs they hate, jobs where their creative potential is stifled and crushed under the weight of meaningless labor performed to make enough money to survive.

The real news is jobs created solely to provide profits for those who don't work at all, or for a corporation which is nothing but a bankbook.

The precious unredeemable time of our lives is sacrificed for numbers in bankbooks.

The real news is elderly people rotting away in dilapidated Old Folks' Homes or in spare rooms in their children's houses, unwanted, resented, feeling they might as well be dead. The real news is in the millions of people who don't get enough to eat, who receive inadequate medical care, who suffer and die from diseases which could be cured and should never have been contracted in the first place.

The real news is when there's a giant traffic jam on the Bay Bridge because the market economy and capitalism require profit and there's no profit in safe, comfortable, efficient, rapid public transportation. The real news is that there are hardly enough parks and playgrounds for a fraction of our children, that

© Martin Glass

schools are falling apart, overcrowded, repressive, irrelevant and hated by the children imprisoned there.

The real news is that guys are getting beaten by sadistic psychopaths in prisons and army stockades all over the country, kids watch hours of obscene commercials on TV, women are forced to waste their lives in shopping and cooking because private consumption is the syphilitic deity of our society.

The real news is that people who can't take it any more—and they're mostly black or poor whites—are called mentally ill and given shock treatment or mind-killing drugs.

The real news is that ten thousand women die every year in the United States from slipshod expensive abortions, because this system doesn't permit half the population to decide what goes on in their own bodies, doesn't provide for any way outside of the decayed institution of marriage for children to be cared for.

The real news is that cops who murder black men are given medals and a guy found with two joints gets ten years.

The real news is that guys are being forced to kill their brothers in Vietnam.

The real news is that all the important decisions made in this country are made by maniac insects with dollar signs engraved on their beady inhuman plastic eyeballs. We see their pictures every day on the business pages in their newspapers.

The real news is that Huey Newton is in jail and Richard Nixon isn't. . . .

QUESTIONS FOR DISCUSSION

1 What were the strengths and weaknesses of Woodward and Bernstein's teamwork on the Watergate assignment?

2 How does the new journalism differ from traditional, "objective" reporting?

3 Do you accept the validity of Epstein's analysis of news? What additional or contrary lines of analysis can you develop?

4 The criticisms of the news systems made in the McHugh and Glass articles were made in the late sixties and early seventies. Are such criticisms valid today? Why or why not?

PROJECTS

1 Invite to class an editor of a local newspaper. Prepare interview questions that will help you determine that paper's:
 (a) emphasis on interpretive reporting
 (b) attitudes toward youth in the news
 (c) emphasis on contemporary music
 (d) political biases.

2 Conduct a comparative news analysis by taking a specific news item and comparing its treatment and coverage in several media. You might include the following:
 (a) newspapers—local, national, and "underground"
 (b) magazines—news magazines, **Ramparts** (or similar publication), and a special interest magazine
 (c) television—local and network
 (d) radio—hourly news or special report

Compare treatment by these media on such aspects as depth of coverage, bias or point of view, prominence and amount of coverage, and whether it is a byline story or not (personally reported or wire service).

advertising

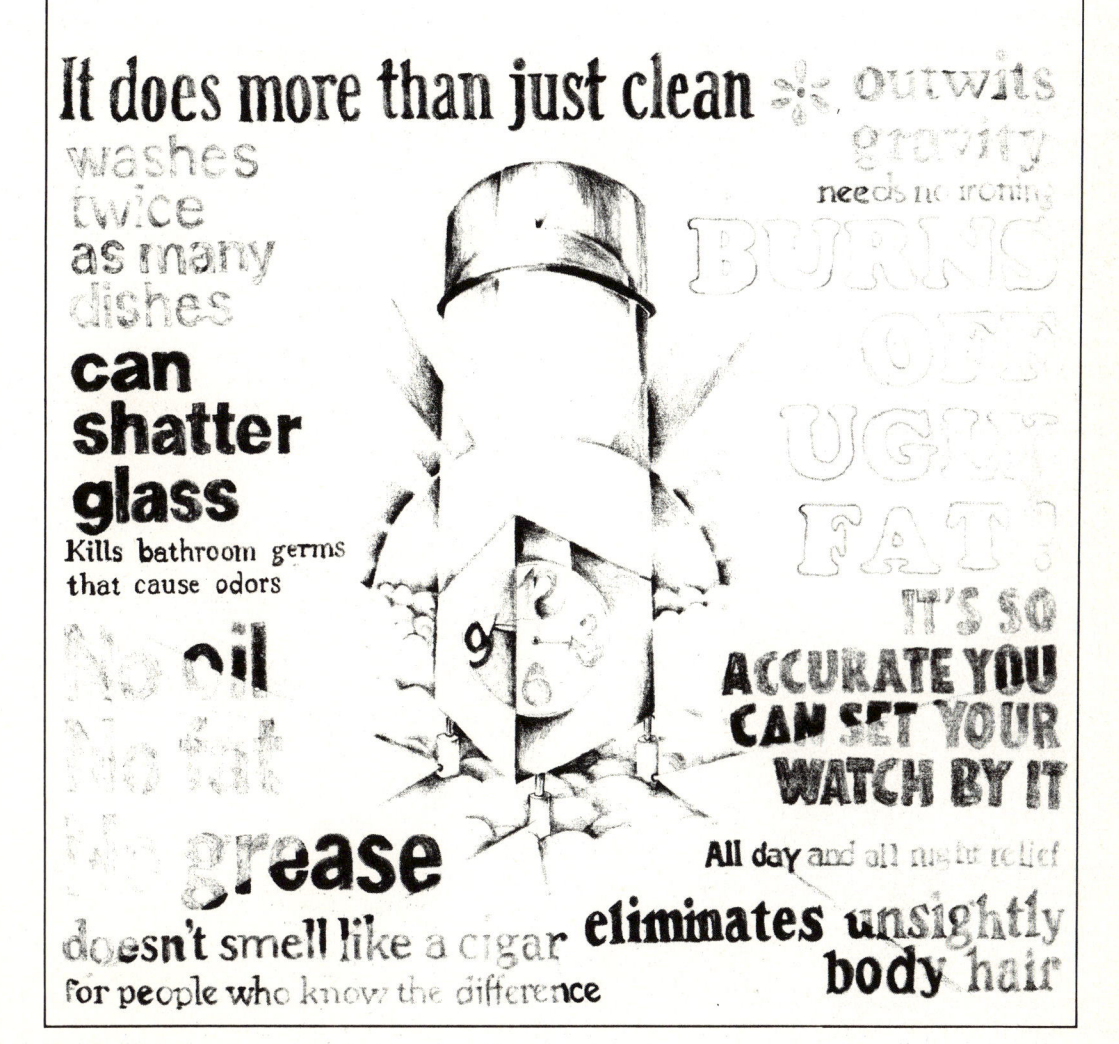

It does more than just clean ❋ outwits gravity

washes twice as many dishes

needs no ironing

BURNS OFF UGLY FAT

can shatter glass

Kills bathroom germs that cause odors

No oil
No fat
No grease

IT'S SO ACCURATE YOU CAN SET YOUR WATCH BY IT

All day and all night relief

eliminates unsightly body hair

doesn't smell like a cigar
for people who know the difference

sex and advertising

CHARLES WINICK

More than a generation ago, Philip Wylie created a sensation when he suggested, in *Generation of Vipers*, that a central message of much advertising was, "Madam, how good are you in bed?" The latent message of much current advertising is, "Dear Sir or Madam, our product can help you be more sexually with it." And, "sexually with it" now has many more meanings than when Wylie's book appeared.

It has more meanings because Americans are, for a variety of reasons, more receptive to sexual connotations in auditory and especially visual stimuli than ever before. Larger sociological factors such as increases in leisure and women's employment, ideological developments like the encouragement of individualism and free expression in costume and growing acceptance of relativity in morality have contributed to the greater acceptance of sexual material.

As Americans engage in more foreign travel and attendance at college, they tend to be more emancipated. Frankness is prized, especially in the younger people who constitute an increasing part of the population. Young preadolescent girls who play with mannequin dolls like Barbie and Dawn are rehearsing sexual fantasies, which can be implemented in dating behavior during their teen years.

Books by Kinsey and Masters and Johnson and some permissive Supreme Court decisions have helped to routinize the discussion of sexual material. As television becomes ubiquitous, our threshold for visual stimulation is lowered. As life becomes grimmer, Americans tend to seek a conceptual countervalence or isostasy of sexual material. Because the media contribute so substantially to our knowledge about the grimness of life, it is especially appropriate that the media carry advertising which is so heavily sexualized.

IMPORTANCE OF ADVERTISING

How important is advertising to Americans? A landmark study by Raymond A. Bauer and Stephen A. Greyser concluded that advertising is largely taken for granted by most people, who accept it as a necessary component of everyday life. It has little salience, something like the weather.

The typical consumer pays some attention to an average of seventy-six advertisements a day, although he is exposed to many more messages. Advertising provides a continuously available form of sex education in that it conveys images of the conduct of men and women. These images help to mold our impressions of appropriate behavior and appearance, and may be far more influential than conventional sex education and family life education. The typical child entering the first grade today has already spent more time watching television than he will devote to the classroom during the next six years. And between one and two of every ten minutes of that television time go to advertising.

Some idea of comparative impact can come from a comparison of the amount spent on advertising with our budget for education.

In 1971, this country spent $20.5 billion on advertising, or more than half of the $36.45 billion outlay for all elementary and high school education. In terms of formation and modification of attitudes toward sex roles, it is probable that advertising ultimately has more effect than formal education on the subject.

FANTASIES

One effect of advertising is to encourage sexual fantasies. Maidenform brassieres demonstrated that a pure sexual appeal, presented in an atmosphere of fantasy, could be successful. The famous "I dreamed I was a _____ in my Maidenform Bra" series was acceptable to women because the exhibitionistic situations shown were part of a dream, and who can be responsible for their dreams? The brassieres were white, as if to underscore the virtue of the dreamer. The slogan was so widely accepted

---

"Sex and Advertising" by Charles Winick. Used by permission of the author.

that on the night of June 9, 1964, after an official dinner, when Mrs. Lyndon B. Johnson inadvertently locked herself out of the second floor of the White House and was forced to go downstairs to the state floor, facing the possibility of meeting some of the departing guests at 1:30 a.m. while wearing her robe and slippers, she thought of the advertisements and noted in her diary "I went to the opera in my Maidenform Bra."

Advertisers whose products involve some actual contact with young women often feed fantasies by hinting at their accessibility to men. Lufthansa ads show lovely stewardesses who imply that they and not sauerbraten are attracting men to the airline.

National Airlines, with an advertising budget much smaller than its larger competitors, made them envious with the enormous success of its advertising slogan ("I'm Cheryl—fly me to Miami"). Each National plane was given a provocative female name matching that of the toothsome stewardesses who posed for the photographs and television commercials. Women's Liberation groups have objected to the sexual appeal of the advertising, but to no avail.

Another fantasy which is fed by advertising is that both single and married men are always in a state of sexual readiness, alert to every attractive woman. A commerical for Diet Pepsi-Cola shows a slender young woman, who is presumably building her meals around the product, strolling along. One man is so excited by her appearance that he falls into a river. Another man, in a scene which is almost too literal to be symbolic, rises from his chair and then collapses to the ground. The announcer cheerfully reminds us that "if you want men to do a double take, drink Pepsi."

Sophisticated consumers may marvel that "before and after" advertising still seems to reach its target. Yet, a number of personal product advertisements still show a person, usually a young girl, who is dancing happily with a young man until he happens to get a whiff of her breath or glances down at the dandruff dotting her hair. The young man then hastily terminates their contact. In a typical advertising message, the woman consults a friend who accurately diagnoses her condition and recommends the advertised product. The next scene usually shows us the original couple dancing together or holding hands with the young lady holding a bottle of the advertiser's product and volunteering to the audience that she eliminated her problem with dandruff or odor as a result of learning about the product from her friend. Such advertising would appear to pose difficulties of belief, but is still quite prevalent.

"Before and after" advertising illustrates the fantasy component of many of the marketing appeals for products related to sex appeal. The implication is that the product contains a kind of magic which can radically transform a user into a remarkably seductive person who will get her man.

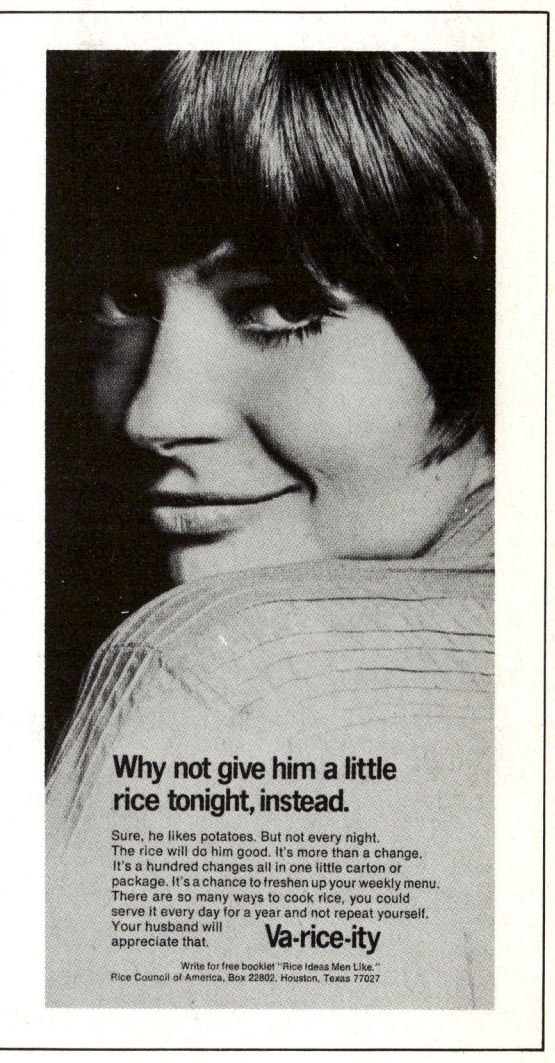

Why not give him a little rice tonight, instead.

Sure, he likes potatoes. But not every night. The rice will do him good. It's more than a change. It's a hundred changes all in one little carton or package. It's a chance to freshen up your weekly menu. There are so many ways to cook rice, you could serve it every day for a year and not repeat yourself. Your husband will appreciate that.

Va-rice-ity

Write for free booklet "Rice Ideas Men Like." Rice Council of America, Box 22802, Houston, Texas 77001

Advertising 123

Landing a man is still presented in a conventional way, with the woman attracting a man almost magically by her radiations and physical attractions. Women's Liberation has not made much of an impact on advertising.

YOUTH

Just as Women's Liberationists are currently protesting the manner in which women are shown in advertising, the half of our population over twenty-seven might complain about its severe underrepresentation in almost all media.

One of the impressions gained from any systematic study of sex in advertising is that young people are doing most of what is happening. Relatively few models seem to be over twenty-seven. This emphasis on youth may be contributing to a generalized belief that mature people have no sexual interests.

MARRIAGE AND THE ADVERTISER

Sexual themes tend to be shown in courtship or nonmarital situations. The housewife is generally shown as an unglamorous and frequently unappetizing woman whose peak experiences seem to center on finding a laundry soap or detergent or floor cleaner with magical properties, or hearing about such products from a friendly lady plumber. Wives in advertisements are usually not presented as having much interest in their own husbands, and no awareness of other men. A manufacturer of men's clothing headlines: "Linett makes clothes that interest women—even wives."

Few scenes of marital sexual feelings of any kind are shown, except in travel advertising. What takes place in an exotic locale seems less threatening.

There are relatively few advertisements in which a husband and wife are shown together in other than a chaste situation. When married couples are shown in a bedroom, they wear pajamas, do not ordinarily touch each other, and conduct animated conversations at midnight on the relative merits of toothpaste in reducing cavities.

One recurrent theme is the husband's interest in philandering and the wife's need to make herself more desirable than the competition. A commercial for a low calorie salad dressing shows a husband dutifully pecking his wife on the cheek before leaving for the office. He is then shown, away from home, ogling some pretty girls. The announcer ominously warns the wife, "If you want him home by five, use Frenchette."

SEXUAL INADEQUACY

Some very successful advertisements may be effective because they tap deep-rooted attitudes toward sexual inadequacy. One of the most famous campaigns ever conducted enabled Hathaway to become a significant factor in the men's shirt field, even though it had a very small budget and appeared in a limited number of media. A distinguished looking middle-aged European was shown wearing an eye patch, along with his shirt and tie. On an overt level, the eye patch was a striking and memorable image which facilitated recognition of the brand. But depth interview studies disclosed that the man was remembered. The eye patch communicated to many men that the man was impotent or had other difficulties which blocked full sexual expression. Many a man reacted to the advertisement with the subconscious feeling that "I have sexual problems too, but perhaps I can look as distinguished as he does in spite of my disability if I wear a Hathaway shirt."

A very popular current television commercial which also has both an overt and covert appeal is a series for Alka-Seltzer, for which Alice Playten won an award. Miss Playten is shown as a young bride wearing a sexy costume. She is rhapsodizing over "our first home-cooked meal; tomorrow we'll have poached oysters." Her husband is running to the bathroom cabinet to repair the ravages of the evening's dinner. "I never saw a dumpling that big before," he mutters. "I wanted to impress you," she coos. On the surface level, we laugh because of the bizarre dishes which the bride is concocting. Depth interviews suggest that, on a deeper level, we are laughing because we anticipate that the young husband will be impotent as a result of his gastric distress. There are many popular versions of the ancient wedding breakfast joke, of which this commercial is a variant. In the most frequently told version, the groom looks at the first breakfast prepared by his bride: burned toast, underdone eggs, and cold coffee. "Well," he says, "you can't cook either."

VARIOUS SEX APPEALS

Oral sensuality is appealed to by large numbers of toothpaste advertisers who convey, subtly or explicitly, that the mouth and teeth represent a royal road to romance. Ultra-Brite toothpaste "gives your mouth sex appeal."

Kissing and similar preparatory lovemaking represent perhaps the major form of physical contact between men and women, judging from advertising. Because so many manufacturers of hair products are heavy advertisers, the incidence of amorous couples admiring and touching each other's hair is extraordinarily high.

Discreet physical contact between couples also occurs in cigarette advertising, with its water symbolism. No one knows if advertising copywriters or their audiences are fully aware of or respond to the sexual symbolism of lakes or rivers or oceans. Cigarette companies have often used such themes because they connote coolness, but they also convey connotations of sexual and related themes. That is why cigarette advertising often shows a couple walking or running hand in hand near a body of water.

One relatively subtle effect of advertising could be to repress sexual energy and discourage sexual activity by its continual downgrading of "mess" and "dirt" and its championing of super cleanliness. There is a preoccupation with excessive washing and shampooing and extreme concern about odors of any kind. Yet people are not plastic, and sexual attraction and interaction cannot be antiseptic.

Lack of an odor used to be a major aspect of the sexual appeal of many products. Mouthwashes for many decades stressed that their use blocked odors and left the mouth neutral in terms of smell. More recently, mouthwashes stress the specific smell which they give their users.

Probably the most remarkable shift of this kind has been the content of advertising for vaginal deodorants. The advertising began cautiously enough by referring to the effects of various products in masking vaginal odors, but shifted to extolling the virtues of products which not only cover up but have perfumed aromas. The consumer may well wonder for whom the aroma is intended.

There can be no question for whom the aroma of men's fragrance is intended. If a man uses

> During World War II, when the men went off to wage war, the economy needed more production-line workers. Women were mobilized into the vacuum. The image of women projected through the mass media shifted drastically.... There were more advertisements for the women's branches of the armed services, more pictures of women working alongside men. In fact, the new propaganda was that women were dull mothers if they didn't have roles outside the home. The accent on cosmetics dropped.... The wartime image that was projected was a far cry from the fashion plate mirage projected in the "You've come a long way, baby" ads for Virginia Slim cigarettes.
> —Alice Embree

Hai Karate, the advertising tells us he will have to fight off the women. Golf pro Tommy Bolt assures television viewers that he "likes to smell nice," and the potential of a man who "smells nice" is discreetly suggested in many commercials.

The male as sadist is celebrated by the advertising for Silva-Thin cigarettes. In a typical commercial, a tough looking man is driving a fast car which has a woman passenger. He forces her out of the car onto an empty road, driving off alone with his pack of Silva-Thins. He lights up, presumably enjoying the recollection of his brutality toward the passenger. A woman is only a woman, but a good cigarette is a smoke.

The mini-musical commercials for Virginia Slims, which received an award as the best overall advertising campaign of 1969, disparage men. In one commercial, a man is punishing his wife for smoking, probably around the time of World War I. A sexy modern woman is then shown, swinging her hips as she walks, while a voice sings "You've come a long way, baby." When the woman approaches closer to the camera, she is joined by several other women,

Chateau Martin wine doubtless got an extra fillip of attention from many listeners to its radio commercials, the theme of which, presented in a provocative voice, was "Had any lately?" But the campaign was withdrawn, perhaps because it was generating more smirks than sales. Brut men's cologne boasts that it is useful "after a shower ... after shave ... after anything ... "

A slogan which lends itself to double meanings helps to get the name of a product repeated, which is one goal of advertising. If the context of repetition is vulgarly sexual, the image of the product will suffer.

THE FUTURE

Cigarette commercials are no longer shown on television, so that many of their appeals will increasingly be found in print media. The future will surely witness a great expansion of advertising for cigarettes in magazines, newspapers, and billboards. The greater permissiveness of these media will encourage more sexualized advertising for cigarettes, a product which has almost a tradition of libidinized advertising.

For other products, in all media, there will probably be an increase in advertising involving who presumably help in celebrating her freedom from males.

Men or women are seldom shown in advertisements for products which play a part in sexual intercourse. Limited advertising for one line of condoms began in 1970 and messages in behalf of various proprietary contraceptive products appear in some women's magazines, but usually in comparatively modest space and couched in euphemistic language.

DOUBLE-ENTENDRES

The double-entendre may be remembered and elicit smirks, but there is some question about its sales effectiveness. "The thinking man's filter" was abandoned as a slogan for one brand of cigarettes, among other reasons because it was being used in too many leering jokes. On the other hand, "it's what's up front that counts" and "so round, so firm, so fully packed" survived many joking reformulations. Clairol's famous "does she or doesn't she?" remains an enormously successful slogan, perhaps because of its auxiliary meanings.

126   Media Content

advertising— parity and peter pan

ISADORE BARMASH

THE CONSTANT DILEMMA

Smarting from a mushroom cloud of consumerists' criticisms and crackdowns on advertising claims by the Federal Trade Commission, major consumer-goods makers only partly turned the other cheek in the late 1960s and early '70s. The result of much of it was a pasty mélange of ineffective sales pitch and inoffensive claims. Naturally from both the sales and credibility standpoints, it had the clout of a marshmallow hurled at a daisy in a fifty-mile-an-hour wind.

How to sell, creatively stimulate and still not offend by deceiving?

Wonder Bread, while temporarily deterred from banging away that its product "builds strong bodies 12 ways," adopted a cutesy but less ambitious pitch. Loaves, known as "Fresh Guys," plopped out of stoves and deported themselves in animated antics. Profile Bread was touted as a diet loaf but its only real contribution to weight reduction was thinner slices. So, in a corrective ad, actress Julia Meade pleasantly admitted, "But eating Profile will not cause you to lose weight." And Geritol, no longer allowed to claim that it was just the thing for tired blood, shifted to celebrities familiar to the Geritol generation who proclaimed, "I *feel better* because I take Geritol."

Different, but not very, in principle was Ford Motor Company's radio-television pitch in between product recalls on more than 140,000 Torinos and 900,000 cars and trucks. The pitch was: "Listening Better. Building Better. That's Ford!" Chrysler Corporation's message was a bit more subtle: "Visit your Chrysler-Plymouth

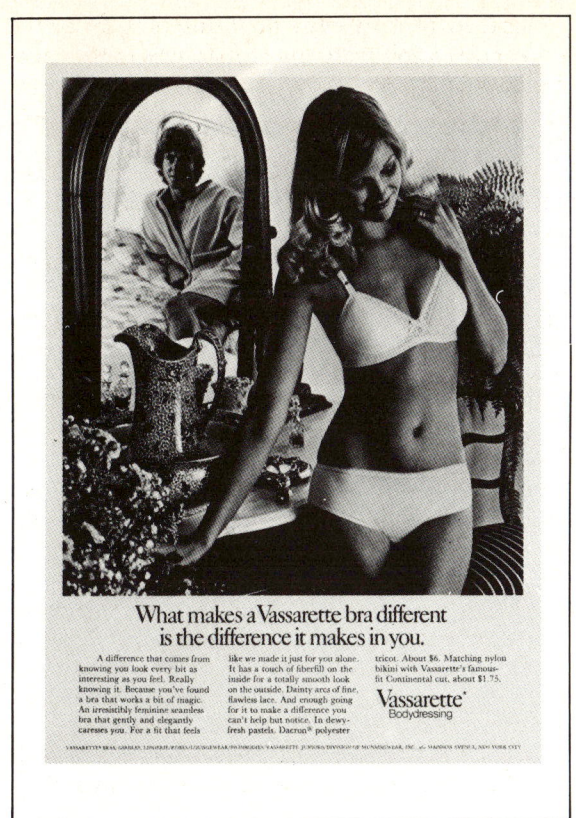

unconventional forms of sexual expression and in themes of sadism and masochism, reflecting larger trends in our society. The future will probably see more sexual contents in advertising, at least until a saturation point is reached.

The likelihood of saturation can be estimated from the experience of Sweden and Denmark. These countries, with emancipated attitudes toward sexual matters, tend to avoid erotic content in advertising, which usually makes a serious and factual appeal. If and when sexual behavior becomes less highly charged in this country, advertising will probably also tend to become desexualized. But such a day seems a long way off.

"Advertising—Parity and Peter Pan" Excerpted from *The World Is Full of It* by Isadore Barmash. Copyright © 1974 by Isadore Barmash. Reprinted with the permission of DELACORTE PRESS.

dealer. He wants to sell you peace of mind. So CALM DOWN!" Why not? Automobile prices did go up annually, despite price controls.

In recent years, the gray pains of parity and the traumatic and financial pangs that accompany both governmental and society censure have saddled leading advertisers and their agencies with many of their most anxious moments in decades. So great has been the pressure and stigma inflicted on Madison Avenue and its clients in the last five years that the constant problem of devising ways with which to make a hundred million American consumers part with their dollars has become a tortured process. In it, the most common solution has been a return to dull, often stupid advertising commonplaces. Gone are the creative sixties—welcome to the dumb seventies.

What brought the advertising business to this sad stage? The largest American service industry, the advertising field, accounts for an expenditure of an estimated $20 billion annually or roughly 2 percent of the country's gross national product. With that degree of financial impact on the nation's mass media, what is the urgency for deception? Only the competition that exists in the marketplace. It is a competition that has grown sharply over the years but which still fails to avoid the reality of parity in many products. It may come as a shock to those who prefer to wear rose-colored glasses, but many products made in America for mass use reflect parity, the state of being equal in virtually every aspect with other products.

The color, trim or detail, packaging, labeling and other inconsequentials may be different but there is scarcely a difference in ingredients in many brands of toothpaste, detergents and soaps, packaged foods, electronics, automobiles, beer, cigarettes and tobacco, ad infinitum. So how can the advertiser increase market share, consumer loyalty, market penetration, shelf space at retail and so forth, when his beloved product isn't markedly different from another's beloved product? By a preemptive claim, of course. The only rub is that the preemptive claim, the claim that literally lifts a product above and beyond the qualifications of any simi-

> Advertising isn't words. And it isn't pictures. It's what you use to make people *behave* the way you want them to. You can't *change* people but you can *channel* them —your way.

128   Media Content

lar products on the market, is no longer allowed on parity products by the watchdogging FTC. Thus, a part of the dilemma is the increasing stringency of governmental policing of advertising practices.

But the advertiser's dilemma has at least two more elements.

One is the client-agency relationship, a rapport represented by a fine skein which is rapidly being torn asunder by the onslaught of jabs from both the public and private sectors. The other is the loss of public credibility in the advertising effort, one of the most disturbing aspects in the entire picture.

So these are the three components of today's dilemma in the advertising business and they are also its three main causes.

But what *really* brought Madison Avenue—and its counterparts elsewhere in other major American cities—to its knees? I suggest that it is the advertising community's Peter Pan syndrome. You know Peter Pan. He was the pixyish boy in the James Barrie play of that name who never grew up. He exists; he lives today on Madison Avenue and among its clients. Advertising never really grew up or seemingly wanted to. Perhaps it is because, in our classic American hard-selling push, no one will let it.

PARITY IN ACTION

Copywriters in anguish, advertisers in a sweat, media beefing up their acceptability staffs and the government and even advertising policing boards studying each ad, monitoring each commercial in a tizzy of concentration. Is that the situation on Madison Avenue these days? Just about.

So project this scene: [*A big advertiser (to be known as B.A.) is meeting with the representatives of his advertising agency, namely the account supervisor (A.S.) and the copywriter (COPY) to draft a new campaign on a food product. The advertising pitch on the product has come under FTC censure and additionally its sales have slipped badly.*]

THE B.A.: What we desperately need, gentlemen, is a message, a theme, that will avoid bringing Washington down on our heads again

> Advertisers claim that they are portraying life as it is, not creating images. But what they are really doing is trying to control consumption patterns.
> A woman who spends all of her time doing housework will buy more cleaners; a woman who works and continues her home-making unaided will buy expensive plastic convenience foods.
> —Susan Luttner
> **Grapevine**

but will increase our tonnage and bring us back to where we were five years ago.

A.S.: Fine, George, we fully understand this and we've already done some preliminary work. The problem, though, is complex as all hell—how to avoid a preemptive claim and at the same time create a dominant identity minus any claim of supremacy.

B.A.: But, dammit, the product is the best in the field. We've tested it out and the results came back affirmatively. Why can't we say so?

A.S.: You can't unless you can produce undisputed documentary proof that it is the best, the unique product. Can you do that, George?

B.A.: Well, we used to say, "Treat yourself to the best—you deserve it!" And then they made us stop using that. Gentlemen, I'll be utterly candid with you, our product is no different from three others on the market but what we have going for us is that we were the first and we used to be the biggest seller. I still say we've got the best franchise with the public and all we have to do is to capitalize on that franchise—to get that loyalty back in actual numbers.

[*Silence reigns for a few moments until the short, fat, bearded copywriter bestirs himself. He bangs a massive pipe against an ash tray and holds up a sheet of paper.*]

COPY: We put together a couple of ideas or three. You see, your product was pitched to an audience of all ages but the biggest sales component was accounted for by kids who liked it for breakfast. Now, if we can get across the idea that adults need at least as much energy as kids in this youthful world—

Advertising 129

culture is our business

MARSHALL MC LUHAN

Ads are the cave art of the twentieth century. While the twenties talked about the caveman, and peopled thrilled to the art of the Altamira caves, they ignored (as we do now) the hidden environment of magical forms which we call "ads." Like cave paintings, ads are not intended to be looked at or seen, but rather to exert influence at a distance, as though by ESP. Like cave paintings, they are not means of private but of corporate expression. They are vortices of collective power, masks of energy invented by new tribal man....

Today, through ads, a child takes in all the times and places of the world "with his mother's TV." He is gray at three. By twelve he is a confirmed Peter Pan, fully aware of the follies of adults and adult life in general. These could be called Spock's Spooks, who now peer at us from every quarter of our world. Snoopy has put man on the moon and brought him back. Four years old may already have become the upper limit of tolerable emotional maturity. (This is not a value judgment; e.g., it would have been self-defeating for me to have said years ago "the medium is the mess-age": such judgments distract attention from the events and processes that need to be understood.)

These richly significant forms are easily obscured and destroyed by the classifiers and moralizers who want to know whether they are a "good thing" or a "bad thing". There are many educated people who consider it a bad thing to study or to understand what goes on in our world.

MARSHALL MC LUHAN

From *Culture Is Our Business* by Marshall McLuhan. Copyright © 1970 by McLuhan Associates, Ltd. Used with permission of McGraw-Hill Book Company.

to sell your product, admit it's not perfect

GARY GREGG

It Tastes Terrible, But I Use It. We have all seen that commercial for mouthwash, but we may not have realized that the admission that the product doesn't taste as good as others would make us have more faith in it. Recent work by consumer psychologists indicates that advertisers should say a few minor bad things about their product to make their claims of superiority more believable.

Robert Settle of California State University at San Diego and Linda Golden of the University of Florida reasoned that consumers attribute an advertiser's claims either to his desire to sell his product, or to the product itself. In the first case, they suggest, the consumer would be uncertain about the actual characteristics of the brand, and thus be less likely to buy it. But if he or she attributes the claims to the brand's excellence, sales should increase.

To test this hypothesis, Settle and Golden developed a series of experimental ads and then asked a group of 120 business students to evaluate them. Half of the ads for each product (a pen, a watch, a blender, a camera and a clock-radio) claimed the product was superior to the leading brand on five main features. The others claimed superiority on the three features that Settle and Golden felt a potential consumer would be most interested in, but admitted that the best seller was better on two less important features. While the students' expectations of how well the products would perform dropped a bit when two features were disclaimed, their increased confidence in the advertiser's claims made up for it.

"At the least," the researchers conclude, "it would be better for the advertiser to disclaim at least one feature of minor importance than to exclude it from the message entirely." So long as the advertiser knows which features his customers regard as important and which they regard as unimportant, he should be less reluctant to include varied claims. "Such a practice," they say, "may tend to make advertising claims of superiority more believable and to relieve some of the public pressure currently being experienced by marketers."

Reprinted from the *Journal of Marketing Research,* Vol. XI, May 1974, published by the American Marketing Association.

"You can't beat Crest for fighting cavities," wheezes the silver-haired druggist in the fade-out of the commercial.

I doubt that there's a druggist in the land who ever uttered those words. And I don't think many people go into drugstores these days asking for advice on which toothpaste to buy. However, if they did, the druggist, who may or may not look like a kindly old gentleman, would probably say: "Buy Crest."

He'd support the Procter & Gamble brand for a very simple reason: It's one of the most profitable products he has in the entire store.

—Milton Moskowitz

advertising—its own worst enemy?

JOE CAPPO

I sometimes wonder if advertising isn't its own worst enemy.

Advertising people will blame their problems on government regulation, on consumerists and perhaps even on the press. But maybe they can find the causes for their problems right in their own offices.

A recent survey conducted for this column by Foote, Cone & Belding indicates that a significant percentage of people feel their intelligence is insulted by some of the advertising they see.

The research showed that 39 percent of the men and 58 percent of the women questioned said they had been insulted by some advertising.

The men mentioned feminine products, toilet paper and detergents as the most offensive.

Women mentioned the same items, but included airlines and "all commercials" as being offensive.

Actually, the numbers really aren't all that important. But why should any significant number of adults feel insulted by any form of advertising?

Aside from personal sensitivities, the important question is:

Does intelligence-insulting advertising sell products? I don't think so. . . .

In an area somewhat related to this, about one-third of the women surveyed said they saw, heard or read advertising that "was hurtful or offensive to them as women."

Once again, feminine products led the way, mentioned by 18 percent. The second largest category, mentioned by 12 percent, were described as "dumb housewife ads."

From the *Chicago Daily News*, July 7, 1975. By permission of the Chicago Daily News and Joe Cappo.

Here are some excerpted comments mentioned by respondents during the survey:

- "Women in commercials look stupid. Degrading. Resent 6-year-old child telling women about a product."
- "Laundry products portray women as stupid, as though clean clothes are most important thing in life."
- "Sanitary protection ads (on TV) are unnecessary. Women's magazines are more appropriate."

[Advertisers] try to convince women to worry about dirt they can't see and odors they can't smell. Even the "progressive" advertisments continue to allocate the housework to working women. "As a businesswoman with my own model agency in New York City," Barbara Stone appreciates how simple Centura Dinnerware is for her cooking and entertaining chores. Although I appreciate this recognition that some women do work I wish advertisers would realize that their products are not exclusively used by women.

—Susan Luttner
Grapevine

madison avenue's response to its critics

BUSINESS WEEK

Rather than provide another frightened defense of the advertising industry, this balanced article notes the marked changes in advertising's reaction to its critics. Advertising agencies, in response to the growing consumer movement, seem to be developing more openness to criticism of the industry. The article presents several views of FTC action against advertising, including such controversial measures as the corrective ad and equal time for counter ads.

Like a slow-moving Saturn V rocket struggling to escape from the earth's atmosphere as it heads moonward, the advertising business has shaken off the shock waves caused by the first blast of consumerism and has moved into a second stage. It is a period of sober evaluation—or reevaluation in many cases—and it differs markedly from the initial period when admen reacted by heaping invectives on the heads of Ralph Nader and the five members of the Federal Trade Commission.

Now, according to people at both the client and agency level, corporate leaders are sitting down with agency heads and creative men, and, perhaps for the first time, are trying to develop mutual goals that go beyond the mere selling of goods or services. The result in some instances is advertising that is deemed "more effective." In other cases, admen themselves may consider their work less effective in selling products; but they acknowledge a different kind of effectiveness: the ads draw no ire from consumer groups and watchdogs of either appointed or unappointed stripe.

Reprinted from "Madison Avenue's Response to Its Critics" in *Business Week*, June 10, 1972. Used by permission of Business Week.

"We have literally taken some campaigns from our agencies that were not what we thought they should be," says Earl Clasen, marketing vice-president at Pillsbury Co., who feels that advertising today must have a corporate role equal to that of personnel planning, legal affairs, and other top-priority functions. "We have carefully explained our position on this to the agency, and better ads have come out of it. It takes time—not necessarily money—and policies and procedures that make sure that corporate philosophies, from the topmost levels, are reflected in advertising."

An assistant advertising director at a major airline notes that when a governmental group questioned an ad recently, "our first thought was one of righteous indignation—'They're way out of line,' and so on. But since then, management has made us take a good hard look at ourselves, and at what we were saying in trying to get business in a very competitive situation. And some of us have come around to thinking that maybe a little closer scrutiny isn't all that bad."

A few months ago, that kind of language would have been considered near-blasphemy on Madison Avenue. Indeed, verbal brickbats were hurled by their fellows at several admen who seemed to have defected to the consumerist "enemy" early in the game. Noted art director and agency president George Lois, for example, was barely appointed to head the New York Art Directors Club when he announced that the organization stood four-square behind a Council of Economic Priorities study that castigated advertisers in *Time* and *Business Week*. The ads, said the CEP, boasted of ecological gains, but the companies doing the boasting were major polluters. Lois' posture drew some angry comments.

So did an address at Fairleigh Dickinson University by Milton Marcus, a vice-president at a small fashion agency, Claire Advertising. Marcus said: "The quality of life in a society is determined by the quality of its culture. Ours is rotten. The advertising industry has helped create it and is continuing to make it worse." Advertising skeptics shook their heads, too, when Arthur W. Schultz, chairman of Foote, Cone & Belding Communications, Inc. tried to find a rainbow in the clouds, and said that if advertising responded *positively* to the consumerism movement, the resultant effectiveness of ads could save all industry $2 billion a year. As people become more confident that ads are truthful, he explained, "there will be a reduction in the numbers and impact, if not the elimination, of many of the charlatans in our business."

THE FTC ATTACK

The word *charlatan* is a dangerous one in an industry where many spokesmen have lobbied over the years for "professional" status similar to that afforded doctors, engineers, and lawyers. But in looking at the aggressive and punitive record of just one body—the FTC—in recent months, even some of the most impassioned proponents of the "good" in advertising might be suspicious of some of its practitioners. Among other things, the FTC has:

- Proposed that American Home Products Corp., Bristol-Myers Co., and Sterling Drug, Inc., which spend about $80 million a year to advertise Bufferin, Anacin, Bayer aspirin, and other remedies, spend 25% of their budgets to "correct" claims made in previous ads.
- Ordered major makers of cough-and-cold remedies to come up with proof of such claims as "Contac provides relief for up to 12 hours" and "4-Way Nasal Spray works faster than other products." Makers of toothpaste, TV sets, tires and others also have been asked for such substantiation.
- Won agreement from cigarette companies to emphasize the Surgeon General's health warning in all print ads. ("We're changing our printing plates now," says a spokesman for a major company whose ads some months after the agreement carried no warning whatsoever, "but it takes time.")
- Moved to eliminate some $73 million in ad spending by cereal makers that, according to the FTC, is unnecessary for sales, serves to drive out competition, and is probably fraudulent to boot.

Where there is so much smoke, there can well be some fire—or so the public and numerous admen themselves have come to believe. "I think much of the industry is getting what it deserves," says Harold Levine, who recently brought former newscaster Chet Huntley into his small agency. The new partner in Levine, Huntley, & Schmidt—who watched thousands of commercials during his eighteen years with NBC-TV—will check out the agency's TV ads from an ethical standpoint. "The clients are delighted," says Levine. And Robert J. Fisher, ad manager at the Ford Div. of Ford Motor Co., endorses FTC interest in advertising: "Their concern has made top management more responsive to pleas for more straightforward, honest ads. It put a damper on some free-wheeling of years past, and it has brought us closer to the guy we should be talking to, anyway."

Such words sound sincere. Yet, under them is a deep-seated fear on the part of many admen that increased governmental regulation of the $20 billion advertising industry would lead to less advertising, fewer product sales, fewer agency commissions.

The fear grew in the past two years as advertising's growth rate, which was about 5.1% annually during the 1960s, slipped to about 4%. General business conditions—the recession—accounted for the slowdown, admen told themselves repeatedly, but in the backs of their minds was another thought: Was the barrage of anti-advertising criticism weakening clients' belief in the value of advertising (and particularly TV advertising) as part of the marketing mix?

The figures tell a yes-and-no-and-perhaps story. Procter & Gamble Co., for example, spent $190.5 million in TV last year, up from $179.3 million in 1970, and American Home Products raised its spending from $67.2 million to $88 million. General Motors Corp. was up, too, from $42 million to $65 million. General Foods, Bristol-Myers, and Colgate-Palmolive all spent less. But did the decreases have economic justification, or had management lost faith in advertising?

Says a General Foods advertising executive: "If we didn't think advertising worked, we wouldn't spend $100 million a year on it." A further indication that the downturn was a temporary one came when the reviving economy caused advertisers' TV investments to surge in the first quarter of 1972: National clients spent about 9% more for network ads than in the same 1971 period, and 10% more for local ones.

Still, admen themselves have increasingly noted that today's advertising is not all that it once was. FC&B'S Schultz, for one, recently pointed out that studies reveal that the industry's repetitive blandishments to "buy this" and "try that" have lost 20% of their effectiveness in the past 10 years. At a Washington (D.C.) meeting last month, a vice-president of Quaker Oats Co. said that for the past two decades, advertising has been seriously lacking "in terms of ethics, in terms of contributions to society, and perhaps even in terms of economic efficiency." Quaker's Vice-President Kenneth Mason proved his point with figures from a special telephone survey of TV viewers: The survey showed that 97% of them did not know who had advertised on six high-rated programs they had watched the night before.

THE KIDS TUNED OUT

Economics Professor Robert L. Heilbroner, a longtime critic of the advertising industry, has a ready explanation for the current seeming lack of effectiveness of advertising. Today's young consumers, he says, are yesterday's TV-nurtured children, who learned almost in infancy that toy and cereal advertisers "lied" to sell their mommies products which seldom lived up to their on-screen image. Heilbroner, who teaches at New York City's New School for Social Research, claims that admen responded to the first indications of disbelief not by making their ads more honest and informative, but by simply hitting harder and more often with what he calls "calculated prevarication." This served only to bring on increased attacks from consumerists, and a growing suspension of belief by the public.

A study released in mid-April by the American Association of Advertising Agencies shows how serious the problem is today. Of some 9,000 students from 177 universities and colleges, 53% told the AAAA that they consider advertising "believable some of the time." Some 57% thought—a chilling thought to the admen—that more government regulation should be imposed on the advertising industry.

Reporting on the study, William H. Genge, president of Ketchum, McLeod & Grove, Inc., looks on the bright side. "The students don't want to ban advertising," he says, "they want to improve it. I regard this attitude as healthy and constructive, and it makes their criticism all the more relevant."

THE ADMAN ALSO IS RESPONSIVE

Admen are listening to criticism these days for any number of reasons. For one thing, many of

MILES KIRKPATRICK

them have accepted *consumerism* as a worthwhile movement, rather than as simply an attack on big business in itself. "I'm a consumer first of all," says Cunningham & Walsh Chairman Carl Nichols, Jr., "and I have a point of resistance to faulty workmanship and products that don't work or do what they're promoted to do."

In some companies and agencies, younger executives are said to be more receptive to discussions of ad criticism. ("I don't buy that," says the ad director of a giant food products company. "I know a chief executive who is sixty-two years old and is more responsive to the whole consumer movement than a lot of kids just out of college.") But a primary reason that attention is being paid to critics of advertising, whether it is admitted or not, is that the industry hopes it can keep the FTC off its back.

The FTC's attacks in the past two years have made some kind of positive reaction mandatory. When Miles Kirkpatrick was brought in to head the FTC early in 1970, the agency set out to establish itself as the "hottest" regulatory body in Washington. It almost had to. Kirkpatrick himself had chaired a study by the American

Bar Association that labeled the commission a "do-nothing agency" blind to the troubles of consumers. An independent study by a group of Ralph Nader's *raiders* had arrived at the same conclusion.

Under considerable pressure from consumers' groups and some members of Congress, as well as from the FTC staff itself to bolster the commission, President Nixon named Kirkpatrick, a fifty-six-year-old Republican, to shake up the FTC. The new chief appointed a young aid, Robert Pitofsky, to head a new Bureau of Consumer Protection—and the two men swung into action. Among their innovations:

Opening the regulatory process to "outsiders" For the first time, consumerist lawyers—such as John F. Banzhaf III, who heads an organization called Action on Smoking & Health (ASH) that was instrumental in obtaining the broadcast ban on cigarette aids—have been made aware that the FTC will listen to their pleas. Numerous lawyers have since petitioned for tough anti-advertising action and have clamored to act as a "friend of the court" whenever the FTC considers ad restrictions.

Stretching the concept of "Unfair and Deceptive" ads Over the years, the FTC has usually attacked claims it believed to be false—Colgate's Rapid-Shave would not help a razor shave sandpaper, Geritol will not cure "tired blood"—but the commission has lately sought to have drug companies and others conduct extensive tests before making any ad claims, even though their products contain individual ingredients that have been known to be effective.

Although the FTC lost one such case against Pfizer, Inc.'s Un-Burn sunburn painkiller, it still wants to restrict claims that are not backed up by scientific data. The agency would also bar ads that imply that a product is unique—for example, "Wonder Bread builds bodies 12 ways"—when such claims could be made by rivals with virtually identical products.

Letting the public itself do more regulating In a number of product categories, beginning with automobiles and continuing through tires, TV sets, cold remedies, electric shavers, air conditioners, and toothpastes (with more to come), the FTC has ordered advertisers to document their claims. The commission's idea is that, by putting the documentation before a skeptical public, the press and consumerists will point accusing fingers at perpetrators of fraudulent claims.

In practice, however, the idea has not worked out very well. Automobile advertisers, for example, flooded the overworked FTC staff with a mass of technical material that has taken many months to evaluate. It concluded that 13 of 75 claims were not supported by empirical data, 21 had incomplete data, and 32 could not be evaluated at all because the terminology was too technical.

Kirkpatrick told Senator Frank Moss (D-Utah), who chairs the Senate consumer subcommittee, that nine of the "no data" claims might be supported by additional data yet to come and that five are being studied by an independent evaluator who also will consider some of the technical claims. Moss has proposed a *truth-in-advertising* bill that would require advertisers to back each claim in an ad with the proof alongside, but he has not won FTC support thus far. And the commission's plan to continue its substantiation investigation until the end of the year indicates that he will not get backing before then.

THE "CORRECTIVE" AD

These efforts, while troubling to advertising executives at major corporations and on Madison Avenue, are not regarded as overwhelming threats. Experience has shown that cases in which the FTC charges deceit take years to wend their way through the commission and subsequent court tests. Already, one company—Sunbeam Corporation—that was asked to substantiate claims in an electric shaver ad, has complained to the FTC of intimidation and a violation of its rights under the First Amendment. Admen know, too, that in practice most controversial ad campaigns are ended long before a final decision is reached and a consent order signed. The real FTC challenge that confronts the ad industry, they believe, stems from three "revolutionary" objectives:

To force advertisers to run costly "corrective" ads that supposedly would counteract any false impressions placed in the public mind by deceptive ads in the past.

To force broadcasters (via Federal Communications Commission rules) to provide free air time for "counteradvertising" messages from groups or individuals seeking to refute product commercials, in the way that antismoking forces were given air time to show the dangers of cigarettes.

To win passage of Senate Bill 986 and House of Representatives Bill 4809, which under Title II would give the FTC authority to issue trade regulation rules that could seriously affect advertising, as well as other industries.

The corrective ads proposal has been controversial for about two years, during which time, the FTC has tried to apply it to cases involving such products as Firestone tires, Wonder bread, and most recently, Bufferin, Excedrin, Bayer aspirin, and other pain-killers. Admen scoff at the suggestion that a client spend one-fourth of his annual budget on ads that would say, for example: "It has not been established that Anacin is more effective for the relief of minor pain than aspirin...." or that "It has not been established that Bayer aspirin is more effective for the relief of minor pain than any aspirin...." The language in both instances was proposed by the FTC, but in the only case thus far in which an advertiser has run "corrective" ads, the wording was left up to the client, ITT Continental Baking Co., and its agency, Ted Bates & Co.

THE "CONCERNED" ADVERTISER

To stave off further complaints and action from the commission—which had objected to claims that Profile bread would aid dieters in losing weight—the baking company put TV spokeswoman Julia Meade on the air last August to clarify "any misunderstandings" that viewers might have reached while viewing Profile commercials over the years. The bread, Miss Meade stated, would not help anyone lose weight—but it was tasty. Despite recurrent rumors that grateful viewers appreciated the new approach, Arthur Ostrove, Continental Baking's ad director recently announced that the ads would be taken off as soon as the one-year penalty period was up. Profile sales in the past year suffered tremendously, he stated—but whether from the

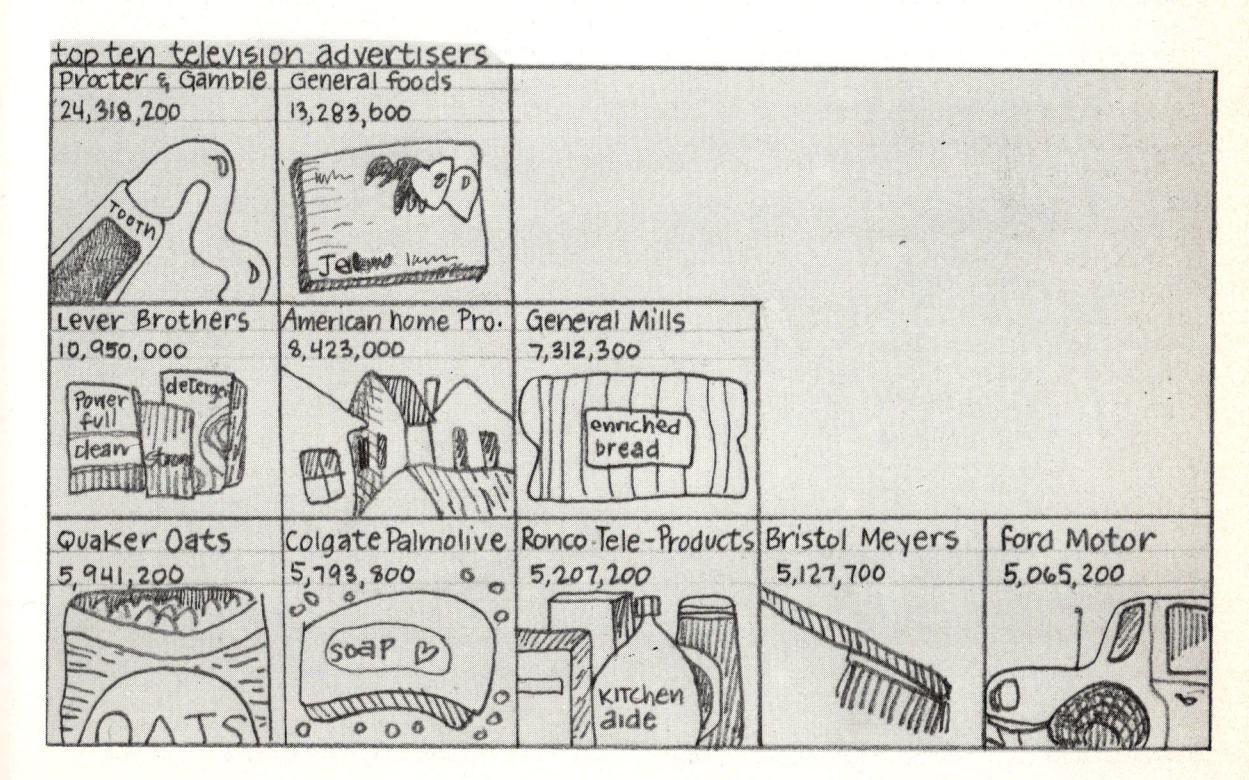

top ten television advertisers

Procter & Gamble 24,318,200	General Foods 13,283,600			
Lever Brothers 10,950,000	American Home Pro. 8,423,000	General Mills 7,312,300		
Quaker Oats 5,941,200	Colgate Palmolive 5,793,800	Ronco Tele-Products 5,207,200	Bristol Meyers 5,127,700	Ford Motor 5,065,200

Advertising 137

commercials or adverse publicity stemming from the original FTC complaint is unknown.

Continental's compliance with the FTC proposal drew fire from other advertisers, who contended that the commission now had a shining example of "an advertiser concerned with truth." And several weeks ago, when a second company, Ocean Spray Cranberries, Inc., agreed to run corrective ads on a claim made in its advertising, *Advertising Age* editorialized vehemently against Ocean Spray President Harold Thorkilsen, who had said the company would have preferred to fight the FTC charges, but "there are times when economics and practicalities dictate that a company compromise on a lawsuit." Such a response, said the trade publication, would make it harder for other companies "with legitimate beefs to win their tilts with the government on another day."

Despite the compliance of two advertisers, the industry at large does not view the proposals for corrective ads as a major threat. They have to be made on a case-by-case basis, and the courts are likely to bottle up individual complaints for lengthy periods, should the advertiser fight back.

It is the counteradvertising proposal that is deemed a real danger by most advertising executives—particularly those at TV stations and networks. As they see it, ecologists would demand free air time to attack car advertising on the grounds that cars cause pollution; organic food advocates could protest chemical additives in frozen pastries, and so on. Various groups and individuals have asked the FCC, which has jurisdiction over the forty-three-year-old "fairness doctrine" under which broadcasters operate, to open the airwaves to their messages against the Vietnam war, ecological infractions, and other controversial issues. The communications body has been studying most of the proposals on an issue-by-issue basis, but last March the FTC made the startling proposal that the doctrine should be applied to advertising messages for products.

Broadcasters, mindful of the $200 million a year they lost once the ban on cigarette advertising went into effect, feel that the antismoking ads which they were forced to put on the air helped bring about the Congressional ban. They doubt that the FCC will endorse the FTC's broad and sweeping proposal, but they realize that it is possible that "counter ad" forces could win out in specific product areas—in detergents, perhaps, or analgesics. And they worry that advertisers might decline to promote their products in the knowledge that someone might get free air time to rebut their claims. Would it not be easier, agency men wonder, for the client to put his budget into newspapers or magazines where he would not face the counter-advertising threat—since print media has no *equal time* or fairness requirements. And, if so, his total advertising budget—and the agency commission—would probably be greatly reduced. (The six major cigarette companies cut their spending 28% last year from $278.5 million in 1970 to $200.2 million in 1971, while domestic consumption of cigarettes rose 3.3%.)

THE FTC WANTS TO MAKE THE RULES

Most bothersome of all is the proposal to give the FTC legislative rule-making power. Peter W. Allport, president of the Association of National Advertisers, says that if the commission gets the proposed authority, "it would no longer need to prove that a given course of conduct or business activity was unfair or deceptive; it could simply issue a rule saying it was, and find you guilty if you violated the rule."

Allport argues that the FTC could issue rules on almost anything: "It could, for example, say that a given advertising-to-sales ratio was unfair, or that advertising to certain markets —children, let's say—was deceptive per se...." The bill that, in Allport's view, would permit this is on "the highest priority" schedule of Representative John Moss (D-Cal.), who chairs the House subcommittee that must consider it first. Moss moved up the priority after the FTC suffered a court setback in April, when a judge blocked a commission rule requiring the posting of octane ratings on gasoline pumps. The FTC has taken the case to the Supreme Court, but a decision will not be reached until next year.

CONSUMERISM IS HERE TO STAY

Much of the FTC activity, advertisers assume (and some FTC lawyers openly admit), is undertaken just to keep the admen on their guard. "What we're trying to do," says Gerald Thain, Pitofsky's director of national advertising regulations, "is get big advertisers and their lawyers to ask themselves, 'Is it worth the risk to try something that may be deceptive?' If the cost of losing is not worth the candle, they are not going to stop."

Thain's phrasing seems to indicate a presupposition that admen normally consider risking a deceptive ad or two. "I've been in the business twenty years," says F. Williams Free, who created the controversial National Airline campaign, attacked by feminists for its "Fly me, I'm Barbara" headlines, "and I've never sat in a creative meeting where somebody said 'Here's an idea I think we can get away with.'" Thomas Dillon, who heads the gigantic BBDO agency emphasizes the same point: "We have seventy-five clients, a lot of them in very competitive fields. In all the years I've been here, I've watched our competition's ads, and so have all the other people on our accounts, hoping to catch them in a statement that we can take advantage of. We haven't been able to do it. We've never been able to catch Procter & Gamble in a lie."

Dillon's outspoken attitude toward the FTC—he believes many of its actions are simply politically motivated—draws respect but not always agreement from other admen. Maurice L. Kelly, vice-president and director of advertising for Eastern Airlines, believes the time for anger and resentment is past. "The consumerism movement is here to stay," Kelly says, "and, frankly, it has accelerated some things that we should have been doing all along."

Specifically, he notes that the airline last fall instituted an "office of consumer affairs" and will open branches at major airports to handle on-the-scene problems. An executive running the office now checks out Eastern's ads, as do the company's lawyers and public relations people. The airline has also moved to clean up its ads, eliminating the asterisks and footnotes that sometimes make it impossible for the average traveler to obtain the advertised low fares.

"Some guys say that if you have to run 'full-disclosure' ads that cover all the restrictions, the ads will be too dull to read," says Kelly. "I don't believe it. There are enough creative people in the business to make an ad interesting, despite any limitations."

Last fall, after dozens of high-level advertising executives trooped to Washington to explain their ways of doing business at an "informa-

TOM DILLON

tional" hearing conducted by the FTC, admen hoped that some of the governmental suspicions would disappear. But, says William Colihan, vice-president of the American Association of Advertising Agencies, "admen walked through the valley of the shadow of death and emerged unscathed"—only to find shortly afterwards that the FTC hoped to broaden its definitions of "unfair advertising."

THE NEW KIND OF ADVERTISING

Now the admen are hoping that their new attitudes will take off some of the heat. In addition to expressing themselves in speeches and public statements, they are putting a new kind of advertising—for many of them, at any rate—onto the air. Shell Oil Co., for example, which long has advertised the "secret ingredients" that give automobiles better mileage, has adopted a "no claims" institutional approach in which it talks of such things as its expertise in making soles for tennis shoes. "And if Shell can do that," says a typical commercial, "think what it can do in its primary business of making gasoline for your car." A Sunoco TV spot admits that most cars do not need its gasoline blend with an octane rating of 260, "but isn't it nice to know that there's a company that makes it?" Other "no claim" ads are appearing for American gasoline (which uses folksinger Johnny Cash to tell about the glories of the open road), Ford cars ("The Torino just might be more car than you bargained for"), Dash detergent, and numerous other products.

THE MOVE TO SELF-REGULATION

In another move, the advertising associations and the National Council of Better Business Bureaus have set up a new and elaborate self-regulatory system. The idea is to correct potentially deceptive or misleading ads before the government storms in. The new National Advertising Review Board, headed by former United Nations Ambassador Charles W. Yost, has already received some 200 complaints from consumers groups and individuals. "Some of the groups have admitted they are testing us," says William H. Ewen, executive director of the NARB, which assembles panels of five adjudicators to discuss complaints with offending agencies and advertisers. The five are drawn from a roster of fifty leading executives both inside and outside the industry. "We hold that the ultimate responsibility for advertising is that of the client, not the agency," says Ewen, who notes that thus far the reaction from both has been extremely positive. It had better be: The NARB says that if an advertiser fails to modify an offending ad once the board has ordered it to do so, the board will turn its findings and the complaint over to the FTC or other regulatory body.

As yet, with panels meeting as often as three times a week, such action has not been necessary. Although some Washington officials, including FTC Chairman Kirkpatrick, have lauded the admen's efforts, the FTC recently moved to set up a special task force to study whether industry self-regulation means much as a general rule. A prior staff study revealed considerable doubt.

Another matter of great concern to the advertising fraternity is that the FTC and the anti-advertising crusaders in Washington have not yet let up the pressure, despite the industry's new conciliatory attitude. Howard H. Bell, president of the American Advertising Federation, recently proposed that the various advertising organizations coordinate industry reaction to the numerous attacks that evidently will continue to come from all sides. *Broadcasting* magazine called Bell's proposal a "battle plan."

THE QUESTION OF FTC'S PRIORITIES

Admen who still want to fight feel that they have plenty of ammunition. BBDO's Dillon, for example, notes that the FTC's own survey of its regional offices shows that only 5.7% of all complaints from consumers were about advertising. Many more were about product delivery, faulty merchandise, and the like. But according to Kirkpatrick, the issue of consumer protection takes up 60% to 70% of the commission's time—and advertising was the prime consumer issue of the past two years. Contemplating the time and money spent by the FTC to criticize Campbell Soup, Wonder Bread, and a handful of other products, adman Bill Free is aghast. "I mean," he says, "that with all the problems facing the country, there must be a priority list somewhere."

NBC and the Television Bureau of Advertising last month furnished what they consider more concrete evidence of the pitfalls toward which the FTC pushes the broadcast industry when it attacks advertising. The commission's belief in counteradvertising, says TVB, could have cost television some $540.4 million of its gross revenues of $3.2 billion in 1970 and would have changed the industry from one that enjoyed $453.8 million in pretax profits to one that lost $86.6 million.

Kirkpatrick, however, shrugs aside the impassioned protests with an observation that the FTC is not asking broadcasters to run a counter-ad each time a controversial product ad is put on the air. Instead, he suggests that a block of time—say, fifteen to thirty minutes weekly—be devoted to countercommercials. Already, an organization called The Stern Concern has prepared several commercials—featuring actor Burt Lancaster—that criticize Chevrolet and seven well-known analgesics. The car commercial was made for the Center for Auto Safety, which is now trying to get it on the networks; the Medical Committee for Human rights, a national doctors' organization, will seek time for the anti-analgesic message. And last month, an FTC staff member called on a convention of pharmacists to seek airtime to warn patients about over-the-counter drugs.

PLAYING WITHOUT ANY RULES

Despite some signs of dissension within the FTC itself—and the possibility that both Kirkpatrick and Pitofsky might return to private law—admen dare not hope that the commission will soon relax its anti-advertising posture. Most unsettling to advertisers and agencies is the fact that they do not know in which direction the FTC will move, or what it will go after. One month it's cereals, the next it's analgesics, the next it's toothpaste. Last year, Walter Bregman, who heads the Norman, Craig, & Kummel, Inc. agency, looked at FTC activity and said: "Let's face facts—we are scared. Today, the guidelines aren't set, we're playing in a high-stakes game, and we don't know the rules."

Since then, many admen have come to feel that there are no rules. In such a game, the safest tack is to join the consumerist movement —even to use it as an advertising theme—and to make ads that have no claims that can be challenged.

One problem with such advertising is illustrated all too well in a remark by Heilbroner. "One of the few ads I've seen that doesn't turn me off," he says, "is that one where they say they're just giving the facts. It's for—uh—a deodorant, I think, called—uh . . . uh . . . hmm . . ."

QUESTIONS FOR DISCUSSION

1 Does admitting your product is not perfect imply a new honesty in advertising? Why or why not?

2 Why does McLuhan refer to advertising as "the cave art of the twentieth century"?

3 Modern advertising is charged with creating dissatisfaction. Why? What alternatives to present forms of advertising are possible?

4 How many ads (or commercials) would you estimate you saw or heard during the past twenty-four hours? How many do you recall in detail? What was your response to them?

5 How would governmental regulation of the advertising industry affect its responsiveness to the consumer? Is this the most desirable method for improving advertising? What other alternatives are there?

PROJECTS

1 Analyze the probable intended audience for a particular magazine's advertising content. Consider:
(a) income bracket
(b) educational level
(c) religious affiliation
(d) housing category
(e) age
(f) sex
(g) political preferences

MINORITY VOICES AND MEDIA

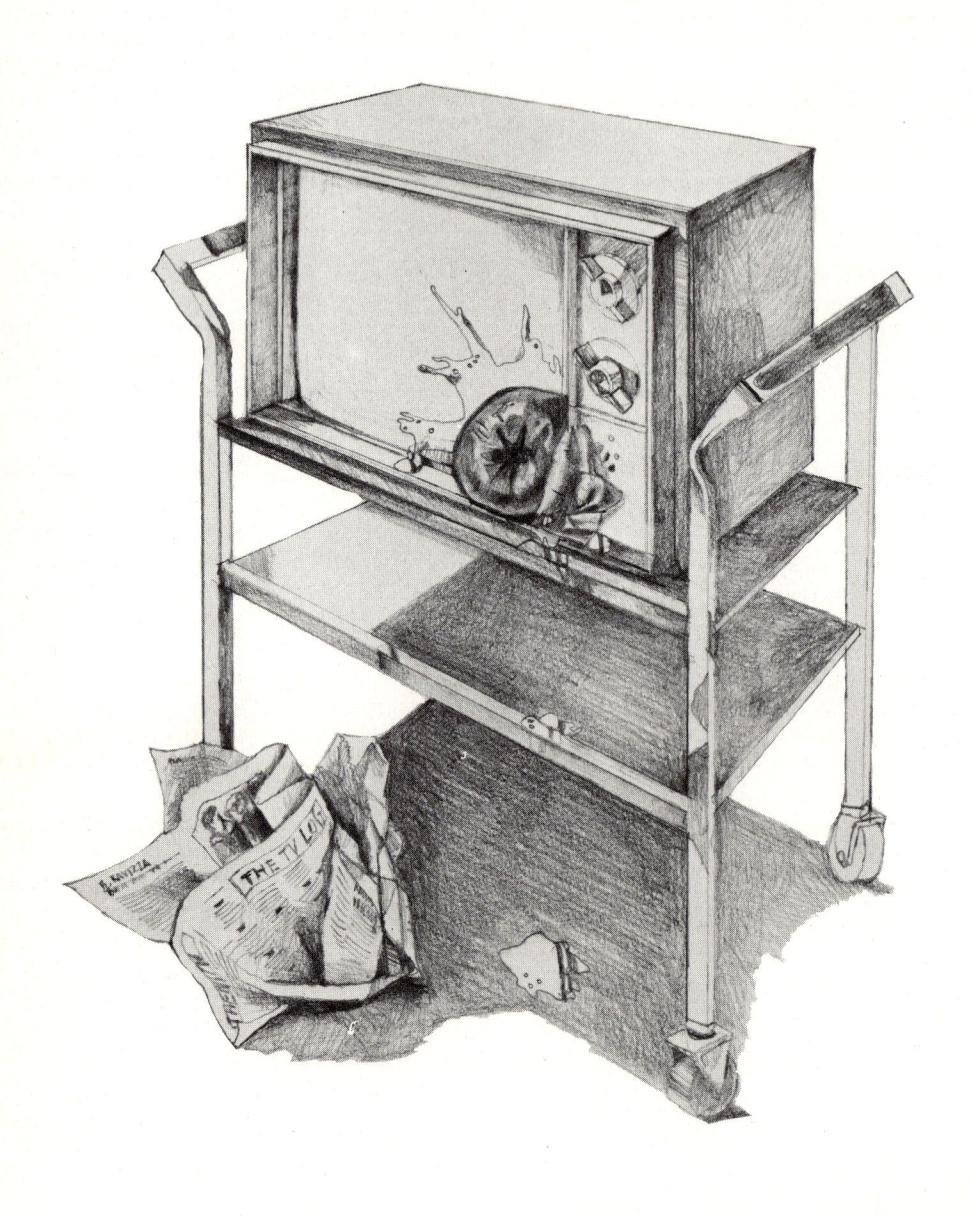

Is Television Making a Mockery of the American Woman?

EDITH EFRON

Journalist Edith Efron summarizes attacks by women's groups on network television's portrayal of American women as stupid, mindless sex objects, never as "whole people." Commercials, entertainment programming, news and talk shows—all are criticized for creating insulting, demeaning stereotypes of women. Today, several years later, much of what Efron and the women's groups complained about still lingers. The author concludes that TV's portrayal of women, "will eventually be 'humanized' in some degree." Eventually seems a long time in arriving.

"You use our bodies to sell products! You blackmail us with the fear of being unloved if we do not buy!"

The strident voice of a young feminist, Marian Delgado, broke through the orderly proceedings of a CBS stockholders' meeting in San Francisco, last April, to the consternation of CBS board chairman William S. Paley and CBS president Frank Stanton, while the latter was criticizing government authorities' "increasing pressures" on broadcasting. Neither of these gentlemen had anticipated the eruption of a new and strangely fierce pressure within their own citadel.

Miss Delgado, speaking for a group of about ten members of the Women's Liberation Front, continued her charge that CBS "abuses" women: the network, she declared, distorted and downgraded women's roles in its commercials and in its general programming. The disruption broke up the meeting—briefly—after which Mr. Paley insisted to the collected stockholders: "We do *not* dislike women." He pointed out that ten percent of CBS's administrative personnel is female. "Tokenism!" scoffed the feminists as they departed.

This little female assault on CBS was gleefully reported by broadcast journalists as an amusing aberration, of no particular significance, by a handful of viragoes. But they were not quite accurate. The Delgado invasion was significant: it was a symptom of an agitation over TV's portrayal of women among a growing number of women of all classes, races and political persuasions, who are joining feminist groups from coast to coast or cheering them on silently.

TV, in fact, has become one of the prime targets of the feminists in their new and aggressive surge for equal rights for women.

In November 1969, 500 highly educated women from cities and campuses in Eastern United States—Baltimore, Boston, Bryn Mawr, Clark University, Cornell University, Penn State, Pittsburgh and elsewhere—met in New York to set up a congress to unite women. At this congress, one workshop concerned itself with women's "stereotyped ... and derogatory ... image most blatantly seen in the presentations of the mass media" and the "misrepresentation by the media of the movement for women's liberation...." Among the results: the creation of an organization called Media Women, a newsletter on the subject, boycotts, and protests such as that led by Marian Delgado.

To discover exactly what the feminists object to in TV, we interviewed a group of them—most of them founders and leaders of feminist organizations, and some of them authors of serious books on women's problems. Some hold very radical positions, some are more moderate. But all are united in an analysis of the damage TV is doing to women. Here's what they have to say:

Commercials, they say, offer a stereotyped and insulting picture of women. "It's disastrous!" says Susan Brownmiller, journalist, a member of Media Women and a TV news reporter for NBC and ABC for seven years. "The image of women in the commercials is that of *stupidity*. They're shown as stupid and helpless."

"They're blatant put-downs," says Anselma

Reprinted with permission from *TV Guide*® Magazine. Copyright © 1970 by Triangle Publications, Inc., Radnor, Pennsylvania.

Del-Olio, actress and founder of the Feminist Repertory Theater in New York City. "They show the woman as a mindless boob and a masochistic slave—either a domestic servant or a sexy handmaiden."

"Commercials are legal pornography!" declares Ti-Grace Atkinson, member of the National Organization of Women and founder of the Feminists. "Women are shown exclusively as sex objects and reproducers, not as whole people."

And Shulamith Firestone, founder of the New York Radical Feminists, and author of *The Dialectic of Sex*, a book being brought out this fall by William Morrow, says, "The ads are creating really weird psychological effects. Women are being led to confuse their sexuality with individuality. What kind of sunglasses or bra they wear, whether they're blonde or brunette, whether there's the right kind of wiggle in their walk, becomes absolutely crucial because their total worth as a human being becomes confused with a surface aspect. The ads are virtually generating erotomania in women."

Similar charges are provoked by the portrayal of women in entertainment programming. Robin Morgan, writer, poet, member of several women's lib groups and mother of a year-old son, says: "The image of women in the plays is *dreadful*. At one pole there's the *I Love Lucy* stereotype, the brainless featherhead, and the sweet, dumb lovable blonde of *Petticoat Junction* and *Green Acres* who's helpless without men. In between, there's the maternal nurturing housewife, like Donna Reed or Julia —passive women who are defined in terms of their relationship to men—as wives or mothers or widows. At the other pole there's the male fantasy of the 'liberated' woman—the chic, hard, cold, sexy swinger with no ties, who obviously sleeps around and is not an economic drag on the man. And there's nothing else. It has almost no relationship with reality at all."

Shulamith Firestone says: "Women are just not *human* in these plays. They're not portrayed as thinking or feeling beings. They're shown as something between an animal and a human. The word 'chick' best captures it."

Is there any view of woman on TV that the feminists like? Yes, there is, but in our era it is unusually rare: it's the strong-minded, courageous heroine. Susan Brownmiller of Media Women says: "There's never been a heroic woman on TV, save for Emma Peel in *The Avengers*. That's the show I watch. I *love* that show! She's the only *strong* woman on television." And Shulamith Firestone says: "The best view of women you get is in movies of the thirties, where you got *strong* women. You can see Barbara Stanwyck portraying a woman who at least has *guts!*"

Commercials and series are not the only targets of the feminists' attack. News and talk shows, too, come in for their share of vitriolic criticism. Of general news coverage, Aileen Hernandez, the president of the National Organization of Women, says, "It is only relatively recently that women appear at all in news shows. You rarely see reports of women who have achieved anything of significance on these shows. Usually when you do see a woman she's involved in the same old claptrap about society or fashion." And Shulamith Firestone elaborates: "News departments don't consider women news. News equals the male government, the male war machine, the male world. There are fantastic women, women of great achievement in this country of whom people have never heard because the networks don't cover them."

Their protests against TV's coverage of Women's Lib itself are violent. They claim that it omits serious content and focuses on the lunatic fringe—a tiny fraction of hysterics with a professed desire to eliminate heterosexual relationships, childbearing, and generally to fold, spindle and mutilate the male of the species.

Anne Koedt, painter and member of the New York Radical Feminists, whose book on female sexuality is scheduled for publication this fall, says "On interviews they always ask you about two things—bra burning and violence! Bra burning is a nonexistent issue in the feminist movement. No one cares! Men just get a sexual kick out of talking about it.

"As for violence, what the male interviewers *really* mean is 'What will you do if we don't *let* you solve these problems?' It's *their* violence they're talking about!" And Anselma Del-Olio says: "The coverage of the feminist movement always contains an element of ridicule. There's all kinds of mocking editorializing, insinuations that we hate men. And on talk shows they surround you with put-down artists!

"But the editing of the film is where it's really at. They do a half-hour interview and take the most far-out thing that you've said—a conclusion which was a logical result of your whole exposition. But very conveniently they cut out all the *reasoning*, which means: they cut out *your* context."

Finally, news-department hiring policies, too, are attacked as "tokenism." Susan Brownmiller says: "I sat there for years and watched agents bring in *models* for news jobs. And I know for a fact that when a woman is considered, the networks are more concerned over her face than her abilities. Directors of news choose men simply in terms of performance, but they tend to lose their standards when it comes to women. And even when they've hired a few token women who are competent, they rarely give them a crack at important assignments."

These are by no means all the criticisms leveled at TV—but they are some of the essential ones. Is there any chance that the feminists—still a tiny minority of American women—will actually succeed in influencing TV if they keep up this barrage? Yes, there is.

Already one loud reverberation has come from the advertising world itself—unsurprisingly from an agency headed by a woman. Franchellie Cadwell, president of Cadwell Davis, Inc., made a speech before a body of professional colleagues recently in which she attacked "these horrendous commercials; created by men for women, that contemporary women find insulting beyond endurance." Under her leadership, Cadwell Davis has conducted a study showing that most American women loathe commercials portraying women as simpletons; and the company has announced a Women's Liberation campaign of its own. In the April 27 issue of the trade journal called *Advertising Age*, the agency published a manifesto, which read in part: "When over fifty-five percent of the women in the country are high school graduates and twenty-five percent have attended college, when women have achieved sexual freedom, aren't they beyond 'house-i-tosis'? At the very least women deserve recognition as being in full possession of their faculties.... We know the rumbles have sounded. The revolution is ready and one of

> ... Television advertisements allot all housework to women. When a beautiful young woman notices "ring around the collar" on a male party guest, the entire crowd glares accusingly at the embarrassed wife. The message is clear: she is a failure as a wife and a woman because she has allowed her husband to appear in public with dirty collars.
>
> Scores of newlyweds worry endlessly when their husbands refuse a second cup of coffee. It never occurs to these women to let the men make their own coffee; instead Mrs. Olson saves their marriages by recommending the proper brand.
>
> —Susan Luttner
> **Grapevine**

women's first targets will be moronic, insulting advertising.... No force has demeaned women more than advertising."

Franchellie Cadwell is not the only powerful woman in the advertising world. Phyllis Robinson, vice president of Doyle Dane Bernbach Inc., and Shirley Polykoff of Foote, Cone & Belding, are just two of the women advertising potentates who take the same stand.

In addition, the entire communications world, which criticizes and influences TV content, is studded with feminist Trojan horses, as various top male editors—such as those of *Time*, *Newsweek* and *TV Guide*—have discovered. And the networks themselves are full of feminist borers-from-within.

Given this fifth column in advertising and communications, backed up by a slowly growing grass-roots feminist movement, it is more than likely that TV's portrayal of women will eventually be "humanized" in some degree. Certainly the men who run this medium are listening with at least one ear to this latest protest group, which includes some of their own wives, daughters and friends—women who have something on their minds besides how white their wash turns out.

Speeding Down the Wrong Track

FREDERICK BREITENFELD JR.

All the current programming questionnaires for broadcasters seem to include the same items:

- What percentage of your programming is for minorities?
- What percentage of your minority programming is locally produced?
- What is the greatest need within the minority community in your market?
- Do you have a system for minority feedback?

Each question assumes more than the one before. We want to help everyone who asks, including the Federal Communications Commission. After all, the FCC itself poses the same questions with the same implicit assumptions: broadcasting licenses are public trusts, and stations must provide programming for minority audiences. Minority programming is essential to any broadcast schedule. The needs of minority audiences must be defined, analyzed and met by broadcasting stations. Minority programming is "in."

But what is it?

One official definition, now in administrative use across the country—at least among public broadcasters—is disturbingly circular: *Minority programs are programs closely identified with the social, economic and cultural experiences of a minority group, and which focus on a need or an interest of the specific minority group with which the program identifies.*

We are asked to list our program offerings that meet the definition, and we try to do it. But it seems strange, somehow, at least for broadcasters who consider themselves educators. We spring from a field in which segregation was declared unconstitutional 20 years ago.

To force integration, we send our children across town in buses in compliance with one set of Federal regulations. At the same time, promoting separatism, we divide our electronic services in order to satisfy another set of Federal regulations.

These past couple of decades have been important to America's social growth. The country was made to realize, at long last, that some of our citizens are getting a raw deal. Some Americans, because of color or origin, had—and still have—a tougher time taking advantage of the alleged equal opportunities that exist in education and commerce.

Those who are being gypped, and are running short of patience, include American Indians, Americans from Puerto Rico, American black people, Americans with Spanish names . . . and others. They are, we are told, the "minority" audiences.

However, will a black dentist respond to minority programming aimed at better opportunities for semiskilled workers? Will an American Indian, unable to get employment at all, watch a sophisticated series on Indian history? Will an Oriental professor of linguistics identify with characters in a drama about an urban ghetto? Will an unskilled laborer of Mexican heritage be helped with a series exploring the roots of Latin music? All programs might pass as forms of "minority" fare, but can "needs and interests" really be defined by ethnic background or race? Probably not. And, in the midst of all this desperate categorizing, what happened to integration?

Those being gypped, for whatever reasons, are mostly *poor people*. They are urban and rural; they are helpless and angry. They need skills and a no-kidding fair chance. The only two factors that really count are ignorance and poverty.

Then what is "minority programming"?

Is it a series on the status of women? Is it third-grade music taught by a black teacher? Is it *Sanford and Son* or *Chico and the Man*?

Sometimes minority programming is described as "by and for a specific racial or ethnic group, focusing on the experience or self-

---

Reprinted with permission from *TV Guide*® Magazine. Copyright © 1975 by Triangle Publications, Inc. Radnor, Pennsylvania.

awareness of that group." The logic is that there is a need to instill pride and a feeling of strength in the people who have been subjects of bigotry over the years. It's good logic, and the cause is laudable. But it screams for separatism, and segregated schools cannot be far beyond.

If we insist that people of only one race or national background should write, produce, act in and watch a program before it is "minority" programming, we are endorsing segregation. Some programming will be for you and some for me . . . and sooner or later, someone will describe them as "separate but equal." While we bicker over it, poverty and ignorance will lie unchanged.

Why, then, do we insist that there is a "minority" program type? Why do we count up the "minority programming" hours? It may be because broadcasters must assure themselves (and the FCC) that they are not bigoted, that this is indeed a land of equality, and that we are erasing sins of our predecessors from the public ledger.

As we try to right the obvious wrongs, as we try to make our programming responsive to our communities and responsible to our constituents, we need reassurance. So we concoct "minority programming" to try to measure our good faith, whether we have it or not.

For the public broadcaster, there are many minorities. A surgeon enjoys learning about both music and the latest in anesthetic devices; an unskilled laborer is in need of a high-school diploma; an industrialist needs a brushup on business arithmetic; a city dweller wants help in getting his apartment fixed; a parent is ignorant of the latest techniques in helping deaf children.

These minorities overlap with every program. These are the audiences for whom we should design "minority programming," and they watch with different skin colors.

It's helping people, and what we call it doesn't matter. Let's just do it.

Women's Pages: You Can't Make News Out of a Silk Purse

LINDSY VAN GELDER

You may have noticed that Brenda Starr doesn't write for the women's page of *The Flash*. When the Girl Reporter is marooned in the steaming Amazon jungle, she does not ferret out the ever-popular woman's angle by interviewing the native chieftain's wife on her recipe for tarantula pie.

"One of the most frequent questions I get," Washington *Post* syndicated columnist Nicholas Von Hoffman has remarked, "is 'Don't you resent being put on the women's page?'" The average newspaper women's page has traditionally been a low-prestige, low-budget, low-paying operation, rife with payola and press agentry. For a great many women journalists—particularly and ironically, for feminists—it has been a purgatory from which to escape.

When I became a reporter in the late sixties, I avoided the women's-angle assignments through a maniacally *macho* willingness to cover train wrecks, riots, *anything* else, and an unfeigned ignorance of conventional women's-pagey topics. (I once stunned an editor by referring to the designer Givenchy as *Guh-vench-ee* instead of Z*hee-von-shee*. Another time, a sister-reporter and I got ourselves fired for protesting assignments to interview the wives of several New York Mets as "Women in the News"—women who, however nice, had accomplished nothing newsworthy.) It never occurred to me that anything meaningful could come out of the editorial department whose beat, after all, includes food, clothing, and shelter. The women's

---

From *Ms.* magazine, Nov. 1974. Reprinted by permission of Ms. Magazine Corporation.

page was for frivolous, boring, puffy, irrelevant, 86-ways-to-make-tuna-casserole news. You know, *women's* news.

Since then we've all had our consciousnesses raised, and to some extent the status of the women's page has improved along with the status of women. So has the quality, at least on the better, big-city newspapers, where the change became apparent after 1970. That year the "women's libbers," as they so chummily call us, grew to a significant national movement (despite press coverage that was hostile, when it was there at all) and the midi-skirt bombed (despite shameless whoring by the fashion writers). Was it possible that readers wanted a new life instead of a new skirt length? Newspapers began covering abortion, rape, child care, alimony, job discrimination, gay rights, and other feminist issues, and taking fresh approaches toward their traditional subjects. Some women's sections—notably those of the Washington *Post*, the Chicago *Tribune*, and the New York *Times*—are now considered by many in the industry to be the best-written, best-read parts of the papers.

So much for the good news. The bad news, arrived at after a recent perusal of dozens of papers from across the country, is that most women's pages are nearly as awful as ever.

For starters, any section that still calls itself a "women's page" is suspect. When the New Orleans *Times-Picayune*, for example, presents the title "Women's Activities: Society/Fashion/Clubs" on a section whose front page is graced by five blown-up photographs of five white fiancées and brides, you get a rough idea of what the *Times-Picayune* thinks about women. (Not to mention the implication that if these are proper women's activities, all of that other stuff in the rest of the paper, like business and politics and sports, is for men.) No, today the slicker practitioners have pages called "Living," "Family/Style," "Scene," "Tempo," and "Portfolio," to name a few—though the editors still call them "the women's pages."

What this too often *means* is that we get caught in a double bind: the name-change may liberate the content, but the section is still a dumping ground for anything the male editors consider a "woman's" story. So we get all the serious news stories about the Equal Rights Amendment, rape-law changes, back-pay lawsuits, and so forth, back among the girdle ads instead of on page one or two or three where they belong.

Or the Washington *Evening Star-News* fashion column that began with an interview with Federal Maritime Commission Chairperson Helen Bentley on her political future, then backed into the fact that Bentley had made her comments at a charity luncheon that included a fashion show. You can't blame the writer for feeling that the Bentley angle made a better lead than the new look in mauve mink fedoras—but if a male politician happened to discuss his future between Super Bowl halves, would the story run on the sports page?

Women's page schizophrenia only trivializes the serious issues of our lives—*Hey, gals, what's* YOUR *bag? Needlepoint, mah jong, or liberation?*—and continues the fiction that women are just one more special-interest group, like the people who read the camera column, instead of half the population. Why can't newspapers have a food, family, furnishings, and fashion page for human beings *plus* front-of-the-paper news stories *plus* features about changing lifestyles that include women's issues? Why do we have to be scrunched into one little newsprint ghetto?

We can begin to make room by chucking out the weddings and engagements—or the "nuptials" and "betrothals," as they say in Societyland. If a Martian decided to research our culture by reading a typical newspaper, she would conclude that every female earthling spent at least several days every month getting married. In addition to the pictures of the brides (why don't they ever print *his* photograph?) we have endless features on debutante balls, wedding etiquette, wedding gown styles, trousseaux, engagement rings, silverware and china, honeymoons, and so on, and so on. The none-too-subtle message—that the main business of women is snaring husbands and that their wedding day is life's supreme shining moment—not so incidentally helps sell a lot of gowns, rings, and sterling silver cake servers, and newspaper advertising linage for same.

Nor are all brides equally radiant in the eyes of the press. CBS-TV newswriter Bryna Taubman, who began her career as a women's page editor in Missouri and Ohio, recalled the typically Byzantine workings of the Cleveland *Plain Dealer*'s wedding coverage: "We had this very rigid formula about the couple's social class. If the bride and groom were from Social Register families, they'd get a big headline, a picture a couple of columns wide, and a fairly long, detailed description of their backgrounds and the ceremony and what the gown looked like. If they were rich but Jewish, or if they weren't rich but had gone to good colleges, we'd run a picture and a shorter article. If they were just high school graduates, no picture."

According to Frank Quine, an associate director of the American Press Institute, which sponsors an annual convention for women's page editors, at least three papers—the Washington *Post,* the Chicago *Tribune,* and *Newsday* on Long Island—have done away with the traditional bridal format and now run only paid ads or classified notices. Other papers have condensed the announcements. "But most of them aren't about to eliminate either the wedding or the club news," said Quine. "They view them as a public service."

"I've spent endless amounts of time explaining to the women's organizations why we don't cover them any more," said Miriam Petrie, the highly respected "Lifestyle 74" editor of the Hackensack, New Jersey, *Record.* "Most clubwomen are honest enough to admit that they don't read the news about organizations they don't belong to, and that they already know the news about their own." About six months ago the *Record* discontinued the bridal photographs. "We did it gradually and we haven't gotten much outrage from the public."

Most small-town and suburban papers are better typified by the Central Maine *Morning Sentinel,* in which a recent women's page included wedding and engagement stories with pictures, an account of a local couple's fortieth anniversary celebration, a story announcing the formation of Pre-Cana conferences for engaged couples, "Dear Abby," "Heloise," two patterns (one "broomstick lace," one "quickie tunic"), and a column on club news. On the same day the society section of the Bluefield, West Virginia, *Daily Telegraph* had much the same fare, plus a local gossip column entitled "Femininely Speaking" ("Have been trying to find time to go by the home of the .... to see that 85-year-old Christmas cactus Mrs. .... has...") and a stupefying collection of what amounted to the minutes of the meetings of the Daughters of the Confederacy, the Ladies Auxiliary to the Old Guard, and nearly a score of other clubs.

> ... I don't know a single woman journalist who has been handicapped by her sex once she did get the job. It's true that a lot of the traits required for reporting—aggressiveness, coolness under pressure, and self-reliance—are bred out of women in this society. From time to time, you **do** have to dodge flying bottles, trip over corpses, and all the rest of the Hollywood bit. In the long run, however, it's the stereotyped female traits that get the story.... Getting people to trust you—as opposed to shoving a microphone in their faces—is where responsible journalism is at today. You've got to have compassion, and all those other "female" virtues. Risking a faceful of MACE to tell what **happened** at a demonstration is not enough. You also have to tell what was **going on**—which usually means a rap with the demonstrators and really trying to see why they're there, whether they're liberating buildings or voting for Wallace.
> —Lindsy Van Gelder

I do not mean to make fun of people in small towns, but it's hard to believe that the dimensions of life in Bluefield are so narrow that women distinguish themselves only as assistant salad servers. And if they are, isn't it the responsibility of a newspaper to broaden them?

Small papers at least have the excuse of small resources; big papers, even the very good ones, have been slow to use their big resources. By newspaper logic, Ralph Nader should have been a "women's page" reporter. Dangerous toys, junky food additives, lethal birth-control pills and IUDs, quack diets, fire-hazardous pajamas, crippling platform shoes, children's worthless car seats, rip-off nursing homes—surely these are the domain of any section with pretensions to covering "living" or "home and family." Though investigative reporting should be every paper's beat, at best these sections have given good coverage to *other* people's muckraking, and press-release consumer guides; at worst they've been the willing flacks for their advertisers and for the status quo.

Most papers are still refusing to call a woman "Ms." if she so prefers; still dishing out cheesecake; still raving on about "career gals" and pert, auburn-haired grandmothers; still running sexist ads; still using women for cheap humor and easy titillation; still asking Billie Jean King when she's going to have a baby; still portraying women as appendages of men.

Even alleged terrorists are ladies first: after noting that Dr. Bridget Rose Dugdale, the suspected Irish Republican Army art thief, holds a doctoral degree, the New York *Times* proceeded nonetheless to refer to her throughout a recent story as "Miss" Dugdale, the "daughter of an English millionaire." Symbionese Liberation Army member Emily Harris was identified by the *Times* as Bill Harris's "wife Emily, a willowy 27-year-old blonde."

Editors and publishers invariably claim that readers *want* to look at brides and bathing beauties and "we're-just-passing-along-the-news, folks"—a standard that conveniently goes out the city-room window when the same editors take it upon themselves to airbrush gory automobile accident photos or to censor profanity. It's also a standard that hasn't been market-researched since the days when a picture of an egg frying on the sidewalk on a hot summer day was the apex of wit.

It's time for a new edition. A living and style section geared to *people,* male and female, is a new frontier. It can be as bright and funny and off-the-wall and informative as the vagaries of modern living allow. The New York *Times,* for instance, has featured articles on jean and T-shirt fashions, the Great Leg Shaving Debate, househusbands, and the fact that people don't eat dinner at the dinner table any more. The Chicago *Tribune* has run a series on the lifestyles of two-career couples and an amusing survey guide to the city's male and female public bathrooms. There's a whole world out there to cover, from men's fashions to children's liberation. Newspapers should be there.

What Do Black Journalists Want?

DOROTHY GILLIAM

They sat shoulder to shoulder in the crowded Congressional Black Caucus hearings, those black reporters, nodding affirmatively if the brother who was speaking was voicing their belief. They shifted restlessly if the witness bogged down in rhetoric. For their standards are high, these black men and women in the white media. And they have a high degree of frustration.

At the March 6-7 session the reporters heard Rep. William Clay (D-Mo.), chairman of the Congressional Black Caucus' hearings on the mass media, saying the media were acting "to perpetuate institutionalized racism." No one knows more than these reporters that what they say or do not say in the media has ramifications for black people far beyond the utterances of blacks in some other white institution. For the media help determine the self image of blacks—and how does a bright, sensitive person reconcile getting his bread from the same source that keeps its foot on his brother's neck? Like the black community, the black journalist is excluded, mishandled, and exploited by the media.

Of course, it rarely comes down as blatantly as that. Few out-and-out bigoted media managers exist. But as Warren E. Howard, an international vice-president of the Newspaper Guild and the first black to serve on the Guild's International Executive Board in the union's thirty-eight-year history, testified:

We most often face publishers tied to a system which they cannot or will not recognize as racist in its employment practices and procedures. It is the system that says, "who me? I don't discriminate. I hire without regard to race, sex, creed, color, etc. In fact,

Reprinted from the *Columbia Journalism Review,* May/June 1972.

I'll hire the first graduate of a properly accredited journalism school who walks in the front door the next time there's an opening and asks for a job. And I'll do it without regard to race, sex, etc." In fact, from some publishers that . . . would come out, "I'll hire the next person with a master's degree and one semester toward his doctorate that walks in the door and convinces me he or she is qualified to be the next chairman of the board, without regard to. . . ."

The fact is that for editors and publishers, the bloom is off when it comes to hiring and promoting nonwhite reporters. For some, it never was otherwise. The history of the media up to the black rebellions of the mid-Sixties indicates where most publishers stood on the issue.

Before 1954, there was near-total neglect of the black community—as well as black journalists—unless the story dramatized some sensational aspect, by and large crime. After the 1954 Supreme Court decision, when the struggle for civil rights equality escalated, the white media helped to make known the wrongs, although they often misinterpreted what they heard and misrepresented what they saw. Then came the riots, and rebelling blacks—fired with the pent-up injustices of long years—roamed their neighborhoods, burning largely the white- and black-owned businesses that had bled them economically. Here was a new phenomenon: white reporters were chased away when they showed up. Obviously newspapers had to have some black faces. Black copyboys and messengers, even, became instant reporters during that period. And most metropolitan newspapers, wire services, and TV stations started taking the hiring of black professionals seriously—more or less.

In the wake of those rebellions, in 1968 the National Advisory Commission on Civil Disorders (Kerner Commission) reported that its "major concern with the news media is not in riot reporting as such, but in the failure to report adequately on race relations and ghetto problems and to bring more Negroes into journalism." It added:

In defining, explaining, and reporting this broader, more complex, and ultimately far more fundamental subject, the communications media, ironically, have failed to communicate. They have not communicated to the majority of their audience, which is white, a sense of the degradation, misery and hopelessness of living in the ghetto. They have not communicated to whites a feeling for the difficulties and frustrations of being a Negro in the United States. . . . If the media are to comprehend and then to project the Negro community, they must have the help of Negroes.

In the intervening years, white illiberalism has grown, the civil rights movement has died, and large segments of the population are in a touchy mood. And newspapers—reflecting this conservatism as well as the economic recession—have lost their enthusiasm for hiring blacks. Some have delayed fulfilling promises to upgrade blacks already on their staffs. And the press has continued to concentrate primarily on conflicts at a time when black power and unity have become black-community themes, and antibusing and Law and Order, whites' themes.

Caught in the dilemma is the black professional in the general media. However you view it, he has problems. He is penned into a situation where whites, refusing to see that they have as great a stake as he in racial harmony in the U.S., push all "racial" stories upon him, all the while doubting his "objectivity." Or, on the other hand, he shies away from these stories altogether and festers quietly, seeing himself—literally—misrepresented. Further, the black community, which has been burned so often that it is crusty, often doesn't trust him. Nor does it grasp the hierarchical gamut the black reporter must run to get news about the black community into print.

I can identify readily with the dilemma, although my own case spanned only part of that developing period of the black journalist on the white newspapers. I came along before the urban insurrections, but the handwriting was already on the wall. When I graduated *cum laude* from Lincoln University at Jefferson City, Mo., in 1957, I applied at my hometown daily, the Louisville *Times*. I was told no vacancies existed or were anticipated, and I was not encouraged to apply for future reference. So I went to work for the black press until I could get "white" credentials: a degree from the Columbia University Graduate School of Journalism.

I was one of two black people in the School's Class of 1961. Within a month, after a trip to Africa, I had two offers from major papers, one of them the Louisville *Times*. I chose the Washington *Post*, which then had a couple of other black reporters on the city staff. Before long, two of us were stacked up behind a lone white reporter writing about welfare and poverty. The senior black reporter on the staff endured being passed over for the Planning beat five times, then left.

Today, eleven years later, the number of black reporters at the *Post* has risen to thirteen—highest of any U.S. daily—yet frustrations have not subsided. In March, in fact, seven black members of the *Post*'s metropolitan reporting staff filed suit with the U.S. Equal Employment Opportunity Commission, charging the paper with racial discrimination. Before the seven did so, nearly all the newspaper's black staff members signed a letter to the newspaper's management, saying in part:

> Nine members of the editorial staff ... wrote you with a list of twenty questions concerning the qualitative and quantitative contribution that black people are being allowed to make in the newsroom and on the pages of the Washington *Post*. They asked why ... so few black journalists have been given the opportunity to advance to some of those positions from which key decisions are made regarding the day-to-day handling of the news. We write now because we wish to make certain the heart of the issue is not obscured by a debate around the narrower question of precisely what that numerical participation ought to be ... black Americans are painfully aware of the lack of participation in the writing of the story of America in a time of change. We could not insist that all matters relative to blacks be written and reported by blacks, anymore than we could countenance the writing of all stories about women by women, all Catholics by Catholics, or all whites by whites. But the lack of black participation in the shaping of the news about the society in which they play so vital a role has led to unfortunate distortions of the basic posture of the community on such vital questions as crime in the streets and the busing of schoolchildren. The complexity of those issues has been masterfully distorted by politicians for political ends in ways that reflect almot nothing of the stake of the black community in those vital questions.

What they might have added—or spelled out more clearly—is that they are, in effect, party to the media's distortion. "They *use* you, man!" one top black reporter remarked in an outburst before a group of black journalism students recently, "and when you get out there—way out there—they often don't back you up."

These were some of the intensifying aggravations which—combined with the idealistic conviction of some that blacks must be black and unified first and communicators second—prompted a group of Howard University students to organize a National Black Communications Conference in March. So it was with some disgruntlement that they heard *Muhammad Speaks* editor Joseph Woodford caution them not to naïvely think that communicators create revolutions.

Throughout the Howard conference, March 3-4, the question whether one could work in the "white" media and at the same time contribute to black progress was a major concern. But at Black Caucus hearings, working professionals engaged much harder issues. Nearly all echoed the line taken by Chairman Clay that "the black media worker and the black movement are grossly excluded, distorted, mishandled, and exploited by the white-controlled news media."

Tony Brown, dean of Howard University's School of Communications and executive producer of *Black Journal*, charged that "the traditional use of mass communications in this country has been for the purpose of oppressing nonwhites and entertaining whites." The result, he said, was the perpetuation of present racial attitudes. "Racism in television has grave ramifications in psychological terms," he added, and he cited statistics that more than 95 percent of 60 million U.S. homes have TV sets, 55 percent of 200 million Americans depend on TV for their news, blacks watch 33 percent more TV than whites, and more than 40 percent of black children believe what they see on TV. "These statistics merely point out the rapid rate of self-hatred rained upon blacks by television," Brown said.

Ethel Payne, Washington correspondent for the *Sengstacke Publications*, criticized the "inaccessibility" of the President to black reporters, charging that [former] President Nixon had "favorites" among the Hill regulars who were given exclusive interviews and that "no such privilege has ever been given a black or minority reporter; nor has the opportunity to question him during a formal press conference arisen."

Rep. Shirley Chisholm (D-N.Y.) strongly criticized the Federal Communications Commission for its apparent lack of concern over the hiring policies in the broadcast industry. She cited Equal Employment Opportunity Commission figures that in the newspaper industry only 4.2 percent of employees are black. In the professional class—the reporters—only 1.5 percent are black. The FCC still has not compiled the reports submitted last May on racial and sexual composition of work forces in radio-TV.

William Wright, national coordinator of Black Efforts for Soul in Television (BEST), called upon the Black Caucus to support legislation that would both decentralize media ownership and abet ownership by groups broadly representative of the communities in which they would operate. He noted that blacks currently own none of the 906 TV stations, and only 2 percent of the 7,000 radio stations in America.

Wright also noted that there now are thirteen bills in the House of Representatives that would make it virtually impossible for blacks or community-oriented groups to challenge stations seeking license renewals. Ironically, the FCC, which is responsible for overseeing the broadcast industry, also favors such legislation. He charged that the FCC's "proposed rules would have the effect of racially restricting the media," and concluded that blacks must move now toward cable TV in order to express their views and culture.

Ernest Dunbar, writer and former senior editor of *Look*, detailed the case of Earl Caldwell, the black New York *Times* reporter who is currently fighting a subpoena obtained by a California federal grand jury that was to investigate the Black Panther Party. "Since it was obvious to black newsmen," said Dunbar, "that Mr. Mitchell, Mr. Kleindienst, and other Nixon aides seemed to feel that the Constitution was but a frail impediment to implementing what the Administration was 'hustling' as Law and Order, and since so-called media radicals were clearly a Nixon target, we expected that black reporters would soon be feeling the heat."

But it was the continuing stereotyped sensation-negative-criminal image that upset L.F. Palmer, Jr., Chicago *Daily News* columnist and commentator. "It's easier to get a piece in on the Panthers or a street gang than on a block club or community news," he said, adding that there was little opportunity for black reporters to deal in depth and detail with basic issues which affect black people." "There's no commitment to put the black man in honest perspective." By the time a story runs the gamut of white editors, he said, often it is "laundered if not eliminated."

The Caucus was told of more than one top reporter who, refusing to be "laundered," was eliminated. Take the case of Samuel F. Yette. Yette was hired on Jan. 1, 1968, by *Newsweek* as a Washington correspondent. He had already worked on four newspapers and two magazines. Yette had appeared on *Meet the Press* several times while on *Newsweek*. Last Christmas Eve he was fired, six months after publication of his book, *The Choice: The Issue of Black Survival in America*. In it he documents how and why he feels the Government has, in the Seventies, acquired the psychic capability for mass black repression—even genocide. Yette has filed racial discrimination suits against the magazine with both the District of Columbia Human Relations Commission and the U.S. Equal Employment Opportunity Commission. The case is now pending.

Cases like Yette's often grow out of accumulated small aggravations—and they are what finally send many black reporters packing. One example is the taping that Don Alexander wanted to do. Alexander was an award-winning reporter for WTTG-TV, the Metromedia station in Washington. He co-anchored the weekend news and helped to conceive and concurrently co-anchor *Black News*, a shoestring operation for which, as one staff member said, "We can't get camera crews to cover things we feel are relevant to the black community." An incident during the same week Yette was fired was the proverbial straw.

Alexander had reserved a time to tape-record an interview with Yette and Tony Brown of Howard University. Less than three hours before the men were due at the studio, however, a news executive told Alexander that the taping time he had reserved had been preempted. The news executive also asserted that the blacks-and-media story had been overdone on *Black News*. Alexander said it was either the taping or him. Management refused to yield. Alexander is now with WCBS in New York.

Ironically, these long-simmering frustrations are surfacing at a time when increasing numbers of young blacks are being trained in journalism. Howard University's School of Communications alone plans to graduate 200 each

Minority Voices and Media 153

year by 1976. What is to be their future, given today's discontent?

Obviously, severe discontent with the news media is not limited to blacks. Many white reporters, editors, and publishers share it. But several elements make the position of black journalists especially perilous—and this is at the heart of the rash suits and openly voiced frustrations. It seems intolerable that still, in 1972, blacks are so grossly underrepresented numerically in American news media and coverage of the black community is so sketchy and negative; that white editors apply standards to news of blacks that they do not apply to whites; that the story is assigned by a white assignment man, judged by a white editor, and read by a white copydesk and news editor. If it is "hot," it goes to the managing editor; if "red hot," it goes even higher. All these decisions are made almost totally by whites.

It is true that a black newsman sometimes must assume the added burden of weighing the loyalty of the black cause against his professional commitment. Yet if there were more black reporters reflecting not only the broad spectrum of views in the black community but also "conveying the truest picture" of what transpires, such tragic stances as those described in a recent *Wall Street Journal* article would not prevail. In an essay entitled "The Black Reporters' Dilemma" [March 23], WSJ correspondent Jonathan R. Laing lamented that many black reporters feel inhibited from "telling it like it is" about black leaders. That certainly is true of some of them. But Laing is from Chicago and should know that one problem is that last year there were only sixteen black editorial employees among 487 in Chicago, so the spotlight is glaring on them. If the percentage of black reporters and editors more nearly matched the percentage of the nonwhite Chicago population, such a situation would be less likely.

Let me emphasize, however, that I do not think black reporters should cover only "black" stories; white reporters should be sent into black neighborhoods, too. When publishers discuss not hiring or assigning black reporters and editors because of their "intense commitment to the black movement," they overlook the fact that whites, just as much as blacks, are involved in the racial struggle. They are the other, necessary, part of the equation. Whites have a stake in perpetuating the racial status quo and usually have just as intense a commitment to their perspective as do blacks.

As Lu Palmer told the Howard student conference, two things must happen to black reporters on white media. First, they must move through the media as advocates for black people. "We must find a way to advocate for blacks as whites have and continue to advocate for whites in the press," he said. Second, activist black reporters and black congressmen must establish a formal liaison to "hammer out together methods by which we can turn white-controlled media into instruments for the advocacy of human rights for all people." Above all, as Earl Caldwell reminded a group of black students at Columbia, despite the psychic costs of working on the white media, blacks should remember one thing: "It's important that you be there . . . that is where the power is."

Caldwell and Palmer are correct; black journalists must continue to fight daily the battles and frustrations built into their jobs. This means sensitizing editors to elevate blacks into positions at every notch of the hierarchy, and pushing to change the behavior and attitudes of their colleagues and the quality of their product. Yet realistically, there is a point beyond which the white-owned media will not venture. And for those black reporters whose ideology won't permit them to work for the general press, there must be a role in the black press.

By and large, the black press also leaves many blacks disenchanted. As Ernest Dunbar told me, "Black newspapers are subject to the same economic pressures from advertisers as are whites, and they can't pay reporters." Then there are the traditionally conservative publishers who, while sensing the need for change, have not found the tools to become more relevant. Now, however, advertising is opening up and a few top-quality magazines have shown that the $30 million Black Market can be tapped. This offers an unprecedented opportunity to remodel and renew the black press. . . .

I would like to see a group of bright, young black journalists acquire a fading black newspaper—anywhere—and dedicate it to tough, interpretative, in-depth reporting. If blessed with sophisticated techniques, it would be read. But the line need not be drawn at newspapers. Public TV also offers an opportunity for trained

> A black on-camera woman has to be not too black in looks, thought, and image.... She gets weaker material than other women. She's not to be taken seriously on camera or off.... Give other black women something to make them think they've arrived. Something they can associate with. How many black women associate with a Diahann Carroll, a Joan Murray, or any of the other black-white women? Women who, in a slightly darker way, exemplify all the virtues of white American womanhood and supposed beauty.
> —Sheila Smith Hobson

men and women to develop a top station and use it as a powerful instrument.

Ben H. Bagdikian, writing recently in the Washington *Post* about the black reporters who are now suing that newspaper, emphasized that remedying the disproportionately small share of blacks in institutional and social decision-making in American society will require an acceleration of hiring, promoting, and on-the-job training—not a new concept. He added:

> And there is no question that to this degree it diminishes the chances for the black's white counterpart. It is, in a sense, unfair to this generation of whites, the same kind of unfairness that was visited on young blacks for ten generations. But sooner or later someone is going to have to pay the moral dues of 300 years of a racial caste system that is destructive of the heart of this society. This is the generation that has been chosen to pay those dues. But let no one think that it is only whites who pay; the young blacks engaged in the struggle pay emotional costs that destroy some of them.

He is right. But one wonders how long white reporters of our generation or any other would stand idly by while blacks are given what has been narrowly construed as preferential treatment. Some black journalists like Yette who feel that the very survival of blacks is threatened in this technological age have given up on the white-owned press and feel the only hope is the black press. If he and the other top black journalists who concur are correct, then the Kerner Commission's forecast of a break between the two societies will become reality.

Now more than ever, it is imperative that publishers look hard at this problem in the broader light of social justice, and make hiring and promoting of blacks a top-priority objective. Only in this way can their perspective on writing the story of America in a crucial time of change be duly recorded, and, more important, their influence be more widely felt.

QUESTIONS FOR DISCUSSION

1 How can your local newspaper change its format in the presentation of what has traditionally been called "women's news"? Give specific examples.

2 What sexual roles or stereotypes do viewers see when watching assorted television programs (situation comedies, detective shows, westerns). How accurate are these portrayals? To what degree do you think people modify their behavior to conform to sexual stereotypes found in the media? Can you see examples of such conformity in your own attitudes and behavior?

3 What picture do the media present of the current women's movement, and how are its participants characterized? Do you feel this presentation is accurate and objective?

4 Does minority programming foster or retard the process of social or racial segregation? How?

5 What options for broadcast access might CATV provide for minority and counterculture segments of the population? How can minorities gain access to CATV systems?

PROJECTS

1 Conduct a survey on campus to determine student opinion on whether all groups are fairly represented in local and national media. Try to get a wide sampling of all groups on campus.

2 Research and identify the qualities and values attributed to people in articles from the mass distribution magazines of the first two or three decades of this century. Compare with a recent edition of **National Lampoon** or **Saturday Evening Post**.

SPORTS

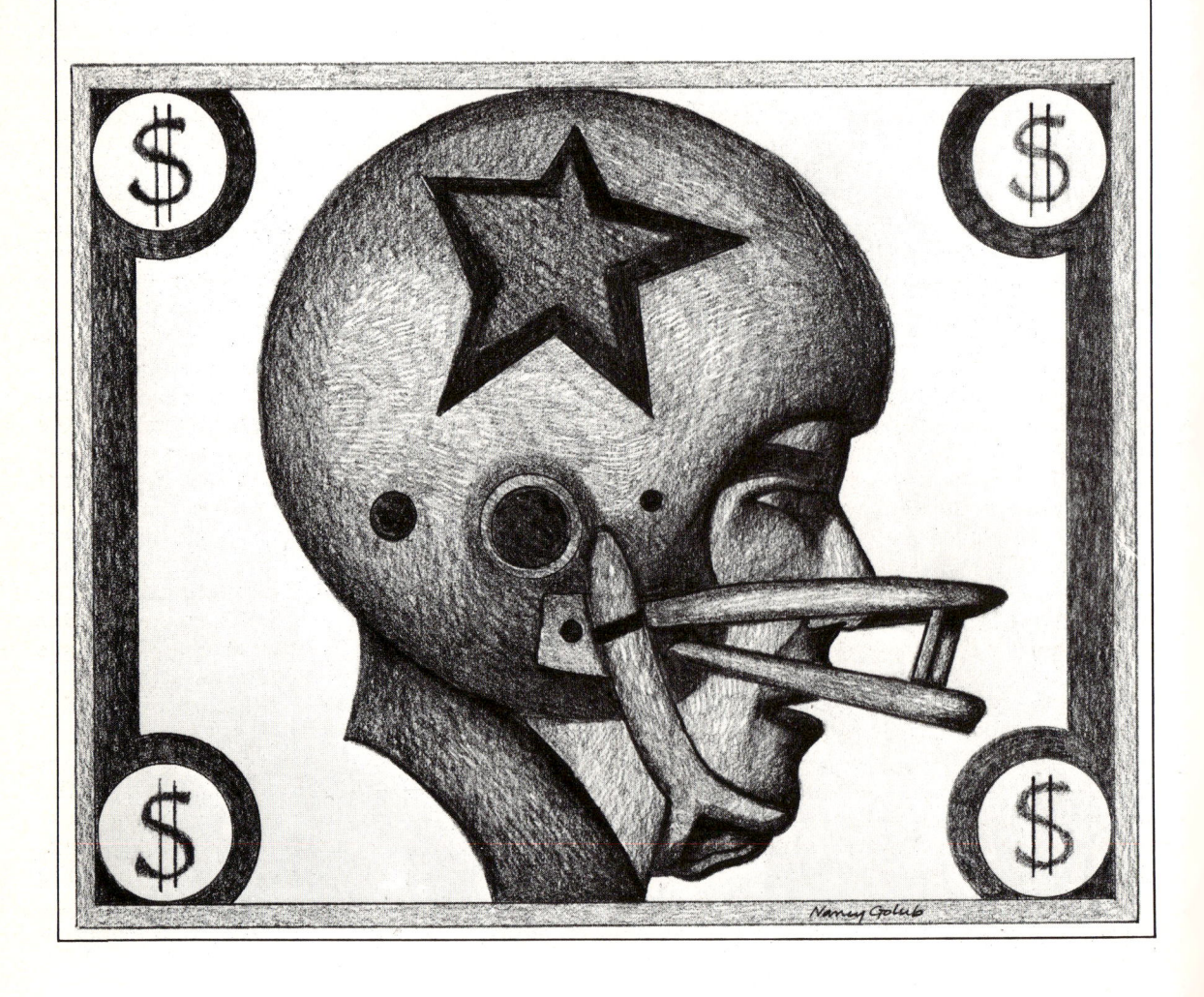

HOW TELEVISION HAS CHANGED SPORTS

WELLS TWOMBLY

Ultimately, the time will come when athletic events will be conducted on gigantic sound stages with studio audiences, who have waited months in order to get free tickets, the only people in attendance. They will be present in order to preserve the decaying myth that sports are for the common herd and not for the electric wowsers who would make life, death, war, starvation and blazing success nothing more than subjects for the wretched camera. There was still a nobility about athletic competition before they debased it, twisted it and reshaped it to meet their special needs. They had no reverence and they taught the rest of us to be irreverent. To our mortal shame, we went along.

It's bad enough that the better of the two professional basketball leagues has conceived a playoff system designed to take the game straight through the awesome heat of summer, straight into the baseball schedule, and right into the time when football teams are gathering their children about them. That is the dreadful sin, because there is no decent reason why the two divisional champions in each conference shouldn't get it over with in a best three-out-of-five series, with the winners to meet in a seven-game finale. Now that has class. Second place teams have no business existing after the schedule ends, but there they are. It is even worse in the National Hockey League, where pickup teams from Moose Jaw, Alberta, seem to qualify for the Stanley Cup festival, the Canadian answer to the eternal winter.

For reasons fair or foul, the Oakland Warriors, who have represented the cloud kingdom of Golden State nobly this season, made it all the way to the last match of their conference competition this year. As a means of punishment for the people who love them for better or worse, for

Reprinted by permission of Wells Twombly.

richer or poorer, the television network decided that their game with the Chicago Bulls be scheduled for six p.m., a time when all true-hearted Californians are locked bumper-to-bumper in holy warfare on the freeway. This means absolutely nothing to the space cadets at the Columbia Broadcasting System. They have this unshakable notion that the only viewers that count live east of the Hudson River. Everything else is Bridgeport, right, booby?

If the network executives are happy out there in Darien, sitting by their pools and sipping a no-vermouth martini at nine a.m., why should anyone around here complain because they either have to take the afternoon off or start for the basketball game at 2:30 p.m. Keeping New Yorkers happy is what the United States of America is all about. If the Canarsie Indians had had stricter immigration laws or better taste about who they sold real estate to, the rest of the nation would have fewer problems.

Television is a hateful instrument. It has tampered with the rules. It has toppled commissioners. It has asked sporting events to restructure themselves to fit the needs of the camera. It has done a million picky things to the point of asking one bowl team to kick off a second time because the first kickoff hadn't been shown because of technical difficulties.

The network crowd has openly offended the sensitivities of athletic purists. The sins are multitudinous. The Professional Golfers Association, seduced completely by big money, changed their marvelous tournaments from classic match play to medal play because it was better suited to television requirements. It may once have been a unique event. Now it's no different than the Shecky Greene Peoria Open. In the rustic years of National Basketball Association telecasts, the Los Angeles Lakers were forced to play a number of 10 a.m. games for the simple reason that they were the only team west of St. Louis and the networks never trusted the difference between time zones.

"This is stupid," said Fred Schaus, then the head coach. "I can't believe that we're doing this. Nobody's ready to go this time of the morning. If they tell me they have to take an official time out when the Lakers are going good, I'm going to refuse it. All they want to do is show an extra commercial. Basketball is a game of momentum. If they do what they want to do, it won't be basketball. That's for sure.

Soon afterwards, Schaus was told to keep his inner thoughts to himself. The network didn't want to hear such obvious heresy. They wanted the coach of the NBA club to praise the glory of the cathode ray tube. After meditation on the matter, good old Freddy recanted.

When they played the first honest-to-gosh Super Bowl in Los Angeles, the deadly serious Green Bay Packers kicked off once, unaware that the National Broadcasting Company was in the midst of spreading culture with an extremely expensive commercial. Word went down to the field that an instant replay was necessary. So Vince Lombardi, defender of the faith and absolute god of honest football, told his club to line up and do it again, this time for the folks out there in videoland.

"Television helps pay the bills," said Lombardi. 'We can't be stupid about this. Cooperating with television is vital. It's something we have to do. Not many franchises could survive on ticket sales alone. It's like everything else in life. . .you have to give something in order to get something."

This is the same Lombardi who considered football somewhat similar to going to church. He saw absolutely nothing sinful about passing the plate for the 16th time, which did not exactly make him unique. It was said that the late, lamented Abner Doubleday, the asserted inventor of baseball, would hurl thunderbolts from the top of Yankee Stadium if anyone trifled with anything so sanctified as the World Series. Charles O. Finley had been a voice crying in the wilderness for years. What he wanted was to play from weekend to weekend with three games on Tuesday, Wednesday and Thursday, which would be performed at night, thereby giving the entire nation a chance to see this great passage of arms.

"They didn't want any part of it," said Finley. "They thought I was absolutely nuts. Then the network adopted my idea and right away baseball said it was the greatest thing they ever head of. They never credited me with being part of it. Television, which pays the bills, snapped its fingers and everything fell into place."

The desire to get in professional sports is incredibly tense, mostly because the money is so

> Both baseball and football broadcasters are apparently frightened of candor and addicted to nice-Nelly happy talk for the simple reason that they're being paid, directly or indirectly, by the teams they broadcast for.
> —Richard L. Tobin

good. Major companies have enormous advertising budgets roughly 50 per cent of them devoted to television. It has been 25 years since a Dick Kazmaier could graduate from Princeton as the nation's best-known back and choose the Harvard Business School over the Chicago Bears even though he was a first-round draft choice. Television makes it possible for teams to make offers nobody can refuse. Every member of the NFL gets 1.7 million dollars from the networks. Baseball is now working on an equally interesting deal. It doesn't televise well, but it is making a cultural comeback.

"I don't think that there's any question that if it were not for television revenue, the average salary would be about $20,000 (it is close to about $35,0000 now) and we would be competing with industry for our best players," said Commissioner Pete Rozelle. "A good player would have to think hard whether he wanted to start with General Motors or Ford as a junior executive or be a starting half-back with the Cincinnati Bengals. It's just possible that we wouldn't be in business."

This is strictly show business, gang. Nothing more. It was suggested as early as 1948 by the late John Tunis, a writer whose imagination seemed powerful at the time, that the finest sporting events would not be held in stadiums. He envisioned the day when 100,000 people would watch the Yale-Harvard football game on a gigantic screen in the Yale Bowl, while the football game itself was played in a zeppelin hangar in Hollywood. It was supposed to be satire. Trouble is, it is perilously close to coming true.

THE SECRET REASONS WHY MEN WATCH FOOTBALL ON TV

A. M. WATKINS

Brace yourselves, girls. All those football games on TV during Christmas and New Year's are just a warm-up.

The really big show is scheduled for Sunday, January 17. On that day, over 60 million Americans are expected to watch the annual Super Bowl game from Miami. It could set an all-time record for people watching a single sports event on TV. It could also set an all-time record for the number of women infuriated over the loss of their men to TV football.

The TV football phenomenon has alienated more women than ever because of the introduction this past season of regular Monday evening games on TV. "It was a long, lost three-day weekend—one after the other," says one pert young blond. Her husband watched from Saturday afternoon through Monday evening with time out, it seemed, only for work during the day on Monday. Burned up, this woman hung a huge black funeral wreath over her front door, emblazoned with the sign: "Football Widow." Her husband mended his ways. He cut his football viewing down to one-and-a-half days per weekend.

Other wives lash out at their husbands for desertion; they damn the TV as an adulterous "other woman" who has stolen their man. Such women naturally are furious and feel rejected, but they often jump to the wrong conclusion, says Dr. Rebecca Liswood of Brooklyn N.Y., noted marital expert and a professor at Adelphi University.

"Women should realize that a man can get great pleasure from the game," Dr. Liswood says. Though he watches, "he can still love you dearly."

Reprinted from "The Secret Reasons Why Men Watch Football on TV" by A.M. Watkins in *Family Circle*, January, 1971.

However, football on TV clearly can be a subversive marital influence. Art Buchwald calls it "Divorce—TV Style."

To understand why men are gripped by TV football fever and what a woman can do about it, *Family Circle* assigned me to query the experts. Here are some of the underlying reasons that they cited:

The Daniel Boone Syndrome. This is probably the No. 1 reason. Dr. Konrad Lorenz, the internationally famed zoologist and author of the best-selling book *On Aggression*, points out that modern civilized man suffers from inadequate discharge of his basic aggressive drive. The typical man is tied to a desk job or other work that requires little expenditure of physical energy.

Yet, the very nature of manhood ordinarily requires that he chop wood, till the soil or do battle in hand-to-hand combat for his woman, and thereby release much of his natural masculine energy (also called "aggression"). It's also related to sexual energy; such innate male energy was easily discharged in the pioneering days of Daniel Boone, but it's no longer possible for most men.

Here is where an action sport like football provides an excellent vicarious outlet for a man's aggressive energy. And watching football enables a man to release such energy in a socially acceptable way.

The Dreams-of-Glory Syndrome. This, in a way, is a subcategory of the Daniel Boone syndrome. Most men must prove their manhood at one time or another. It's particularly important for a young man approaching maturity, says Dr. Bryant J. Cratty of the University of California, Los Angeles, who is also president of the North American Society for the Psychology of Sport and Physical Activity. Dr. Cratty explains that playing football has long served this need, notably for young men in high school and college. Later in life, watching it on television reinforces their masculinity and fulfills their dreams of glory.

The Good Guys Always Win. This third reason stems from the growing, sometimes almost unbearable, pressures of modern life.

Sports

There are crises upon crises—in Vietnam, the Middle East.... Your local school taxes take another jump, and then one of your kids gets into trouble. It can make a man feel terribly frustrated, particularly if he's already experienced a week full of problems at the office. Such travail, explains Dr. Ernest Dichter, president of the Institute for Motivational Research, New York, can be especially tough on a man when it seems that the bad guys always win and the good guys always lose.

That's usually not so with football, where skill, ability and hard work triumph. The rules are black and white and, if you break them, you're penalized. The good guys always win, or almost always. This can provide great solace and satisfaction for a man who has worked hard but is, nevertheless, thwarted and frustrated by depressing local and world events that are beyond his control. Among other things, football provides a healthy release for his frustrations, Dr. Dichter says.

The Male Drop-Out. This is the man who deliberately cops out (a psychologist says "withdraws") on his wife and family, abandoning them for his own fantasy world of football on TV. Sometimes he's a total TV addict, deserting all to watch TV virtually full-time. In effect, the male dropout is thumbing his nose at his wife. Watching football is often "an expression of annoyance or sheer contempt for her," says Dr. Tom McGinnis, New Jersey psychotherapist.

Such men may be unable to love or face up to a close, intimate relationship with a woman. Others are, of all things, sexually impotent. Still others are driven off by a wife who has not fulfilled her marital role, thus causing an angry male animal to seek grim solace from the tube.

To make matters worse, many wives cry foul—the usual words are, "If you really loved me, you wouldn't watch TV!" But a man is deaf to the plea because it's usually hurled at a very crucial time in the game. Some wives retaliate by withholding love (also called sex) from their husbands (which can really initiate marital war when no real grounds for warfare previously existed). And, of course, some women swallow their pride and hurt feelings and say nothing, but nonetheless they're steaming inside.

Clearly, none of these typical responses really helps much. What can a woman do to solve the problem?

First of all, if your man is hooked on TV football, take stock of your situation. Don't feel crushed and unloved. Try to understand the secret reason that applies to your man watching football on TV; then, here are some of the things you might do about it:

• Consider becoming a football fan yourself; i.e., "If you can't beat them, join them." Go wild and try it; you might even like football. Quite a few women do. Television surveys show that roughly one out of every three to four viewers is a woman.

• Try the smother-him-with-kindness approach. Plan your household schedule and family activities not to interfere with a big game. Go overboard and prepare beer and snacks for him while he's watching. This dab-of-honey approach can work wonders.

• Request equal time. A heart-to-heart talk may be necessary. One young wife said to her husband, "Okay, it's fine with me if you watch football. I'm glad you enjoy it. But the kids and I also want you once in a while." He complied, giving his family equal time.

• Do your own thing. Often a woman's problem is that, like her husband, she also feels hard-pressed all day and gets little or no fun and enjoyment to satisfy *her* emotional needs, according to Dr. Laura Jo Singer-Magdoff, president of the American Association of Marriage and Family Counselors. Women are solving this problem (sometimes as an antidote to a man's TV football mania) by taking up needlepoint, sculpturing, learning a foreign language or becoming active in community affairs or politics. "Funny thing," Dr. Singer-Magdoff adds, "the more a woman develops her own thing, the more interesting and appealing she often becomes to her husband."

THE SHAME OF THE SPORTS BEAT

BILL SURFACE

Last summer, Tom Fitzpatrick, whose objectivity helped cost him a sportswriting beat but subsequently won him a Pulitzer Prize as a general columnist for the Chicago *Sun-Times*, decided that the most interesting story of the day would be to accompany one of the paper's baseball writers, Jerome Holtzman, to the Chicago Cubs' game. It wasn't a routine day for Holtzman. He had, in some sports reporters' opinions, betrayed them by reporting precisely what they knew: that the same players who allowed themselves to be quoted as saying that Cubs manager Leo Durocher "has a way of inspiring you" were planting anonymous quotes that they "can't play for that man." Because of this, Holtzman had written:

> After two flops the Cubs are losing, worse than ever, the players are older, softer, better paid and worried about next year's contract.... Sorry kids, the so-called Cub heroes are not heroes at all—they're copout artists.

As a result, Fitzpatrick thought, all he needed to do to obtain some lively material would be to watch the reactions when Holtzman entered the Pink Poodle, a room where sportswriters gather before each game for news and complimentary meals. "Look, Holtzman was an out-and-out defector," Fitzpatrick said. "He had broken all the rules in the baseball writer's book of protocol. He had written what he actually thought and heard. He had contradicted the thinking of the town's eminent sports authorities and leading freeloaders. Sportswriters do not like a colleague who won't play the game and who won't go along with the pack."

As Fitzpatrick described it, Holtzman was greeted warmly by a supervisor of ushers: "That was great, Jerry, just great." The reception in the Pink Poodle was considerably cooler—perfunctory handshakes and such comments as, "Here comes Knute Rockne." ... "Hey, Jerry, are the Cubs going to vote you a full share when you win the pennant." ... "The players and everybody are still talking about it." After that day's game, Fitzpatrick reported, Holtzman walked away from the pressbox whistling "a tune sung earlier by his colleagues ... a parody of a new pop hit ... *Jerry Holtzman, Superstar.*"

The reaction to Holtzman's reporting, though comparatively mild by the standards of investigative reporting, underscores the compromised journalism being offered by all too many sports departments of newspapers and radio-TV stations. Frequently having little relationship to the standards maintained by other departments of a newspaper or broadcasting company, sports reporting has generally become so partial and so predictable that, on many occasions, it resembles more the work of a master of ceremonies than that of a journalist. It is debatable that such reporting satisfies even the sports buff who, no doubt, would welcome revelations about the often-gritty ways a game is played. Instead, he tends to receive a standardized recapitulation of an event, statistics, and either the coaches' praises or complaints.

Except in a few newspapers publishing both a full business section and complete stock market tables, the space routinely allotted to sports is by far the largest in any department of the American newspaper. Television has doubled its coverage of sports events since 1960, and continues to allocate increasing time to them. The three major networks already are committed to televising nearly 1,000 hours of sports in 1972. Largely because of the media's exposure, sports now affect the ambitions of children, the recreational habits of adults, and, sometimes, local governmental priorities. Because obtaining a new team or stadium often arouses civic pride, moreover, fortunes are made by entrepreneurs and elections won by politicians who arrange the transfer of a professional sports franchise or passage of a bond issue for a new stadium.

Reprinted from "The Shame of the Sports Beat" by Bill Surface in *Columbia Journalism Review*, February 1972. Used by permission of the author and Columbia Journalism Review.

Instead of presenting the pros and cons of these trends, however, sports reporters frequently advance an idolizing theme. For every thoughtful report that appears in the sports pages of the *New York Times, Los Angeles Times, Washington Post Newsday*, and a few other papers, innumerable dailies maintain a tone that the *Indianapolis News* unabashedly trumpets. When the Indiana Pacers play a basketball game at home, the *News* uses a masthead containing the line: "Go Pacers Go!"

The fawning over some sports events exceeds even the boldest promoter's claims. A striking example is the Super Bowl game played each January to decide the championship of professional football. When the game was originated in 1967, the National Football League officially named it—on tickets, programs, and trophies —the World Championship of Professional Football. From the first announcement of the game, though, several sports reporters said it was so important that it should be called the "super bowl." Within a few days "super bowl" was used in reports by, among others, NBC, CBS, the *New York Times, Los Angeles Times, Chicago Tribune, Cleveland Press*, Associated Press, and United Press International. A couple of years later Pete Rozelle, pro football's commissioner, announced that although he had been reluctant to call the game "super bowl" lest it sound corny, henceforth so it would be known.

Some commentary is so simplistic that it strains credulity. In his column for the *New York Daily News*, for example, Gene Ward was extolling the glories of artificial turf in stadiums about the time a study released by a professor at the University of Washington indicated that the rate of serious injuries was likely to be fifty percent higher on hard artificial turf than on natural grass. The National Football League Players Association, citing the high number of disabling injuries on artificial turf, demanded that professional teams stop installing synthetic surfaces until their safety could be determined. The Miami Dolphins reported that players had slipped on the slick, discolored turf in Miami's Orange Bowl 114 times in just two games, and the New England Patriots protested that they found the field "unplayable." Moreover, a House Commerce subcommittee investigating the possible hazards of artificial turf had already heard conflicting reports by two manufacturers about prior safety claims. Still, Ward wrote:

> It was obvious that labeling synthetic turf as more dangerous than natural grass is a fallacy. ... The size of the score against the Patriots would appear to negate the logic of their protest. I have to wonder why it is that colleges, which have put in far more synthetic gridirons than pros, haven't joined the protest march. ... Georgia Tech authorities loved their new $309,999 Astroturf carpet. ... I was in Florida over the weekend for Army's Friday night match with Miami on the Orange Bowl's Polyturf and didn't hear a murmur of complaint from either team. It was a thrill-packed tussle, too.

Except for public disagreements about players' salaries and contracts—a seasonal staple on sports pages—it is hard to find really incisive reporting about the increasingly troubled business side of sports. General reporters, whom sportswriters often call "hatchet men," experience little difficulty in identifying many such problems. The *Wall Street Journal*, for example, noticed that some team owners who are customarily identified as "sportsmen" have engaged in payoffs to or business arrangements with members of organized crime. *Sports Illustrated* has repeatedly found that some teams are torn by insubordination, drugs, or racial conflicts. *Life* reported that some professional athletes have associated with prominent gamblers or been wrongly blacklisted by some owners. *Psychology Today* has offered a thesis contradicting one advanced by many sportswriters: Successful athletes tend to have a "low need to take care of others" and are not "builders of character." Magazines as diverse as *Esquire, Reader's Digest, TV Guide,* and *Newsweek* have shown that professional football heightens its appeal with sanctioned violence that often is concentrated on maiming the quarterback.

And the type of investigative reporting done by the *Philadelphia Evening Bulletin* (it published details of a secret contract used by the American Basketball Association to illegally sign an All-American player at Villanova University) remains as rare as baseball's no-hit games. If the subject has damaging overtones for the home team, even critical reporting tends to be so tolerant that a few sportswriters have built reputations among their colleagues as *hard-hitting* by taking firm positions on transitory issues—whether an umpire should have decided a baseball was fair or foul or whether an aging quarterback on a distant team can throw as far as he once did.

Once a glamorized team owner is declared bankrupt or an athlete is arrested, publicly implicated in a scandal, or seriously injured, newspaper sports departments will cover it. Yet even then there is a noticeable lack of followup. Many sportswriters imply that they really don't understand the business aspects of sports or that they don't even want wire-service copy on the subject in their sections. From their conversations, it appears that many share the opinion expressed in a sports column by the *Chicago Sun-Times'* Bill Gleason:

> Will the Supreme Court please sit down and do something about the [baseball] reserve clause? Quickly? Abolish it ... sustain it ... but get it off the sports pages of the nation. ... I am sick of reading about the reserve clause, about pension plans and bankruptcy proceedings. Let's have a ruling ... so we can get back to reading about the games professional athletes play.

Some sportswriters similarly dislike reading what disenchanted athletes say about how games are played—a muckraking book under a former athlete's byline is attributed to a "social leper" or a "man who hates sports." A case in point is the recent *They Call It a Game*, by Bernie Parrish, a former Cleveland Browns' defensive back who admittedly hopes to drive several prominent men from professional football for allegedly blacklisting him. Though the book is intemperate and sometimes inclined to innuendo, it offers enough facts about debatable labor practices, untidy associations of some owners, and apparent laxity on gambling to have received a favorable review in *Life* and a balanced column by Robert Lipsyte in the *New York Times*, and to have been the basis for a lengthy federal grand jury investigation of pro football's alleged violations of anti-trust laws. Instead of attempting to disprove Parrish's most serious charges, most sportswriters who mentioned the book emphasized themes such as the "possibility of a libel suit against Parrish," or, as one put it, that he was looking for "a seasick remedy.... I'm going to be ill."

Because of the way U.S. sports are usually reported, clubowners have far more control over what material reaches some sports desks than editors might realize. Often reporting on one team or sport throughout his career, a sportswriter generally must function in an atmosphere that seems more clubby than businesslike. If a sportswriter covers a major college football team, he knows that a standing ritual is the small press party at which other journalists and announcers socialize with the teams' publicists, coaches, and athletic director. When a reporter covers one of the twenty-four major league baseball teams, he is given the team's card admitting him to private lounges in stadiums, such as the Cleveland Indians' Wigwam or the San Francisco Giants' Curley Grieve Room (named for a late sportswriter), there to sit with other writers and team executives as he hears information that the club wishes to reveal and enjoys complimentary liquor and/or dinner. The food is often viewed as a prerogative, though reporters usually can charge their papers $10 to $15 a day for food while traveling.

If a sportswriter avoids the free meals, he still can find it extremely difficult to socialize repeatedly with a team and then be the only journalist to report its faults or present a true characterization of a tough-talking coach. The writer is in an even more uncomfortable position if he has maintained a friendship with players and, even just occasionally, faces the alternative of reporting or ignoring a negative fact. C. C. Johnson Spink, publisher of the *Sporting News*, the weekly trade paper, attributes major objectivity problems in part to these friendly relationships.

"Here we have sportswriters who take their wives and children to spring training with the team," he says. "He and his family socialize with the players' families. He goes out to movies, breakfast, or to and from the game with the players. Many reporters' wives are in social events with players' wives. What you have is a big, happy family. Of course you don't read that the player ever drinks, curses, or misses practice. One St. Louis Cardinal before he was traded was nothing but trouble all year long. But it wasn't reported. Nobody wanted to rock the boat. A reporter should avoid this situation because I suspect that anyone involved in this type of friendship would find it difficult to blast people who deserve blasting."

Feeling like part of a team, unwilling to annoy friends on it, can lead to an enjoyable life. When reporters become "house men"—the name their colleagues use for writers who always support a team's management—they plainly enjoy status. They are recognized on sight by the league commissioner and asked by a team's owner or leading executive if they need an interview with a prominent athlete or a couple more tickets for friends—even when influential men complain that they cannot buy tickets. A club's publicity director feels free to ask the sportswriter to dramatize a rivalry to stimulate sale of tickets for a meaningless exhibition game or to write that tickets are available for a limited time—without disclosing the poor location of the seats. "I used to be a pro football publicity man and it was surprising how easy it was to have someone slip something into the paper or on the air," says John Steadman, sports editor of the *Baltimore News American*.

Aware that readers are frequently deceived by sports teams, Steadman has infuriated the Baltimore Colts by providing loyal fans a forum to protest the requirement that they buy three tickets to meaningless exhibition games in order to qualify for tickets to regular-season football games. (The result: though they were pro football's champions, the Colts had the league's lowest attendance for their exhibition games in 1971.) "Sure I've been intimidated for taking a stand against this unethical practice," Steadman admits. "But it would be against every principle a reporter is taught if he let his readers be exploited by the usual pol-parrot talk on tickets for practice games." A few other sports editors have begun to show more caution about tickets. *The New York Times* sports department, for example, not only mentions sometimes whether available tickets are on an arena's second or third level; it also has published an in-depth article on how scalpers control quantities of tickets to popular games.

Sportswriters can be ingratiated in various ways. So far, no paper has been found which refuses to allow its staff sportswriters to be selected by professional leagues to write either an "authorized" history of their sport or contribute chapters to the coffeetable books that they produce, and only San Francisco, Oakland, and Milwaukee are known to have papers which prohibit service as official scorers (for a fee of $35 a game) in major-league baseball—which plays a minimum of 1,944 games a season. Some colleges and professional teams also pay loyal reporters what is called the "fast fifty" (but sometimes is $100) to superficially revise a story into a one-page feature for their programs. Professional teams hire sportswriters who cover their games to write or edit their annual yearbooks. Some men who promote college basketball doubleheaders pay $25 to a reporter to act as "official scorer" even though the opposing teams have their own scorers.

For many sportswriters, columnists, and sports editors, there are regular allotments of tickets; and, for some, periodic checks from a team, race-track, or college athletic department for being a "consultant." During the Christmas season, it is common for promoters to affirm their appreciation by sending faithful reporters, columnists, and sports editors the usual radios or electric razors, hams or liquor, $100 or $250 gift certificates. Some such gifts are returned or refused by sportswriters, but others express concern over their lack of status when left off a Christmas list.

With so many reporters wanting to accommodate friendly owners, teams have been protected from negative news for so long that even slight criticism brings violent reactions. Sportswriters who irritate club officials have been harassed in such petty ways as being excluded from an owner's weekly cocktail party or told that they cannot leave their typewriters in the pressroom along with those of other reporters. Or a publicity man may make only a feeble attempt to call an uncooperative sports reporter for a press conference. Retaliation comes fastest from teams which have enjoyed virtual immunity from local criticism. Aware of Chicago Bears owner George Halas' influence with certain journalists, sports copy editors for one Chicago newspaper used to jest after taking phone calls that Halas had just requested that a headline over a story be increased to four columns in the next edition.

As bland as many sports pages seem, however, they scarcely approach the partiality that is generally called *play by play* sportscasting in radio and TV. Since removing its ban on radio broadcasts in 1939, major league baseball has increasingly controlled broadcasts and telecasts of its games, to the point that it now has a prerogative comparable to the Democrats and Republicans being able to hire all announcers for their national conventions and ensuing election campaigns. With no apologies, baseball clubs (and subsequently football, basketball, and hockey teams) either hire or maintain absolute approval over hiring of the men who describe their games on a local or regional basis. Such broadcasts aren't being permitted as a public service; beer, automobile, gasoline, and other commercials during the broadcasts bring each of the twenty-four major league baseball teams an average of $1 million a season.

Leaving little margin for the sportscaster to err, an executive of every club monitors telecasts and, in most instances, furnishes explicit instructions that go so far as to forbid cameramen from following foul balls into empty parts of a stadium and thereby reveal sparse attendance. In his regular briefing the next day, an announcer frequently receives orders from the public relations director on how he can improve the team's image.

Except for injuries (which foster a theme of tough luck), even negative news that may creep into a sports page is scarcely, if ever, mentioned. Cameras which are quickly aimed at the heroic reception for someone hitting a home run are automatically pointed away from fights in the stadium, a player's tantrums, or a manager showing disgust when a player has obviously loafed. Even when the sound of the crowd indicates that an incident is being censored from a telecast, most clubs righteously refuse to show it.

Accounts of the home team's performance are so unabashedly favorable that, in many cities, it seems possible to offend a sports announcer by accusing him of being objective. Jack Brickhouse, a big, friendly man who has announced sports events on Chicago's WGN for twenty-three years, typically punctuates his TV descriptions of Chicago Cubs games with "Atta boy Ernie!" or, when a Cub hits a home run, an exuberant "Hey! Hey!" When fans stop him along Chicago's Michigan Avenue to ask "How are we [the Cubs] gonna do?", the "we" can be taken literally: Brickhouse is a member of the Cubs' board of directors.

Meanwhile, across town, the Chicago White Sox management, reasoning that the solution to their declining attendance not only rested upon a hustling new manager for the 1971 season but also a hustling new announcer, hired as their radio announcer Harry Caray. A knowledgeable veteran from St. Louis, Caray promised to "talk a million people into the park by painting an exciting picture—a feeling among people that they're in the park." Caray had a personal reason to feel excited as the White Sox's attendance doubled during the first season that he broadcast their games: "I got a base salary from the White Sox," he told *CJR*, "but on top of this, I got a $10,000 bonus from them for every 100,000 in attendance over 600,000. We drew 841,000 people so I got two bonuses [$20,000] and just missed a third."

Caray's style, while by no means critical, does differ somewhat from others in that he will admit that a White Sox has struck out four times in a game. "I don't have any designed criticism, and I want the White Sox to win," he says. But you can't talk so favorably about everything *all* the time that you sound intimidated by the owner. If the fans don't believe what you say about the action, they won't believe your commercials—then you can't sell sponsors. It's unfortunate that some men go way too far in protecting their teams."

At the network level, media participation in sports events being "reported" can be even more blatant. During professional football games, for instance, broadcasters have sideline stage managers to stop games at various points in order to present a minimum of sixteen commercials during each game. In pro football's Super Bowl, a referee was told that a commercial was being telecast when the Green Bay Packers kicked off to the Kansas City Chiefs and that, consequently, the Packers would have to repeat the

Sports 165

kickoff. They did. Directors have also asked, through the sideline managers, a football player to grimace to show that he is in pain or, as an NBC director recommended, to "have a doctor lift [a player's] left shoulder so that his face will show. Does he need some oxygen?"

Militant former football players such as Bernie Parrish claim that the National Football League can have any announcer removed from telecasts of its games. While announcers vigorously deny this assertion, it seems obvious that they provide no visible reason for a league commissioner—or most players—to even be piqued. In the 1971 Super Bowl, for example, the Baltimore Colts and Dallas Cowboys made so many major errors (eleven) that the *Sporting News*, a weekly trade paper, was moved to call it "a comedy of errors" and *Sports Illustrated* to view it as the "Blunder Bowl" that was won "by default, not design." NBC's Curt Gowdy, however, his voice rising for emphasis during the play-by-play telecast, called it "one of the greatest games I've ever seen."

Such superlatives are used so often that it seems fans have been conditioned to expect them. When asked if anyone complained about sports announcers, William Ray, chief of the Federal Communications Commission's Complaints and Compliance Division, said: "We don't get any complaints about this at all—that's the catch. We act on specific complaints. But we don't have the resources to monitor games. We don't examine contracts and don't know if professional football has a veto over who announces the Super Bowl. We do know, though, that the problem of sports announcers on club payrolls—or subject to the veto of clubs and being paid cheerleaders—has been going on for thirty years. Even back when Judge Landis was the baseball commissioner, he threw an announcer off a national World Series broadcast because he had criticized an umpire.

"While the current situation generally doesn't violate any rules, it does raise two questions: 1) Are the stations disclosing who's paying certain people? 2) Are station licensees abdicating their responsibility to review and see that program material isn't false or misleading? We know there are a lot of problems in sports broadcasting and have started a file on it. We plan to take it up with the Commission. But we've just been preoccupied with issues like cable TV and the Fairness Doctrine."

If answerable to a station instead of a team, announcers seem likely to offer a far greater ratio of negative news than otherwise. Perhaps the clearest example is *Sports Huddle*, a weekly discussion program on station WEEI in Boston whose participants visualize themselves as sports ombudsmen. They may be guilty of pranks such as calling the Two O'Clock Club in Baltimore to ask—on a not-unfounded assumption—whether some of the Boston Red Sox are present. But they venture so often into such basic questions as why certain sports arenas continue to deteriorate while ticket prices continue to rise that, they say, clubowners have threatened to sue them. Weston Adams, president of the Boston Bruins, has publicly denounced the sportscasters because, he explains, "They were becoming extremely personal and I don't feel that has any place in anyone's broadcasting."

The reason for the unusual brashness? The program is conducted on a parttime basis by three men (Ed Andelman, Mark Whitkin, and Jim McCarthy) who have jobs outside of sports. Much as they profess to like sports, the three men have declined feelers about becoming full-time sports announcers on the premise that, once they begin fraternizing with the team, they would no longer be genuine sports *reporters*.

There are indications from some sportscasters that, even should they want to practice more journalism and less salesmanship, the system inhibits it. Perhaps the most memorable example occurred during the last week of the 1966 baseball season when Red Barber, whose tempered criticism distinguished him from most baseball announcers, was told by a New York Yankees executive that he could not report that only 413 fans were sitting in a stadium that accommodates nearly 70,000. His pride wounded, Barber went on to comment that "whatever" the attendance is, "it is the smallest crowd in the history of Yankee Stadium." Barber ventured the comment, he explained in his recent book *The Broadcasters*, because he was convinced that New York's morning papers would cover the game "with pictures of the yawning emptiness of Yankee Stadium." It may be a coincidence, as the Yankees management contends, but four days later they told Barber that he would not broadcast any more Yankee games.

Though neither the Yankees nor any other team can escape responsibility for such firings, controlled broadcasts reflect even more on the stations which tolerate them. When arranging terms of a broadcast, it seems obvious, a station or network should consider whether the rating or income it will receive is worth the price of its journalistic independence. As ABC Sports president Roone Arledge, who advocates an all-network agreement on ground rules for purchase of sports events, recently told Melvin Durslag of *TV Guide* [Nov. 27, 1971]:

Once a promoter gets paid he should have nothing else to say about the selection of announcers, the tone of the telecast, or the comment offered by those on the air. The news departments of the three networks will not tolerate interference in their everyday coverage. If NASA were to tell them, for instance, that they would be accredited to cover a space shot only if they promised to say nothing critical, and if NASA had announcer approval, the networks would scream "censorship." Why must such practices be permitted in sports?

In the print media, veteran journalists take some comfort in the fact that sports departments, for all their faults, are generally more objective today than ever before. During the Babe Ruth and Ty Cobb eras, baseball clubs openly paid travel expenses of most reporters who covered them. (But such reporting was frequently balanced by individualistic columnists who did not travel with a team.) James Roach, a veteran of forty-one years in sports department —the last fourteen years as sports editor of the *New York Times*—believes the situation unquestionably has improved, and that more papers are attempting to enforce a new policy:

"*One*—you assign intelligent men to cover teams in a square-shot way. Then you edit the copy—or gently chide the reporter—if he gives you the obvious hometown rah-rah. *Two*—we have a good rule at the *Times* about travel expenses. If an event is worth going to, it's worth paying for. Of course, this eliminates the press junket that gives a sportswriter a holiday and the chance to write about a horse race that needs publicity. You have to pass up that hotel's trip to Florida this winter to do a column about those big fish that are really biting. You don't take the free ride to a winter resort to cover a new golf tournament that's supposed to be loaded with celebrities. You stick to this rule even though the trips get more enticing each year. I just turned down an expense-paid trip to Tahiti to cover a waterskiing championship."

Publisher, editor, and sportswriter associations, however, have been slow to involve themselves in such issues, even to promulgation of ethics codes specifically applying to the sports beat. Baseball and football writers associations concentrate on matters such as who should be permitted into a pressbox, or whether radio-TV reporters should be allowed into postgame interviews or have access to now-prohibited areas. And the National Collegiate Athletic Association has not been known to reprimand a university athletic department for paying, in various ways, newspapermen for perpetuating the favorable image that can assist in recruitment of star athletes.

Where broad reforms have occurred they usually have originated outside the sports department. When the Louisville *Courier-Journal* and *Times* consolidated their sports departments, for example, the merged department was placed under supervision of a new executive sports editor, Earl Cox, who had not covered many of the area's popular sports teams. Then, in a departure from tradition, the papers' sportswriters were prohibited from accepting the usual free whiskey or blocs of tickets. Moreover, reporters have seldom been allowed to cover one team so consistently that they feel like integral parts of it.

"We quickly found that we got more realistic journalism and less pulling for the home team by rotating staff writers on different teams," Cox says. "Even then, you have to be prepared to rotate anytime a reporter walks around insisting that *we're* really going to clobber 'em tomorrow night."

The *Sporting News'* C. C. Johnson Spink agrees that, wherever possible, periodic reassignment of reporters should be tried to foster objectivity. "A sports editor or the managing editor of a big daily paper should see that his sports reporters are as businesslike as a good cop on a beat," he says. "You'll hear a reporter maintain that he can't get personality material on players unless he is well acquainted with them. Good cops and good reporters have a pretty fair record of getting information from people they've never met before. And the ball clubs need publicity; they're not going to boycott the reporters for very long. Also, while I feel the majority of reporters are *not* on teams' payrolls, I believe that the paper's management should inquire into—and draw the line against—sportswriters who are paid by clubs for such jobs as editing or keeping statistics. Working for a team you cover is a conflict of interest."

Such changes clearly would help. Meantime, though, the general situation might best be typified by sportscaster Bob Prince's happy reports about the Pittsburgh Pirates: "*We* had 'em all the way."

> The number of radio and television hours devoted to major league baseball is staggering. By the time the sport's 850 radio stations and 215 television outlets finish broadcasting at the end of this season, more than 430,000 hours of air time will have been filled. If a person were to take in all the games that will be broadcast, he would have to spend every minute of every day for the next 48 years listening or watching.

QUESTIONS FOR DISCUSSION

1. How has television altered the way amateur and professional sports are played?

2. Should team management have the option to select the sportscasters who announce their games? What should be the relationship between the sportscaster and the team?

3. What are the relative advantages of print coverage of sports events over live broadcasts? Of broadcasts over print?

PROJECTS

1. Tape record the pregame warm-up programs on three major sports events. Analyze the comments and interviews, including the following points:
   (a) attitudes toward the "win-at-any-cost" ethic
   (b) reporter bias toward home teams
   (c) any additional valid information that may have been provided as a result of the warm-up?

2. Analyze the coverage of a specific local sports event by the local media. Do you find any biases for or against local teams? If so, give specific examples. If a particular writer or commentator seems relatively free from such bias, can you explain how such objectivity is maintained?

MEDIA CONTENT PROJECT

1. As a class project, monitor and log the following types of television programs:
   children's programs
   adventure programs
   situation comedies
   adult dramas

   Determine the following: (a) the percentage and number of advertising messages per half hour, (b) the number of violent episodes per half hour, (c) the number per half hour of leading figures by sex difference, (d) number per half hour of support figures by sex difference, (e) number per half hour of leading figures by racial difference, (f) number per half hour of support persons by racial difference. What conclusions can you draw based on the data you gathered?

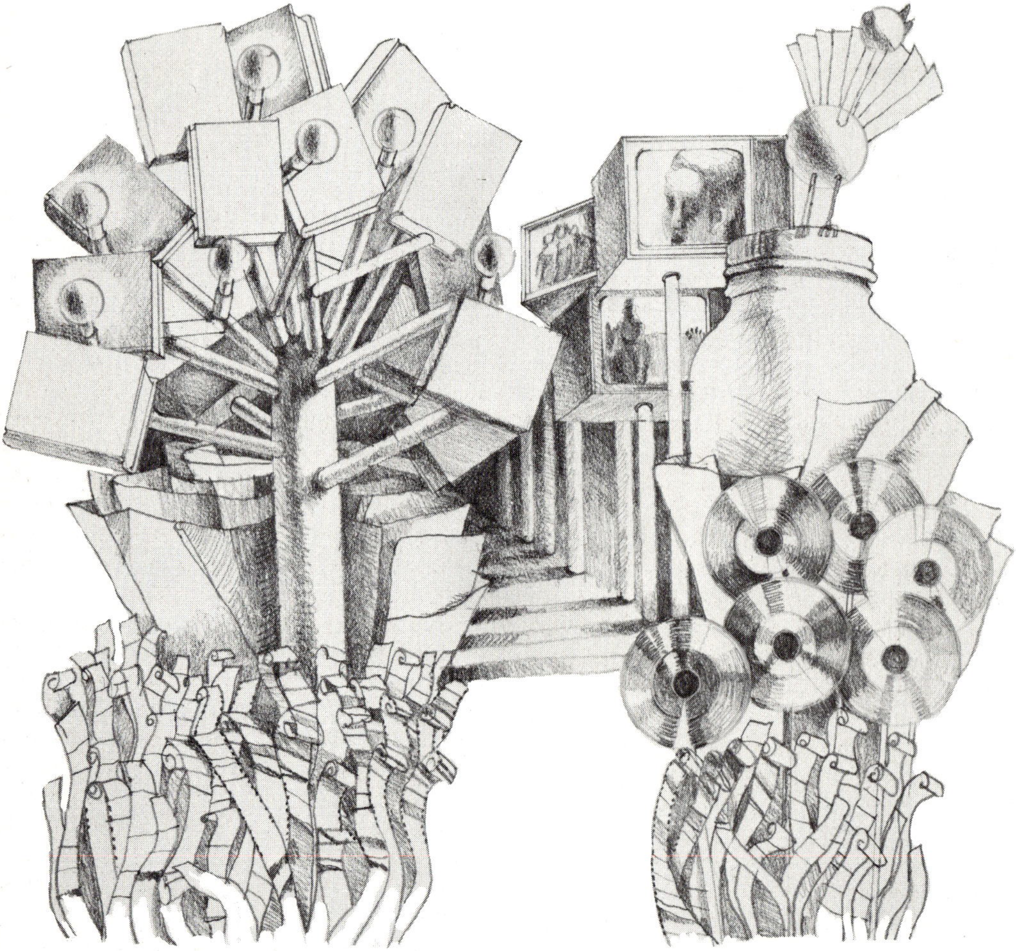

MEDIA ENVIRONMENTS

Media content resides in institutionalized environments. If we are to survive in a complex, ever-changing, media-based world, we must be aware of those environments and how they affect our lives.

The observation that media is an invisible environment loses its validity when the individual learns to use and interpret media at levels beyond the surface. Learning to recognize media forms and content in relation to greater society stimulates new perceptions of the nature of media and clarifies the reasons why some of the most powerful sectors of society have expressed concern about the media. To understand why the major media are adjuncts to virtually every concentration of wealth and power in the nation, one must comprehend the extent to which major media often determine the models of behavior that people ascribe to and emulate. It should then come as no surprise that the effort to force media to do the bidding of this or that power bloc is ongoing, nor that serious observers of society continually petition major media to alter their content to become more beneficial to the common good.

Politics, economics, and education have been substantially altered by the emergence and continuing development of electronic technology. That technology, no matter how sophisticated, cannot by itself alter the institutions to which it is applied. Many of our institutions whose foundations were established during the agricultural and industrial periods of our history are now attempting to function in an electronic age. The electronic information environment is very much with us today.

Can a reporter fairly serve the public good if he or she is forced to divulge the source of confidential information? Should the press's responsibility to inform the people have priority over the government's need to keep certain information confidential? Do the media barons have a right to manipulate our minds in a way that best serves a mercantile business community? These crucial inquiries and debates are ongoing in relation to today's media environments.

Another significant controversy involves the potential threat to privacy of our new media technology weighed against the American public's right to know. The success we have in solving such problems will be determined largely by our awareness of the possible solutions. This section is intended to help you, as a student of media, better recognize the social environments in which the mass media function.

Politics, Censors, and the Media

Nancy Golub

Power Struggle: President Versus Press

THEODORE H. WHITE

The major, institutional power blocs in our society are brought into focus in this unique analysis by Theodore White. The conflict point is the Nixon presidency, but the forces have been generating since the turn of the century. This article from **The Making of the President, 1972,** *pre-dates Watergate which became an explosive climax point in this ongoing power struggle.*

What lay at issue in 1972 between Richard Nixon, on the one hand, and the adversary press and media of America, on the other, was simple: it was power.

The power of the press in America is a primordial one. It sets the agenda of public discussion; and this sweeping political power is unrestrained by any law. It determines what people will talk and think about—an authority that in other nations is reserved for tyrants, priests, parties and mandarins.

No major act of the American Congress, no foreign adventure, no act of diplomacy, no great social reform can succeed in the United States unless the press prepares the public mind. And when the press seizes a great issue to thrust onto the agenda of talk, it moves action on its own—the cause of the environment, the cause of civil rights, the liquidation of the war in Vietnam, and, as climax, the Watergate affair were all set on the agenda, in first instance, by the press.

In a fundamental sense, today more than ever, the press challenges the Executive President, who, traditionally, believes his is the right to set the agenda of the nation's action. Power, said Karl Marx over a century ago, is control over the

---

Excerpted from *The Making of the President*, 1972 by Theodore H. White. Copyright © 1973 by Theodore H. White. Reprinted by permission of Atheneum Publishers and the author.

means of production; that phrase, said Arthur Schlesinger, Jr., recently, should be changed—power in America today is control of the means of communication.

And it was for this control that Richard Nixon warred with his enemies of the press all through the election year, and beyond.

One could best explain the nature of this struggle in 1972 by making an imaginary diagram of the American power structure at the turn of the century and comparing it to the American power structure as the post-war world came to its end.

In 1900, as William McKinley prepared for his second term, the American power structure could be described in pure Leninese. At the pinnacle of power was Wall Street—finance. Wall Street centralized American national action—it decided where mines would be opened, railways built, what immigrant labor should be imported, what technology developed. Wall Street set the agenda of national action without discussion. At a second level was the Congress of the United States—doing the will of the great financiers, enacting the necessary laws, repelling the raiders of prairie discontent. On a third level was the series of largely undistinguished men who until 1900 had held the figurehead office of President of the United States for thirty years; their chief power, beyond the expression of patriotic piety, was to deploy a minuscule professional army and navy against Indians and Spaniards. The American clergy exercised some moral power, best expressed in such issues of national political importance as temperance. Behind came all the other power ingredients—a decorative Supreme Court, the early labor unions, the corrupt big-city machines, the universities. Then the proprietary press—for the press was then a proprietorship, something owned by businessmen for making money.

By 1972 the power structure had entirely changed. The most important fall from power had happened to finance; businessmen might get fat, as they still did in 1972, by wheedling subsidies from national or state governments, but they were now a lobby that came hat-in-hand before a legislature and executive to whom once they had dictated. Labor, big labor, had risen to almost equal political power. The clergy had declined in power even more than big business. Congress, too, was a major loser in the

Politics, Censors, and the Media 173

power game—seventy years of domination by vigorous, aggressive Presidents had reduced its self-respect and, even more critically, the respect of the public. The Supreme Court had reached a peak of control over the national agenda in the 1960's; but its power was beginning to fade again as the seventies began. Universities were among the big gainers in the power hierarchy—universities now surpassed big business and big labor as centers of American innovation. But the two greatest gainers in the reorganized power structure were the Executive President and his adversary press, or, as one should more properly phrase it in modern America, the "press-television complex."

Both tried to operate under what they considered traditional rules, but American life had made that impossible.

What made it impossible was a number of things. The classical word-on-paper press was being concentrated into fewer and fewer hands, into news-gathering oligopolies.* Joining the word-on-paper press had come the infinitely more potent, even more concentrated power of the national television networks. And in both another change, more subtle but vital, was going on: a new appreciation by journalists themselves of their own role, their own responsibility, their own dignity. Once they had been hirelings of their proprietors, employed to articulate or consolidate opinion or, at the very most, to entertain the masses with their reporting. At some point in the 1960's, however, they had begun to see themselves as creators of news—not the recorders, but the shapers, of events, with a self-constituted responsibility to history. The great men of this new journalism might, at a bar with their friends, nostalgically insist that they were reporters like the rest of the fellows; they might show their tattered press cards, reminisce about police stations they had covered from Paris to Kansas City, or recall the idiosyncrasies of the men they had worked for, from Roy Howard to old Hearst to Harry Luce. But they were not reporters any longer. In television, men like Cronkite, Sevareid, Chancellor, Smith had, and recognized, no responsibility to any boss or institution—duty bound them technically only to their deadlines, and conscience to their self-constituted responsibility to the American people. So, too, the senior national reporters were still left free to describe the world as they saw it in the word-on-paper press. Concentration of press outlets made those journalists who still enjoyed a free outlet ever more powerful, and in their own eyes ever more responsible for values. The texture of their reporting had changed, too. Before World War II, the natural progression of a reporter's career had taken him from the sports shack to the political clubhouse; sportswriters had a flair for vivid copy and personalities, and such great artists as Heywood Broun and, later, James Reston were models for many others. Journalists who reached the summit of their profession after the war were, however, immensely more educated men than their predecessors, far more at home in the university seminar than at the police line-up or the football locker room. Their learning and their moralities made them a formidable group.

In the eyes of Richard Nixon and the administration, this concentration of power took on another cast. He could see, as every President before him saw, that somewhere in the press he would find a natural adversary. But within the new concentration of power, the significant heights of influence had been "seized" by men of a world-view, and of a culture, entirely alien to his own. These were the adversary press. Its luminaries not only questioned his exercise of power, as all great American journalists have done when examining a President. They questioned his own understanding of America; they questioned not only his actions but the quality of his mind, and his honor as a man. It was a question of who was closer in contact with the mood of the American people—the President or his adversary press? Neither would yield anything of respect to the other—and in Richard Nixon's first term the traditional bitterness on both sides approached paranoia.

Again, we must go back to sketch background. . . .

The modern age of journalism began in the United States at the turn of the century—and with it the modern age of American politics, responding at first slowly, then ever more rapidly, to the new audience brought to political in-

---

*See "The Rush to Chain Ownership," by Robert L. Bishop, in the *Columbia Journalism Review*, November/December, 1972.

volvement by the changing technologies of news delivery.

It is easiest to approach this change in journalism by glancing at the commerce, structure and technology of 1900—for commerce and technology were, over the next two generations of American life, increasingly to change the news-gathering business until in the 1960's it climaxed in the explosive force of national television. A number of related developments had been maturing in the decades just before Theodore Roosevelt became President. There was, first, the completion of the railway network, which linked America from coast to coast to provide manufacturers for the first time a continental market. Manufacturers, by 1900, could ship stoves, furniture, oil, beer, machinery, timber, housewares anywhere in the country. But to explore the reachable new market and sell their wares, they needed a national advertising medium. Until the turn of the century no such medium had been available. Local newspapers, when they carried what they called "foreign," or out-of-state, advertising, printed ads for small package goods, like patent medicines or books, that could be shipped easily. Now, with bulk goods coming in, like washing machines, carpet sweepers, stoves, automobiles, all finally transportable, the manufacturers could deliver all across the country—if they could find a voice, a horn, a trumpet to tout their goods.

Technology had also made the horn ready. The development of the high-speed rotary press which could spin off several million copies a week had made mass printing possible. And coupled with this technical magic was the development of the halftone photo-engraving process which could illustrate text, and thus entrance the semi-literate native Americans of the day as well as the immigrants who could read little or no English. Publishers could now print, illustrate and circulate millions of magazines, and sell pages to advertisers for huge sums—if only they could find editors with talent enough to capture the imagination of a whole nation.

The men the publishers found (and frequently the editor and the publisher were the same man) were editors of an entirely new breed. Editors of national magazines required a different eye span and thought frame from editors of newspapers. Their medium* was different, its audience larger—in fact, nationwide. For the first time, a breed of journalists was required who could think beyond the interests of New England, or the Midwest, or the Cotton Country, or the hometown. As they sat there in New York at their desks, the mind's eye of such men had to sweep the nation as, previously, only the mind's eye of a Wall Street financier or the President had done. Moreover, their time frame was different from the time frame of newspaper editors of the era. News until then had been just that—the record of what happened in the twenty-four-hour cycle. Newspapers reported what had happened yesterday. But for magazines, the time frame was what was *happening*—what had been happening last week, last month, the last three months, which would continue to be news, and relevant news, next week, next month, perhaps even next year. Newspapers captured only the event; magazines captured the swell and roll of events. Corruption of municipal governments was not just the local story of a sheriff caught dirty-handed yesterday accepting a bribe; corruption of municipal government was part of a nationwide phenomenon, a disease of the system, and it interested people everywhere. The trusts were not just local gougers—they were national monsters, whose purposes and plans could be made clear only by looking at them nationally; the despoliation of nature was a national problem, not a local offense. And these national problems, once they were identified and exposed and their cast of characters described as villains or heroes, made vivid national reading—as vivid in California as in Maine.

---

*"Media" is a word invented by advertising agencies. Essentially, it is a phrase in the advertising man's sales pitch to manufacturers about the cost-effectiveness of their advertising dollar. A maker of goods has just so much money to be budgeted for reaching potential customers—and advertisers measure the reach in Cost-per-Thousand, or so many dollars per thousand of potential audience. "Media" is a quantitative, commercial term and measures the relative effectiveness of spending to reach such thousands via newspapers, magazines, radio, television, billboards or direct mail. "Media" is an outsider's term, and no journalist thinks of himself as a member of the media. The author will do his best to avoid the use of the word "media" in the rest of this book and refer to members of the news community by the old-fashioned word "newsmen."

The magazines thrived, and as they thrived they changed American politics. The great writers and editors of the muckraking era of the 1900's—Lincoln Steffens, Frank Munsey, S.S. McClure, Upton Sinclair, Ida Tarbell, Ray Stannard Baker—are the ancestors of every important investigative reporter since then. More than that—they and their editors, for the first time, jostled big business and the clergy for control of the national agenda, forcing politicians to respond to the concerns the "muckrakers" had raised. In doing so, the muckrakers moved the nation to pass its first consumer legislation, its first environmental legislation, to control the money supply and banking system, create a first-class navy, reorganize its tax system.

The dominance of the magazine as the overbearing news-master of American thinking reached its apogee, perhaps, in 1940 when three publishers of the East, the masters of *Time* and *Life*, of *Look*, of the *Saturday Evening Post*, the dominant magazines of the day, created a man called Wendell Wilkie, decided he should be the Republican nominee of that year—and then imposed him on that party. Few naked exercises of press power can compare to their feat except, perhaps, the imposition of John Garner as Vice-President on the Roosevelt ticket in 1932 by publisher William Randolph Hearst.

But by 1940 the predominance of the magazines was already threatened, for news had been freed from its bondage to the printed word, and had gone electronic. By 1940 Franklin Roosevelt had found that radio was the simplest direct appeal over a hostile printed press to the ears of the American people. Roosevelt learned to use radio not only artfully—for no Republican could match the ring of his silver tone on air—but also with trickery. Friends still recall his glee at the out-foxing of Thomas E. Dewey one evening on radio in the campaign of 1944. Roosevelt reserved time for a quarter-hour radio address on the National Broadcasting Company network; his rival booked the following fifteen minutes to exploit Roosevelt's listening audience for his reply. But Roosevelt spoke to clock time for only fourteen minutes—then left one full minute of paid time in dead silence after his remarks. The listeners frantically twiddled their dials, searching for sounds on other wave lengths; and the millions, who found other stations as they twiddled, were simply not there when the Republican candidate, Dewey, came on the air to speak.

Electronics are like that—subject to manipulation by experts in a way the printed press is not. But electronic journalism is more than that—it is the human voice, the human personality, there in the room with the listeners, supported by the most elaborate effort to gather all news, all information, all reality into ten-, fifteen- or thirty-minute time packages with incomparable impact on the individual mind. Television has a life and vitality of its own beyond manipulation. The Second World War lured the nation to radio—Edward R. Murrow intoning "This is London," or voice-casting from a bomber over Berlin; William L. Shirer broadcasting from Berlin and Compiègne. Radio was part of the home atmosphere from D-Day on; by 1960 radio had been multiplied by television; and by 1972 television was where American politics took place.

By 1972, 50,000,000 grown-up Americans sat down each evening to learn of their world as the massive resources of the three great networks delivered their three visions of that world in capsulized twenty-three-minute packages. Ninety-six percent of all American homes held TV sets. A Roper survey declared that 64 percent of all Americans now got most of their news from television, with radio, magazines and newspapers sharing the rest; and they trusted television by two to one over any other medium for credibility. And between this newest and most potent form of news delivery, on the one hand, and the President, on the other, was growing up an institutional hatred.

Richard Nixon never ignored television; had suffered at its hands; would continue to suffer. But by 1972 he had learned how to use the instrument against its masters. As President, he could conscript its time and the attention of its audience—the rules of the game required that when he went to China or to Moscow, television must show what he was doing; the rules of the game stipulated that if he chose to speak on an issue of state—Vietnam, prices, busing—he was news, and television had to give the news air. But though he could command the time of the instrument, he could never master, or even win to friendship, the personalities who controlled television for all the other evening hours of the year. There was the continuing adversary. "We came in talking togetherness," said Pat Buchanan in 1971, the President's sage and scout on the news front, "and now they attack us for divisiveness. But we can talk togetherness until we're blue in the face. It does no good if every night they see on the tube blacks attacking whites, or whites attacking blacks, students in demonstrations, picket lines, war riots. The tube is doing it, the tube is dividing us. The AP and the UPI put out a complete news service every day, and editors can pick and choose how they make up their front pages from what the wires bring in. But the networks lay down a half-hour news show that every station *has* to use all across the country. It's as if the AP put out one boiler-plate front page every morning which every single newspaper had to use unchanged."

It was the struggle over the agenda that bothered Buchanan—and over and over again the struggle between President and press came down to this struggle. Who controlled what went before the American people? Did a candidate—a Democratic candidate as well as Nixon, the Republican—have a right to expect that the newsmen would present what he said as he said it? Or did the newsmen have the right to choose what they thought was important in what he said? Who chose? Who decided what truth and news were, what people would talk about?

In November of 1969, Vice-President Spiro T. Agnew had made the administration's case public in one of the most masterful forensic efforts in recent public discourse:

"A small group of men, numbering perhaps no more than a dozen anchormen, commentators and executive producers, settle upon the twenty minutes or so of film and commentary that's to reach the public.... They decide what forty to fifty million Americans will learn of the day's events in the nation and in the world.... We do know that to a man these commentators and producers live and work in the geographical and intellectual confines of Washington, D.C., or New York City, the latter of which James Reston termed the most unrepresentative community in the entire United States. Both communities bask in their own provincialism, their own parochialism. We can deduce that these men read the same newspapers. They draw their political and social views from the same sources. Worse, they talk constantly to one another, thereby providing artificial reinforcement to their shared viewpoints."

Was authority in the press and in television really centered in the cities of New York and Washington, where in truth, as Agnew described them, a limited, definable group had become the leadership elite of the news-gathering profession?

No conspiracy had concentrated this elite in the New York-Washington centers. Commerce and technology had done it, to create a change in American journalism as profound as had ushered in the muckrakers seventy years before—and even more unpredictable in result.

The figures did not really expose the nature of the change. Just before World War II, there had been 1,878 daily newspapers in the United States. By 1971 that number had fallen to 1,735—apparently no great change. What had changed, however, was proprietorship—great and powerful groups were gobbling up individual papers all across the country, linking them to one another and to radio-TV franchises. Local competition of daily newspapers had all but ceased in 1972; at the time of the muckrakers, 60 percent of all cities had enjoyed daily a choice of two or more rival newspapers; by 1972 that number had dwindled to 4 percent. Autopsy of the apparently small number of papers which had died was more significant. The most important of them had died in the large metropolitan centers of the nation where the city problem boiled and news competition had been keenest. Los Angeles, which had had four newspapers at the end of the war, had only two by 1972. Chicago had been a town where four proprietors divided the daily press; in 1972 Chicago still published four newspapers—but now only two proprietors controlled them. San Francisco had had four newspapers; by 1972 there were only two. In the Presidential year 1972, Newark, New Jersey, was to lose one of its last two daily newspapers.* Washington, the same year, was to lose the Washington *Daily News*, leaving the city's opinion and information to be divided between the Kauffmann-Noyes family (of the Washington *Star*) and the Graham family (of the Washington *Post*). Boston was to lose, in 1972, the Boston *Herald-Traveler*, having already long since lost the Boston *Transcript*, the *Record*, the *Post*, and remained now with the Boston *Globe* and the *Herald-American*.

Television—and, to a lesser extent, the craft unions—had been strangling the older forms of news delivery in the big cities. Television delivered the news quicker, more attractively, with more talented manpower than the older news-delivery system could afford. Television offered news sauced with a visual drama that words could not match; and drew off the advertising dollars, as well as the audience, which had sustained rival systems of news delivery. Television wrote the end of the general national magazine's hegemony over American thinking—in 1969 the old *Saturday Evening Post* had been scuttled; in 1971 *Look* Magazine died; in 1972 *Life* Magazine, that majestic creative force of photo-journalism, was to die, ending the postwar world in American periodical journalism, too.

The geography of the newspapers that survived in the United States required entirely new definition. The need to make a profit and stay in business had sorted them into groups that could better be defined culturally or commercially than by regional, sectional or political interest. There were newspaper chains that published straight news to make money and were efficient at both—the Newhouse chain, the Cox papers, the Scripps-Howard, Knight, Gannett, Ridder chains, the Cowles papers, several papers in the Hearst chain. Such commercial chains accounted for 60 percent of the daily circulation of the country. There were also, across the country, simple, barefoot individual proprietorships whose ideas had changed little since the time of Warren Gamaliel Harding, himself a publisher, proprietor of the Marion, Ohio, *Star*. These spanned the right end of the opinion spectrum, from stovepipe-hat conservatism (like the Copley or the Pulliam papers) to the rock-throwing, pistol-packing Neanderthal quality of a paper like the Manchester *Union Leader*, which dominated New Hampshire.

The administration had little to worry about from the "proprietary" press which controlled so large a share of the country's daily circulation. Ninety-three percent of all papers that endorsed a candidate in 1972 endorsed Nixon—753 dailies, with 30,500,000 in circulation, supported him as against only 56, with 3,000,000 circulation, for McGovern. "Out There," where lay his spiritual home, Nixon was reported cleanly and fairly, in his own terms. The gentle rounds of Herbert G. Klein, Nixon's Director of Communications, were smoothly devoted to explaining to the press leaders of Out There what the Nixon Presidency was all about—and Klein was both persuasive and effective.

What neither Nixon nor Klein could reach or affect was a specific cluster of newspapers, all lumped together by them under the convenient rubric "Eastern Liberal Press." Geography contradicted the neatness of this rubric, however, for this crowning cluster was spread as far west as the Los Angeles *Times*, held a beachhead in Chicago with the Field papers, reached south to the Louisville *Courier-Journal*, as deep into the interior as the St. Louis *Post-Dispatch* and added these logotypes to the obvious Washington *Post*, *New York Times*, Boston *Globe* and Long Island *Newsday*.

All of these were immensely profitable newspapers. Having survived the competition of television, having established their community leaderships so solidly that nothing could shake their advertisers, they were immune to any hostile pressure except from their unions, or outright government legal persecution.

---

*The condition of press and public affairs in New Jersey can only be regarded as tragedy. New Jersey, the eighth largest state of the Union, had been deprived in the 1960's of its only VHF television franchise, thus leaving it the only state without a video outlet of its own. The death of the Newark *Evening News* closed down even further the ability of New Jersey's citizens to find out what is going on in their own communities. New Jersey's politics has come to rank among the most sordid, squalid and disgusting in the chronicles of state politics. Between the 1968 and 1972 Democratic conventions, no less than six members of the 1968 New Jersey delegation were convicted of felonies. Cursed with unmanageable problems of industry, race and suburbanization, none of its citizens can easily find out what is happening in New Jersey today. The state is a national sadness, the stamping ground of demagogues and ignorants.

Yet an even more important characteristic marked them: All these great enemies of the Nixon administration were family-owned or family-controlled publications. And between this "baronial" press and the proprietary press is a difference of spirit far greater than that between a state teachers' college and an Ivy League university.

The newspaper families of the baronial press are the last great aristocracy in American life. If there is an elite in America, a truly self-recognizing *noblesse*, it is the great families who own and manage the outstanding daily publications of the nation.

One used to be able to see them all in the flesh in unforgettable display at *The New York Times's* annual reception on the tenth floor of its mausoleum at Times Square, when the Associated Press each spring gathers publishers from around the country for its annual meeting. The Sulzberger family would receive as befitted the Grand Dukes of Manhattan, Arthur Hays Sulzberger sitting in his chair, his consort, Iphigene, standing beside him, both nodding graciously and extending their hands to the other noble families of the realm as they strode proudly in. There were the great personages from out-country, the Grand Duchesss of Los Angeles, Mrs. Norman Chandler; the Grand Duchess of Washington, Mrs. Philip L. Graham; there were the earls, counts, countesses of lesser but still courtly blood—the Taylors of Boston, the Binghams of Louisville, the Fields of Chicago, the Pulitzers of St. Louis, the Ridders of the Midwest. They were to be distinguished, by bearing and disposition, from those publishers who worked for powerful but publicly held commercial enterprises where family lineage was either absent or, like the Newhouses, too fresh in power to have acquired patina. As politicans and diplomats watched, the great family figures would circle, flanked by small courts of their own famous writers, stars or editors. If swords, costumes and decorations had been permitted, one might have transferred the personages to a levee at Versailles when the nobility of France was assembled in the Hall of Mirrors—and they would have been at home. And among such families, the proudest in carriage and bearing were those who had come to be bracketed as the "Eastern Liberal Press."

What characterizes these hereditary newspaper barons is something not too difficult to define—a sense of patrician responsibility, a sense of the past both of their own communities and of their nation, and an invulnerability to common fears, common pressures, the clamor of stockholders and advertisers that weaken the vigor of lesser publishers. They understand power better than most politicians; their families have outlived most political families, locally and nationally; they can make politicians—and, on many occasions, break them.

What follows from the pride of these publishers is, however, more subtle, more difficult to define and, in terms of the clash between them and Richard Nixon, the operational fact: They insist on their own concept of honor and style. The families that own the great newspapers of the Liberal Press have the taste, and the purse, for the finest news-writing; they invite from their staffs elegant, muscled, investigative reporting. In this field, they outclass all other newspapers; their quality is evident every day on their front pages; they have survived, and their competitors have perished, because of this quality. These families regard their star reporters as almost sacred—as great racing families regard their horses, horse-handlers and jockeys. Men and women are proud to work for such publishers; their reporters set the style for all other reporters everywhere who hope, someday, to have their prose appear in such newspapers. In a sense, the great organs of the Liberal Press have escaped from the direct control of the publishers who own them and belong to the journalists who operate them for the owners. There is no way the Nixon administration, or any other administration, can reach or influence their reporting, their assessment of the agenda of the nation's unfinished business, their challenge. They are independent not only of Mr. Nixon, but of all pressures except the internal self-criticism of their own communities. They live in a world of their own.

If, in the 1972 campaign, one had drawn up an imaginary hate-list at the White House, one would have had to rank an order somewhat like this: first, the Washington *Post*; second, the Columbia Broadcasting System; third, *The New York Times*; fourth, the Hanoi regime; fifth, the Saigon regime; sixth, American universities;

seventh, the Indian government—and so on down the line until one came to George McGovern, the rival candidate, somewhere between tenth and twentieth. (Reviewing this imaginary list one day, a White House friend, who declared it to be preposterous, said to me: "You ought to get the Boston *Globe* in there somewhere—if it were important enough nationally. It's even worse than the New York *Post*—because it's better.")

The three top names on the imaginary hate-list deserve special examination.

The Washington *Post* had been a moribund conservative newspaper until purchased by financier Eugene Meyer in 1933. It had persisted with a feeble flicker of vitality and much deficit financing as a secondary newspaper until management passed in 1948 to Mr. Meyer's son-in-law, Philip Graham, who acquired control of *Newsweek* and invigorated both the newspaper and the magazine until they became major national forces. It was, however, only when direct authority passed to Mrs. Katherine Graham, on the death of Philip Graham, her husband, that the Washington *Post* acquired that exuberance of reporting which made it the chief enemy of Richard Nixon. Mrs. Graham, one of Washington's great hostesses, a shy and beautiful woman of enormous power, manages her empire as Queen Elizabeth managed England—by choosing vigorous men and sending them out on the Spanish Main with freebooters' privilege to seek targets of opportunity. The seadogs Katharine Graham chose when she took over her domain in 1964 were buccaneers of the caliber of Drake and Hawkins, men of quality who enjoyed a good fight. Her two chief admirals, Benjamin C. Bradlee, the executive editor of the Washington *Post*, and Osborn Elliott, editor of *Newsweek*, two Harvard men of the same generation, proceeded to recruit staffs of their own characteristic vitality and style, and, between them, helped change journalism in the sixties.

It is Bradlee and the Washington *Post* that concern us most here—for the Washington *Post* hates Richard Nixon, and Nixon hates the Washington *Post*, and they are locked like two scorpions in a bottle, determined to destroy each other. It was the *Post*, more out of zest for the hunt than any political malice, that made the Nixon administration its target. With gusto, total dedication and courage, its reporters made the Nixon administration their prey—and as they cried "Talley-Ho," the rest of the press pack followed. As the Washington *Post* uncovered the spoor of the Watergate scandal, word was relayed to Mrs. Graham that John Mitchell, the former Attorney General, had declared that "Kay Graham would find her t-t in a wringer" if her staff carried on. Mrs. Graham folded her arms, figuratively, over her bosom and supported her staff. It was for her a question of losing the loyalty of her troops, on the one hand, or perhaps, on the other hand, of being squeezed out of her substantial broadcasting properties by a hostile government. She chose in lonesome gallantry to support her staff, and the Watergate investigation went on.

The Columbia Broadcasting System, second on the imaginary hate-list of the Nixon administration, was another news-gathering institution which had acquired its own internal dynamic, subject to little more management control than cost-accounting. CBS was not to be compared to the baronial press in corporate structure—it had become a widely held public corporation, quoted daily on the New York Stock Exchange. But three men had made it great. Two of those were William S. Paley, chairman of the board, and Frank Stanton, its former president, who regarded the network as their own property, which it had long since ceased to be. The third man had been Edward R. Murrow, one of the great journalists of the twentieth century. Paley and Stanton had had their problems with Murrow's intractable integrity over many years; yet they had been proud of him. He was not only the chief decoration of their News and Public Affairs division, but also a spectacularly able organizer and chooser of other men. Murrow had created for himself, and for the broadcasters he chose, a position *vis-à-vis* management which held simply that management's only control was to fire them or cut them in pay; he and his broadcasting team could not be told what to say, or what the news meant. Murrow's professional fathership of names that came to be reference points in the history of television news reads like this: He had first employed Charles Collingwood and Howard K. Smith in Europe, fresh from Rhodes Scholarships. He had added to his staff Eric Sevareid, in Paris, at the age of twenty-seven. He had put to work in television Fred W. Friendly, at the age of thirty-two. He had been the original sponsor of William L. Shirer, David Schoenbrun, Chet Huntley and other still-glittering or once-famous names who created news television. Of the great men of television, only Walter Cronkite had not been moved forward by an assist from Murrow somewhere along the way.

But to all of them, as well as Cronkite, Murrow had bequeathed something more important than opportunity and fame: He had bequeathed a sense of conscience and importance with which neither management nor government might interfere. Murrow's concept of public advocacy had emboldened him to ignore timid management and launch the attack that destroyed Senator Joe McCarthy; he had spoken for blacks against government, for the poor against the landlords, for the hungry against the establishment. And at CBS, a huge corporation more vulnerable than most to government pressure and Washington reprisal, he had left behind a tradition that the reporting of news and public affairs was to be what its correspondents and producers wanted it to be, not what management sought to make it. Paley and Stanton honored this tradition. It was as inconceivable for them to lift the telephone and tell a Cronkite or a Sevareid what to say as, for example, for the Elector of Saxony to tell Johann Sebastian Bach how to compose his music or to play his tunes at the court's next chamber-music gathering. When they went on air, the CBS newscasters held absolute, unrestrained power.

There remained next on the imaginary hate-list the press organ most difficult to characterize—the most important of them, *The New York Times*.

The Nixon administration and its spokesmen insisted that they did not hate *The New York Times*. It is difficult for anyone to hate *The New York Times*; but *The New York Times*, the best newspaper in the world, is the major power force in American thinking—and it can kill, without malice, simply by a reflex of its muscles. Where the reporters of CBS and the Washington *Post* could be described as being out of the control of their proprietors, *The New York Times* could be described as being, in critical areas, out of the control of its own management, too. For the *Times* lives at the center of a closed loop—lives in the Manhattan world of opinion makers, and it is impossible to say how much the Manhattan opinion makers influence the *Times*, and how much the *Times* influences the opinion makers. . . .

The New York Times is not the hometown newspaper of New York—New York is many hometowns, and the *Times* serves several of them; far more are served by the New York *Daily News*. But the *Times* is the hometown newspaper of all men of government, all men of great affairs, all men and women who try to think. In the sociology of information it is assumed that any telephone call made between nine and noon anywhere in the executive belt between Boston and Washington is made between two parties both of whom have already read *The New York Times* and are speaking from the same shared body of information. Whether in finance, music, clothing industry, advertising, drama, business or politics, it is accepted that what is important to know has been printed that morning by *The New York Times*. The *Times* is the bulletin board not just for the city, but for the entire nation's idea and executive system. It is the bulletin board for book publishers, who decide what books may be incubated from its dispatches; it is the bulletin board for the editors of the great news magazines, who speed their correspondents to the scene of any story the *Times* unearths; it is the bulletin board of all three national television networks, whose evening news assignments, when not forced by events themselves, are shaped by ideas and reportage in the *Times*. . . .

But *The New York Times* was more than a great instrument for reporting news. It was also the most powerful voice in the national culture. Its critics of art, books, theater, music, movies, dance, its Sunday *Book Review* and cultural sections were to the cultural marketplace what the Dow Jones ticker is to Wall Street.

On the *Times*, as on most other publications, these departments deal in value judgments; and the values which dominate the *Times* are not those of "Out There." They are the values dominant in New York's centers of culture, values shared by the major university campuses. These values, as we have noted earlier, were strongly anti-war from 1967 on, highly tolerant of radical youth and black militancy, and in polar opposition to those of the President. . . .

For the Nixon administration, the Washington *Post* was a recognizable enemy, out to get it. *The New York Times* was different—it was the spreader of elusive values that completely contradicted the administration's own: the values of Manhattan, of the universities, of the opinion set, of the intellectuals—the subtle, corrosive values which had, somehow, taken over television's minds and, through television, set up the chief opposition the administration recognized in the campaign.

The values of Manhattan's *avant-garde*, and the university, television and opinion centers they influence, are matters for another book—on American intellectual history. In the campaign of 1972, however, those values were the values the administration saw itself as opposing: the judgment of all its performances against an unreachable perfection of attainment, the art critic's measure of all things by their symmetry of composition; the derivative intellectual scorn of men who profess a higher morality than those who must compromise with reality or settle for less than perfect in order to make things work now. Words are the fuel of politics. In 1972 the words of patriotism, honor, family, peace-and-quiet, law-and-order—as well as the blunter, harsher words that describe the cruel front of race clash in American communities—were essential dividers in the political contest between the liberal cause and the conservative cause.

Power is to liberals, said someone, what sex is to Puritans—liberals loathe it, yet lust for it; distrust it, yet itch for it. The key belief of liberal intellectuals, shared with conservatives, is that power, in the hands of any but their own kind, conceals a hidden wickedness. In the case of Richard Nixon, liberals were not only convinced of the hidden wickedness of his use of power, but affronted by his manners, his speech, his style. For years, thus, climaxing in 1972, Nixon felt himself relentlessly pursued by such intellectuals, who thereby displayed to their own friends and admirers their courage, their superior virtue, their pious orthodoxy. The election of 1972 as it unrolled outraged liberals—it proved that Richard Nixon read the mind of the country better than they, that he was closer to the country's throb. The tragedy was that, however great his achievements—and they were spectacular—his management of power in the place closest to him was flawed exactly as liberals expected it to be. A crime had been committed in his name, authorized by men of his choice. The unveiling of the Watergate scandal was on the way—and when it broke, it would entirely erase whatever credit balance was his in the proceedings between him and the Liberal press.

We have thus the pattern of opinion in the campaign of 1972—a proprietary press across most of the country overwhelmingly in favor of Richard Nixon; a "Liberal Press" in several great metropolitan centers freed of the dictates of its proprietors; and an opinion center radiating out of New York, its ideas carried on the back of *The New York Times*'s indispensable reporting, and influencing at the center most of the major news magazines, all of the book publishers, all of the sectarian magazines of opinion and, most importantly of all, the world-view of the great national news networks. . . .

The President feigned indifference to the press and New York-based television networks. And, indeed, he behaved as he insisted he must—he must act by his own instincts and judgments, not heeding what the nets and liberals said. Yet a reporter could never rid himself of the realization that the hostility of the Liberal Press obsessed Nixon.

Across the street from the White House, in Rooms 122 to 127 of the Executive Office Building, there had been installed under the management of Dr. Lyndon (Mort) Allin, a political-science graduate of the University of Wisconsin, an elaborate center for press surveillance. There the White House view of the press was daily shaped; and the shape the press made of itself was, to the Nixon command, frightening. Each day a staff of four, assisted sometimes by eight volunteer clipping ladies on the top floor of the Executive Office Building, monitored, reported and clipped the news-and-opinion flow of the nation. News tickers clacked; video-tape monitors stood by to record the television news shows; newspapers and magazines piled up from all over the country, stacked on tables, desks, wastebaskets, shelves, until the offices looked like a paper-baling operation in a junk shop. And out of this each day Allin and his staff prepared for Pat Buchanan, who passed it on to the White House, a summary of what television was saying, what the wire nets were reporting, what the opinion magazines opined, what the columnists and commentators commented.

Each day the Allin scrutiny examined fifty key newspapers among the 1,700 dailies in the country. These included, of course, all the famous names of the notorious "Liberal Press." They also included what Allin described as "the stalwarts" which would be with Nixon "no matter what"—the Detroit *News*, the Dallas *Morning News*, the Chicago *Tribune*, the New York *Daily News*, minor newspapers in Jacksonville and Orlando, Florida, Then followed the "generally sympathetic newspapers"—the St. Louis *Globe-Democrat*, the Houston newspapers, the Fort Worth *Star-Telegram*, the Los Angeles *Herald-Examiner* and the San Francisco *Chronicle*. Then followed the neutral papers, which played the news straight from the wire services, but whose editorials and comment might go either way. And once below the top fifty newspapers of the country, support for the President grew overwhelmingly.

Apart from the country press, however, the view from the White House was dismal. The networks were all of them generally regarded as "bloody," with CBS the most hostile and, in White House eyes, ABC the most reasonable. The syndicated commentators and columnists were filed by name—forty of them—with their key dispatches all preserved for the record; the columnists were, of course, generally hostile. Worst of all, however, as seen from Allin's paper-barricaded lair, were the opinion periodicals.

The surveillance center received some forty-two major periodicals of opinion and reportage. They ranged from *Human Events* (hostile to Nixon from the right—*Human Events* believes Nixon is soft on Communism) to Manhattan's *Village Voice* and the *New York Review of Books* (hostile to Nixon from the left—they treat him as if he does not belong to the human race). In between came all the rest, the finest of American thinking, intellectual conception and cultural values—*Time, Newsweek, Life, The New Yorker, Atlantic* and *Harper's; Saturday Review, New Republic, Nation, National Review;* the *Progressive, Intellectual Digest, Current, Kenyon Review, Partisan Review, Commentary, Ms., Esquire*. Of these forty-two opinion reviews received in 1972, two were published in Europe (the *Economist* in London, the weekly *Le Monde* in Paris); one was published in Wisconsin (the *Progressive*); and all the rest were published in the belt of resistance to Nixon—Boston (1), Washington (7) and New York (all the rest). Apart from the business magazines (*Dun's Review, Forbes, Business Week*) and the periodical stalwarts (*Reader's Digest, U.S. News & World Report*), the panorama with one exception—the *National Review*—ranged from distrust to suspicion to contempt to disgust. The nation's opinion makers, centered in the Boston-New York-Washington area, loathed the president.

Each day the Allin rooms summarized this vast outpouring of material for some thirty members of the White House staff, all of whom needed to be approved by H. R. Haldeman for receipt of distribution. Allin's staff worked around the clock, from seven in the morning until one the next morning. The top two pages of the report, prepared by Buchanan himself, who arrived at seven, always summarized the three evening news shows on television and whatever the major wire services said of note. Then followed twenty to thirty pages of summary of other television shows (*Today* or the CBS Morning News) and the gleanings from the fifty major newspapers. And on Mondays, to start the week, there was a special summary of the opinion journals and the commentators, a bitter dosage for the President. "I just don't understand," said Mort Allin after two years on the job, "how the hell he can sit there and take this shit day after day." . . .

There was never any concerted, planned-out response by the Nixon administration to what it considered press hostility. The President himself, by 1972, had completely tuned out the adversary press and television. They no longer influenced him. His adversaries had pursued him so relentlessly over so many years that whatever they said could be discounted as malice or fiction—even the Watergate affair. Which was tragedy. . . .

Mr. Nixon had by the beginning of 1972 arrived at a personal assessment of the problem. All his major impacts on the American people in his first term had been made by an appeal over

Politics, Censors, and the Media   **183**

the concentrated voices and influence of his very real enemy, the Eastern Liberal Press. His speech of November 3rd, 1969, on Vietnamization of the war, had been sneered at by his enemies—but had turned out to be a triumph, judged by the response of public opinion. His announcements of his trip to China, of wage-price controls in 1971, followed by his own trip to China in early 1972, convinced him that the critically important elements of the news-delivery system in America would bleach out all his thoughts except those expressed in fact and deed. Thus, his campaign of 1972 would be carried to the American people by leap-frogging the news system itself.

The Nixon campaign baffled the news system as few others had done before.

The leading candidate was simply unavailable for questioning.

He had given only eight formal press conferences in his first year in office; in 1970, the number had dropped to four; in 1971 he had moved up to nine press conferences; but in 1972, election year, he had dropped that number to seven. From Franklin Roosevelt on, Presidents had found the press conference the easiest, quickest way of reaching the news system and provoking reaction—they had averaged, until Nixon's time, from twenty-four to thirty-six press conferences a year. Richard Nixon reduced that average to seven. He preferred to reach the people directly, by TV and radio, with the pageantry of the Presidency in action.

1972 was a year when Nixon dominated the airwaves—Nixon from Peking, Nixon from Shanghai, Nixon from Moscow, Nixon from Kiev, Nixon from Hawaii, Nixon greeting foreign chiefs of state. For those who wanted more substance and less pageantry, Nixon had another channel—the campaign radio address. He had first experimented with radio in 1968 and had found paid half-hours, in terms of dollar cost, the most effective way of delivering a serious theme. By 1972 he had, thus, abandoned the telethon, the question-and-answer period, which had once been a staple of his campaigning. In 1972 he was to deliver no less than thirteen daytime radio addresses (plus one in the evening), usually on weekends. With sober, carefully prepared stands on the major issues as he saw them, he reached usually one to three million people per broadcast, and he provided with the texts the background material that the out-country press could digest as policy. If the nation wanted drama, there was the President on TV; if the editorialists demanded that issues be clarified, there were the radio speeches they could read. His public record and theoretical proposals were delivered to the American people better than any candidate's had been before.

But for the newsmen, reporting the President was a chore. The news corps had grown in number as the number of newspapers in America shrank. By 1972 their number was almost self-defeating—graying veterans and college editors all jostled in a mob in which every second hand seemed to sprout a microphone, and the booms, cameras and sound poles of television crews clubbed any head not alert enough to duck in time. If one followed the President and was very lucky, one might be made a pool member, one of the revolving five men or women allowed to sit in the rear of Air Force One. There, occasionally some member of the White House inner staff might wander back to say hello and even vouchsafe real information. On the plane you might actually see the President—a newsman scrambling down the rear steps could alight in time to view the President as he came down the front steps of the plane. But the rest, the swollen horde that had now become the trail of all campaigns, were sentenced to the press buses.* And the press buses, two, three, sometimes four, would stretch a quarter-mile behind the President in procession, too far back for their passengers ever to see the man in the flesh, who was audible, if at all, only on the loudspeaker in the bus, from which the voice of a pool man up front might relay what was happening on the trip they were covering. It was easier to cover the President on campaign in 1972 by staying home and watching television with the rest of the people—which was the way the President wanted it.

Mr. Nixon had planned his strategy long before the nomination of George McGovern; the strategy ignored all Democratic candidacies as

---

*A fresh view of press coverage of the 1972 campaign was published in the fall of 1973 in a most entertaining book by Timothy Crouse called *The Boys on the Bus*, published by Random House.

well as the conventional news-delivery system. But even had the Nixon strategy been planned with George McGovern as the intended victim, it could not have trapped his Democratic rival better. McGovern's philosophy of "open politics" was not merely verbal. It reflected the deep personal conviction of George McGovern and his entire staff, and was in turn reflected at every level of his campaign. It was reflected in the pleasant, companionable atmosphere of his plane, where he and his staff were almost always available for direct questioning, and where the cloth partition between the candidate's personal forward section and the large rear press section could always be breached by a smile. It was reflected even more in his Washington headquarters, where his staff had been trained to be straightforward with newsmen, and thus invited them to explore every crevice of privacy and report each rustle of discontent. The press covered McGovern with stifling thoroughness—partly because he invited it, partly because it was, as one reporter called it, "the only show in town." Analyzing his defeat, McGovern said bitterly, after the campaign was over, "I was subjected to the close, critical reporting that is a tradition in American politics. . . . Yet Mr. Nixon escaped a similar scrutiny. The press never really laid a glove on him, and they seldom told the people that he was hiding, or that his plans for the next four years were hidden. . . . Not a single reporter could gather the courage to ask a question about the bugging and burglary of the Democratic National Committee. . . ." The press was to make up for that shortfall in 1973—but by then it was too late to do George McGovern any good. . . .

There was, however, the other level of contest—the ongoing fight between the President and the press which an election could not settle: control of the agenda. The Washington *Post*, followed by the Columbia Broadcasting System, followed by *The New York Times*, had decided they would place squarely on the agenda of public talk the matter of corruption in government and, specifically, corruption of power in the Nixon campaign.

Once there, it could not be removed, and would become the tragic Watergate story.

How "Fair" Should TV Be?

NAT HENTOFF

Recognizing the problem of limited access and the need for varying opinions to be expressed on radio and television, the FCC instituted the Fairness Doctrine in 1948. In this article Nat Hentoff outlines the issues involved and states the position of the broadcast industry that the Fairness Doctrine is an unwanted government intrusion into broadcasters' First Amendment rights.

Last February, ABC-TV refused to televise an already-taped Dick Cavett show with guests Abbie Hoffman, Jerry Rubin, Tom Hayden and Rennie Davis. In response to queries from newspaper reporters, ABC's management explained that the network "had an obligation to insure fairness and balance under requirements of the Federal Communications Commission." And Cavett's four guests, ABC management continued, "made controversial remarks about the U.S. judicial system, continuing hostilities in Southeast Asia, Watergate scandals and the use of revolutionary tactics."

The offending program would be aired, ABC said, only if Cavett sliced a half-hour out of it and, in accordance with what's known as the Fairness Doctrine, used that time to interview one or more people who are manifestly conservative in their views.

Cavett at first refused, then succumbed reluctantly after the network canceled the original show. When it was finally aired on March 21, it not only had been altered slightly, but for rebuttal purposes two right-wingers—Jeffrey St. John, a CBS political commentator, and Fran Griffin, Illinois chairwoman of Young Americans for Freedom—had been tacked on.

Reprinted by permission of the author and publisher from *Lithopinion* No. 34, the graphic arts and public affairs journal of Local One, Amalgamated Lithographers of America (New York). © 1974 by Local One, A.L.A.

The Fairness Doctrine became law in 1949, when Congress amended the 1934 Communications Act to insist on the obligation of broadcast licensees "to afford reasonable opportunity for the discussion of conflicting views on issues of public importance." The air, after all, is public; and the public should have access to broadcasting facilities using its air.

Television- and radio-station owners, and not a few news reporters and analysts in broadcasting, objected. Nobody, they reasoned, certainly not the government, can force a newspaper or magazine or book publisher to give space to those who consider a particular article or book "unfair." So why shouldn't television and radio, like the print media, have the same inalienable First Amendment rights to voice views freely?

In 1969, the Supreme Court appeared to have answered that question for some time to come. In its *Red Lion* decision, the Court proclaimed that "a licensee has no constitutional right . . . to monopolize a radio frequency of his fellow citizens." Furthermore, the Court emphasized, "It is the purpose of the First Amendment to preserve an uninhibited marketplace of ideas in which truth will ultimately prevail, rather than to countenance monopolization of that market . . . [by] a private licensee."

ALMOST EVERYBODY APPROVED

The *Red Lion* decision caused general rejoicing among liberals, most centrists and even a sizable number of conservatives who, while usually of the view that private enterprise and government regulation are antithetical, decided that in the matter of the public airwaves, only the government can effectively mandate that there be a real public forum for clashing ideas. (Many conservatives, after all, hold it as an article of faith that broadcasting is dominated by "left-leaning" reporters and analysts, and the *Red Lion* decision gave promise of some "balance" on the people's air.)

As a civil libertarian, I too was among the rejoicers. One of my own articles of faith has long been that owning a radio station, and especially a television station, amounts to having a license to make a hell of a lot of money. The least that broadcasting ownership can do to justify all those profits is to give dissenting citizens free and fair access to their channels.

My "heresy," with regard to the Fairness Doctrine, began to take shape in November 1972, when I read a dissenting decision by David Bazelon, Chief Judge of the United States Court of Appeals for the District of Columbia Circuit. Bazelon, who warred frequently with Warren Burger when the latter was on that appeals court, is a pre-eminent civil libertarian. He is also one of the few judges in the country who, like William O. Douglas, writes with marvelous and witty lucidity. We all have our prejudices, and one of mine has been best summarized by J. Mitchell Morse in *The Irrelevant English Teacher* (Temple University Press, 1972): "Style is a matter of intellectual self-respect. To write well, a certain moral courage is essential."

I would pay more attention, for instance, to William Buckley if he were finally to recognize that ormolu rococo reveals a talent for self-inflation but has little to do with writing or thinking well.

It was not, however, on aesthetic grounds that Judge Bazelon's decision in *Brandywine-Main Line Radio, Inc.* v. *Federal Communications Commission* shook me up. What Bazelon was saying made unnerving sense—both common sense and constitutional sense.

The case at issue concerned the FCC's refusal to renew the license of radio station WXUR in Media, Pa. The station was under the control of Rev. Carl McIntire, a fustian preacher whose views are well to the right of those of, let us say, Barry Goldwater and Savonarola. The FCC claimed that WXUR had failed to adhere to the Fairness Doctrine, pointing out that in decapitating WXUR, it was only doing what the Supreme Court, in the *Red Lion* decision, had mandated it to do.

Bazelon's dissent is worth close attention because it gets to the core of a rather complicated question. The First Amendment is designed to allow the citizenry as wide and robust a range of views as partisans can come up with. Accordingly, the Fairness Doctrine would appear to be eminently in line with the First Amendment. The people's right to hear diversity of opinion, and to express their own opinions, must surely have primacy over the First Amendment rights of those who own radio and television stations and of those who are regular staff reporters and commentators.

THE RIGHT TO BE DISRUPTIVE

It is not, however, all that simple. First of all Bazelon noted, the FCC, by forcing WXUR off the air, had deprived its listeners of *that* station's ideas, "however unpopular or disruptive we might judge these ideas to be." (Or, as Justice Douglas has pointed out, "Under our Bill of Rights, people are entitled to have extreme ideas, silly ideas, partisan ideas.")

Hold on, though. Let us grant that those who determine policy for a station do have the right to express even such noisome ideas as those of Rev. McIntire. What, then, can be wrong with forcing such ownership at least to share its channel with those who oppose its ideas?

Bazelon answers by observing that it is very difficult for a station such as WXUR to be held firmly and continually to the Fairness Doctrine, since "the monitoring procedures which the FCC requires for identification of controversial issues are beyond the capacity of a small staff, or a shoestring operation." This burden of equal time, he added, involves " . . . very critical First Amendment issues indeed. The ratio of 'reply time' required for every issue discussed would have forced WXUR ([if the FCC had allowed it to continue, in strict conformity to the Fairness Doctrine] to censor its views—to decrease the number of issues it discussed or to decrease the intensity of its presentation. The ramifications of this chilling effect will be felt by every broadcaster who simply has a lot to say."

A specific example which Judge Bazelon might have cited has to do with a complaint filed with the FCC in 1971 against KREM-TV in Spokane, Wash. The viewer invoking the Fairness Doctrine was Sherwyn M. Hecht, who was irritated by the unfairness, as he saw it, of KREM-TV's failure to provide sufficient air time to those citizens of Spokane opposing a local bond issue to raise money for a projected "Expo '74" undertaking.

Ultimately, on May 17, 1973, the FCC decided that Mr. Hecht's complaint was unwarranted. In the meantime, however, the station had to spend some 480 work-hours of executive and supervisory time satisfying the FCC that it had indeed been fair on that issue. This did not include supporting secretarial or clerical time. As a station official said rather wearily, "This represents a very serious dislocation of regular operational functions and is far more important in that sense than in terms simply of the dollar value of the salaries of those engaged in our self-defense."

That's too bad, an advocate of the Fairness Doctrine would say, but this kind of expense and dislocation is a necessary part of the cost of being a responsible—and responsive—broadcaster. If there is indeed a danger that some small stations might go under because of this financial weight, it could be possible for noncompeting stations (stations in different cities) to share expenses in hiring a full-time team of people expert at responding to FCC inquiries.

DIG WE MUST

In any case, this economic argument against the Fairness Doctrine surely can't apply to metropolitan stations or to the networks. However, Richard Salant, head of CBS News, disagrees. In an interview with writer Fred Powledge for the latter's American Civil Liberties Union report, *The Engineering of Restraint: The Nixon Administration and the Press*, Salant spoke of network economic and dislocation problems inexorably linked to the Fairness Doctrine, no matter which administration is in power: "We get a letter [from the FCC, notifying the network of a complaint from the public] and everybody has to dig. The reporters, the producers of the show, everybody has to dig out stuff and try to reconstruct why they did what they did. . . . If nothing else, it takes you away from your work. And when it is the government, through the FCC, moving into areas of program content, the effect is *chilling*. We have more lawyers than we have reporters."

It is when broadcasters, including reporters, argue against the Fairness Doctrine on the ground of its "chilling" effect that we move from matters of economics and personnel disarrangement to a fundamental First Amendment question. As Judge Bazelon emphasized in his dissenting opinion on the FCC's expunging of

WXUR, "In the context of broadcasting today, our democratic reliance on a truly informed American public is threatened if the overall effect of the Fairness Doctrine is the very censorship of controversy which it was promulgated to overcome."

Is there evidence of a chilling effect because of the Fairness Doctrine?

Louis Seltzer, president of WCOJ, a 5,000-watt radio station in West Chester, Pa., wrote the American Civil Liberties Union last year in an attempt to persuade it to stop supporting the Doctrine. "The Fairness Doctrine," Seltzer argued, "is *unfair*. As a practical matter, I know that it has served to muzzle this station for 25 years. An example: We aired only one or two [shows] of a well-produced series put out by the Anti-Defamation League of the B'Nai B'Rith on 'the Radical Right.' Why? Simply because airing these programs would open the floodgates to a paranoid response from the 'nut' groups. . . . True, we could refuse to run the reply programs on the basis of their patent untruth, but this would cost us a $10,000 lawsuit up to the Supreme Court of the United States, and even then there would be a possibility of losing. . . . This station is not small, but it not that large. We have neither the time nor the money to devote to such Joan-of-Arcian causes."

One obvious response to Mr. Seltzer's words is that the First Amendment exists for the benefit of "nut" groups too, but the point is that he did decide not to run the full series rather than get embroiled in a lawsuit.

A CHILLING BALANCE

Another illustration of the Fairness Doctrine's negative effect was that Cavett show decision. Richard Salant, who on the basis of his doughtily independent record would not, I think, have censored that program, has observed in answer to another request for the kind of "balance" that ABC-TV asked of Cavett: "Suppose the English governor had told Tom Paine that he could go ahead and publish all he liked, but at the back of his pamphlets he would have to allow the governor's assistant to publish *his* views to guarantee that the pamphlet had given the other side. That would have preserved Tom's right of free speech, but far from being an implementation of the First Amendment, it would have been just the opposite. You would have to consider it a restriction upon speech if, in order to print a broadside, Tom Paine had to present not only his own views but also those of someone arguing on the other side."

During the same week in which ABC-TV, in fear of the Fairness Doctrine, exercised prior restraint on Dick Cavett and his four controversial guests, a number of radio stations throughout the country refused to broadcast a new recording by the singing team of Seals & Crofts. The song, *Unborn Child*, argued against abortion. The station executives who censored the song from the public air explained that they did not want the hassle of providing equal time to pro-abortion spokespeople.

A recurring point made by Salant is that the *publicized* examples of station and network self-censorhip are only a small percentage of such management decisions which no one ever gets to hear about. "When one's very survival in one's business—broadcasting—depends on licensing by the government; when the penalty for error and for government disagreement is not a fine, but capital punishment [the loss of your operating license], does anybody think for a moment that there are not those who have said, 'Let's skip this one, let's not make waves, let's stay out of trouble'?"

Even in his own organization, Salant, who is more supportive of his investigative reporters than any other network news chief, has "a constant fear that somebody down the line—reporters or producers or somebody—will think 'Gee, we've caused such headaches to management, or to ourselves, in having to dig out all this stuff, when the lawyers come around, I'll play it easy for a while.'" Salant even sent a memorandum to his news staff telling them he considered self-censorship a "high crime."

Salant may not know it, but the memorandum didn't work in all cases. An official at WCBS-TV in New York has said—not for attribution, of course—"Sure, there are enough pressures in this business; who needs trouble from the FCC?"

A classic case of FCC interference with a network news operation began with a complaint by a small but vigorous organization called Accuracy in Media (AIM), accusing NBC-TV of not being fair in its 1972 documentary, *Pensions: The Broken Promise*. AIM told the Federal

Communications Commission that the program had been unbalanced, focusing on the deficiencies of private pension plans and not providing equal time to those pension plans that actually do protect the retired worker. The FCC agreed, and in May 1973, wrote NBC: "It does not appear that you have complied with your Fairness Doctrine obligation" to give both sides of controversial issues.

HOW TO BEAT THE BLAND

NBC is appealing that decision, maintaining that if the FCC ruling stands, investigative reporting on television will be markedly curbed. Attorneys for the network have emphasized that "to the extent the FCC staff's opinion requires ever greater accountability to the government itself, it is simply inconsistent with the long history of disassociation and even antagonism that has characterized the relationship between government and press in our country." Television journalists, NBC went on, would be forced "to engage in a kind of thinking and practice which has nothing to do with journalism. It would impose, as well, a variety of other less-obvious sanctions—the inhibiting effect upon television journalists and producers of being obliged to justify to their superiors and to the Commission the work they have done; the immense amount of time required—time better spent in preparing new programming—in preparing a 'defense' to similar charges; the ever-present threat to license renewals inherent in such rulings; and the like. In short, the issue is not alone whether television journalism will be too bland; it is whether it will be free enough not to be bland."

Ironically, in a footnote to its decision affirming the complaint against NBC by Accuracy in Media, the FCC staff had accurately observed that "for years prior to the broadcast of *Pensions*, neither NBC nor the other networks, to the best of our knowledge, had telecast any program dealing extensively with private pensions. There was little discussion in any general circulation print media and [there were] no widely distributed books on the subject. In fact, there was no apparent public discussion, much less controversy, apart from that of a relatively small number of experts, businessmen and government officials who take a professional interest in the subject. There had been hearings in the last Congress on the subject, but NBC was breaking new ground journalistically on a subject about which the public, at that time, had little knowledge."

So, by way of encouraging new groundbreaking by television journalists, the FCC thereupon demanded that NBC give time to "the other side."

Meanwhile, Abraham Kalish, Executive Secretary of Accuracy in Media, wrote a letter to stations affiliated with NBC, reminding them: "If you carried *Pensions: The Broken Promise* and you have not given your audience a program that showed the other side of the issues, you have not fulfilled your obligation under the Fairness Doctrine. I am sure that you are anxious to fulfill that obligation. NBC may wish... regrettably... to challenge the FCC on the Fairness Doctrine issue, but it is the licensee, not the network, that *may have this used against him in any challenge to a license renewal.* NBC has an obligation not to play games with your license. We urge you to tell NBC that." [Emphasis added.]

ANTEDILUVIAN ENTREPRENEURS

The message was well aimed. As a network correspondent—again, not for attribution—notes, "All along the line there are individual owners of affiliated stations who are antediluvian, moneymaking, conservative-thinking entrepreneurs. The network sends them something like CBS's *The Selling of the Pentagon* or NBC's *Pensions: The Broken Promise*, and they get very, very worried."

Richard Salant, for attribution, puts it even more starkly: "The affiliates have the perfect right under the law to turn down everything from the network that they don't want. They can put those of us in news completely out of business by turning the faucet. The government knows it can scare the pants off almost any broadcaster—certainly the affiliates. It takes an awful lot of guts for management to ignore these attacks because they can literally mean station owners will lose their economic life."

In one of the affidavits included in NBC's petition with the Court of Appeals for the District of Columbia, in its attempt to have the FCC decision on *Pensions* overturned, the network points out that this particular program won the prestigious George Peabody Award for public service in television as "a shining example of constructive and superlative investigative reporting." Furthermore, in March 1973, *Pensions* received a Christopher Award for "television news calling public attention to a much-neglected social issue." In May of that year, there was also a National Headliner Award for the program, followed in June 1973 by a Certificate of Merit of the American Bar Association.

Nonetheless NBC—unlike, let us say, *The New York Times* if it had printed a similar report on pensions—has to defend itself against the government. Reuven Frank, an NBC News executive with a remarkable track record for investigative journalism on television, says mordantly that the FCC's decision means that "we in television news must never examine a problem in American life without first ascertaining that we have piled up enough points on the other side—a little bank account of happiness to squander on an area of public concern. Otherwise, we should be overdrawn, and would have to schedule a program in payment of the debt.

"Must I and others charged with the responsibility for documentary programs," Frank continues, "review each proposed subject to see not only if it needs doing and can be done but whether we are *entitled* to do it? Must a search be made each time of the entire history of the network and its programs to determine whether enough has been presented saying there is no problem, so that we can be licensed to do a program saying there is a wee problem after all? Anyone I could hire for this would not be worth having. On the other hand, it will be a boon for travelogues."

David Brinkley adds: "To be found guilty of 'unfairness' for not expressing to the government's satisfaction that most people are not corrupt or that most pensioners are not unhappy is to be judged by standards which simply have nothing to do with journalism."

A WET BLANKET ON BOLDNESS

And Bill Monroe, Washington editor of the NBC News' *Today* program, articulates the anxieties of many news broadcasters on other networks and independent stations: "The very knowledge that the obstacle course seen in the *Pensions* ruling exists has an inevitable wet-blanket effect on reporters and producers. The FCC, while speaking for boldness, turns around and punishes those who practice it. It is thoroughly understood in the industry that the most likely outcome of bold journalism is trouble with the FCC: a penalty, amounting to harassment, in the form of an official request for justification, in 10 or 20 days after a program has been aired, that the program is in compliance with the Fairness Doctrine. Any newsman who has seen the effort a broadcast executive and his staff must make to prepare an answer to such an official request can only assume that his boss, as a human being, would have a desire to minimize such official challenges in the future."

Joining in NBC's petition to the Federal District Court was J. Edward Murray, associate editor of the Detroit *Free Press*, and a past president of the American Society of Newspaper Editors. By way of example of how inhibiting a fairness doctrine applied to print media would be, Murray says: "Newspapers, including the Detroit *Free Press*, investigate and expose policemen who are on the 'take' in the dope rackets. If an equivalent weight or time must be given to policemen who are not on the 'take,' the whole campaign becomes so unwieldy and pointless as to be useless. Must the good cops get equivalent space with the bad cops?"

As of this writing, NBC's case for First Amendment rights for its news staff is still in the courts. "Even if we win," an NBC reporter observes, "you can be sure that the next time someone comes up with an idea for a tough exposé, the brass is going to think quite awhile before it gives us the go-ahead, and then they'll probably impose their own 'fairness doctrine' on us."

Whatever the courts do decide, those who fervently support the Fairness Doctrine continue to argue that broadcast and print journalism cannot be equated because anyone can start a newspaper but radio and television channels are limited. Therefore, there *has* to be government supervision of "fairness." This is a venerable contention, but it no longer is germane to the real world of communications. In his dissenting opinion in the WXUR case, Judge David Bazelon pointed out that, as of September 1972, the number of commercial broadcasting stations on the air was 7,458. By contrast, as of Jan. 1, 1971, there were only 1,749 daily newspapers in the country.

"Nearly every American city," Judge Bazelon wrote, "receives a number of different television and radio signals. Radio licenses represent diverse ownership; UHF, local and public broadcasting offer contrast to the three competing networks; neither broadcasting spectrum is completely filled. But out of 1,400 newspaper cities, there are only 15 left with face-to-face competition."

THE ROLE GOVERNMENT SHOULD PLAY

The scarcity argument—that Federal officials have to insure "fairness" in television because there are so few channels—is no longer tenable. Does the government, then, have any legitimate function in television? Sure, says Justice William O. Douglas. It has a duty with regard to television—as it has concerning the printed media—to prevent monopolistic practices. That it has largely failed in this responsibility in relation to newspapers (most recently, through the Newspaper Preservation Act, which gives them limited but substantial exemption from antitrust laws) does not mean that the government ought to abdicate this duty concerning television. If, for example, one group of station owners is a predominant force in a particular region, that ownership should be divested of some of its telecasting facilities.

Federal authorities are also, Justice Douglas notes, responsible for "promoting technological developments that will open up new channels. But censorship or editing or the screening by government of what licensees may broadcast goes against the grain of the First Amendment."

Another necessary function of government is to make sure that channels don't intersect. Seeing to it that Channel 2 in any given city doesn't cut into Channel 4's picture has nothing to do with the First Amendment. In this respect, the government's role is like that of a traffic cop keeping motorists in their proper lanes.

There is also nothing destructive of the First Amendment in the current efforts of various groups to see that fair-hiring practices—including equality of access to broadcasting jobs by minorities and by women—are adhered to by television stations. That kind of pressure is also being applied to newspapers, and it is entirely constitutional.

My thesis—that those who would also have the government intervene in programming to assure "fairness" are wrongheaded—has another dimension. Emboldened by these forays into broadcasters' First Amendment rights, people who decry the "unfairness" of newspapers are pressing for "access" to print media.

On Feb. 4, 1974, Senator John McClellan of Arkansas suggested that Congress consider mandating that newspapers publish the replies of public figures who are attacked. Let the head of *that* camel get into the tents of newspapers and magazines, and those editors who are already timid—and they are not few—will make sure that their reporters stick to "safe" stories, like "color" features attendant on the annual Indianapolis Speedway race. In 1972, David Burnham of *The New York Times* wrote a long, devastating article on police corruption in New York City—a piece that forced an extremely reluctant Mayor John V. Lindsay to establish the independent Knapp Commission to dig into the subject of cops on the "take." Would that story have had nearly as much impact if the *Times* had been compelled to give equal space and position to a story quoting the Police Commissioner about how many honest cops there were on the force? Furthermore, that kind of requirement might well persuade a less independent newspaper than the *Times* not to publish a story on police corruption in the first place.

TOWARDS DEEPER MUCKRAKING

Will television become less bland—at least in its news and documentary divisions—if it is emancipated from the Fairness Doctrine? There are no guarantees, but the strong likelihood (and I speak from many years of coverage of television journalism) is that those with a taste for muckraking—Richard Salant, Reuven Frank, Paul Altmeyer at ABC-TV, and many others—will feel a lot freer to dig a lot deeper.

I asked Richard Salant that question while researching this article. He responded:

If we had full First Amendment freedoms, . . . the benefits to the public would be precisely the same benefits it now receives from the full application of the First Amendment to print journalism. For papers run by timid, lazy or greedy entrepreneurs, the First Amendment may not do a hell of a lot of good. So, too, in broadcasting.

But at least . . . no timid broadcast management could cop out on the ground that they might get into

Fairness Doctrine problems with the FCC, or risk a lot of lawyers' fees, or even run the danger of losing their license.

Whether the Fairness Doctrine is a real or an imagined Sword of Damocles—and it's real enough for a lot of broadcast journalists—it also serves as a shield for some broadcasters who want to duck hard investigative reporting. I am persuaded, but obviously cannot yet prove, that the brooding omnipresence of the Fairness Doctrine *does* indeed affect the state of mind of some reporters, some editors, some news executives, if only because they know that if they don't watch out, they're going to have to spend an enormous and unfruitful amount of time and money transcribing old broadcasts and searching them out to provide material for the lawyers who have to respond to complaints and to FCC 20-day letters.

There can be no concrete proof of how much bolder and braver television journalism may become if it finally is fully protected by the First Amendment, but surely it's an option worth taking, particularly since, as Judge Bazelon emphasizes:

Most Americans now consider television and radio to be their most important news sources. Broadcast journalists have grown up. They see it as in their interest to be guided by the same professional standards of 'fairness' as the printed press. There is no factual basis for continuing to distinguish the printed word from the electronic press as the true news media.

And that analysis, I contend, is fair enough—for all.

TV in Election Campaigns—A Call for Changes

ROBERT D. SQUIER
JANE M. SQUIER

Following are excerpts from a letter published November 3, 1972, by the Forum for Contemporary History and written by Robert D. Squier and Jane M. Squier, political consultants who directed TV operations for leading Democrats in both the 1968 and 1972 campaigns

In our experience with campaign consulting, we have seen television move politics out of the political back room into the family living room. The broadcast media, primarily television, have made it possible for the first time in our history for candidates to have direct and personal communications with every probable voter. Unfortunately, the problem is that most of that communication has been stuffed into the sausage-like skins of spot advertising—a format invented years ago by advertisers and their agencies to sell consumer products—and the costs have been unbearable.

Has this come about because politicians and their managers deliberately chose this kind of communications? Not really. Instead, it's our contention that this is all that's available to them and that the whole system is skewed in the direction of this kind of static-filled communication. Virtually no availabilities are provided for more serious and thoughtful messages. But that puts us a bit ahead of the story. Let's assume the politician's eye as he looks at the full spectrum of televised political communications available to his campaign.

First, he can usually count on coverage of his more visual and provocative movements by the

Copyright © 1972, The Communications Company, Bethesda, Maryland, Reprinted by permission.

192   Media Environments

news departments of local (or network) television systems. What finally appears on the home screen is approximately from 45 to 90 seconds of material from a rally, a speech, or some other visual event.

Most stations have a rule-of-thumb approach to this coverage, and it is all very cut and dried. If you visit their media market [the geographic area covered by their broadcasts] about once a week, in a statewide race, for example, they will cover you if you make it interesting and easy for them to get it on the air. This means scheduling nothing that you expect them to cover after 2 p.m. in most markets. Otherwise, you will get the rip-and-read treatment, which is wire-service copy read over a color slide with commentator in the foreground.

Many candidates, in the past few years, have taken to supplementing this coverage with videotape handouts. This is a version of an old campaign staple, the press release, dressed up for television. The use of this technique has stirred some controversy, but as long as the material is identified as coming from the candidate (which is more than a lot of newspapers do when they run verbatim versions of linear campaign "flackery") it meets the FCC's regulation.

Stations will use the material, and as long as they don't hand over their editorial right to decide what is news, we can see nothing wrong with the practice. Frankly, we would rather see a 60-second statement of a candidate's views on a pertinent issue than an image spot of his walking by the water with his dog at heel and coat slung carelessly over the shoulder.

A second way a candidate can use the medium of television, as mentioned earlier, is through adapting the formats and limitations of consumer advertising—by boiling his messages and/or his personality down into 10, 20, 30 or 60-second spot announcements. This is, by far, the most prevalent method of communications, and during the last few weeks of any political year, even the most casual television viewer can expect to be bombarded with these little "messagettes."

A third method is to accept the infrequent offers of free time that some stations provide, to make his case in a more responsible length. It is also possible to accept televised-debate offers which give him a chance to present his case to the public in direct juxtaposition with that of his opponent. A fair number of stations offer this time but then abandon the project when one of the opponents, usually the incumbent, refuses to cooperate.

The most glaring example of this practice has been the lack of televised debates in the last three presidential races. The issues raised in debate aren't always those that the public needs for rational decision making, but personally, we would still prefer Quemoy and Matsu [Asian offshore islands that figured in Kennedy-Nixon debate] to the tricky little production commercials of Nixon's November Group, or the carefully edited listening sessions that Guggenheim Films spliced together for McGovern.

The final method is for candidates to purchase program-length time and make their cases in a format conducive to thoughtful communications. We have recently seen the president of a prominent ad agency, who admittedly has had no experience in political campaigning via television, lambaste the poor spot in favor of five-minute or longer programs. Before he departed on the lecture circuit, he could have saved himself a long trip by stopping off in the office of one of his time buyers. Had he done this, he would have discovered that time segments longer than 60 seconds are rarely available. Few stations will sell longer lengths to candidates because they don't want to risk the lower ratings that usually lead out of such programs.

So there you have the system. Can it be changed to better serve our needs? We think it can. Television is not only the most effective of our communications media, it is also the only one that is *owned by the people*. This is an incredibly simple but so often overlooked fact.

The people own the airwaves and, through a Government agency, bestow on broadcasters a free license to use them. But there is another point—the license is accompanied by an order that the airwaves be used in the public interest.

CANDIDATES PAY WHAT AMOUNTS TO A RANSOM

Something seems strangely wrong here. We, the people, own the electronic media, and we ought to be able to use them when it serves our collective purpose. As the system now operates, candidates for public office must pay what amounts to a ransom to broadcasting stations in order to conduct the most important transaction of a democracy—an election campaign.

The Campaign Reform Act of 1971 ... was a long-overdue first step to combat this system of ransom and payment—but it was only a step. Like all reforms, it brought with it new problems that must be solved with the experience we have all shared in this year's campaign.

Let's see what we got for our legislative efforts:

The new law puts a ceiling on broadcast expenditures for candidates in all federal elections. It is a ceiling that at least makes the rules of access to the airwaves equal for all candidates, not just equal for those who can afford to pay the dues. More importantly, it has moved political candidates from the status of least-favored to most-favored clients—when they go to rent back the airwaves from broadcasters—by requiring that time be sold to them at the lowest commercial rates.

Now, what has become of the dire predictions about what this would do to the financial stability of the broadcasters? The broadcast business, in fact, is a financially healthy and thriving industry that pays virtually nothing for the use of the airwaves during the 90-plus weeks every two years not covered by this legislation. And even during political campaigns, stations only return a portion of the time to the public; and that is required to be at a discount, not as free time. Add to this the fact that program time has been reduced to accommodate more than the level of advertising normally acceptable under their own code of good practice. When broadcasters tally up their profits and losses for the period covered by this election, we will see that they once again have profited handsomely for their part in the democratic process of elections.

One of the problems with this whole question is that political candidates and their parties have helped to confuse the issue by their willingness to deal with television as an advertising medium rather than as a way to effectively communicate their political ideas. So, in order to talk about this sensibly, let's try to separate these two areas and call one of them program-length television and the other television advertising.

What we are specifically proposing is a reform in the program-length area, and that is that candidates for public office be provided substantial amounts of prime time—either free or at drastically reduced rates—in order to make their case in any way they see fit to the American public.

We see no reason for a further reform of the candidates' use of television as an advertising medium. Candidates for public office who could have access to responsible lengths of broadcast time, and still feel that their most effective way of communicating with the voters is through product-oriented advertising, should be allowed to do so. They should, in our view, have to pay the same price that manufacturers pay in order to market their products. This is now possible through existing law. But if they make the decision to present their case in program-length appeals, we feel they should be encouraged to do this either at drastically reduced rates or free of charge. We would, in effect, be subsidizing a system which would encourage candidates to use this more responsible channel of communication.

A PLAN TO BETTER SERVE THE PUBLIC

So, in brief, we propose the following: (1) Broadcasters, network and local, should set aside a significant body of time to be made available to candidates for public office for the purpose of paid and unpaid program-length political programs. (2) All political spot announcements would continue to be classified as advertising and would be covered under the existing law.

If such a system doesn't work on a voluntary basis, Congress should be prepared to legislate this idea into being in time for the 1974 elections. A reasonable timetable, it seems, would be to first measure how much time broadcasters have made available this year for responsible-length appeals, paid and especially unpaid. Secondly, if access and free time are not forthcoming, then it is clear that more federal regulation is indicated from those wonderful folks that brought you the Campaign Reform Act of 1971.

Hopefully, while all of this is going on, newscasters will take a hard look at themselves and come up with better ways to cover political candidates. One idea might be to set aside a specific campaign-news half-hour period at the end of the regular news each night. This could be salvaged for the political season from the time which was returned to local broadcasters by the FCC when it was decided that too much time in each evening's schedule was being dominated by the networks. Presently, most stations are filling this half hour with ancient and threadbare reruns.

A campaign-news program could make use of videotaped interviews, confrontations between candidates filmed at outside forums, and real live debate. Local and state press corps have got to find new and imaginative ways to bring political-campaign news to their audiences, or they will become increasingly more irrelevant to the process.

Television is the most effective means of political communication yet invented and, because of this fact, it is going to remain the single most important element in campaigns. It is now time to make this instrument better serve our political process.

Has Public Broadcasting Lost Its Nerve?

HARRY J. SKORNIA

The exuberance and national focus of public broadcasting was noticeably slowed in the early seventies when the Nixon administration vetoed a major funding bill, followed by a shake-up in top management of the Corporation for Public Broadcasting. Has public broadcasting been politicized by the purse strings—a fear of many people since its inception in 1967? Harry Skornia provides a hard look at this broadcast system and cites disturbing issues and questions that are in part created by the lack of long-term funding of public broadcasting.

As one of those who fought, prayed and hoped against all odds for "education's own stations," this pioneer looks at what they are doing today with more than passing interest. Regardless of how forgotten many of the "old pioneers" and visionaries may be personally, much of our blood—and reputations—are in this movement called public television.

So I have a special perspective when I ask: What have public television's programmers done to our child? How well is public broadcasting fulfilling the promises we made, of what "we" would do with it, if we got it—in endless testimony during year after discouraging year?

My own involvement with this movement spans 35 years. I often wonder how we persevered, in view of the opposition. Specifically, I recall:

The broken promises of commerical broadcasters who said that they would always take "good care of education's needs," and who

Reprinted by permission of Dr. Harry J. Skornia

then proceeded to oppose separate frequencies for education, to discontinue their own education departments in favor of higher profits, and to boot educators' programs from one useless time period to another.

The near-destruction, during the thirties, of educational broadcasting as the number of AM stations dropped from its previous high of 200 to somewhere closer to 20.

The battles of struggling, small stations as FM came into being. [I recall in particular one game little station, WBOE in Cleveland, which began life as an experimental "UHF AM" in the 40 megacycle band; paid for the non-standard, special-order receivers needed by the schools to receive this "school of the air"—just in time to see FM come along; changed its license to FM (still in the 40 megacycle band); and started again—only to have the 40 megacycle allocation changed to the 88-92 megacycle band.]

The efforts of commercial broadcasters, in several Midwest areas, to delay the arrival of educational television.

Throughout many of these years, there was no one to fight for educational broadcasting, to keep alive the hope of one day having it, or to make "promises" when asked what we'd do with it, other than a little band of us dedicated pioneers, then college administrators and national leaders—rallied by the Joint Council on Educational Telecommunications, under men like Richard Hull and Ralph Steetle—came upon the scene to provide the needed clout, supported by grants from the Rockefeller, Kellogg and Ford Foundations.

Now, of course, those years have quietly taken their place in the histories of broadcasting, and public broadcasting has taken *its* place as an established, if often unsettled, force in American communications. From my own vantage point, any list of plusses and minuses in public broadcasting today would have to begin with this plus: We *are* alive and kicking.

A second encouraging sign is the feeling of fraternity—of being part of a movement. I cannot yet say a profession; those who know of our efforts toward real professionalization can attest that we still have far to go in this area. But we are numerous—and there are many great and talented educators and broadcasters among us.

A third accomplishment is the pioneering efforts in American Samoa and Micronesia—which are in many ways unique in the world. We can well be proud of the Rex Lees, Wilbur Schramms, Vernon Bronsons and other unnamed heroes whose health, as well as dedication, went into them.

A fourth great contribution is specifically public radio's *All Things Considered*. I have for some time called this America's best news and public-affairs program. I believe this opinion is becoming more widely shared, particularly among opinion leaders around the country.

There are many other projects and uses of the media—in the form of TV colleges, open universities and other break-throughs, of which we can be proud. Let us not forget them.

There are also some things that bother me about the current scene—particularly about public television. Perhaps, when addressing an audience of professional readers, it would be more productive to focus on these. And perhaps, since I'm speaking of *our* creation, you may accept from me—whose loyalty should be beyond question—some rather blunt concerns that, from outsiders, you would call unfair. As a reminder, I was on the firing line for quite a while, took my bumps, and know how *hard* it is, against the many odds.

Certainly, many of public broadcasting's problems up to this time have been attributable to the lack of a permanent, dependable, continuing financial base. At the time Newton Minow's efforts were succeeding in getting the bill through to require all sets shipped in interstate commerce to have UHF, I hoped (and many of us badgered Congressmen) to get also an excise tax on each set, which would be an allocated tax, specifically earmarked to support *public* broadcasting.

During the years even distinguished advertising educators like Charles Sandage of Illinois have recommended that excess profits in broadcasting go into a kitty into which less favorably situated stations might dip for funds to enable them to do the sometimes unprofitable public interest programs in frequently unprofitable areas, on which our nation's survival depends.

When the Ford Foundation announced it was getting out of public broadcasting after admittedly generous and indispensable support for many years, I hoped that they (perhaps with other foundations) might consider an endowment of at least a few hundred million dollars, large enough to provide minimum security to public broadcasting if it lived only on investment income from it, leaving the capital or "seed money" intact until new sources like those mentioned above could be developed.

What we need for *all* stations—especially community stations—is a practical equivalent of the frequently undramatic line-item status in the regular budget that the stations of many (especially land-grant) universities already enjoy. Modest as the broadcasting budget is at the University of Illinois at Urbana in Champaign, for example, it is (though perhaps not yet in priority, when *reductions* come) virtually as *secure* a line-item in the recurring, state-appropriated tax funds of the total University as budgets for heating, or any of the other instructional or operational departments. In some large state university and network systems, and in numerous public school systems, similar relative *security* (I did not say equality, or affluence) prevails.

But not for community television. To engage in a bit of personal reminiscence again, many readers may not know the genesis of the idea of the Community TV station. Without claiming credit for any part of the idea, let me describe what we in U.S. Military Government (in consultation and cooperation with our British and French colleagues) in 1946 to 1948 designed as the structure of West German broadcasting.

First, there was to be no federal system, and no government hand in it. A public corporation was created for each separate state or "land" in West Germany. Each corporation was made up of representatives equally of all the principal social, economic, educational and ethnic groupings of each state: labor, agriculture, the various religious denominations, the various educational levels and institutions, women, youth groups, etc. West German broadcasting was not to be the instrument of any one group (government, business, religion, labor, education) but of the *whole* society: *public* as opposed to government or political.

I believe many critics today feel that the West German system is one of the best in the world, but it is so principally because, *built into the system*, was a set tax, so the *public* paid, and knew it was the *direct supporter* of German broadcasting.

That feature, the set tax, was retained from earlier German history under the Weimar Republic. It provided adequate financing, and even bought the first receivers that went into the schools. That feature of *most* free, democratic broadcast systems in the world is precisely the feature which the U.S. community TV station, does *not* have. And that critical difference, for these stations, has spawned a great many compromises or betrayals of the public interest which I discuss below.

Until, or unless, permanent and dependable recurring financing is built into this part of the system, many of the most unique members of the public TV system (the community stations) will be doomed not only to be among the most cowardly, but also to engage in practices that smack of pure commercialism. It is fortunate that public broadcasting has begun to seek—as a crash project of urgent priority, to *solve* the problem of financing. For as long as public TV in many localities is doomed to pass the hat, conduct auctions (for the success of which the aid of "personalities" from the commercial media is needed), and adopt a variety of near-commercial practices, public TV will be a lady whose virtue is of necessity *partially* compromised. Public broadcasting, as a movement, today is forced to co-exist, with smiling tolerance, with the most shameful behavior on the part of its commercial counterparts. This situation is nothing less than intolerable. If continued, it will be fatal.

We, who fought for public TV, realized that no system is perfect. Each system contains its taboos. The commercial system protects its friends and sponsors: business and business practices. The corporation becomes "we," and government "they." To escape commercials, there is public TV or Pay TV. The latter is still free enterprise, but it makes it possible to pay directly, in money, instead of in attention, time, some call it blood—i.e. in the form of commercials.

Even the most securely financed educational public TV has its taboos. Imagine a University of Illinois Public TV documentary on some of the shameful politicking of the General Assembly, which appropriates its funds. Or on the Governor who can reduce or "line veto" various appropriations. Or a documentary by the Community TV station, on the shenanigans of the city of Chicago which controls, in whole or in part, the budgets of many of its educational institution members.

Of course there is no perfect system. But there is room for courage and intelligence within our imperfect system. Here, bluntly listed, are some of the national problem areas that I think public broadcasting must attack.

VIOLENCE

The Payne Fund in 1933 documented in a dozen volumes (some authored by people like George Stoddard, later President of the the University of Illinois and Chancellor of New York University) the connection between violence in *films* and delinquency in girls, boys, adults and institutionalized criminals. Today, most TV is films.

The Catholic Church, Western German and Japanese researchers, and several volumes of UNESCO studies have further proved causative connections between TV violence and real life violence. The world has become incredulous at commercial TV's continued use of violence in the U.S.

The 1962 and 1963 Dodd Committee Hearings provided evidence that this problem was reaching frightening proportions. Immediate steps were promised.

The recent Pastore Hearings on the Surgeon General's Report on TV Violence and Children had the Surgeon General, on the record, declaring that there is no longer any question of the causative connection between TV violence and real life violence, and that the time for action is now, if our nation is to survive. In all these hearings, the networks were there. But this, in a sense, is their Watergate. The videotapes they made have never been aired. What is worse: public television has apparently concurred in this criminal concealment. The 56-minute film produced by the Canadian Film Board, with the specifics suggested above—*has not been shown on Public TV in the U.S.*, to my knowledge, except on station KVST-TV in Hollywood, on whose board I happen to serve.

I personally offered this film, or a video tape of it, to our Chicago Public TV station. Perhaps they needed the "good will" of the network stations too much for fund-raising to dare to show it. In any case it has never been shown except for the hundreds of non-TV group showings arranged by friends and former students of the author.

Under the rug with it are the 1974 hearings—with the testimony of Leo Singer, President of Miracle White, seeking to lead a movement for corporations to refuse to sponsor programs of violence. Un-aired too, are Annenberg Dean George Gerbner's TV Violence Index explanation and early results.

The millions of crippled lives resulting from this network practice—the millions of maimings and deaths that are occurring—cry out for public TV to expose this shameful practice. One may claim the need to "live to fight another day." But what kind of a virtuous life is it for public TV if this crime—and kow-towing to network and industry pressure, and gun lobby power—reduce public TV in effect to misprision of felonies? Is this kind of life worth living? Where is our integrity?

ENERGY

The oil industry scandal cries out, finally, for documentaries that do not engage in the double talk heard from commercial TV documentaries—double-talk that is more than counterbalanced on commercial networks by intensive "institutional commercials" from the companies themselves. Yet public television is silent. The reason is obvious in the scores of non-commercial commercials by Mobil, Exxon and others who "support" (i.e. purchase immunity to exposure on) public TV.

We are urged to save electricity. At the same time TV commercials "push" hair dryers, curlers and other electricity-using instruments, many of which use more electricity than all the light bulbs in many a home. Not a word on public TV about this hypocrisy. Why? Perhaps because "Sunday programming on this station is made possible by (a grant from) Commonwealth (or Consolidated) Edison"?

DRUGS

There are various studies available on TV as a "drug pusher." On a 1973 program Art Linkletter indicated that some 40 percent of all abdominal surgery (for ulcers, internal bleeding, etc.) was caused by aspirin. Yet aspirin, with little protest from public TV, is pushed on probably every commercial station in the nation as irresponsibly as if it were candy.

NUTRITION

The danger to teeth and general health arising from the huge amount of sugar being packaged and sold as foods and beverages (in cereals, snacks, soft drinks) is no secret. Surely Kellogg, Coca Cola and other such grants are not enough to purchase public TV's silence in this area, too? If so, whose interests is public broadcasting protecting? If the "sponsors," under whatever guise, are the same on commercial as on public TV, who is to look after the interests of those the sponsors deceive and exploit? How is America to be kept from achieving malnutrition in the midst of plenty, while wasting precious materials which might help the rest of the world achieve a decent standard of living—or at least survival?

POLLUTION

Does "contribution" from a steel company "bribe" public broadcasting not to do documentaries on the steel industry's role in polluting the air and water of America? Can a motor company purchase immunity by being a "big giver"? How livable is this condition? Once "built in," how reversible is this habit of compromise with our integrity?

ATTENTION/CONCENTRATION/FRAGMENTATION

The education job we hope to do depends on citizen ability to understand, concentrate, and be the ultimate policymaker of the nation.

How compatible with this are commercial practices in which there are hundredfold repetitions of promotion for products one can't possibly use or find relevant—in my case girls' hair preparations and a myriad others—which can develop in us, if we are to preserve our sanity, only inattention. The ratio of the the unwanted to the wanted has become so high that the *usual* condition is likely to be "tuned out"; we "awaken" from this state often, to find the "tune-out" has also deprived us of some small but part of the "mix."

In short, with the fast-moving, interrupt "bits" emphasis of the media, how are we to preserve the sustained concentration which some problems—and our nation—frankly need? More concentration on candidate qualification and issues might have spared us Watergate and many other mistakes.

Fragmentation also has reduced our expectation, or tradition, in communications to bits too small to satisfy sustained or significant needs.

Sesame Street had in a sense to imitate *commercial* approaches, because children had been conditioned and left by commercial TV with short attention spans, the expectation of small bits and nuggets of information repeated ad nauseum, and hysterically paced. The BBC, where children were not so conditioned, noted this fragmented pacing and (dis)continuity. This is far different from what *Seasame Street* would and could be if such commercial TV conditioning were not present. Have we, the educational community, simply to live with this conditioning of our children without protest or even mention of what commercial TV does?

VALUES/CELEBRITIES/MODELS

It is interesting to compare who the *models* of success, admiration and imitation are *now* (largely entertainers and sports figures) with those of pre-TV days. TV makes celebrities, of course, just as in music it "makes" a hit by its simple repetition, almost regardless of quality.

In my football days at Michigan State our hero was Knute Rockne. "Rock" taught that, even if your team lost, if certain individuals played over their heads, and achieved by discipline and spirit levels *they* had never before achieved, you had, in that sense, won. How you played the game was a crucial criterion in sport and life.

In professional football (and politics: cf. Wagergate) "winning is the only thing," to quote not only Vince Lombardi but Mitchell, Haldeman, Ehrlichman and others.

Just as Japanese broadcasting devotes whole series to ethics, morality and values, should public broadcasters not concern themselves with these factors—and protest at the destruction which commercial media models are wreaking on American moral fibre?

ENCE/TRIVIALIZATION

...n network officials refuse to ...e in the violence problem is ... terms. What they parade as ... the "three spoon test," the ...eezing toilet paper to see ...r not or "proving" a product's ... from its own label. How *can* one convince people who call this evidence?

At prime time do we discuss nutrition, poverty, political candidates and issues, or population problems? No. Our radio-TV students found, from a frequency study of commercial TV (including commercials) that the principal problems of America are smelly feet, underarm perspiration, dingy hair, slipping dentures, yellowing teeth, hemorrhoids, and stomach acidity (from eating too well!).

How can public television interest the population in other problems, while the commercial media, with hardly a protest, are allowed to say "these are the ones?"

POLITICS/ECONOMICS

How tolerably can public television co-exist with the deceitful conventional wisdom that says that money is the measure of success or qualification? Or how effective a political system can we have when it is the kind of big money made necessary by television that gave us Watergate, and makes it virtually impossible for a non-millionaire (or a candidate not "sold out" to millionaires or special interests) even to run?

Must public television not recognize that *any money* for campaigning by TV is immoral and indecent in a land where networks earn profits of millions and percentage profits in the hundreds, if the statements were not "rigged"? Must we not join the other *civilized* democracies in eliminating this shame and perversion of our political process before democracy and politics become permanently incompatible?

Or is it really necessary that economics be the least understood problem and science in the nation, and the most poorly explained? Why not have a try at reducing this "science" to understandable dimensions, even if those who profit most from keeping it esoteric and confused resist such an approach, because it would weaken their present status, which they find good?

OTHERS

A discussion such as this one could go on to consider models of "conflict resolution," and the need for us to be about developing skills in this area.

Or "ascertainment" of community needs, which I feel is as essential for educators as for commercial broadcasters, deserves consideration. Programming without ascertainment is like medication or surgery without diagnosis. Japan, Britain, and Germany, not forced by any FCC, or charter, have "town meeting" type panels weekly, with millions (not just a few leaders) consulted daily about the ideas, needs and expectations from broadcasting. That's the two-way feedback we need.

Or *language*: under FTC threats commercial TV has designed a new type of ambiguity of language which prevents the deceitful advertiser from being "nailed." The only thing is that inexactness and ambiguity have risen to such a level that when students or others need *precision* and *exactness*, it is nearly impossible to find; language, as the currency of communication, is being so debased that our classrooms and programs are bogged down with "speakers" flailing the air helplessly in their effort to communicate, nearly every other word of their speech being "I mean," "you know," "right on" or similar substitutes for communication. Before verbal communication breaks down further, should public television not begin to recognize this problem, not only in its own back yard but in the total environment?

These few examples may or may not be trends. Personally, it seems to me that there has been a reduction of muscle and courage in what is beginning to call itself the public broadcasting "industry." (I used to press for it to call itself an institution.)

Weren't there some pretty muscular "counterads" a few years ago? Where is this consumer effort today? Weren't we pretty excited about setting meaningful professional standards, perhaps for the world, for the broadcaster-journalist role we envisaged? Are we laying off because professionalism means lots of things you won't do for money—and, right now, we need money?

What worries me is, I've seen this sort of thing happen elsewhere before. At my age you've seen a lot, if you've stayed alert. I saw Nazism come to Germany, with fewer freedoms each summer I cycled through the land.

I've seen broadcast systems sampling "commercialism," and finding the full, effete feeling pleasant—and drifting more and more into a life of easy and expensive living.

As we come to see the finer and finer staffs and facilities we can have and the awards we can win, and even the documentaries we can do (but not on too controversial subjects), by taking a little from big business here and going along with big commercial practices there, isn't it a great temptation to leave until we are financially more secure meeting the violence (and therefore the big commercial TV boys) problem, or the gun control problem, or the problem of what commercials are doing to our attention factors?

Such a trend as the present one soon becomes irreversible. Affluence rarely if ever brings courage. If there is to be courage, it will be there now, however lean the budgets.

The drift into ease is so pleasant that soon the values of public broadcasting may become pretty hard to distinguish from those of commercial TV. If so, where has our child gone? What were we fighting for?

The Carnegie Commission was right in asserting that financial security would be essential if public broadcasting is to make a real difference in America. At present it is making only a partial difference, and that difference does not seem to be increasing as much, or as fast, as we who fought for it would like.

Let us hope public broadcasting may devote its best brains to solving the financial insecurity problem which seems to be spawning increasing moral cowardice in treating gut issues in America.

We've whipped many problems. Now, let's solve the financial one before the status of a prostitute, or lady of easy virtue, becomes permanently acceptable.

In the April 1974 *Center Report*, Dr. E. Grey Dimond, Provost of the University of Missouri-Kansas City Medical School, observes: " . . . The United States has not developed an effective code of morality and ethics. Crime, drugs, venereal disease, unemployment, racism, school dropouts, broken families, alienated children, alcoholism, graft, political conniving are almost all at the highest of any country in the world. The United States has become an *old, young country*."

Has this condition any connection with the fact that public broadcasting in the U.S. enjoys only a fraction of the per capita financing it enjoys in most countries (Britain, Japan, West Germany, Canada), while commercial broadcasting enjoys the greatest (and some would say most irresponsible) profits, power and freedoms of anywhere in the world?

Whatever may be your reply to that question, isn't it essential that a new birth of courage, a rejuvenation of goals and deeds must come soon if democracy, human dignity and decency are to survive here?

> There's talk of a revolution. A social revolution. It has started and is progressing. Television, one way or the other, is going to be a part of that revolution. And it is going to be an unwilling part. Television exists in this country for two reasons: money and audiences. Money puts the physical productions on the air, but audiences keep them there and keep the flow of money coming.
> —Sheila Smith Hobson

The Decision Is Tentative

BENNO C. SCHMIDT, JR.

The Caldwell decision in 1972 was strongly criticized as a violation of a news reporter's freedom of speech and confidentiality of information sources. In this analysis of the issue, Benno Schmidt, Jr. points out that the Supreme Court position is not unyielding and, in fact, leaves considerable latitude for future judicial and legislative activity.

For a little less than a decade, journalism and law have shared a common struggle to accommodate traditional procedures and principles to the development of widespread disenchantment and disobedience in American society. Numerous political, racial, and cultural groups have committed themselves to political or personal goals which they believe transcend the traditional obligations of citizens in a democratic society. While the rhetoric is often more apocalyptic than the action, there is no denying the social importance of these alienated groups. Whether the cause has been the rights of racial minorities, resistance to the draft, protest against the war, or exploration of different levels of consciousness, many groups—both organized and spontaneous—have advocated and often acted in disregard of law. Other traditional sources of authority, such as family, schools, or church, have been vigorously challenged. The media, as readers of the *Review* need not be reminded, have not escaped this distrust.

The *Caldwell* decision, encompassing three cases joined together for adjudication, is a microcosm of the difficulties of both journalism and law in responding to the alienation of many groups in this country. It is an intersection of journalism and law of the sort which, with disquieting frequency in recent years, has come to be viewed as a collision between competing interests. The idea that the interests of journalism and law are naturally antithetical, in this instance or any other, is ominous. Of course, much error and injustice are done in the name of law, just as much that is tawdry and worse is accomplished by reporters and the media. There will always be conflicts when either journalism or law offers a short-sighted view of its real interests. But thoughtful persons in each profession must make the effort to understand and accommodate the legitimate interests of the other. What, in brief, are the legitimate social interests of journalism and our legal system as exemplified in *Caldwell*?

Knowledge must be available about dissident groups before social institutions can respond to them in a rational and principled way. Disregarding any issues of justification concerning these groups' rhetoric or actions—issues of great variety about which there is ample room for disagreement—most persons would agree that decisionmakers at all levels have both underestimated and misunderstood the disenchantment which exists in many quarters. Whatever disagreements we might have about dealing with alienation and disenchantment are academic until we have access to information. For this knowledge we must depend on the individual efforts of journalists who try to penetrate the suspicion and hostility of protest and underground groups. These efforts will be substantially impeded if the reporter's subjects feel that anything he learns will become available to those social institutions to which they are opposed.

The difficulties of covering important protest groups should not be exaggerated. Few significant dissident groups are interested solely in being let alone. Most embrace a responsibility to reform society at large, and thus find useful whatever media attention they can attract. Conflicts between suspicion of the media and the desire to propagate information through it have resulted in individual reporters' being given knowledge on condition that other information or the identity of certain sources not be divulged. Journalists always have made use of promises of confidentiality in probing beneath the surface of

Reprinted from the *Columbia Journalism Review*, Sept.–Oct. 1972 by permission of Columbia University and the author, Benno C. Schmidt, Jr., Professor of Law, Columbia University School of Law.

press handouts, outright lies, and self-serving secrecy. But my impression is that the use of confidentiality in digging out stories is now more extensive than ever. Certainly, to the extent that the practice is a condition for coverage of disenchanted groups in our society, it has greater social value than ever before.

On the other hand, the legal system has important interests at stake in overcoming promises of confidentiality when they stand in the way of prompt and accurate detection and prosecution of crimes. The grand juries which subpoenaed the three reporters involved in the *Caldwell* decision occupy a traditional and important place in law enforcement. It has long been the proud boast of Anglo-American law that no person is too high to escape the obligation of testifying to a grand jury. This unlimited obligation is an important guarantee of equality in the operation of criminal law. Thus, courts have historically been unsympathetic to claims that certain kinds of information should be privileged from disclosure before the grand jury. Only the privilege against self-incrimination and the attorney-client privilege have achieved general recognition from the courts of the U.S.

In *Caldwell*, the Supreme Court was presented with a collision between the interests of journalistic freedom—interests accorded a constitutional dimension by the First Amendment—and the fundamental social interest in enforcement of the criminal law. Most observers seem to think that the Court forthrightly rejected the journalists' claims in favor of upholding the investigative powers of the grand jury. I believe the decision is more tentative. The Court clearly rejected any journalists' privilege in the particular circumstances of these cases. But there are signs that the Court may be more sympathetic to the privilege if it is asserted in different circumstances.

Let us look more closely at the three cases at hand. One case involved two stories describing the activities of drug users and sellers in and around Louisville; a second, a report on civil disorders in New Bedford, Mass., for which the newsman covered a Black Panther news conference and spent about three hours inside the Panther headquarters to cover a police raid which the Panthers expected but which never occurred; and a third—the best known of the cases—a report on activities of the Black Panthers in Oakland and San Francisco for which Earl Caldwell taped interviews and wrote articles in *The New York Times*.

In all three cases, the reporters declined to provide requested information to a grand jury. Caldwell, however, did not claim that a reporter should be completely free from official investigation with respect to all kinds of confidential information about possible law violations. He and the *Times* made the narrower argument that "so drastic an incursion upon First Amendment freedom" should not be permitted unless the Government could show a "compelling governmental interest" in the reporter's testimony. Such an interest, they submitted, could be demonstrated if the Government convinced a court that the reporter probably has information relevant to a specific violation of law, that the information sought could not be obtained from sources other than the reporter, and that, as a general matter, the subject matter of the investigation is of overriding interest to the Government.

Unlike the reporters in the other two cases before the Court, Caldwell found relief in the lower courts. The U.S. District Court denied a motion to quash the subpoena, but ordered that Caldwell not be required to testify about any confidential sources or information received while gathering news. Caldwell still refused to appear before the grand jury, maintaining that his appearance alone would jeopardize his relationship with the Black Panthers since they would not know what had gone on in the secret session. The District Court held Caldwell in contempt, but the Court of Appeals for the Ninth Circuit sustained an appeal, holding that the First Amendment gave him the right to refuse to appear in the absence of the Government's showing of some special necessity.

The opinions of a closely divided Supreme Court pretty well span the spectrum of possible First Amendment responses. The majority opinion, authored by Justice White, first argues that requiring reporters to testify before grand juries about confidential sources involves no "intrusions upon speech or assembly, no prior restraint or restriction on what the press may publish, and no express or implied command that the press publish what it prefers to withhold." Official inquiry is simply an "incidental burdening of the press," resulting from enforcement of civil or criminal statutes of general applicability; citizens generally have an obligation to tell grand juries anything they might know about commission of crimes—the sole exception being the Fifth Amendment right of any witness to refuse to testify about matters that might be self-incriminating. Thus, these cases present an issue akin to valid general laws—such as general tax statutes or labor relation statutes—being enforced neutrally; in such tax or labor cases, objections to enforcement because of incidental burdens on First Amendment activities have properly been given little weight.

The reporters argued for a special privilege because of the consequences of compulsory testimony: the flow of information would be significantly diminished from news sources preferring to remain confidential. However, White argues, not all news sources insist on confidentiality, and reporters may never be called to testify before a grand jury even when they have received information in confidence. Moreover, informants who have insisted on confidentiality often have a substantial interest in dissemination of news which would outweigh any fear of investigation. Thus, the fear of substantial drying up of news sources is speculative. But, White argues, even if some constriction in the flow of news should occur, the public interest in investigating and prosecuting crimes reported to the press outweighs that in the dissemination of news about those activities when the dissemination rests upon confidentiality.

The majority refused to accept Caldwell's claim that the State be required to meet three tests before requiring a reporter's testimony: 1) that there is probable cause to believe that the reporter possesses information relevant to a specific violation of law; 2) that the information sought cannot be obtained by alternative means from sources other than the reporter; and 3) that there is compelling and overriding interest in the information. White meets these arguments with a rather simplified theory of the grand jury's appropriate purposes. They include, first, an investigatory function in determining whether a crime has been committed, and second, a need to review all available evidence to determine whether prosecution is appropriate. Third, he suggests, the Government always has a compelling interest in information about the violation of any of its criminal laws; courts are not in a position to choose the criminal activities which are important enough to justify investigation into a reporter's confidential information.

White also argues that acceptance of the reporters' privilege would lead to undue confusion in future cases. The potential difficulties include defining the categories of newsmen who qualify for the privilege—a troublesome problem in light of the traditional doctrine that the liberty of the press extends to pamphleteers, lecturers, and almost any author, as well as clear cut journalists. In addition, whether there is probable cause to believe a crime has been committed, or whether the reporter has useful information which the grand jury cannot obtain elsewhere, pose extremely difficult judicial determinations. Finally, courts cannot assess the governmental interest in particular information by weighing the value of enforcing different criminal laws. This would engage the courts in an essentially legislative value judgment of various criminal laws.

The majority opinion clearly rests on the notion that the subject of reporters' privilege is an appropriate one for legislative or executive consideration. It notes that several states already have passed statutes embodying a journalists' privilege of the kind sought, and that the U.S. Attorney General has fashioned a set of limiting rules—guidelines— governing subpoenas which embody some of the standards Caldwell advanced.

After seemingly rejecting both the theoretical and the empirical arguments for a journalists' privilege, the majority opinion concludes with an enigmatic suggestion that the door to the privilege may not be completely closed. "Newsgathering," the majority notes obliquely, "is not without its First Amendment protection":

[G]rand jury investigations if instituted or conducted other than in good faith, would pose wholly different issues for resolution under the First Amendment. Official harassment of the press undertaken not for purposes of law enforcement but to disrupt a reporter's relationship with his news sources would have no justification. Grand juries are subject to judicial control and subpoenas to motions to quash. We do not expect courts will forget that grand juries must operate within the limits of the First Amendment as well as the Fifth.

The majority's whisper of encouragement is echoed, if not clarified, in a brief but potentially important concurring opinion of Justice Powell. He emphasizes "the limited nature" of the Court's holding, and states that "we do not hold that . . . state and federal authorities are free to 'annex' the news media as 'an investigative arm of government.'" No "harassment" of newsmen will be tolerated, Powell continues, if a reporter can show that the grand jury investigation is "not being conducted in good faith" or if he is called upon for information "bearing only a remote and tenuous relationship to the subject of the investigation." Moreover, judicial relief could be forthcoming if the reporter "has some other reason to believe that his testimony implicates confidential source relationships without a legitimate need of law enforcement."

What Powell seems to be saying is that the claim of reporters' privilege must be balanced against society's interest in law enforcement in a highly particularistic, case-by-case manner. In a footnote, he reminds us that Caldwell asserted a privilege *not even to appear* before the grand jury unless the Government met his three preconditions. Powell rejects this notion that the State's authority should be thus tested at the threshold. Instead, he seems to suggest that the balance can better be drawn when actual questions are put and the reporter refuses to answer. Presumably, Powell agreed with the decision reached in the other two cases because, although questions were actually put, the reporters in those cases rested their right of refusal on an absolute journalists' privilege rather than on an *ad hoc* demonstration that the particular questions were improper.

Four Justices dissented. Justice Douglas expressed his own categorical view and Justice Stewart wrote a more balanced opinion for himself and Justices Brennan and Marshall.

For Douglas, the proper decision is a simple reflection of his absolute view of the First Amendment: "There is no 'compelling need' that can be shown which qualifies the reporter's immunity from appearing or testifying before a grand jury, unless the reporter is implicated in a crime." Douglas thus endorses an absolute privilege: since no answer can constitutionally be compelled, there is no need to require even an appearance. Douglas rejects as insufficient under the First Amendment Caldwell's and the *Times'* position (which he characterizes as "amazing") that the journalists' privilege should be balanced against competing needs of the Government. Douglas has no doubt about the unfortunate consequences:

Forcing a reporter before a grand jury will have two retarding effects upon the ear and the pen of the press. Fear of exposure will cause dissidents to communicate less openly to trusted reporters. And, fear of accountability will cause editors and critics to write with more restrained pens.

Justice Stewart wrote a careful but impassioned dissent. Stewart's starting point is the broad right to publish guaranteed in our society by the First Amendment, from the 1921 landmark decision in *Near vs. Minnesota* to last year's decision on the Pentagon Papers. From this right to publish, Stewart deduces a corollary right to gather news. This right, in turn, requires protection of confidential sources "as a matter of simple logic once three factual predicates are recognized": (1) newsmen require informants in gathering news; (2) confidentiality is essential to creation and maintenance of a newsgathering relationship with informants; and (3) unbridled subpoena power will deter both informants from divulging sensitive information and reporters from publishing.

The journalists' privilege which Stewart would protect is not absolute. The interest of the Government in investigating crime is substantial, and Stewart believes it can properly outweigh the journalists' privilege if the Government can show: (1) that the information sought is "*clearly* relevant to a *precisely* defined subject of governmental inquiry"; (2) that the reporter probably has the relevant information; and (3) that there is no other available source for the information.

Stewart concludes that the Court's decision will in the long run impede rather than advance efficient law enforcement. Law enforcement officials benefit from dissemination of news about illegal or questionable activities. Thus, for Stewart, the Court's decision is a "sad paradox":

> [T]he newsman will not only cease to be a useful grand jury witness; he will cease to investigate and publish information about issues of public import. I cannot subscribe to such an anomalous result, for in my view, the interests protected by the First Amendment are not antagonistic to the administration of justice.

What conclusion, then, can be drawn about the future of journalists' privilege? Despite what might appear at first to be the Court's flat rejection of the privilege, I believe that both extreme constitutional positions are ruled out. Obviously, the Court has rejected, by an effective 8 to 1 vote, the view advocated by many newsmen and adopted by Justice Douglas that journalists should have an impenetrable shield against official inquiry into confidential sources. Less apparently, a working majority has also rejected the opposite extreme: that journalists can claim no special protection under the First Amendment but should be treated like any person with knowledge of illegal activity.

Justice Powell's concurrence reflects at the very least an open mind about extending to newsmen a qualified privilege to refuse testimony that would jeopardize confidential relationships. Powell seems to recognize that a journalist has an important interest in protecting confidential sources. But for Powell the legal context is critical to balancing this interest against society's vital interest in law enforcement. He wants a concrete record of particular questions about a specific confidential relationship before he attempts to reconcile the reporter's First Amendment claim and society's interest in detection and prosecution of crime.

Thus, Powell rejects the invitation in *Caldwell*, we can assume, because he believes that, in constitutional terms, not all grand jury questions are the same, not all journalists are the same, not all confidential relationships are the same, and (perhaps) not all crimes are the same. Relevant differences, in Powell's view, can be gauged only when the issue is at a riper stage than in *Caldwell*, where the reporter had failed even to appear, or than in the other two cases, where the reporters rested their non-compliance on an absolute claim of privilege.

If this reading is correct, Powell, in a future case—perhaps in *Caldwell* if, on remand, it moves to specific questions and refusals to answer based on concrete arguments about particular sources—may shift to join the four dissenters in upholding a journalist's claim that the First Amendment justifies a refusal to disclose confidential information. I suspect that we have not heard the last word from the Supreme Court on journalists' privilege.

Other developments may be expected. The three cases decided all had to do with reporters' testimony before grand juries. Neither the majority nor any of the concurring or dissenting opinions discussed the constitutional status of grand jury subpoenas *duces tecum*—orders compelling the production of tapes, notebooks, outtakes, first drafts, and other forms of tangible evidence. The subpoena initially served on Earl Caldwell was of this sort: it ordered him to produce for the grand jury notes and tape recordings. When he objected, the Government agreed to reduce the scope to an order to testify.

While the opinions do not so indicate, it is conceivable that the Court may find journalists' work product subject to a greater range of constitutional protection than is accorded his testimony. Required production of notes, tapes, or first drafts might seem more directly in conflict with freedom of the press than compelled testimony in that the quality of the actual article, report, or newstape disseminated to the public is more directly affected. If journalists' stock in trade can be as freely compelled as testimony, then journalists will be constrained in the initial writing, filming, or taping, when freedom and flexibility are most necessary if the quality of the final product is not to suffer. The Court might therefore find a greater threat to the First Amendment in subpoenas requiring production of tangible work product, and strike the balance more on the side of journalists' privilege than it would for testimony.

The final prediction to be drawn from *Caldwell* is that there will be renewed legislative activity. In difficult constitutional problems, the Supreme Court's response often reflects an assessment of legislative or executive competence to deal with the problem. The Court's treatment of

> ... the established American press has in the past ten years and particularly in the past two years performed precisely the function it was intended to perform by those who wrote the First Amendment of our Constitution. . . . Perhaps our liberties might survive without an independent established press. But the Founders doubted it, and . . . I think we can all be thankful for their doubts.
> —U.S. Supreme Court Justice Potter Stewart

journalists' privilege is in this tradition. The majority opinion notes that some states have accorded some degree of statutory protection to a journalist's confidential sources and information. Moreover, Justice White points to Atty. Gen. Mitchell's 1970 subpoena guidelines, which almost meet the tests urged upon the Court by Caldwell and the *Times*. The majority makes quite clear its view that defining and protecting journalists' privilege is much better suited to legislative than judicial treatment. White's opinion catalogues the subtle problems of rulemaking and line-drawing (is every pamphleteer and would-be author a "journalist"? what crimes are "serious" enough to warrant investigation into a journalist's confidential sources?) that the majority feels can be more sensibly handled by general legislation than by case-by-case response. Deference to a legislative solution, the majority obviously feels, is realistic in this instance because of the media's political power. The press and the state and federal legislative bodies should respond to the Court's invitation. The best hope for the media is clearly in the nation's legislatures.

Despite the predictable cries of outrage against the Supreme Court's decision, it should be remembered that the Court's rejection of the journalists' privilege may not be as complete as it appears. Courts have traditionally opposed the creation of evidentiary privileges because such barriers clog necessary investigative and adjudicative processes. Therefore, the chances for judicial creation of a sweeping privilege were not good.

On the other hand, there is no doubt that the publicity given the Court's decision will dry up some news sources. Particularly if overzealous prosecutors abuse their power to try to require journalists to divulge confidential information, the consequences for a probing and independent press are troubling to contemplate. The Court has said it is not unconstitutional to compel a reporter to appear before a grand jury to testify about confidential sources. This does not mean that frequent resort to the practice is a good idea.

QUESTIONS FOR DISCUSSION

1. How does the structure of the mass communications industry influence public and governmental bodies in a democratic society?
2. Your freedom of expression is guaranteed by the First Amendment. How can you gain access to the mass media to exercise this freedom?
3. What role should the media play as watchdog of the government? The government of media?
4. What restrictions do the media place upon themselves regarding their associations with corporate interests? How are these restrictions manifested?
5. Broadcasters maintain they are not afforded the full First Amendment freedom of expression enjoyed by print media. Why? What specific regulatory document is cited by broadcasters as proof of such restrictions? What arguments are cited to justify this document? Which position do you agree with?

PROJECTS

Analyze a local television or radio station to determine:
(a) Does the station editorialize frequently?
(b) Does the station endorse political candidates and issues?
(c) Has the station been summoned to provide air time under the provision of the FCC Fairness Doctrine? Under what circumstances?
(d) Do you feel the station is fair to all groups in your community? Give specific examples to support your answer.

MINDS, MANIPULATORS, AND MEDIA

Contamination: Propaganda and the News

DALE MINOR

The inability to draw a strong, sharp line between journalism and show business—which is ultimately to say, between fact and fiction—is one of the most critical problems in modern-day American journalism because of the crucial role television occupies in conveying news. The case should not, of course, be overstated, and it is the opposite of my intention to foster paranoia toward the press; my purpose is, rather, to point out what are serious dangers to the press. The quality of television news, both in terms of the caliber of its people and the professionalism of its standards, has improved considerably over the years. But that improvement falls somewhat short of revolution. Probably the most hopeful aspect of the picture is that many television newsmen—reporters, producers, and news executives alike—have become increasingly aware of and vigilant toward these problems and vices and the special responsibilities they bear.

One of the difficulties after drawing the line between fact and fiction is in making the viewer aware of it, and this is a part of the problem over which the newsman and the television news departments have absolutely no control. The problem arises because fiction—outright, announced fiction—can look very much like fact and often purports to be or to represent fact. What we find in the "entertainment," or avowedly show-biz, side of the equation is a reversal of the fact-fiction relationship. Theoretically, television has two functions vis-à-vis the viewing public: to inform them and to entertain them, with great predominance given the latter. Theoretically, the two functions are separate,

From the book *The Information War* by Dale Minor. Copyright © 1970 by Hawthorn Books, Inc. Reprinted by permission of Hawthorn Books, Inc., 70 Fifth Avenue, New York 10011.

but as we have seen, in reality the values and practices of show-business impinge upon and corrupt the process of informing. In like manner the desire to inform invades the area of entertainment, and a host of regular network television programs, particularly dramatic series, have become fiction-*cum*-propaganda, consciously or inadvertently developing and nourishing attitudes among viewers which affect their reception of information provided by journalists—sometimes creating a built-in hostility to that information, but in any case tending to wash out whatever line might exist between fact and fiction on television. This process is accelerated by the imperative of realism and "authenticity" in dramatic presentations, even of the most banal sort (actually, the more banal the program, the more important those values become).

Take, as the most prominent and flagrant example of this phenomenon, the great gaggle of television dramatic series devoted to the trials and tribulations of policemen. A few that spring immediately to mind are *N.Y.P.D.*, *Adam-12*, *Dragnet*, *Ironside*, and *The F.B.I.* All of them are technically well done fictional propaganda vehicles for specific police departments (New York City, Los Angeles, San Francisco, and of course, the Federal Bureau of Investigation) as well as for law-enforcement groups and attitudes in general. Possessing the ideal ingredients of danger, action, and simple but effective ready-made plots, the genre has always been a sure-fire winner, but it seems exceptionally successful today with so much public concern over crime in the streets, student uprisings, civil-rights and antiwar demonstrations, and the general issue of law and order. Now, the line between serious fictional drama and reality has always been provisional at best. As art, the former is involved with "truth" as much as, and to a depth inaccessible to, fact-bound journalism; in the same manner comedy and satire have always been intimately involved in the subject matter of journalism. They are individual and independent visions of truth and the meaning of reality, to be judged as such, free of any other considerations or responsibilities. The dramatic series named above, however, are about as independent as the editorial board of *Pravda*. Not only are such shows dependent on the political and social views and attitudes of network executives and advertisers, but, more importantly, they are dependent on the views and public-relations interests of the organizations they portray. The case of one such program reveals a general pattern.

David Susskind's production company developed and produced *N.Y.P.D.* The subject matter, policemen and their work, was already a proven success, as was the gimmick of using "actual case histories" for the story basis (both established by the original *Dragnet* series of prehistoric times; *Dragnet* also established, with its twelve-word vacabulary and its pseudo-documentary style, the effectiveness of the illusion of "authenticity"). *N.Y.P.D.*, however, was going to add a couple of wrinkles. It would (and did) incorporate a black cop in its cast of detectives. And it would be rigorously authentic, to the finest details, in its portrayal of police work in New York City, i.e., it would be a model of technical realism. For this purpose the producers required the full cooperation of the *real* N.Y.P.D., the New York Police Department, and that cooperation was forthcoming—but with strings. Before it would agree to the scheme, the real-life N.Y.P.D. demanded the right to cancel shows it disapproved of, not simply at the time they were completed and put in the can but up until two weeks prior to their scheduled broadcast—presumably in case somebody changed his mind, or in case Jacques Nevard, N.Y.P.D.'s minister of information, was late in screening the episodes.

For some viewers such a story may come as a surprise. For others it simply documents a situation that has long been palpably obvious, and for them it is self-evident that similar procedures are to some degree in force in the case of other series that rely on the cooperation of the organization they portray. No one who watches *The F.B.I.*, however occasionally, could imagine a truly critical look at the bureau and its operations in one of the show's episodes. One cannot conceive of *Dragnet* or *Adam-12* approaching the question of policemen and their work from any but an inside, public-relations viewpoint. This kind of abject prostitution is not entirely the invention of television. It has long been a standard procedure in the movie industry, where whores are made when they are not born.

This is particularly true in war movies requiring (as most all of them do) the cooperation of the Army, Navy, Marine Corps, or Air Force. *Dr. Strangelove* not only could get no cooperation from the military, but it was lucky not to have been made the object of a pacification program. *The Green Berets,* on the other hand, got so much cooperation that one would not have been surprised to learn that the Vietnam war had been set back six months on its account. The movies, however, do not double as the nation's principal source of news and information; and the frequency, availability, and consequently the power of television create a much more serious conditioning problem than the storied corruption of the movie industry ever could.

This is not just a convenient example. The police problem is one of the most serious, complex, and perilous issues facing contemporary American society. A report published in June, 1969, by the National Commission on the Causes and Prevention of Violence found that across the nation the police were becoming politicized and polarized to an extent that endangers the structure of democracy. The report, prepared under the direction of Jerome H. Skolnick, of the Center of the Study of Law and Society at the University of California at Berkeley, documented the growing political power of police organizations (a power far out of proportion to their numbers), the effectiveness of such organizations in pressuring political institutions, their tendency to equate dissent with subversion, and a growing public acceptance of both the attitudes and the extracurricular political activities of these public servants in blue. It is not cop-baiting to observe that, for reasons often beyond the control of the overburdened and underpaid policeman, the attitudes and activities of the police and their effect on the rest of society pose not just serious but critical problems for democracy in our time. But how are the millions who regularly view these television dramatizations and are emotionally and intellectually affected by them to view an objective study of, say, the basic disputes between the police and ghetto dwellers? They have seen, time and again, every variety of police critic—demonstrator, reporter, reformist politician—not only portrayed in consistently unflattering and unsavory roles but also, with equal consistency, linked to the causes of rising crime rates, disrespect for authority, and the general dissolution of American society. The Neanderthal social theories of J. Edgar Hoover, Sam Yorty, and the average chief of police come alive several times a week on the home screen as dramatizations of "true case histories from the files of...." In this respect one cannot divorce television news from the quality and integrity of television entertainment. It is little wonder that a medium which spends so much of its time and energy developing such an audience and which has acquired such a financial stake in the goodwill and cooperation of law-enforcement propagandists is less than reckless in presenting news and public-affairs programs that challenge either.

The problem does not confine itself to the attitude of the average television viewer toward only the police and their critics. Television news executives can talk about the independence of their operations all they like (and they like to a great deal), but those operations can never be very independent of the attitudes and values developed in the average viewer by the medium's overall product, whether the issue be crime in the streets, the Vietnam war, or Presidential politics. This is one area the television networks might consider when, and if, they contemplate the apparent contradiction between their immense power to influence public opinion (which is a fact, in spite of its use by Spiro T. Agnew) and the widespread public support for Agnew's attack on their news presentation.

Independence is also compromised by sponsor attitudes, such as those cited by a representative of Westinghouse Electric (which has its own network) during the darker days of blacklisting:

> We buy "Studio One" as a package from CBS through our agency, McCann Erickson. These two businesses, as well as all of us at Westinghouse, have a great stake in our capitalistic society. It is therefore in our own best interests never to engage in any activities that would jeopardize the free-enterprise system.*

---

*John Cogley, *Report on Blacklisting*, Vol. II: *Radio-Television* (New York: Fund for the Republic, 1956), p. 30.

And Harry J. Skornia in *Television and the News* quotes a president of Columbia Artists Mangement as laying down the following rule for performers:

> The public performer ... must observe an axiom of show business, which is not to engage in contentious nonconfromism ... Active participation in politics .... is incompatible with his profession. ... Judgment of a performer's behavior is on a public-relations level. Wherein merit may lie on any question is irrelevant.

Considerable changes have taken place in the industry since those gems of wisdom were uttered, but hardly a revolution. Going back to the contrasting treatment of the Smothers brothers and Bob Hope, the former presumably "jeopardized" the system, whereas the latter did not. In the context of the second quote, Hope's plugging of the Johnson Vietnam policy was obviously an engagement in conformism, whereas the brothers Smothers had been guilty of "contentious nonconformism." The fact that much of any network's revenue comes from people holding such attitudes creates a perilous atmosphere for the operation of an independent, "call the chips where they fall" news department.

The intrusion of show-biz values into informational programming, the need to include elements of conflict whether they exist naturally in the subject matter or not, the compulsion to emphasize the dramatic and focus on the bizarre at the expense of distorting reality, and the attempt to fabricate drama where it is not sufficiently present dangerously compromise the integrity and credibility of television news and must inevitably deepen public mistrust and hostility toward the press, even as they succeed in attracting viewers and raising ratings. These corruptions are matched by the ideological conditioning of audiences by entertainment programming. Taken together, they constitute a major reason why, as Robert MacNeil states, "relatively few documentaries really delve into the acute problems of our time," and why the electronic press today, while under attack from several directions, lacks the moral courage necessary for an adequate defense.

TV Violence: How It Changes Your Children

VICTOR B. CLINE

ITEM: Shortly after a Boston TV station showed a movie depicting a group of youths dousing a derelict with gasoline and setting him afire for "kicks," a woman was burned to death in that city—turned into a human torch under almost identical circumstances.

ITEM: Several months ago, NBC-TV presented in early-evening, prime viewing time a made-for-TV film, *Born Innocent*, which showed in explicit fashion the sexual violation of a young girl with a broom handle wielded by female inmates in a juvenile detention home. Later a California mother sued NBC and San Francisco TV station KRON for $11,000,000, charging that this show had inspired three girls, ages 10 to 15, to commit a similar attack on her 9-year-old daughter and an 8-year-old friend three days after the film was aired.

ITEM: A 14-year-old boy, after watching rock star Alice Cooper engage in a mock hanging on TV, attempted to reproduce the stunt and killed himself in the process.

ITEM: Another boy laced the family dinner with ground glass after seeing it done on a television crime show.

ITEM: A British youngster died while imitating his TV hero, Batman. The boy was hanged while leaping from a cabinet in a garden shed. His neck became caught in a nylon loop hanging from the roof. His father blamed the TV show for his death—and for encouraging children to attempt the impossible.

These are just a sampling of many well-documented instances of how TV violence can cause anti-social behavior—instances that are proving that TV violence is hazardous to your child's health.

© 1975 Downe Publishing Inc. Reprinted by permission of Ladies' Home Journal.

TV broadcasters can no longer plead that they are unaware of the potential adverse effects of such programs as *Born Innocent*. During the last decade, two national violence commissions and an overwhelming number of scientific studies have continually come to one conclusion: televised and filmed violence can powerfully teach, suggest—even legitimatize—extreme antisocial behavior, and can in some viewers trigger specific aggressive or violent behavior. The research of many behavioral scientists has shown that a definite cause-effect relationship exists between violence on TV and violent behavior in real life.

When U.S. Surgeon General Jesse Steinfeld appeared before the U.S. Senate subcommittee reviewing two years of scientific research on the issue, he bluntly concluded,

> The overwhelming consensus and the unanimous Scientific Advisory Committee's report indicate that televised violence, indeed, does have an adverse effect on certain members of our society. . . . It is clear to me that the causal relationship between televised violence and antisocial behavior is sufficient to warrant appropriate and immediate remedial action. . . . There comes a time when the data are sufficient to justify action. That time has come.

The Federal Communications Commission was ordered by Congress to come up with a report by Dec. 31, 1974, on how children can be protected from televised violence (and sex). Hopefully, some concrete proposals will develop.

The television moguls have repeatedly paraded before various Congressional subcommittees over the last ten years, solemnly promising to reduce the overall amount of violence programmed, especially in time slots that had large numbers of child viewers. However, if we look at the data compiled throughout the 1960's and early 1970's, we find very little change in the average number of violent episodes per program broadcast by all three networks. In one study, the staff of U.S. Congressman John M. Murphy of New York found NBC leading the pack with violent sequences in 71 percent of its prime-time shows, followed by ABC with 67 percent and CBS with 57 percent.

With more and more mega-violent films coming to TV from the commercial theater market, as well as the increasing violence injected into made-for-TV movies, we find that the promise of television has been shamelessly ignored. In too many TV films, we see a glorification of violence that makes heroes of killers. The primary motivation for all of this is money and the fierce scramble for ratings. Thus the television industry's "repentance" for past wrongs, occurring after major national tragedies such as the assassination of the Kennedy brothers and Martin Luther King, Jr., with the transient public outrage and demand for change has been all ritual with little substance.

We are a great free society with the power to shape our destiny and create almost any social-cultural environment we wish, but as the late President John F. Kennedy put it, "We have the power to make this the best generation in the history of mankind, or the last." If one looks at crime statistics, we find that we are by far the most violent of all the great Western nations. Our homicide rate is about ten times greater than, say, the Scandinavian countries', or four times greater than Scotland's or Australia's. There are more murders per year on the island of Manhattan or in the city of Philadelphia than in the entire United Kingdom, with its nearly 60,000,000 people. Violent crime has been increasing at six to 10 times the rate of population growth in this country. And interestingly, if one analyzes the content of TV programs in England, we find that their rate of televised violence is half that of ours; in the Scandinavian countries it is much less even than that.

Thus one of the major social-cultural differences between the United States with its high homicide and violence rates and those countries with low violence rates is the amount of violence screened on public television.

"MONKEY SEE, MONKEY DO"

Much of the research that has led to the conclusion that TV and movie violence could cause aggressive behavior in some children has stemmed from work in the area of imitative learning or modeling which, reduced to its simplest expression, might be termed "monkey see, monkey do." Research by Stanford pyschologist Albert Bandura has shown that even brief exposure to novel aggressive behavior *on a one-time basis* can be repeated in free play by as high as 88 percent of the young children seeing it on TV.

Dr. Bandura also demonstrated that even a single viewing of a novel aggressive act could be recalled and produced by children six months later, without any intervening exposire. Earlier studies have estimated that the average child between the ages of five and 15 will witness, during this 10-year period, the violent destruction of more than 13,400 fellow humans. This means that through several hours of TV-watching, child may see more violence than the average adult experiences in a lifetime. Killing is as common as taking a walk, a gun more natural than an umbrella. Children are thus taught to take pride in force and violence and to feel ashamed of ordinary sympathy.

According to the Nielsen Television Index, preschoolers watch television an average of 54 hours a week. During one year, children of school age spend more time in front of a TV set than they do in front of a teacher; in fact, they spend more time watching TV than any other type of waking activity in their lives.

So we might legitimately ask, What are the major lessons, values and attitudes that television teaches our children? Content analyses of large numbers of programs broadcast during children's viewing hours suggest that the major message taught in TV entertainment is that violence is the way to get what you want.

WHO ARE THE "GOOD GUYS"?

Another major theme that many TV studies have shown to occur repeatedly is that violence is acceptable if the victim "deserved" it. This, of course, is a very dangerous and insidious philosophy. It suggests that aggression, while reprehensible in criminals, is acceptable for the "good guys" who have right on their side. But, of course, nearly every person feels that he or she is "right." And often the "good guys" are criminals whom the film happens to depict sympathetically, as in *The Godfather*. Who is "good" and who is "bad" merely depends on whose side you're on.

Studies by McLeod and associates of boys and girls in junior and senior high school found that the more the youngster watched violent television fare, the more aggressive he or she was likely to be. Other studies revealed that the amount of television violence watched by children (especially boys) at age 9 influenced the degree to which they were aggressive 10 years later, at age 19.

The problem becomes increasingly serious because, even if your child is not exposed to a lot of media violence, the youngster still could become the *victim or target* of aggression by a child who is stimulated by the violence that he or she sees on TV.

And criminals are too frequently shown on TV as daring heroes. In the eyes of many young viewers, these criminals possess all that's worth having in life—fast cars, beautiful, admiring women, super-potent guns, modish clothes, etc. In the end they die like heroes—almost as martyrs—but then only to appease the "old folks" who insist on "crimes-does-not-pay" endings.

The argument that you can't get high ratings for your show unless it is hyped up with violence is, of course, not true—as 20 years of *I Love Lucy* and, more recently, *All in the Family, Sanford & Son, The Waltons* and scores of other shows have demonstrated. Action shows featuring themes of human conflict frequently have appeal, yet even they needn't pander to the antisocial side of man's nature or legitimatize evil.

The hard scientific evidence clearly demonstrates that watching television violence, sometimes for only a few hours, and in some studies even for a few minutes, can and often does instigate aggressive behavior that would not otherwise occur. If only 1 percent of the possibly 40,000,000 people who saw *The Godfather* on TV were stimulated to commit an aggressive act, this would involve 400,000 people. Or if it were only one in 10,000, it would involve 4,000 people—plus their victims.

Some parents believe that if their children are suitably loved, properly brought up and emotionally well-balanced, they will not be affected by TV violence. However, psychiatrist Fredric Wertham responds to this by noting that all children are impressionable and therefore susceptible. We flatter ourselves if we think that our social conditions, our family life, our education and our entertainment are so far above reproach that only emotionally sick children can get into trouble. As Dr. Wertham points out, if we believe that harm can come only to the predisposed child, this leads to a contradictory and irresponsible attitude on the part of adults. Constructive TV programs are praised for giving children constructive ideas, but we deny that destructive scenes give children destructive ideas.

It should also be noted that the "catharsis theory" in vogue a few years ago, which suggested that seeing violence is good for children because it allows them vicariously to discharge their hostile feelings, has been convincingly discarded. Just the opposite has been found to be true. Seeing violence stimulates children aggressively; it also shows them how to commit aggressive acts.

The author of this article has conducted research studying the "desensitization" of children to TV violence and its potential effects.

In our University of Utah laboratories, we set up two six-channel physiographs which had the capacity to measure emotional responsiveness in children while they watched violent TV shows. When most of our subjects saw violent films, those instruments measuring heart action, respiration, perspiration, etc., all hooked up to the autonomic nervous system, did indeed record strong emotional arousal. We studied 120 boys between the ages of 5 and 14. Half had seen little or no TV in the previous two years (hence had seen little media violence), and the other half had seen an average of 42 hours of TV a week for the past two years (hence a lot of violence). As our violent film, we chose an eight-minute equence from the Kirk Douglas prize-fighting film, *The Champion*, which had been shown many times on TV reruns but which none of the boys tested had ever seen. We considered other, more violent films, but they were too brutal, we felt, to be shown to children—even for experimental purposes. The boxing match seemed like a good compromise. Nobody was killed or seriously injured. Nothing illegal occurred. Yet the fight did depict very graphically human aggression that was emotionally arousing.

These two groups of boys watched our film while we recorded their emotional responses on the physiograph. The results showed that the boys with a history of heavy violence-watching were significantly less aroused emotionally by what they saw—they had become habituated or "desensitized" to violence. To put it another way, our findings suggested that the heavy TV watchers appeared to be somewhat desensitized or "turned off" to violence, suggesting the possibility of an emotional blunting or less "conscience and concern" in the presence of witnessed violence. This means that they had developed a tolerance for it, and possibly an indifference toward human life and suffering. They were no longer shocked or horrified by it. It suggested to us the many instances of "bystander apathy," in which citizens in large urban areas have witnessed others being assaulted, yet did not come to their rescue or try to secure aid or help. Or incidents such as the My Lai massacre, in which American soldiers killed Vietnamese civilians. This suggests an unfeeling, indifferent, noncaring, dehumanized response to suffering or distress.

In any event, our research has presented the first empirical evidence that children who are exposed to a lot of TV violence do to some extent become blunted emotionally or desensitized to it.

Since our children are an important national resource, these findings suggest that we should teach them wisely. The kinds of fantasies to which we expose them may make a great deal of difference as to what kind of adults they become, and whether we will survive as a society.

The author, who is a psychotherapist and who treats many damaged children and families, was then faced with the problem of what to do about his own TV set and his own children, who regularly watched TV and had their favorite programs. The evidence had been stacking up in my laboratory—so what should I do about it at home? The thing that finally turned me from being the permissiven tolerant, "good-guy" dad to the concerned parent was the realization that whenever my children looked at TV for any lengthy period, especially violent action shows, they became frequently touchy, cross and irritable. Instead of playing outside, even on beautiful days, discharging tensions in healthy interaction with others, they sat passive for hours, too often hypnotized by whatever appeared on the tube. Frequently, homework didn't get done, chores were neglected, etc. One Saturday morning I was shocked to find my bright, 15-year-old son watching cartoons for four straight hours, having let all chores and other responsibilities go. It was then that we finally decided to turn off the TV set on a relatively permanent basis.

"NO TV" IS A TURN-ON

When we announced this decision, we found ourselves faced with a family revolt. There was much wailing and gnashing of teeth. It was as if the alcoholic had been deprived of his bottle, or as if we had suddenly announced that no more food would be served at our table.

However, the "storm" lasted only one week. Interestingly, during that week, the children went outside and played with each other and the neighbors much more, a lot more good books got read, homework was done on time, chores got finished, and the children got along with each other better. And very interestingly, the complaints about "no TV" suddenly stopped at the end of that week. Now, several years later, we do occasionally look at TV—some sports specials, a good movie, something required for school, even a mystery. But it's almost never on school nights—and it is no longer an issue in our home. Nobody feels deprived. It's now just not a major part of our lifestyle.

It should be stated, in all fairness, that television has the potential for great good—to teach children pro-social values and behavior, such as sharing with others, controlling one's impulses, solving problems through reason and discussion, being kind and thoughtful. Such programs as *The Waltons* suggest to me that such content can have wide popular appeal and be commercially marketable—if done with talent, care and commitment. In other words, television could be used for far more constructive programming than we have seen in the past. For the time being, parents should, in my judgment, be very cautious about what they expose their children to on television (as well as in movies). If something particularly objectionable is broadcast during children's prime-time hours, there are three things that can be done: 1) turn the television set off; 2) phone your local station expressing your concern; 3) write to the program's sponsor, indicating your objections (the firm's address will be found on the label of his merchandise).

The evidence is clear: a child's mind can be polluted and corrupted just as easily as his body can be poisoned by contaminants in the environment. Children are essentially powerless to deal with such problems. This means that the responsibility for effecting change rests with every adult citizen. Meaning you. Meaning me. Meaning us.

Saturday's "Kidvid Ghetto"

F. EARLE BARCUS

By not having paid enough attention to the relationship between the child and the television set, we have given over a great deal of responsibility for the education and socialization of the child to salesmen. Each Saturday morning for years, advertisers have been seducing young children into wanting toys, cereals, vitamins, snacks, and other products. That is their job, and they do it effectively.

Why seduction? When one considers that young children have no purchasing power, then one realizes that children are simply being used as tools to get their parents to spend money. Since young children have not developed that discriminatory cynicism which seems necessary to evaluate claims of advertisers, they become easy marks.

This seduction is accomplished not only through formal sales messages directed toward the child, but by the whole framework of children's television programming which has developed. I would like to report something of the nature of this programming and advertising matter from studies I have made of children's television on Saturdays.

Last year, I videotaped nearly twenty hours of cartoons, comedies, adventures, and commercials from what one television critic has called the "Kidvid Ghetto"—Saturday mornings—on four commercial Boston television stations. Three stations carried mostly network programs; the fourth was an independent UHF station.

Measurements of mass media performance relate both to questions of quantity (availability of content) and quality. One important aspect of quality is diversity of fare, for with diversity we at least have some choice.

The first striking feature of children's programming, however, was the lack of diversity. Nearly seventy percent was network programming, twenty percent recorded, and the remainder locally produced. Overall, eighty-eight percent was entertainment. All recorded material and ninety-four percent of network fare were entertainment. Two-thirds of all program time used animation techniques of the *Bugs Bunny/Roadrunner* variety. Thus, seven out of ten minutes was comedy drama (mostly cartoons), another one of ten minutes was devoted to crime, action, or adventure drama.

Also illustrating a lack of diversity was the subject matter of the programs. Eighteen basic subject classes were used in the analysis. Of these, only three accounted for two-thirds of all time in the stories. One-third of the story time dealt predominantly with crime or its solution, followed by plots in which interpersonal (usually physical) struggles between characters or stories of the supernatural (ghosts, witchcraft, magic) predominated. In contrast, there were no stories about domestic (home and family) problems, religion, race and nationality, education, business, or literature and the fine arts. Only minimal amounts of time were devoted to historical topics, government and public affairs, love and romance, nature and animals, armed forces and war, or science and technology.

Informational non-story programs focused on four subjects: science and technology, race and nationality, literature and the fine arts, and nature and animals. Although these accounted for more than two-thirds of informational programs, such programs accounted for less than two hours of total time for all four stations.

In recent years there has been much concern over the amount and effects of television violence. Our study was not addressed to the larger issue of how much, or in what way, such violence might influence young people. Rather, we tried to describe the extent, types, and results of whatever violence appeared in the children's shows. Perhaps the best summary of my impressions is that most of the violence is simply unnecessary—seemingly it is used as an easy device around which to construct a program.

The popular impression that violence on tele-

Reprinted from *The Progressive* magazine. © by the Progressive Inc.

vision has been curtailed in recent years is not supported in the study. For example, it was something of a surprise to find that in more than eight out of ten story segments there was at least one recognizable act of violence, and in thirty percent, violence "saturated" the stories. ("Saturation" means that if one takes away the violence, there is no reason for the story in the first place.) The following shows the extent of violence in these dramatic segments:

The Extent of Violence	No. of Stories	Per cent
Stories saturated with violence	24	30
Violence subordinate or incidental	41	52
No violent acts in segment	14	18

These figures include only recognizable physical violence such as shooting or hitting with weapons, or kicking, punching, or banging of bodies without weapons. Verbal abuse and threats of violence were not counted.

Even in the stories in which no direct act of violence was noted there were sometimes suspenseful or potentially frightening situations, including, in one case, a parachute which failed to open, and in others "chase scenes" in which the threat of violence was present. Overall, more than half of the stories included active "chase scenes," and twenty percent included obviously frightening or suspenseful situations.

Much of the violence took place in a humorous context. Sometimes "laugh tracks," designed to cue the audience as to what was funny, were used.

A most interesting trait of the violence on children's television is that seldom does anyone get hurt. Overall, we found only eight stories in which there was a death or permanent injury of any kind, and of these only three were a direct result of interpersonal, physical violence. Many characters were flattened, beaten, run over, or blown up, but almost all miraculously survived with no visible aftereffects. The exceptions included a cat that disintegrated and a canary that committed suicide.

Thus, although there is an abundance of violence, one might be left with the impression that violence is harmless since little permanent damage is done to the characters. One of the main reasons children's television is like it is—violent, active, humorous, and simple—is that the programs are not really an important part. The stories are there to attract and hold the child to the set for the *real* message of commercial television—the advertising message.

Through a complicated and unique set of industry demands, the National Association of Broadcasters Code permits more commercial material in children's programs (i.e., sixteen minutes per hour since it is non-prime time) than is recommended for prime television time (in which twelve minutes are allowed).

In 1,125 minutes of Saturday children's television we monitored, nearly one in five minutes was devoted to commercial messages—either for products or promoting future programs. There were 406 messages. Were these spread evenly over all programming, they would average one commercial message every 2.8 minutes.

In 1,125 minutes, fifty-seven companies advertised ninety-nine products in 132 separately designed commercials, and, with repeated showings, these appeared 311 times.

In June, these ads were divided among six product categories, with twenty percent to twenty-four percent devoted to cereals, toys, candies/sweets, and other foods/snacks. The remainder consisted of miscellaneous products, including medicines/drugs/vitamins (one percent) and other (mostly adult) products (eleven percent). Product advertising is highly seasonal, of course. In a November, 1969, study by Ralph Jennings of the Office of Communication, United Church of Christ, for example, fifty-seven percent of all commercials on Saturday children's television were for toys, compared with the twenty-two percent we found in June.

We also found that if there is a choice of where to place the commercials, the odds are more than two to one that they will be *within* (interrupting) programs rather in station-break segments *between* programs. This is where program promotions and non-commercial announcements are more likely to appear.

Many commercials, if not blatantly deceptive, are at least potentially misleading. Although few direct appeals to children such as, "Go ask your Mommy to buy this," were found in our study, several other dubious commercial practices were. These included endorsements by celebrities, commercials given by the host or characters of the program, brief qualifying phrases, the use of "free" cereal premium offers, special photographic techniques which included close-ups and "worm's-eye" views to distort size perspectives, and speeded-up photography to enhance the appearance of speed.

Cereals, which have come under question as to nutritional value, often use nutrition as a major selling point (forty-four percent made nutritional claims). More frequently than nutrition, the appeal of *sweetness* is used (fifty-three percent). The cereals are "sparkled with sugar," have a "secret sugar-frosted coating," are "honey-sweet." One goes further. General Mills' "Count Chocula" cereal is "monstrously sweet."

When these same appeals to taste and color are made for iron-enriched vitamin pills or other children's medications, the dangers are even more apparent. In this connection it is ironic that some of the flavored aspirin and vitamins for children are labeled *Keep Out of the Reach of Children*.

The most striking feature of the commercials is the lack of product information given. A good exercise the next time you watch a toy ad is to try to answer the following questions, which seem important from the consumer's point of view:

What is it made of? How big is it? How exactly does it work? How fast does it go? How much does it cost? Does the price include the accessories? How much practice does it take to use it? Is it designed for a certain age group? How long will it last? Will it break if I step on it? Where can I buy it?

We tried to keep track of some of these points. In only six of the 132 separate commercials was the price given. In only three were dimensions given.

The content of commercials lies not only in their formal messages, but also in the built-in assumptions about the good life and depictions of the characters and their activities.

Thematically, "fun" is an important aspect of many ads for children. We found "fun on a stick," things which were "fun to make," and "fun to eat." Children were told to "join some friends and have some fun," to "get in on the fun," and to eat "the first frozen dinners with fun in them."

Closely related are "coolness" and "popularity" themes. One Dawn Doll commercial begins, "When you're popular, it's easy to make friends." Dawn is popular—and has many friends (all sold separately, of course).

Implicit messages are included in the depiction of characters in the commercials. By sex, males outnumber females about three to one. Female characters are associated with dolls, primarily. For boys, speed, noise, and power are frequent appeals: "Make your bike roar," "just listen to them scream," and "speed enough to burn" are some examples.

Analysis of characters by race revealed just one commercial with a black-only character, and two others had Indians. About three out of four commercials had white-only characters; the remainder were "integrated," often showing a black or Oriental youngster in a group of children.

Most of the above examples of commercial practices come from taped or filmed thirty- or sixty-second ads. In local programs, the opportunities and temptations to utilize such practices may be even greater.

It is fairly common for the hosts on local children's programs to sell spots on their shows. Thus, the selection of the host may well be as much for his or her sales ability as for being a good programmer for children. This practice puts the host in the position of impressing a new advertising account with his ability to move the product; to do so he may personally endorse or otherwise promote sales when perhaps he should be worrying about his child audience.

Product and program integration in a nationally syndicated pre-school children's program, *Romper Room*, is a case in point. Many mothers consider this one of the better children's programs on commercial television. For several years, however, local teacher-hostesses across the country have used *Romper Room* as a platform for promoting Romper toys. In a detailed study of one week of one of these programs, thirty-six percent of the time was devoted to playing with, demonstrating, or displaying brand-name toys, almost all of which were identifiable Romper Room-Hasbro products, in addition to formal commercial announcements for toys and other products or services. Adding the formal messages to the informal toy play, forty-five percent of the time was spent in product promotion.

There were several ways in which this was done. The teacher-hostess of the program described the toys as "very special," referred to them as "our" toys, urged children at home to get the toys so that they could play along, and demonstrated them in some detail for the children at home. Sometimes the same toys played with on one day were advertised the next. The teacher also gave some of the commercials herself. Even the "prayer" segment was used. After a one-minute dairy commercial, the "teacher" and children recited the prayer, "God is great, God is good, let us thank Him for our food." She then said to the children in the studio, "Now you may have your Tropicana Orange Juice from the Pleasant Hill Dairy." That is a pretty good endorsement. There may be some fairly obvious lessons for children in all of this, some of which even the advertisers and manufacturers would not want to foster intentionally.

One thing the child needs to assume is that consuming and having things is good. It makes you special, gives you status, and gains you friends. Fred Rogers, producer-performer on the PBS program *Misterrogers' Neighborhood*, made an important point in a national symposium on the effects of television programming and advertising on children. (This and other articles selected from this symposium have been published in a 1971 Avon paperback entitled *Action for Children's Television*.) Taking the view that a caring adult must mediate life experiences for the child, including those experiences gained through television, Rogers said, "I am convinced that the sense of feeling worthwhile, the sense of being able to make a difference by who we are inside, is essential to living." He tries to do this through song and verse, and quotes a song called *It's You I Like*:

"It's you I like
It's not the things you wear.
It's not the way you do your hair,
But it's *you* I like,
The way you are right now.
The way down deep inside you,
Not the things that hide you,

Not your toys
(They're just beside you),
But it's you I like."

This is not the message of commercial television, however. From commercial television, the child learns that "fun" is extremely important. Not just any kind of fun, of course, but that which can be provided by products and programs. He is told you can get something for nothing in free offers and by the practice of deemphasizing price. He learns to want, but not to discriminate. He is not prepared, by example, to ask questions.

Perhaps most serious, however, is what he learns through experience. Letters from mothers to Action for Children's Television and to the Federal Communications Commission have reported many instances of children who, after buying television-advertised toys which look like steel but are made from cardboard, after buying dolls which break when you hug them too tightly, and after eating those sweetest of cereals which taste of chemicals, may be learning not to believe what people tell them.

Research on five-to-twelve-year-old children's reactions to television advertising by Scott Ward of the Marketing Science Institute, Cambridge, Massachusetts, has indicated that with age, children decrease attention given to television commercials and make more negative and fewer positive comments about them. This indicates that the young child may be learning to be cynical and suspicious of advertising claims. For the advertiser, this may not matter, however, since there is always a new crop of youngsters to form the market for those same toys and cereals.

In a statement at the hearings on Modern Advertising Practices conducted recently by the Federal Trade Commission, I argued that advertisers and companies should develop a better code of practices and guidelines which would include giving more information to the consumer, less time for commercial interruptions on programs, and other "improvements" in the practice of advertising to children. Since then, I have reconsidered. I have reconsidered partially on the basis of one logical argument based in historical fact in our culture. It is this:

It has long been recognized that in many

areas children may need the special protection of the law and society. We feel that children are not yet capable of decisions in some areas and protect them in others. We have child labor laws, age limits on voting, drinking, and signing legal contracts, and have reached some agreement to restrict their exposure to certain literature and motion pictures through the rating system.

The question, then, is this: If humans need to be twenty-one to sign a rental agreement, eighteen to vote, and fifteen to obtain a driver's license, at what point do children become fair game for the advertiser?

This question was partially answered by Melvin Helitzer of Helitzer Advertising, Inc., in those same FTC hearings. Referring, as marketing people generally do, not to children but to the "youth market," he said:

"Child's play *is* hard work. And just reaching the right youth group is no easy assignment. There are really six distinct age spans: infant (0–2); pre-schooler (2–4); primary grades (5–9); pre-teen (10–13); teen (13–16), and college students (17–21). Each of the six age groups requires a carefully individualized approach—in words, music, product comprehension and appeal."

One can only wonder what new approaches can be used to reach the 0–2 year age market. Action for Children's Television (ACT), formed in 1968 as a group of four mothers concerned about their children and television, launched a campaign to improve children's television and educate others as to what is going on. Now a national organization, ACT has recently petitioned the Federal Communications Commission for rule making in the matter of children's television. (The FCC has estimated that more than 100,000 letters have been received in connection with this petition, which, as these matters go, is a remarkable response.)

The petition urges the adoption of the following rules to govern all programming for children:

One There shall be no sponsorship and no commercials on children's programs.

Two No performer shall be permitted to use or mention products, services or stores by brand name during children's programs, nor shall such names be included in any way during children's programs.

Three Each station shall provide daily programming for children and in no case shall this be less than fourteen hours a week, as part of its public service requirement.

In the third proposed rule, three age groups are specified for which programming shall be provided (pre-school, primary, and elementary), and a range of hours when such programming should be aired is suggested.

Obviously, adoption of such rules would require a great readjustment in thinking and planning by networks and stations. New sources of revenues for stations and networks would have to be found if the media could not financially support this amount of public service programming. These might include credits to companies which support program production in lieu of spot announcements (as is now done in brief announcements on public television stations), public support, foundation grants for program development, or some form of government subsidy.

Other readjustments are easier to make. Some things have already happened. Recently, CBS announced that Captain Kangaroo will no longer give commercials himself on his program. Ideal Toy Company has reported that it has shifted its commercials from Saturday morning children's programs to adult programs. There are also rumored changes in the National Association of Broadcasters' guidelines for advertising to children.

Advertisers and television executives are fond of pointing out that parents are the most important factor in controlling the lives of children. This is partially true, of course. The same parents who would object to a door-to-door salesman who might ask for a few minutes to sell their child toys or candy should be equally apprehensive about the salesman who does this each Saturday when their child is watching television. Parents, therefore, must exercise more influence, not only on the child, but also on the advertisers, the Government, and the television industry, to help correct abuses which they perceive.

The governmental regulatory bodies, the FCC and FTC, also share the responsibility and

> On October 24, 1974 . . . the FCC issued, instead of rules, a 37-page policy statement of "guidelines", designed to 'clarify' broadcasters' responsibilities in programming for children and advertising in children's programs. Suggested guidelines include: (1) There shall be a reasonable amount of programming for children, a significant portion of it educational and international. (2) Children's programs should not be offered only on weekends. (3) Special needs of pre-school children should be recognized. (4) Time alloted to commercials per hour should be decreased (by Jan. 1, 1976) to 9½ minutes weekend mornings; 12 minutes during the week. (5) There should be a clear separation between program material and advertising (6) There should be no host selling.

should provide the proper safeguards for children both as viewers and consumers by helping to promote better programs and advertising practices.

FCC Commissioner Nicholas Johnson recently recommended to a Senate committee that the permissible number of commercial minutes be reduced by half, and that two commercial minutes be removed from every half hour containing violence and be made available at no cost to professionals to program information to children about the adverse consequences of violence.

Finally, the advertisers and the television industry must assume responsibility for the potential effects of their programs and messages. It is often argued that it has not been proven that these programs are *harming* children. Would it not be as reasonable that the burden be put on broadcasters to demonstrate how they are *helping* the child? Moreover, broadcasters cannot be allowed to shift the complete responsibility onto parents by the simple suggestion that "they can always turn off the television set." Broadcasters use public airwaves by virtue of their licenses and have the responsibility for providing program services to keep that license.

In the final analysis, we need a revision in the policies and procedures governing children's television. We must find a way to separate the advertising influences from the content of children's television programs. It is ludicrous to measure the success of a children's program by the number of commercial messages which can be sold in it. Program producers should insist on the freedom to program for the child, not the sponsor. It is difficult enough for an adult to produce, write, or act in programs which assume the perspective of the child, consider his needs and wants, and translate these into quality children's programs. That a producer at the same time design programs into which twelve commercial announcements can be inserted makes his job nearly impossible.

QUESTIONS FOR DISCUSSION

1 Does televised violence stimulate violence in our everyday lives? If so, how? If not, why not?

2 Do the media have too much influence over the processes of social decision-making? What evidence can you cite to support your position?

3 Cite ways in which the major media are utilized to manipulate or alter public opinion?

4 How do the media influence people's daily lives? Give specific examples.

PROJECT

1. Evaluate your own attitudes toward:
   (a) doctors, lawyers, police
   (b) male and female sex roles
   (c) various lifestyles that exist
   (d) education, religion, family life

Can you see any ways in which your exposure to mass media have affected these attitudes? Cite specific examples.

OWNERSHIP, ECONOMICS, AND MEDIA

The Rush to Chain Ownership

ROBERT L. BISHOP

The "good old days" included a lot of seamy journalistic history but they did have one advantage: competition. Newspapers were never what they should have been, but even small towns had two or more, each keeping an eye on the others and on the public interest as they saw it. Now head-to-head competition is almost dead, and even separate ownership of morning and afternoon papers is practically gone. We are well along toward wiping out independent ownerships of both newspapers and television stations, to the point that consolidation often means capitalistic cannibalism—one group or chain swallowing another. And much of this has come about because of U.S. tax laws.

Consider these points:

1. The percentage of American cities with competing newspapers fell from about 60 percent in 1910 to 15 percent in 1950 and now is less than 4 percent.
2. The percentage of daily newspaper circulation held by group newspapers rose from about 43 percent in 1950 to more than 60 percent in 1972.
3. Annual revenues of the ten largest daily newspaper groups are estimated at about $2.2 billion—approximately one-fourth of the total for the entire industry. They also have one-third of the circulation.
4. Cross-media owners (holders of print and broadcast properties) control 36 percent of all daily newspapers. They also own 25 percent of the TV stations, 8.6 percent of AM radio, and 9.5 percent of FM radio. Almost all the AM stations are in the top ten markets.
5. The combined holdings of groups, cross-media owners, conglomerates, and firms related to the mass media encompass 58 percent of daily newspapers, 77 percent of TV stations, 27 percent of AM and 29 percent of FM stations.

The state of Michigan offers some concrete examples. Within two years, two Michigan chains have been bought by Gannett and the largest independent paper was purchased by Panax—leaving only two independents with more than 20,000 circulation. The twenty-five independent papers that survive account for only 11 percent of the total state circulation. I exclude the Detroit *News* because, although it is legally independent, it owns three TV stations and has extensive family ties to Booth, Hearst, and Scripps-Howard. Other recent newspaper sales include the Niles, Mich., *Star* to Ridder Publications and the Ypsilanti *Press* to Harte-Hanks.

Neighboring Ohio has similar conditions—independent papers account for 24 percent of the circulation, if one includes the Cincinnati *Enquirer* and Columbus *Dispatch*. Scripps-Howard, following a court order, sold its interest in the *Enquirer*—since resold to an insurance and land company—and the *Dispatch* operates under a joint printing and business agreement with the E. W. Scripps *Citizen-Journal*. About twenty-one different groups have footholds in Ohio through sixty-three daily newspapers. The largest number—ten—is held by Lord Thomson, the British press magnate.

(Broadcasting, which becomes more and more important as the only possible competing editorial voice in many communities, is, if anything, worse off. For example, of the thirty-one transfers in fiscal 1971 which exceeded $1 million each, only two were to individual ownerships rather than to groups or cross-media owners. The thirty-one transfers involved twenty-nine TV stations and twenty-six radio stations. Even counting the less profitable UHF stations, the network O and O's and the seven largest groups probably got more than one-third of station revenue, not counting revenues which went to the networks directly. This means that less than 7

Reprinted from the *Columbia Journalism Review*, November/December 1972.

percent of the stations get one-third of the money, and a far greater share of profits.)

Both newspapers and broadcasting stations are falling to conglomerates. All three of the networks could be termed conglomerates because of their interests in other media, rental cars, baseball teams, theaters, etc. But twenty other conglomerates have broadcast interests, including General Tire, aerospace contractor Avco, Nationwide Insurance, and Kaiser Industries. Newspaper owners include the Jefferson-Pilot insurance company, Capital Cities Broadcasting, Field Enterprises, and the Houston Endowment, Inc., owner of the Houston *Chronicle*, the largest paper in Texas. As Ben Bagdikian pointed out in the *Atlantic* in 1966, the Endowment also has important interests in thirty-two corporations and a majority interest in twenty-five. These include banks, hotels, office buildings, and real estate.

Nor is the picture any brighter in cable television—regarded by many as the last hope for a competitive mass medium. Half of all cable subscribers, or 2.5 million people, are served by one of eleven U.S. CATV companies. When pending mergers are completed, six companies will serve one-third of the subscribers. Fourth largest is Cox Cable Communications, which is linked with Cox Broadcasting and under the same general ownership as Cox Newspapers. Tenth and trying hard to grow is Time-Life Broadcast, Inc., which is selling its over-the-air properties to make room for cable. About 42 percent of CATV is owned by other media interests, according to *Broadcasting* magazine; broadcasters own 30 percent, newspaper publishers 7 percent, and telephone companies 5 percent.

Some communications principalities have far-reaching tentacles in all media. The empire headed by James Cox, for example, is in the top ten in newspapers, broadcasting, and CATV.

Cox has both the morning and afternoon papers in Atlanta, Ga.,, West Palm Beach, Fla., and Dayton and Springfield, O., his father's old political power base. He also has papers in Miami, Palm Beach, and a 47 percent interest in both Daytona Beach papers. The only Cox paper facing local competition is the Miami *News*. Even the *News* has the evening field to itself and is sheltered in a joint operating agreement with the Knights' Miami *Herald*. Circulation tops a million and Cox newspaper revenues probably hit $120 million annually, with revenues after taxes of $14 to $20 million.

Cox Broadcasting reported revenues of $65.3 million for 1971: a $15.8 million profit before and $8.1 million after taxes (a respectable but not overwhelming return of 12 percent after corporate taxes). Company earnings, after taxes, amounted to almost one-third the net value of all property, plant, and equipment, or 13 percent on stockholder's equity. More important to the stockholder, however, is the fact that his equity has grown by $44.3 million since 1964—up almost two and a half times.

Two-thirds of Cox's income comes from broadcasting: five VHF stations in the top thirty markets, together with four AM and four FM radio stations. Fifteen percent of revenues comes from publishing. (CBC owns 98 percent of United Technical Publications, with magazines like *Electronic Products* and *Office Products News*; its National Auto Research issues a weekly automobile price guide, the *Black Book*; *Industrial Machinery News* is the largest publication of its type; and Amphoto is the largest publisher in photography.) Seven percent of revenue comes from program distribution and production: CBC's Bing Crosby Productions produces such winners as *Willard* and a son of *Willard, Ben*; CBC syndicates *Hogan's Heroes* and *Ben Casey*; and last year it produced *World Series of Golf*, on NBC.

Program production is a natural interest for any cable operator. CBC owns 56.3 percent of Cox Cable Communications, Inc., fourth-largest system in the country. Cox Cable has twenty-nine different systems with about 230,000 subscribers. It already returns about 10 percent on revenues before taxes.

The Cox interests are not unique. Every newspaper group in the top ten has substantial interests in other areas, especially broadcasting. Knight Newspapers probably has the least outside involvement—five weeklies, a transportation company, a newspaper supply company, an advertising firm, and an interest in one TV and eight radio stations through Summit Radio Stations. (The TV station is Akron's only station, and Knight has the only daily newspaper. Another station has been authorized but never built.)

Another example of a media empire is the Times Mirror Co. Its anchor is the Los Angeles *Times*, but the *Times*, the *Daily Pilot, Newsday*, and the Dallas *Times Herald* account for less than half of Times Mirror's total revenue. The stable also includes several publishing companies which issue law books, medical journals, Bibles, *An American Jewish Cookbook*, and trade books such as Gay Talese's *Honor Thy Father*. Lumber, plywood, and paper come from Times Mirror forests and mills. *Popular Science*, maps, aviation products, educational and travel materials, commercial printing, a Dallas TV station, and twenty-one CATV systems contribute further to total corporate revenues of $524 million.

All these diverse interests give leading media groups a tremendous impact on the economy. If one takes into account both the media and non-media revenues of the ten largest broadcasting organizations and the ten largest newspaper groups, the total is near $15 billion. And that, obviously, is just a small measure of their potential influence.

Nor is a recitation of each company's holdings the entire story. A cursory look at most of the large broadcasters or publishers reveals many connections with other interests, either through directors who serve in more than one company or through family ties.

Take the Cowles family. One branch, headed by John Cowles, Sr., owns the Minneapolis Star and Tribune Co. Its interests include 50 percent of *Harper's*; four newspapers, including the Minneapolis *Star* and *Tribune*; a TV station in Hutchinson, Kan.; and a 47 percent interest in a Minneapolis radio-TV-CATV combination. John Cowles' family shares, with his brother Gardner Cowles, ownership of the Des Moines *Register* and *Tribune*. That firm operates a radio-TV combination in Des Moines, a TV station in Daytona Beach, Fla., and an AM and FM station in Memphis. (The sister TV station is operated by *The New York Times*.) Gardner Cowles, who formerly published *Look* and other magazines, in turn owns a 23 percent interest in *The New York Times* through stock exchanged after *Look*'s demise.

But the trail does not end there. The Minneapolis broadcasting company is held jointly with the Ridder family, publishers of the St. Paul *Dispatch* and *Pioneer-Press* and fifteen other dailies. (On the side, the company has eleven California weeklies, radio stations in Aberdeen, S.D., Colorado Springs, Colo., radio and TV stations in Duluth, Minn., and commodity news market wires.) Ridder is a minority stockholder in the Seattle *Times*, which in turn owns both papers in Walla Walla. And serving on the Ridder board of directors is Lee E. Owens, president of Owens Publications, with dailies in Richmond, Whittier, and Berkeley, Calif. Also on

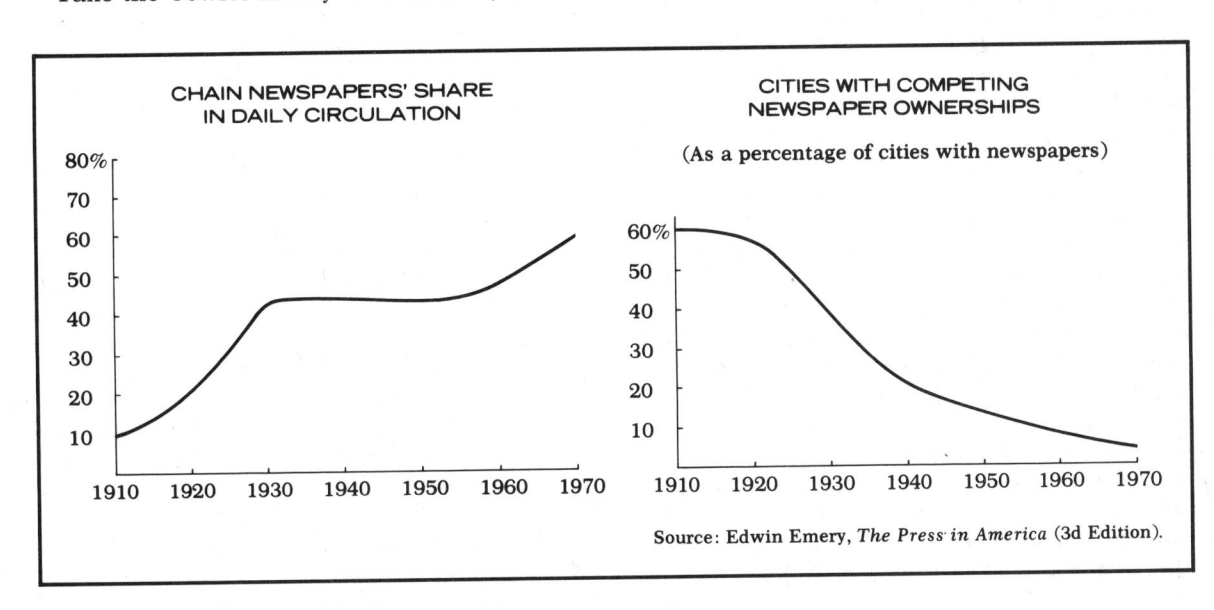

CHAIN NEWSPAPERS' SHARE IN DAILY CIRCULATION

CITIES WITH COMPETING NEWSPAPER OWNERSHIPS

(As a percentage of cities with newspapers)

Source: Edwin Emery, *The Press in America* (3d Edition).

the Ridder board are the chief executive officers of Burlington Northern, Inc., and the Bank of California.

The Mormon Church furnishes another well-known study of interlocking interests, vaguely related to even the Los Angeles *Times* through Times Mirror. The church owns real estate, department stores, life insurance, trucking, sugar plantations, and more than 600 farms, forty mills, factories and salvage stores, and Florida land. Bonneville International Corp. is a wholly-owned subsidiary which owns two TV and eleven radio stations, including one shortwave. It also has a nonvoting interest in Times Mirror.

The church's daily newspaper, the *Deseret News*, has a joint operating agreement with the Kearns-Tribune Corp. Kearns-Tribune owns 35 percent of a TV station in Salt Lake City, and another, owned by Columbia Pictures, is associated with K-T and the church in a CATV venture. K-T also owns a portion of Los Angeles' Times Mirror. In addition, K-T shares its TV station ownership with the Glasmann-Hatch interests (the only paper in Ogden, Utah, eight radio stations and two more TV stations in Utah, Montana, Idaho, and Hawaii, plus CATV systems). Utah probably is more completely under the control of a communications combine than any other state in the Union.

The board of directors of the Times Mirror company is a story in itself. The firm had sixteen directors in 1971, most of them outside officials from enterprises such as North American Rockwell, TRW, Inc., Republic National Bank of Dallas, Northrop, and law and securities firms.

One also could discuss the Washington *Post*'s link to *The New York Times* through joint interests in the International *Herald Tribune*; the *Post* and the Los Angeles *Times*' tie through a joint news service; the ramifications of the Hearst Corp.; or the various links between Scripps-Howard, the Scripps League, Howard Publications, the Buckner News Alliance, the Detroit *Evening News*, John P. Scripps Newspapers, their broadcasting arms, and United Press International. But even without doing so, it is easy to see that a fairly small community controls a tremendous share of America's communications network. And there is no doubt that the trend is to consolidation, not diversification.

Is such concentration bad? The answer is not inevitably and invariably yes. A proprietor's actions are more important than the form of incorporation. John C. Quinn, group vice president for news in the Gannett group, made a good case for group ownership before the 1972 assembly of the International Press Institute:

> Newspaper concentration may multiply the anxiety over evil; it also increases the capacity for good. And a publisher's instinct for good over evil is not determined by the number of newspapers he owns. A group can attract top professional talent, offer training under a variety of editors, advancement through a variety of opportunities, long-term careers on newspapers with a variety of size, geography, publishing cycle, and readership needs. It can invest in the research and development and nuts and bolts experience necessary to translate the theories of new technology into the practical production of better newspapers.
>
> Concentrated ownership can provide great resources; only independent local judgment can use these resources to produce a responsible and responsive local newspaper. That measure cannot be inflated by competition nor can it be diluted by monopoly.

Quinn may be correct in saying that only a group can provide the capital, the technology, and the management to keep a local newspaper competitive with other advertising media. He is certainly correct in saying that a group owner may be as much a saint or rascal as an individual owner. He is not correct in implying that the managers of a public corporation are as free to take unpopular and unprofitable stands as an individual owner. As one executive in a publicly held corporation recently lamented, "Now I'm expected to make money from the photo department and the morgue!"

The fiduciary relationship of an editor is a new consideration in the debate over concentration, however. Generally, American theory has agreed with Quinn that big owners can be tremendous influences for either good or evil. But with one eye on human nature, we have chosen to have a lot of little rascals keeping an eye on one another. The theory was that Great White Fathers are scarce, and that it was better to confine each owner to one slice of the media pie in one locale. Our practice, of course, has been quite different. We have abandoned local competition and are in the process of wiping out regional competition.

As Quinn said, concentration puts enormous financial, political, and social power in the hands of a few people. Some are primarily newsmen, concerned with what goes between the ads as well as what pays the bill. Sale of a paper to the Knight group, for instance, generally means an increase in quality. But some other chain owners are strictly businessmen who happened to get into communications. These include men like Samuel I. Newhouse, or the notoriously indiscreet Lord Thomson, who is fond of comparing newspapers and television stations to a cash box or a license to print money.

Worst of the lot are the manipulators. Walter Annenberg was certainly among this crowd until selling his Philadelphia papers to Knight. William Loeb of the Manchester, N. H., *Union Leader* may be the worst illustration left.

The second reason for opposing such concentration is the danger of cross-media ownership and local or regional monopolies. These abound throughout the country, as shown in a recent study by Paul Jess of the University of Michigan. In 1970, Jess says, seventy-two of the 1,500 U.S. cities with daily newspapers had no competing ownerships, though they had both print and broadcast facilities. One owner clearly dominated eighty-three other cities. Seventeen of these cities were between 50 and 100,000 in population; eight had more than 100,000 people.

Among cities with no competition were Santa Cruz, Calif. (32,000 people), Stamford, Conn. (109,000), and Bloomington, Ill. (66,000). One owner was dominant in cities like Tacoma, Wash. (154,000), Akron, O. (275,425), and Newport News, Va. (138,000).

Granted that many of these communities can receive other broadcast signals, or subscribe to newsmagazines or regional newspapers. But this ignores a newsman's most important function—keeping an eye on his own community. So what if we can find out what is happening in Nepal? What touches us every day is our local government, our local schools, our local social problems; these are things we can do something about.

A single owner may cut off sources of information deliberately or indirectly through not providing enough newsmen to do the job. Whether the news is unreported because of an industrialist who sits on the board of directors or because of an absentee owner more intent on black ink than black problems makes no difference.

LEADING NEWSPAPER GROUPS (1971)

	Circulation	Gross Revenues (In Millions)	Profit After Taxes (In Millions)
Tribune Company	3,631,451	$479.0	$13.5
Newhouse	3,370,785	450.0*	18.0*
Knight	2,204,000	271.4	16.1
Scripps-Howard	2,264,502	250.0*	12.5*
Gannett	2,197,997	238.4	19.7
Hearst	1,709,288	160.0*	9.0*
Times Mirror	1,686,556	523.8	34.9
Cox Newspapers	1,014,662	120.0*	7.0*
Cowles Publications	901,648	100.0*	6.0*
New York Times	891,460	290.9	9.4

*Estimates

Note: All figures include non-newspaper operations except Cox Newspapers (Cox Broadcasting and Cox Cable are separate, publicly held companies).

Source: *Robert L. Bishop*

Corporations and groups are much like real live publishers in their personnel policies. Some—like Booth, Knight, Gannett, and Times Mirror—hire first-rate men. Others—like Cox and Thomson—pay more attention to getting the most work for the least pay. One of the Ridder family candidly told a brilliant young assistant that there was no future for him in the business: "What we need is a constant supply of mediocrity."

Thomson stands willing to lose between $2 and $3 million a year to keep the *Times* of London alive. (Losses now are reported to be down to a more manageable $1.5 million.) But his smaller papers spare no economy. One Thomson alumnus tells how Thomson drove more than 100 miles years ago to convince him that it was in his best interests to take a space-rate cut from 10 cents to 8 cents an inch!

The third reason for opposing concentration is that problems of one region not reported there may never be aired in other parts of the world. Most of the news which moves over the wire services or the networks originates in a tip from a local newsman. If no competent newsman is there, the story dies—or smolders until it becomes another Watts or Laos. Consolidation is a worldwide phenomenon and it brings the threat of interference with even international news.

A fourth reason is purely commercial—ad rates go down with competition. In a monopoly situation, all one need do to increase profits is raise advertising rates, with no compulsion to plow the added revenue into editorial improvements.

What causes newspapers and stations to merge? Sometimes the answer is rooted in pride—at one time Lord Thomson would buy almost any paper because he wanted to own more than 100. He more than got his wish; his empire now includes about 170. Thomson also bought the *Times* of London not only because he thought he could make it profitable again but also because he saw it as his "monument."

But the main reasons for mergers are economic and apply in every industrialized society. Tax structures are designed to encourage capital formation and industrial growth. This has meant steep income taxes but a low capital gains tax. U.S. rates on personal income go as high as 70 percent; capital gains are taxed at one-half the individual's ordinary rate, up to 25 percent (35 percent for corporations). The reasonable person's response to this incentive is predictable: take as little out of the company in the form of salaries or dividends as possible, while trying to increase the value of the company or its stock.

The Panax Corp. of Michigan illustrates the advantages of this tactic. During twelve months in 1970-1971, the corporation sold a daily, a weekly, and a radio station for capital gains, after taxes, of $1.3 million. The proceeds enabled Panax to merge with the Macomb *Daily*, largest independent paper in the state except for the Detroit *News*, and another group of seven suburban weeklies. Capital gains recorded for 1971 were almost four times the net income from operations. Small wonder that President John P. McGoff closed his annual message by saying:

> By borrowing, buying, selling, merging, and building, your Company has emerged as a viable, growing, and profitable publishing organization. It is a policy that has served us well. We plan no change in direction.

VARYING COSTS OF BUYING A $5 MILLION NEWSPAPER

SOURCE OF FUNDS	COST
Corporate profits paid to individual in 50% tax bracket	$19.4 million
Personal income in 50% tax bracket	$10 million
Corporate earnings	$ 9.6 million
Corporate capital gains	$ 7.7 million
Individual capital gains	$ 6.7 million
Stock swap, price/earnings ratio of 25, paper selling at 25 times earnings	$ .0*
Stock swap, price/earnings ratio of 50, paper selling at 25 times earnings	$ 5 million gain for buyer*

*Does not allow for buyer's gain in new basis for depreciating the newspaper plant, which could provide another $500,000 tax shelter.

Source: *Robert L. Bishop*

Harte-Hanks, in becoming a publicly held stock company recently, illustrated two more ways to obtain capital gains. In "going public," H-H established a market and a price for its stock; thus shareholders could dispose of part or all of their holdings whenever they chose—at the capital gains rate. More importantly, the market established a high price for the stock, making it much easier to acquire other papers through mergers and stock swaps. It was as though every dollar of H-H assets had suddenly become worth $1.50.

Why does a newspaper or broadcasting group go public? Certainly the disadvantages are sobering. The owner has to reveal many of his financial secrets. If the stock offering is more than a small one, he must meet fairly stringent requirements from the Securities & Exchange Commission. The expenses of underwriting are considerable, and there is the possibility of annoyance from unhappy stockholders.

Still, dozens of owners have taken the path to the brokers. Some obviously had to raise more capital than they could as individuals. Others sought to give the company life beyond their own years and, in the process, to avoid some of the tax problems which so easily beset proprietors. A primary motive is to raise values before proposing mergers through stock swaps. Usually an entrepreneur gets a business going, establishes a growth rate (which may come from acquisitions), and then sells stock. Typically the public pays ten to twenty times the price per share paid by the entrepreneur. For example, an electronics company went public a few years ago. The founder bought his stock at $1 per share, his key executives bought at $10 a share, and the public, at $20 a share.

When the Harte-Hanks group went public this year, it had physical assets and cash valued at $20 million after depreciation, and current liabilities and long-term debts of about $14 million. The company and a group of private stockholders sold a little less than 10 percent of the outstanding common stock for $7.6 million. Within a month, because Harte-Hanks has been actively acquiring other newspapers, the stock went from an initial $21 to $33 per share—theoretically enriching those who held stock before the public offering by more than $32 million.

Growth is the key word in stock pricing. Harte-Hanks sold for thirty-eight times its 1971 earnings per share—or, if one counts an extraordinary gain of $1 million from the sale of securities in 1971, twenty-seven times earnings. The stock is priced this way because: 1) not much is available, and 2) it looks as though the company will grow rapidly. Since 1967, earnings per share (not counting extraordinary items) have gone up by one-third, and, because H-H is buying everything not nailed down, investors feel that earnings will continue to grow. Dividends play little part in setting stock prices—Gulf Oil or U.S. Steel pay much higher dividends than H-H, but their stock sells for nine times earnings because investors see little growth there and many pitfalls.

Gannett, the most acquisitive American chain in years, has been able to use practically every method of merger and purchase known to Wall Street. At the end of last year, the company had more than $118 million in retained earnings and almost $27 million in cash and marketable securities available for cash purchases. Tax-free stock swaps have been more profitable, though. Last fall, when Gannett purchased the Honolulu *Star-Bulletin* group, its stock was selling for some $60 per share. Assuming that the organization was valued at twenty-five times its earnings, with 1971 earnings per share as a base, each share would have been worth about $42 rather than $60. The value that stock-watchers put on growth saved Gannett almost one-third in acquisition costs.

Similarly, last June when Gannett acquired the El Paso *Times*, its shares were bringing $76—thirty-five times 1971 earnings, or about $25 per share more than the best stable newspaper stock and $35 per share more than a quality issue like Booth Newspapers. The growth premium thus was almost 50 percent. In short, Gannett's stock-market performance probably saved the chain something like $28 million in the purchase of sixteen newspapers.

If newspaper groups like Gannett follow the historical cycle of companies like the original Hearst empire or the more recent conglomerates, they will eventually level off and then begin to spin off companies. Sometimes a company must trim down because it has taken on more of a management problem than it can cope with. Other times it comes a cropper over too much debt, which has a way of coming due in an advertising drought. Some conglomerates have fallen apart because their fabulous growth rates have been due to acquisitions and fancy bookkeeping. They bought staid, conservative companies for ten to fifteen times their annual earnings, and their glamour alone pushed their stock prices upward.

A new subsidiary often shows dramatic gains in earnings. In some cases this is due to increased efficiency in management—typical when a family-owned newspaper is sold to a modern group—but in many cases the gain is through changes in accounting procedures. The new subsidiary will switch to accelerated depreciation—often worth millions in stated earnings through big tax deductions.

Depreciation is one of the most important facets of the sale of mass media facilities. The depreciation concept is an honest recognition that things do wear out or become obsolete and that a business must replace its equipment or go out of business. However, if a business changes hands, it usually turns out that some items are worth more than they were to begin with, at least for income tax purposes. Panax, for example, in the thirty-eight months before sale of the Ypsilanti *Press* to Harte-Hanks, wrote off more than $250,000 in depreciation on the plant while putting approximately $52,000 into property, plant, and equipment. But the property appreciated by more than $1 million after taxes.

Depreciation schedules play a much more important role in the constant exchange of broadcasting companies, especially radio. There depreciation and interest payments are used to make the station show a loss, which can be subtracted from the owner's ordinary income. Then the station is sold for a capital gain. The gain is reinvested in another "money-losing" station, relieving the owner of even the capital gains tax. The game can go on indefinitely, with the only real worry that someone will raise the capital gains rate or maybe abolish it altogether. According to the FCC, 1,388 radio stations showed a tax loss in 1970. But more than half reported payments to owners and depreciation charges which together exceeded their losses, and at some 411 stations payments to owners alone exceeded losses.

Even more important than reinvested capital gains has been financial leverage—the art of borrowing money in order to buy properties which have a higher rate of return than the interest on the loan. Between July 1, 1970, and June 30, 1971, William F. Buckley's company, the Starr Broadcasting Group, Inc., increased its long-term debt almost $8 million at interest rates of up to 9.75 percent. But the group and its subsidiaries had net earnings of $961,924 (after taxes but before profits from the sale of radio stations) on a total equity of $3,553,204—or a return of 27 percent. If, instead of borrowing, stockholders had put up all the capital, return on equity would have been 7 percent.

Another source of funding for expansion is retained earnings. These are profits, on which the corporate tax has been paid, which are held in the company for any business purpose. Very often this purpose is to lengthen a chain. If an individual outsider wishes to buy a newspaper or station, he probably will bid with money on which both corporate and individual income taxes have been paid. A corporation, however, may bid with monies generated by depreciation or capital gains—which may be completely tax-free—or retained earnings, free from personal income taxes. It takes no genius to see which bidder can pay more.

Some large companies have enormous retained earnings: Time, Inc., for one, had more than $220 million at the end of 1971. Westinghouse has more than $1 billion in retained earnings, with $91 million in cash and marketable securities and another $166 million in other investments. Capital Cities Broadcasting Corp. has almost $87 million in retained earnings. The acquisition opportunities that such hoards offer are obvious.

What can be done about the decline of independent newspapers? Even maintaining the status quo will not be easy; improving on it will be even more difficult. But neither task is impossible.

1. The enormous, preferential treatment given to capital gains must be eliminated or severely limited. Otherwise we may well end up with one huge chain operating stations and publications as though they were supermarkets, root beer stands, or outlets for advertising the company's own products. At this stage in our economic development, there seems little necessity to treat capital gains so generously; they should be taxed at the same rate as personal income, though collections might be spread over several years.

2. Corporate income taxes should be graduated, just as personal income taxes are. Most companies pay exactly the same rate, regardless of whether they make $1 million or $50 million. (The tax is 22 percent on income up to $25,000; 48 percent over $25,000.) And most tax loopholes work in favor of the larger company.

3. The rules on retained corporate earnings should be enforced. Companies often have cash and securities equal to one-fourth of their annual income. Until 1959, the IRS rule of thumb was that a company must pay out 70 percent of its income to its owners. Perhaps we should return to some such guide, since growth companies usually pay only nominal sums.

4. Depreciation should not be allowed until equipment is actually replaced or sold. The difficulty in regulating depreciation allowances is

distinguishing between items which are wearing out or becoming obsolete, and those increasing in value. Probably the most equitable way would be to figure a tax credit on the basis of what actually happened to the asset.

5. No monopoly rent should be allowed, either for publishers or broadcasters. The concept of monopoly rent is easily illustrated. John S. Knight paid twenty times earnings for the Philadelphia *Inquirer* and *News*, with very little of that due as a cash down payment. For the noncompeting Macon, Ga., papers, he paid twenty-six times earnings. Had the Philadelphia papers had the market to themselves, they would have been worth at least $14 million more—or an additional 25 percent. This premium is monopoly rent.

Similarly, in broadcasting, the Atlanta *Journal* founded WSB-TV, and sold it in 1950 for $525,000; in 1953, the station was resold for $1.5 million; in 1962, $2.25 million; and in 1967 $12.89 million. Probably 80 percent of the price was due to the partial monopoly granted by the public.

Eliminating capital gains would reduce these prices, but there is no reason why the public should not participate in any gain. A simple solution would be to forbid the transfer of broadcast licenses. Or one could adopt the British solution—government ownership of broadcasting facilities, which are then rented to programming companies at fairly high rates. Or one could tax unearned gains on the ground that the public is part owner of the station's most valuable asset, its license.

6. For publication sales, some sort of Monopolies Commission is needed—but one with far more power than the harmless British version. Such a commission would immediately be attacked as an infringement of press freedom. But why allow entrepreneurs to use what they call freedom of the press to kill the very thing the First Amendment seeks to shield?

A Monopolies Commission might require that publications be advertised for six months before a sale could be consummated with any other media owner, and that first consideration be given an individual ownership if a reasonable bid could be found. If the company had to be sold to a competitor or a group, the Commission would determine the fair market value of the paper or magazine and declare the remainder subject to an excess profits tax.

7. The one-to-a-market rule should be enforced in both cable and conventional media. Only a few locales can make a convincing plea for cross-media ownership in today's competitive marketplace.

8. The federal government should help solve distribution problems for magazines and local newspapers by restructuring postal rates. These rates should encourage small publications which depend more on subscriber income than advertising revenues.

9. Restrictive business practices should be prosecuted. Syndicated material, for instance, is often held off the market just to keep a publisher's competitors from getting it.

Dr. Jon G. Udell, director of the Bureau of Business Research and Service at the University of Wisconsin, has written:

The free press of the United States rests on two foundations:
—The First Amendment, or the right to report the news.
—Economic security, or the means to report the news.

I agree wholeheartedly. But I must inquire as to the economic security of those papers merged out of existence, and to the First Amendment protection of those readers and listeners whose right to know is subordinated to the right to make a financial killing.

A THIRD FORCE IN BROADCASTING: THE GROUP OWNER

WESTON C. PULLEN, JR.

Today, in both radio and television, so-called "group operators" are licensed to own and operate more than 1,400 broadcast facilities—a third of all commercial television stations and 25% of the radio outlets. By and large, the group operators—although the term sounds suspiciously like some sort of sinister syndicate—have established excellent records of public service, as testified to by that very recent FCC Chairman whose accolades to the broadcasters were not exactly strewn like rose petals in our paths. The value of a group operation lies in that hoary equation, "The whole is greater than the sum of its parts." Just as Army divisions in the field draw on Army headquarters for elements which add to their efficiency (although front-line troops will tell you in no uncertain terms where to dispose of a theory like that), so do group-owned stations receive support and sustenance from their group headquarters, and vice by all means versa.

From government, there is a seeming harassment of group operators, and hence a challenge to the concept under which they operate. We believe this attitude is a hangover from the days when political philosophy equated bigness (of anything but government) with evil. Today, the world of business and the world of communications is enormous and complex; huge and multi-faceted organizations like General Motors, Procter & Gamble, RCA, DuPont, General Electric and many others have demonstrated beyond dispute that size and efficiency complement rather than battle each other. Astronaut Cooper would not have orbited far if NASA had chosen its contractors from mom-and-pop electronics manufacturers. It takes a Rip Van Winkle to argue that bigness equals monopoly.

In the broadcasting business, multiple owners can be a much-needed third force between networks and individual licensees. I believe they are the best hope of challenging network power and innovation; group operators can provide more services than can single stations, and they can add to the texture of their local television and radio services many threads of broadcasting service that might otherwise never be available to their audiences.

Time-Life Broadcast, for instance, maintains a full-time Broadcast News Bureau in Washington. So do the networks. Their manpower is greater; they are better equipped to relay instantaneously the top national and international stories that originate in the Capital. But those stories must be of equal interest to all the network's affiliated stations and their audiences; network news judgments are predicated on a national audience.

What happens to those dozens of daily developments in Congress, the Administration, and the Supreme Court that need to be known by citizens of a particular region? The story of a Titan missile contract award to the Martin Company in Denver has little interest to the viewers and listeners in 49 other states, hence has little chance of surviving the network news editor's blue pencil. But it has great interest in Colorado, and the Time-Life Broadcast News Bureau is on hand to report it. Ditto for the fight for the Indiana dunes, the fate of San Diego's aircraft industry, the fortunes of Michigan's political leaders, the decisions affecting Minnesota's taconite deposits and a hundred other news stories lying just beneath the surface headliners that the network skims off each night.

When the Broadcast News Bureau of Time-Life is augmented by the skillful, specialized *Time*, *Life* and *Fortune* correspondents who work out of our Washington bureau, a formidable array of talent becomes available for meaningful broadcast reports to our five television and radio stations. Thus, the fact of Time-Life Broadcast's ownership of its limit of VHF television stations not only fills a gap in news service

---

Reprinted from *American Broadcasting: Introduction and Analysis: Readings.* College Printing and Publishing, University of Wisconsin–Madison.

to audiences in five regions, it also adds dimensions to that news service that no other group could add.

There are as many different philosophies of group operation as there are groups operating. Some believe in leaving decisions to local managers, some in making them at headquarters. Some believe in group programming, some in strictly local buying. Some have gone into program production for syndication, some have not. All insist on public service for the cities in which they are licensed to operate, but their definitions of the elusive term vary widely.

At Time-Life Broadcast, we believe in strong local management with near-100% autonomy in making decisions that affect their local operations. We believe in a total broadcast service, encompassing all the facets of radio and television. We believe in stimulating and actively supporting creative programming at the local level, with especial emphasis on the use of remote pickups. We urge our management and staffs to participate actively in community affairs, and we support our managers in vigorous programs of editorializing on local issues. All of this is natural and right, because of the nature of broadcasting and the nature of Time Incorporated.

But because we are part of one of the great news organizations of the world, we further believe that Time-Life Broadcast stations have a duty above and beyond covering local news and serving their local institutions in the public interest. We feel it our responsibility to reach out beyond our signal areas for the information our audiences need to know.

Thus, our support of the most exciting way of teaching French by television we've encountered, Dawn Addams' easy-to-take *En France* film series which starts in the fall on all our stations and in syndication to more than twenty-five others. And thus, the Time-Life Broadcast public service project on Civil Rights, to demonstrate the ability of group broadcasters to act swiftly and boldly in the public interest. We produced a series of "spot" appeals to individual conscience and reason from national leaders in many fields, with the endorsement and participation of President Kennedy, and made them available to all TV and radio stations in the U.S. without charge. It is hard to conceive of projects such as these being carried out by any single station.

We respectfully submit that these activities, and the many being carried on daily by our fellow group operators, do indeed inject a "third force" into the service television renders its audiences, and that our unique contribution lies in providing the spark and the savvy—to say nothing of the budget—for that service.

CBS Inc. earned $24 million in the first three months of 1975. That was up 15 per cent from 1974 and it was the most money ever made by CBS in its first quarter.

RCA Inc., the owner of NBC, earned $17 million in the first three months of 1975. That was down 46 per cent from 1974 and it was one of the worst first-quarter showings in modern RCA history.

So why does CBS, with less than half the sales of RCA, make more money, especially when both companies have similar lines of business?

CBS airs programs and sells advertisers time on those programs. It doesn't bother to make the television sets that receive those programs. Its broadcasting operations account for about one-half of sales but 75 per cent of profits.

RCA, on the other hand, is a major maker of television sets. In the color market it's outsold only by Zenith. Its broadcasting operations, represented by NBC, account for only 15 per cent of total sales.

—Milton Moskowitz

Media Monopolies: Is Bigness a Curse?

WALTER PINCUS

When a reporter comes up with a story of his own, it will be carried by whoever employs him—a newspaper, a radio or television station, a magazine. If he is lucky another publication or the networks will pick it up and relay it, but usually it dies a quick death. In the course of my career I have tried to promote the idea that newspapers, magazines and television should work together, so that important stories any of them originate can have the same broad impact as, say, a Presidential press conference. This sharing of stories could be done locally by newspapers that own television and/or radio stations.

But if you try to set up that sort of collaboration, you run up against a barrier. A friend of mine who owns a radio and television station as well as a newspaper once confided to me that it was his Washington lawyer who recommended a separate identity for the newspaper and radio-TV staffs. The lawyer did not want it to appear that single ownership meant a news monopoly, although in the end that is what it really was. To take the best from the newspaper and put it on television, or vice versa, might result in a better informed public, but in the case of my friend it could only be done on a regular basis if someone else owned either the paper or the station.

Some years ago I did a study of news reading and listening habits among college-educated, medium-income men and women in Minneapolis. The Cowles family owns the city's morning and evening newspapers and a radio and television station there. I thought they did a good job on all of them. Nevertheless a common complaint among almost all those interviewed was that if the Cowles did not approve of a story, it could not get printed or aired. In that instance, but not in all, I thought the complaint unjustified. But would that same opportunity to "manage" news exist if some other company or individual owned either the newspapers or the radio-television stations in Minneapolis?

On January 2, the Justice Department asked the Federal Communications Commission to hold up renewal of radio-television licenses for three stations, each all or partly owned by a company that owned a newspaper in the same city. One was in Des Moines (the Cowles interests); the other two were in St. Louis (the Pulitzer Publishing Co. and the Newhouse chain). The department wanted public hearings held so that it could be determined whether continued operation by the present owners would "perpetuate the high degree of concentration in the dissemination of local news and advertising." Two months earlier the department had asked that a similar hearing be set by the FCC for radio and television stations in Milwaukee owned by that city's sole newspaper company. The coverage of the Des Moines story was significant. *The New York Times* ran a wire service report on the day of the filing and nothing else in the days that followed. No mention was made by the *Times* of the fact that Cowles Communications, Inc., which owns the Des Moines station, also owns an interest in the *Times*. *The Washington Post*, which noted *its* television station ownership in a second-day story, placed strong emphasis that day on a statement by former FCC Commissioner Nicholas Johnson that the Justice Department move was part of a "war on the media." That Johnson is now running for public office in Iowa, where the Cowles newspaper and the Cowles television station are dominant, was overlooked.

Diversified ownership of radio, television, newspapers and cable television would, in the best of times, be difficult for any government agency to further, even if the desired end is greater variety of news coverage and editorial opinion. The basic constitutional safeguard of the First Amendment limits what Congress, the White House and the courts may do. On top of that, diversifying ownership in a given town or city may run counter to a long-term economic trend toward media monopoly. In the past twenty years we've seen a great many newspap-

---

Reprinted by permission of *The New Republic*, © 1974 The New Republic, Inc.

ers that resisted that trend go under. Many local newspapers in self-defense have bought into local radio stations and, in turn, become the licensees for the first television stations. And local newspapers and television stations are often the developers of cable TV systems.

As of three years ago, according to the American Newspaper Association, 96 television stations, 229 AM radio stations and 151 FM stations were owned by newspapers in the same cities and towns. In almost every major city—New York Chicago, Washington, Philadelphia, Detroit, San Francisco, St. Louis, Cleveland, Baltimore, Atlanta, Des Moines, Minneapolis, Dallas, Milwaukee, Houston—one or more television stations are owned by local papers. In many smaller cities monopoly is more pronounced. In Topeka, Kansas, for example, Stauffer Publications, the company that owns the morning and evening newspaper, also owns the major television station and AM and FM radio stations. The legal counsel of Stauffer Publications is majority stockholder in the local cable television system—which he bought from Stauffer, who got the original CATV franchise. In Atlanta the Cox Newspapers own the only morning-evening papers and a radio and television station. Cox is now seeking a waiver to permit continued ownership of the CATV system. The Justice Department is opposing the waiver.

Any serious contemplation of a government-sponsored media diversification policy comes under instant suspicion these days, because the administration's campaign for "diversity" has seemed a cover for an attack on what the President and his staff consider "unfair" journalism. In a White House memo written in October 1969, Jeb S. Magruder, then working on the President's public relations staff, advised H. R. Haldeman that in the preceding thirty days, the President had requested on twenty-one occasions that specific actions be taken to counter what he considered "unfair news coverage." "Begin an official monitoring system through the Federal Communications system as soon as Dean Burch is officially on board as chairman," was Magruder's first suggestion. "If the monitoring system proves our point [apparently that the TV networks treated Nixon news unfairly], we have then legitimate and legal rights to go to the networks, etc., and make official complaints *from the FCC*."

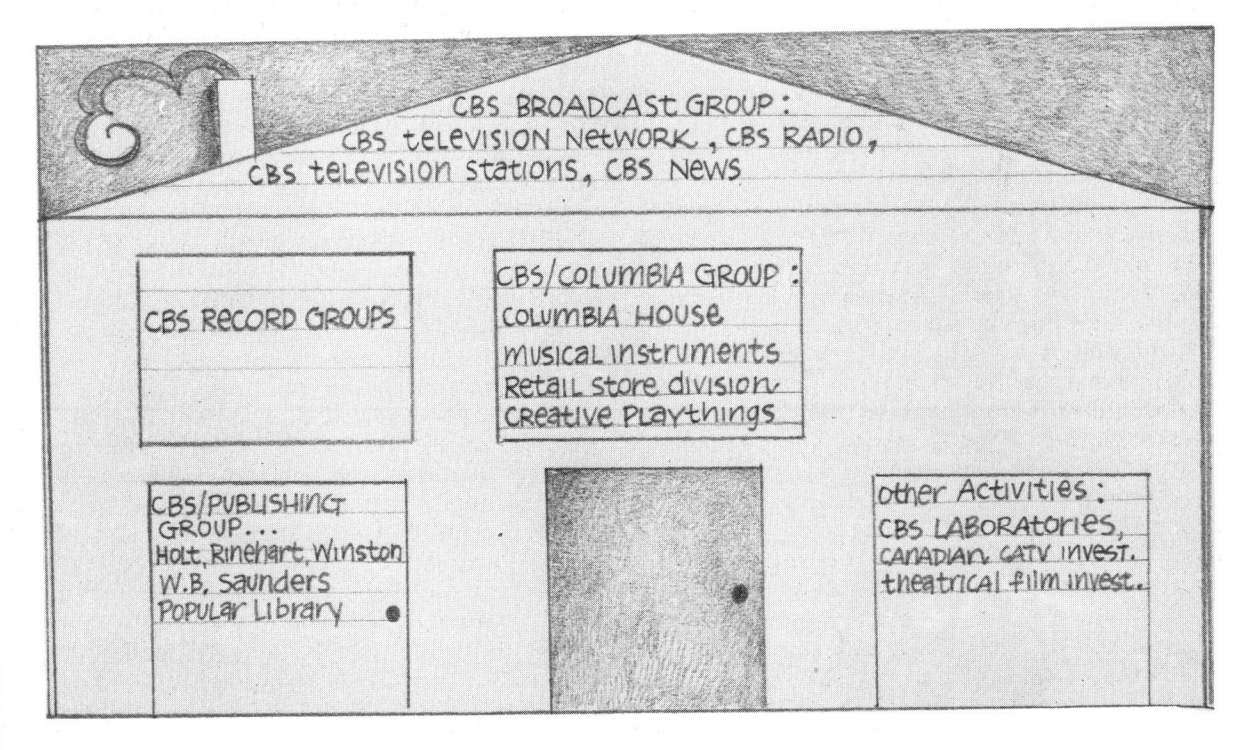

CBS BROADCAST GROUP:
CBS TELEVISION NETWORK, CBS RADIO,
CBS TELEVISION STATIONS, CBS NEWS

CBS RECORD GROUPS

CBS/COLUMBIA GROUP:
COLUMBIA HOUSE
MUSICAL INSTRUMENTS
RETAIL STORE DIVISION
CREATIVE PLAYTHINGS

CBS/PUBLISHING GROUP...
Holt, Rinehart, Winston
W.B. Saunders
Popular Library

Other Activities:
CBS LABORATORIES,
CANADIAN CATV INVEST.
THEATRICAL FILM INVEST.

Ownership, Economics, and Media   235

Magruder's second recommendation was more pertinent to the question of diversity: "Utilize the [Justice Department's] antitrust division to investigate various media relating to antitrust violations. Even the possible threat of antitrust action I think would be effective in changing their views in the above matter," *i.e.*, "unfair'" coverage. Magruder's memo made plain that the administration saw in diversity—or in the threat that the White House was going to insist on more of it—a means of lessening criticism.

Whether the White House crew knew it or not, professionals within the Justice Department's antitrust division were already interested in media monopolies, as were several Democratic FCC commissioners. Well before Richard Nixon was elected, the FCC in 1968 under prodding from Robert Bartley and Nicholas Johnson proposed barring owners of full-time AM, FM or television stations from purchasing another outlet in the same city. The Justice Department that year asked the FCC to go a step further, requiring multi-media owners—particularly those with newspaper properties in the same towns as their radio or television stations—to divest themselves of all but one mass media outlet. In 1968 also, Justice moved against a Cheyenne, Wyoming media monopoly, winning a consent agreement that required the newspaper owner to divest the radio-television properties.

Thus when Magruder & Co. started looking for ways in 1969 to implement their ideas, they found ready support at Justice and the FCC. In March 1970 the FCC adopted its rule limiting future station ownership, and at the same time it set out to devise a further rule based on the Justice Department's 1968 suggestion that all newspapers be forced to sell radio-television properties owned in the same town or city. That initiative was sidetracked as a result of heavy attack from publishers and the radio-television industry. Studies were produced by the industry to prove that divestiture would bankrupt the companies. Dozens of congressmen and senators, prodded by the media back home, forwarded requests to FCC or Justice for status reports on the proposal. The newspaper publishers' organization noted that after more than a year of study and eighteen volumes of exhibits, only five individuals or groups—the Justice Department, a group of law students, a professor at Hofstra University, three academics at Stanford and one church group—had openly approved the concept: "No one has come forward with any showing that the public interest would be forwarded by forced separation of daily newspapers" to accomplish "the abstract of diversity." And the publishers went on to say that diversity "would only add to the plethora of separate and antagonistic voices already existing in the local market." Lawyers for other media monopolies made the point that stations owned by newspapers generally provide better news coverage than those not so owned. In the case of small towns, "under separate ownership," one writer noted, "the stations could not hope to approximate the newspaper's news staff."

It is an old story. In December 1940, when Republican-owned newspapers dominated the fast-growing radio industry, President Roosevelt sent this memo to the then-chairman of the FCC, James L. Fly: "Will you let me know when you propose to have a hearing on newspaper ownership of radio stations." Roosevelt was angry over the manner in which radio stations, particularly the *Chicago Tribune's* WGN, were handling his fireside chats. An FCC investigation was started. Several years later some new rules were promulgated, one of which limited an owner to one radio station per city. The rule required divestitures by some. It also forced the National Broadcasting Company, which had two radio networks of its own, to drop one.

Today the Justice Department's petitions argue that advertising control of the market is so great that on their face the news media monopolies work against the public interest. That does not, however, meet the more troublesome question of news domination. Justice has suggested that newspapers trade stations among themselves, getting rid of those in the same city where they publish and acquiring stations elsewhere. That would keep intact the expertise on the newsgathering side, permit radio-television income to support papers in trouble, and perhaps enliven local competition for news and the best men to cover it.

IT'S A FAMILY AFFAIR (PART 2)

MICHAEL SHAIN

This section of Michael Shain's study of the music business explores the economic relationship between the record industry and radio. Interviews with spokesmen from both industries provide some insights into just how records become hits and recording artists become stars, a process that has not changed measurably since this article was written. Though each business has its own unique capabilities and problems, their audiences and markets are "so overlapping that for all intents and purposes, they are the same."

ASCAP has survived those anti-trust suits of the forties; radio has survived the lawsuits by Fred Waring and the other members of the National Association of Performing Artists of the same time; BMI* broke the monopoly on music performance rights over thirty years ago, and live music has been gone from radio longer than most broadcasters care to remember.

There are still vestiges left from those tumultuous days. WCFL (AM) Chicago still has to use members of the musicians union to spin records; the old issue of radio paying performance rights to the record companies and performers is back again in the form of a new copyright bill pending before Congress; there's still a "potted palm" station in Portland, Ore. (KOIN[AM]), with a live studio orchestra.

But by and large, the scene from then to now is totally unrecognizable. When the record industry finally discovered that airplay didn't really hamper record sales but actually boosted them, the courtship between records and radio began.

*Broadcast Music, Inc.

Reprinted from "It's a Family Affair" by Michael Shain in *Broadcasting Magazine*, December 27, 1971. Used by permission of Broadcasting Magazine.

Jac Holzman, president of Elektra Records: "The bulk of radio is irrevocably wedded to the music industry. We need each other desperately. We both have a story to tell. We both tell our story with the aid of the other. And yet, the distance we maintain is surprising. And there seems to be, perhaps, more distrust and a lesser sense of the reality of the situation from the side of the radio men."

Ever since the inception and proliferation of radio, it has served as the major form of exposure for music product. Since the early fifties and the advent of network TV, music has been radio's major programming tool. Although stations depend heavily upon the record companies to supply them with proficient, exciting music virtually free of charge, radio management has never really been willing to recognize or accommodate its dependency.

Jac Holzman: "Radio sometimes acts like a person who's living in your house and living off your hospitality but is embarrassed about it. And as a result gets testy."

Record men, on the other hand, have never shown much embarrassment about trying to influence the methods by which radio runs *its* business. Witness the Bill Gavin programming conferences of the last several years. Despite a conspicuous effort to keep the annual meetings from becoming "a head-hunting party for the record industry," the music business far outdistances radio in attendance at such affairs.

Neil Bogart, president of Buddah Records: "I have a vision where the radio station guy says: 'OK. I'm ready to battle. Send in the next war group.' And in walks the promotion man who unloads his bombs. The radio man sends up his artillery: 'But I got Gavin Reports.' Or: 'You need a battle plan to get a record played.' ... "

Promotion, like the rest of the music business, has changed greatly in the last ten years. The days of the "personality" promotion man are gone. It is true that promo men of the past have brought this distrust on themselves through deceptive practices, "hype" and, most blatantly, payola. The program director-promo man relationship is subject to the pressures of a highly competitive business, much the same as beset other men in similar jobs in the entertainment field. (The film distribution-theater and publisher-newsstand relationships are two parallels that come to mind.)

Ownership, Economics, and Media

Neil Bogart is one of the best men to talk to when looking for insight into the promo game. In a little more than four years, he has built Buddah from a small label, totally dependent on MGM for distribution, into a major independent company, an autonomous operation owned by Viewlex Inc. Buddah began its independent career with a string of financially successful "bubblegum" hits (Buddah coined the term, by the way) in the late sixties—*Yummy-Yummy* and *Chewy-Chewy* among the top sellers. In the last two years, however, it has advanced strongly into R&B with a new division, Hot Wax, and some bright new black artists, The Honey Cone, Bill Withers and Curtis Mayfield (formerly of the Impressions).

Between Mr. Bogart, with his amazing talent for recording successful singles, and Cecil Holmes, Buddah's national promotion manager and twice winner of the R&B promotion-man-of-the-year award from the Gavin radio programming conference, the company's growth, mainly via its AM hits, has been phenomenal.

Neil Bogart:

If promotion people would understand that their job is not to trick or force a radio station into playing a record but be able to communicate with them, and be able to point out the goods of playing a record then I think promotion men would get more records played. We're very careful not to force an issue. If a radio station doesn't want to play a record, we'll prove the record some place else, hopefully, and come back. But promotion people, by forcing themselves in the past, have made enemies, or set up separate camps.

On the other hand, radio—again, a generalization—automatically takes it for granted that when a record guy calls, it's a hype. As a consequence, they often keep their guard too high to be able to communicate back to the serious promotion people. There are parallels to the Israeli-Arab situation: They're at peace but they're never at peace. And it shouldn't be that way, it really shouldn't be that way.

I think the level of record company people has improved tremendously. The professionalism that is displayed by promotion men is such that the radio industry has never seen. They should open their eyes and look around and see that most of us *are* professionals, with professional jobs."

Lou Adler is one of the premier producers of pop music. He is such a powerful force that he can demand his own label wherever he goes. During the early sixties, while working for ABC Records, he began the Dunhill division of that company with what is credited as the first protest hit, *Eve of Destruction* by Barry McGuire. Later, he enhanced his fame producing the Mamas and the Papas. Today, he works for Jerry Moss and Herb Alpert at A&M records, where once again he has his own label, Ode. The first record on Ode was *If You're Going to San Francisco*, a hit that did as much as any other to popularize the flower generation. New on Ode, and produced by Mr. Adler, is Carole King, perhaps the closest thing to a superstar there is in pop music today.

Lou Adler's end of the music business is primarily creative. But he is a student and a fan of radio and a former associate of Chuck Blore, the noted ex-program director now head of his own radio commercials company. Mr. Adler's consistent success with new talent has been inextricably tied to Top 40 radio.

Lou Adler:

The secret battle that is waged between radio and the record business all through the years is 'Who's on top?' And it changes. In 1961, '62 and '63, radio was on top. In 1964, with the Beatles, Mamas and Papas, Dylan, Lovin' Spoonful, the record business started dictating the product. Whenever you get a lull in excitement in the record business, radio takes over.

And it takes so long to condition radio, that you can have a superstar and it might take you two years to teach radio that it *is* a superstar. Carole King sold 6,000 *Writer* albums up until the time *Tapestry* came out. Now, she's close to 300,000 on *Writer*. It didn't get better; it got exposed. That battle is always waged. As long as there's a lull, they'll [radio] dictate to you what they want to hear. If you try something different, getting it played becomes very difficult.

The soft sound, they call it—James Taylor, Carole King, Carly Simon—all those people were kept back. It was the same thing with the Beatles. The Beatles had plenty of records before [they were played on the air]. It's not the public that turned them down. The public never heard them. Radio ears are a lot farther behind than record ears, which they should be. But I don't know if they should be *that* far behind.

238   Media Environments

If there is one common denominator between the record industry and radio, it is, of course, music. But from that one point on, the paths of the two begin to diverge, the knowledge that one industry has of the other begins to dim. It would seem axiomatic that the manufacturer of razors would know what was happening with the guys who make blades.

That is not the situation in music and radio. There is practically no dialogue between these two billion-dollar businesses. There is no common ground where they can meet. The number of times a year that they talk to each other can be counted on one hand. Yet the audience and market for radio product and record product are so overlapping that for all intents and purposes they are the same.

Jac Holzman is a candid man. Before becoming president of Elektra records, he owned two radio stations, WCCC-AM-FM Hartford, Conn. But broadcasting didn't interest him as the music business did.

Jac Holzman:

The thing about the music business that is unlike radio is that radio does not function as much off the cuff as the music business does. Methodologies of doing business in music shift from day to day. There can be five ways of doing the same thing, each of them a little bit right. You're constantly on the line to make intuitive judgments involving large sums of money. If anybody asked me what it was that I do as president of a record company on a day-to-day basis, the only answer I could give them is that I make it up as I go along. And I don't think radio is like that.

In radio, as you adopt a format, you have to think it out very, very thoroughly, because you're dealing with a totality of a concept. A record company is dealing with 20 to 150 individual artists, all of whom are their own reality. Sometimes they impinge on the reality of the whole and sometimes they don't.

The one area of the music business and the radio business that is close to the same is that there are an incredible number of non-innovative copycats out there, somehow making a living.

Clive Davis, president of Columbia Records:

Record companies can more readily explore the full range of creativity of artists. Whereas radio, being licensed, has many more restrictions. So you get censorship involved where radio is concerned. Therefore, they do have a different kind of responsibility and I'm not looking down at all upon the problems that they have. As far as I'm concerned, we have an obligation to our artists that there are things that we have to put on records, and I believe very strongly that we should. You can make the same analogy between book companies and books. And you find that radio stations cannot play a lot of the material that the artist might want to expose, as far as thoughts are concerned.

Mr. Davis's point is an important distinction to keep in mind. There is no contact with artists—with the exception of promotional appearances—at the station level. Radio is not in the business of finding and exploiting musical talent. It has left that responsibility to the record business. Radio is perhaps the only form of entertainment that—for the most part—does not directly involve itself with artists.

By and large, the record industry is much more understanding of the problems of and differences about radio than has been shown here. The companies within it are acutely aware of the reasons behind radio's comparative conservativism. A record company can be started in a garage with $500, while a radio station in a market of any size represents a capital value of several hundred thousand dollars and up. Radio stations are regulated by the government; record companies are answerable to no one but their creditors. Most of all, the record people realize that radio stations make no money by selling records, a job they do extremely well, but by selling advertising based on the size of their audiences.

But as times have changed the music, and music has changed the times, the music business has become more emotionally committed to its music than it was before. The enthusiasm generated by the pop music of the sixties finally turned on the companies that were supplying it. Management at the record companies got progressively younger. The new executives, promotion men, marketing and publicity experts were coming from the ranks of the "children of the Beatles." And now, those people are asking that same kind of commitment from the people who expose and showcase their product, the people in radio.

QUESTIONS FOR DISCUSSION

1. In what ways do the media romanticize drugs? What effect does this have on drug use and attitudes surrounding it?

2. Shamberg asserts in his article that drugs are a symptom not of decadence but of adaptation, that drugs are providing a new "software." Is this assertion valid?

3. The major media have often been accused of making us a nation of pilltakers. Is such a charge justified? Should there be restrictions on all drug-oriented advertising?

4. What options for broadcast access might CATV provide for minority and counterculture segments of the population? How can minorities gain access to CATV systems?

5. Why is there an underground press in a free society? Why did it emerge in the 1960s? What service to society does it provide?

PROJECT

1. The class should be divided into committees to interview managers or owners of local media, with each committee responsible for a different medium. As a group, develop interview questions to help you determine what percentage of the total revenue of each medium comes from advertising and who are the largest advertisers. Can you see any direct effects of this advertising revenue on the policies or functioning of the medium itself?

EDUCATORS, MEDIA WATCHERS, AND MEDIA

THE SWORD IN THE STONE

MARTIN T. DUCHENY

Anyone could have predicted that the technology would be most easily assimilated by the young. The informational media explosion was particularly alluring. The kids were soon splashing around in it like ducks in a pond, while their elders sat on the shore staring at their new webbed feet as if they were the damndest contraptions in the world.

Naturally enough, the first classroom attempts to use the technology of the informational explosion were less than spectacular. "Visual aids" most of them were called, since everyone knew that only teachers taught. The gadgets, if they behaved themselves and remembered their places, would be allowed to stay and help out from time to time.

Unfortunately, not many of these innovations helped students to learn. And the kids, more and more frequently, turned to commercial print, film, radio, television and the telephone for their information and education. Soon, as Marshall McLuhan observed, students came to regard school as a breach in the process of education, and as a waste of time.

If a spin-off of the informational explosion was to alienate students from the institutions of education, reasoned some, these same tools of the informational explosion could be used to reunite them. The science of applying these tools to the process of learning came to be called educational technology.

Precursors of this new science started with the idea that each person learns differently. This in itself was not so novel a concept; many teachers already accepted it. The problem came when the teacher tried to practice it. In order to teach 30 students on an individual basis, a teacher had to be 30 teachers. Since this obviously could not happen, most teachers shot for the middle and hoped for the best. The new technology, the prophets said, could change all that. With thoughtfully planned use of technology, one teacher *could* become 30 teachers. In fact, 30 *students* could become 30 teachers.

Certainly that sounded promising. Students would become interested in school again. They would learn more efficiently. Both teachers and students would be freed from much of the monotony and frustration of education. There might even be a cost reduction. Surely, this was worth looking into . . . and so, they did.

The first real milestone came in 1970. It was the Commission on Instructional Technology's study *To Improve Learning: An Evaluation of Instructional Technology* (Sidney G. Tickton, ed., R.R. Bowker Co.). After considering much information, the Commission decided that the development of educational technology should be a matter of national educational priority. Their major recommendation was that a National Institute of Instructional Technology (NIIT) be established.

The NIIT was to have two functions: research and motivation. As a research center, it would set up a "library of learning resources." This "library" would identify software shortages and hardware needs, help existing libraries change themselves into learning centers, and provide access to instructional material and educational management data.

The second major role of the NIIT was to be motivational. Since NIIT could never hope to further the cause of educational technology by itself, it would strongly influence and encourage teachers and administrators to investigate, understand and use educational technology. Producers, programmers and technicians would be trained and employed through the encouragement of NIIT. Finally, education and industry would be brought together to speed advances in the design and application of technology to learning.

The price tag for all this, the Commission estimated, would be approximately $565 million. While this sum was already almost five times the 1970 expenditures for research, develop-

---

Reprinted from *Media & Methods*, Jan., 1975 by permission of North American Publishing Co.

ment, and application of educational technology, the Commission saw an even bigger future. By 1980, the expenditure should be approximately $2.5 billion or more, making education's investment in research consistent with industry, health, and agriculture.

As with most commission reports, this one started much thinking, but little else. While a National Institute of Education (NIE) did finally come into existence, the National Institute of Instructional Technology did not—nor did anything like it. And NIE was limited to a handful of demonstration projects. Presumably it was the projected costs which left the immediate future of educational technology looking like a slow-motion runner. But if money was to be the first hurdle, it would be small by comparison with the indifference and antagonism of educators.

In 1972, the Carnegie Commission on Higher Education issued *The Fourth Revolution: Instructional Technology in Higher Education* (McGraw-Hill Book Co.) The Commission acknowledged that the implementation of electronic technology as a teaching/learning tool (the "Fourth Revolution") was faltering, and that just the first step—overcoming a "grossly inadequate supply" of quality software—would demand money and the uncompromising commitment of educational leadership.

With this as background, the Commission recommended dividing the nation into seven regions and establishing a cooperative learning technology center in each region. The centers would have a production unit to design, plan, and produce instructional programs; a resource unit to act as a library and information system; a distribution unit actively engaged in the design, implementation and evaluation of teaching/learning segments; and a computing unit to provide core storage and on-line computing services for management, administration, and instructional use. Each center, the Commission projected, would cost $35 million to start and $150 million in annual operating expenses. The report recommended that the government pick up the tab for all the start-up expenses, plus one-third of the operating expenses for the first ten years.

The Commission realized that, even with these inputs, educational technology could not hope to succeed without understanding and commitment from the ultimate users. They therefore recommended (1) that contact with the methods of educational technology should begin in high school, (2) that the training of prospective teachers should include educational technology as part of the curriculum, (3) that colleges and universities should offer rewards to teachers who use educational technology, and (4) that these institutions should supplement their staffs with technicians and specialists who could advise and assist those teachers implementing the new approaches.

As with *To Improve Learning*, *The Fourth Revolution* painted a picture of exciting possibilities. The funding and the guidance and the encouragement did not come, however. The enthusiasm from within remained but a dream.

In 1973, the Ford Foundation published *An Inquiry into the Uses of Instructional Technology* (James W. Armsey and Norman C. Dahl, The Ford Foundation, New York). Teacher resistance, the report said, was the most formidable obstacle. It grew from a real or imagined inability to work with educational media and systems technology. Teachers saw their work pattern threatened and their professional position demeaned as their art was recast as a science. Encouraging this resistance was a pervasive ambiguity about the goals of education and the process of learning.

The report noted that hardware manufacturers had flooded the educational market with often redundant, inappropriate, incompatible, and generally poorly designed equipment which soon faded into obsolescence. After such a harsh lesson, even the most progressive and affluent school systems were reluctant to invest in new machinery. The other problem was the absence of abundant and proven software. Educational publishers and producers had found the software industry far less lucrative than the production and sale of expensive hardware. The job of production all too often fell to the users, who had minimal production facilities and inadequate experience and technological expertise. Using the resulting home-made productions, many teachers felt justified in pointing out the unsuitability of *all* educational media as teaching/learning experiences. And there is no conclusive research to change their minds.

The Ford Foundation report made no call for new federal agencies or for the appropriation of specific sums for educational technology. It did, however, outline the conditions for the success of educational technology. Before using technology, educators must examine education to determine what it does and how it does it. Only with concrete objectives clearly before them can they hope to use the multitudinous alternatives presented by educational technology. After education has clearly defined its objectives, and at least briefly considered the many possibilities for reaching them, it must alter its administration, staffing, equipment, and facilities, as far as it is able, to at least *allow* the application of as many of the means of educational technology as possible.

Key among the conditions of success was the desire on the part of teachers to use educational media, along with a strong emphasis and encouragement from administrators. Teachers must participate in and support educational technology or it will be doomed to failure. Equally important was measurement and evaluation, since, without being able to prove itself, the value of educational technology would remain a matter of opinion.

The Ford Foundation report only lastly, and with tasteful passiveness, mentioned money. "Finally," it said, "adequate resources must be provided at the beginning and for the duration of the project. Instructional technology is expensive. Adequate financial resources are critical."

The report gave no real answers to the questionable future of educational technology, but it did at least uncover some of the right questions for evaluating its obscure present: Do teachers believe in educational technology any more now than they did when the Commission on Instructional Technology or the Carnegie Commission wrote their reports? Do administrators encourage it? Is industry still exploiting technology? Is anyone willing (and able) to pay for it?

With questions like these we might discover where educational technology stands today. Obviously there is no simple answer. There may not even be a complex one. In fact, even the "experts" give surprisingly mixed responses.

Donald Ely, professor of education at Syracuse University and consultant to the Association for Educational Communication and Technology, is one of the more optimistic in interpreting the present. "The field of educational technology has become established," he said. "It is no longer a stepchild of the educational program." He feels that educational technology has found its place within the curriculum of schools and colleges throughout the country, that it is accepted. Noting that we have come a long way in the past ten years, Dr. Ely feels that the next ten years will be a "period of synthesis when we will gather together all that we have learned, and move toward new and greater impacts on American education."

Harriet Lundgaard of the Educational Media Council, with somewhat more restraint, called for patience and fortitude. "It is just going to take time and hard work," she said. Not dismayed that expensive media programs have not been implemented, she indicated that even the commissions making such recommendations did not expect more rapid progress. In fact, she doubts that a "major national media thrust" would be particularly advantageous to educational technology right now. She sees, instead, as a key to the future, a far greater need for development and interaction between the "highly fractionated" elements of educational media.

Verne Stadman of the Carnegie Commission on Higher Education holds a considerably more guarded opinion. He sees educational technology as "a little ahead of where it was in 1970 . . . but not very much." Nor is his outlook particularly promising. He sees the absence of recognition by teachers and administrators as undermining the essentials of educational technology. Financial problems continue to present insurmountable obstacles. "In a time of financial stringency, it is difficult for administrators to encourage the development of new technologies . . . The argument that technology at its current stage is best used as enrichment instead of economy will not be heard in financially difficult times." In the absence of large doses of financial support, what does he feel will convince teachers and school administrators to join the cause of educational technology? "Only successful conversion by the convinced and committed—not, I am afraid, a very potent force."

The opinions range from "we have arrived" through "we are making slow but methodical progress" to "we are almost standing still." None of these descriptions, however, fit the long-predicted technological revolution. Nor did they even vaguely fit the projections of either the

Commission on Instructional Technology or the report of the Carnegie Commission on Higher Education. Something is obviously happening, but it is not the fourth revolution the Carnegie Commission had hailed.

The dictionary defines a revolution as a thorough-going, fundamental change which proceeds from the very foundations and essentials of the thing changed. If education has changed fundamentally, or is on the verge of doing so, it has kept the secret masterfully. Certainly there is change; movement is taking place; new knowledge is being methodically added to the bulk of human understanding of educational technology. Yet, change is not progress, and progress is not revolution.

In spite of the "progress" of the past years, the essential questions still remain to point accusingly at unfilled prophecies: Where is the leadership in the cause of educational technology? Why are teachers still resisting as before? Where is the financial support? The picture is one of a would-be revolution at best, but without an acknowledged leader, without popular support, and without enough money.

In the face of this bleak present, educational technology seems to have armored itself by becoming an institution, an organization, an establishment. In this way it talks to itself reassuringly, implying that unlistening teachers and recalcitrant librarians are doing the best they can.

Since, as an organized body of knowledge, educational technology can make "progress," revolution seems far too much work to be inviting. Now it can become Educational Technology with capital letters, and set rules and guidelines, and replicate itself.

The prophets have contended that the revolution is about to begin. Perhaps it is already over; a short insignificant takeover of a few minor roles in education, its occurrence recognized, its importance obscured, its effect upon the culture lost in the morass of everyday changes.

The issue has never been whether educational technology will survive. Technology is with us, and that is certain. The real issue is the place and the scope of educational technology. Will it survive as a miscellaneous servant or as an emperor? Will it be a cog in a worn machine or the master mechanic?

The sword, it seems, is still stuck in the stone.

HOW COMMUNITY PRESS COUNCILS WORK

DONALD E. BRIGNOLO

Twenty-two years after the Commission on Freedom of the Press suggested the establishment of an evaluative agency for the mass media, pilot community press councils were operating in Bend, Ore., Redwood City, Calif., and Cairo and Sparta, Ill., under the auspices of the Mellett Fund for a Free and Responsible Press, a non-profit corporation. The objective was to demonstrate the utility of press councils as a two-way communicative link between the press and the public and to encourage more responsible press performance without infringing upon established freedoms.

These new press councils are best described by one editor as voluntary, private, non-governmental, lay citizen groups meeting in unfettered, uninhibited, objective and responsible criticism of the press with a view to forcing upon the proprietors of the media a measure of self-discipline.

Although the Mellett Fund experiments have ended, all but the Redwood City press council have been restarted on a permanent basis.

Internationally, press councils are not a new phenomenon. As early as 1916, Sweden formed the Press Fair Practices Commission to serve as a mediary between the press and the public. Since that time about fifteen countries have set up press councils or courts of honor. In most nations, the press council is seen as a protector of freedom of the press and as a means of estab-

---

Reprinted from *Seminar*, a Quarterly Review for Journalists by Copley Newspapers, December 1969. This is Freedom of Information Center Report No. 217, published by the School of Journalism, University of Missouri at Columbia.

lishing a dialogue between the newspaper and the readers.

J. Edward Gerald of the University of Minnesota described the characteristics of the effective overseas press council:

- It is a private body designed to ward off government pressure upon the press.
- It operates as a buffer between the press and the public and between the press and government.
- Its membership is composed of balanced representation of the community and media.
- It has no statutory power and relies on public support after reporting its deliberations and decisions.
- It appears to function best in nations where newsmen avoid all forms of extremism.

Proponents of the press council idea in this country usually point to the successful European councils as a model. They say that a press council induces a sense of responsibility in the newspaper publisher; allows the newspaper to explain *why* it operates as it does; permits the public to make their complaints, desires and needs known to the publisher; and increases understanding of the newspaper.

Meanwhile, opponents of the press council idea argue that newspapers are already engaging in self-criticism and self-discipline, thus a council is unnecessary; the press council may fall into the "wrong" hands, such as those of politicians or government; and the council idea would infringe on freedom of the press.

In the United States, the vast contemporary dialogue about press councils is rooted in the 1947 report of the Commission on Freedom of the Press, also known as the Hutchins Commission, named after its chairman, Robert Hutchins, then chancellor of the University of Chicago. The 133-page document, highly critical of the press, contained a recommendation for the creation of an independent agency "to appraise and report annually upon the performance of the press."

The Hutchins Commission recommended a national continuing commission, but none has been established to date. This report may have sparked the press, more than twenty years later, to awaken to its responsibilities and set up local press councils in the United States.

Adherents of the local press council say there is no way to make a national press council function effectively in the United States because of the preponderance of local newspapers. "Even state and regional press associations have their difficulties," Richard Tobin has said.

William L. Rivers of Stanford University stated in an interview: "There is still a yearning for a national press council, but a local case would have to be a big one for a national council to deal with it." In effect, a national council would be compelled to examine some 1,750 newspapers or a large sample of them.

The community press council, composed of local citizens and media representatives, has been advanced many times since the Hutchins report, with varying degrees of longevity and success.

The first local press council on record is the Colorado Editorial Advisory Board, set up in 1946 by Houstoun Waring of the Littleton (Colo.) *Independent*. For six years, eight newspaper editors met with eight critics, each representing a different field: sociology, journalism teaching, economics, psychology, political science, public opinion polling, race relations and international relations. Since that time, the media executives have sponsored an annual Critics Dinner, attended by ten leading citizens "to tell us what they would do if they were editor," Waring said. The Colorado Editorial Advisory Board, as we shall see later, was restarted in 1967 as a permanent press council.

In 1958, another pioneer press council was established for a brief time in Santa Rosa, Calif., by Dr. Chilton R. Bush of Stanford University. The Citizens Advisory Council, as it was called, was composed of community leaders who were to meet quarterly to evaluate the performance of the *Press Democrat* the local newspaper.

The press council idea circulated spasmodically during the 1950s and early 1960s. In 1963 Barry Bingham, president and editor of the Louisville *Courier-Journal* and *Times*, proposed the creation of a local press council to act as a public forum for the newspaper and the readers. Bingham did not set up a local press council but established the nation's first fulltime "ombudsman" for a newspaper. This is an official to whom the [public] can complain and who has power, though an employee of the newspaper, to request change or addition.

The Association for Education in Journalism (AEJ), which met in Boulder, Colorado, in the summer of 1967, energetically revived the press council idea. The dialogue generated at that convention gave impetus to Houstoun Waring and Garrett Ray of the Littleton (Colo.) *Independent* to restart the Colorado Editorial Advisory Board, this time as a permanent community press council.

The Littleton Press Council was established on Nov. 16, 1967, as the first contemporary community press council to be operated from the start on a permanent basis. Since that time, the ten-member group has met quarterly with newspaper representatives to criticize and advise on newspaper performance. For example, the council has criticized the newspaper for inferior typography and for placing obituaries on the front page. On another occasion, the council requested the need for more student reporters "to keep the community aware of what students are doing." The Press Council has also urged the newspaper to crusade for better vocational training on the high school level and to foster more community beautification.

The Littleton Press Council is a non-experimental venture, thus no tests have been made to determine the effect, if any, of the council on the newspaper. Two of the obvious effects are: (1) the introduction of youth news and elimination of column rules; and (2) the creation of a Youth Advisory Council, an outgrowth of the press council. According to publisher Garrett Ray, the youth council helps the newspaper "to keep in touch with what young people are doing and thinking."

The press council movement in this country was given a forward thrust by the Mellett Fund for a Free and Responsible Press, an independent, non-profit corporation which, from Sept. 1967 through Oct. 1968, financed experimental community press councils in selected cities. General councils were supported in Bend, Ore., and Redwood City, Calif., administered by Stanford University; other press councils were set up in Cairo and Sparta, Ill., directed by Southern Illinois University. The objective was to promote a continuous dialogue between the representatives of the community and press, without infringing on press freedom, and to demonstrate the overall usefulness of a press council.

In addition to the community press councils, the Mellett Fund also financed summer racial councils in 1968 in Seattle and St. Louis, to contribute to the need for "communication across racial lines" called for by the National Advisory Commission on Civil Disorders. The Seattle Communications Council, composed of both print and broadcasting representatives, was administered by the University of Washington School of Communications. The University of Missouri Center for Community and Metropolitan Studies administered the St. Louis summer council. The final results of the racial councils and the year-long experiments are forthcoming from the Mellett Fund. Undoubtedly, the Mellett councils represent the first systematic attempt in this country to demonstrate the utility of the community press council.

The Mellett Fund for a Free and Responsible Press was created through a bequest of about $40,000 from Lowell Mellett, newspaper editor and columnist, to the American Newspaper Guild to be used to encourage responsible press performance without infringing on press freedom. In turn, the Guild set up the Fund as an independent corporation to further the aims of the bequest. Press critic Ben H. Bagdikian was named president of the organization, which is located in Washington, D.C.

On Sept. 24, 1966, the Mellett Fund officers adopted the press council idea and established some basic ground rules for the proposed experimental councils. One rule was that the council could have no power to effect change in the local newspaper. Bagdikian said the council "could study, discuss or vote, always with the publisher as a member of the group. But the paper retained discretion over its own contents." Another rule was that the administration of each council—its design, implementation and final report—would be in the sole hands of a university journalism professor who had a strong practical newspaper background.

On July 21, 1967, the Mellett Fund announced a grant of $16,250 to Dr. William L. Rivers of the Stanford University Department of Communication to administer year-long pilot press councils in two cities. Rivers is the author of two journalism textbooks and *The Opinionmakers,* a book on Washington journalism....

Rivers wanted cities of moderate size. So he isolated the town of Bend, Ore., (population 12,000) and a suburban city, Redwood City, Calif. (population 60,000). He also obtained the cooperation of Robert W. Chandler, president and editor of the *Bend Bulletin,* a newspaper with a daily (except Sunday) circulation of 7,800, and Raymond L. Spangler, publisher of the *Redwood City Tribune,* a daily with a circulation of 21,000....

On Sept. 15, 1967, the Mellett Fund made a second grant, this time for $8,786, to Dr. Howard R. Long, chairman of the Southern Illinois University Department of Journalism, to administer two more experimental press councils. Dr. Long, who is editor of the quarterly, *Grassroots Editor,* was assisted in the project by an SIU faculty member, Dr. Kenneth Starck, who served as field director and moderator of the council meetings. The University later provided an additional $5,123 to support the pilot projects.

Long and Starck wanted press councils to function in cities representing different social and economic settings. One choice was Cairo, Illinois, (population 9,348), a racially tense community which has just begun to climb out of an economic decline. About 38 per cent of the population is black. By contrast, Sparta (population 3,452), the other study site, is only 10 per cent black and has a teeming economy based on a mixture of agriculture, railroad and small industries.

Another reason for selecting the communities: both daily and weekly newspaper operations are represented and the publishers pledged their full cooperation. The *Cairo Evening-Citizen,* a five-day-a-week newspaper with a circulation of 6,600, is published by Martin Brown. The other publisher is William H. Morgan, who puts out the Sparta News-Plaindealer, a weekly with a circulation of 5,381.

Long and Starck decided to vary the formats of the press councils to determine whether different procedures have any effect on the operation of a newspaper. In Cairo, the council was "directed" that is, it functioned with minimum local publicity. At the first meetings the members were given background information about the role of the press in society. Later a system was devised by which members could vote by secret ballot to reflect their sentiments on the performance of the newspaper. In Sparta, the press council was "non-directed," that is, members were encouraged to search on their own for the role of the newspaper in society and the proceedings received maximum publicity.

The criteria for membership were that persons should be active in the city or represent a wide variety of community interests. Starck recruited members following interviews with persons whose names had been suggested by various community citizens. Each council consisted of fifteen persons. Starck said: "Individuals with extremely militant racial positions were avoided." The active council members in both cities included housewives, school officials and business and professional people. Five Negroes were represented on the Cairo council; three served on the Sparta council....

The discussion topics came in two bundles: (1) those dealing with the newspaper, such as its function in the community and questions pertaining to production and policy; and (2) issues dealing with the whole community, such as water pollution or race relations. "Most of the time these issues were intermingled," Starck said, "the only difference being whether the newspaper or the entire community served as the discussion base." Some of the questions asked by Council members were: "What is the policy in printing names of juveniles in stories?" and "Exactly what is—or should be—the newspaper's role in our community?"

Various methods were employed by the administrators of the Mellett Fund press councils to evaluate the possible effects of the experiments. At Stanford, Rivers and Blankenburg used similar procedures in both cities. They employed the questionnaire in the "newsmaker" surveys mentioned earlier. The items asked for the respondent's evaluation of the story, the degree of "seriousness" of any error noticed, and how well he was acquainted with newspaper staff members.

The administrators also measured all council members early and late on their attitudes toward the newspapers, using a modification of the Brinton-Bush-Newell questionnaire which measured twelve dimensions of newspaper quality such as racial and religious fairness and the general area of satisfaction.

"These tests made it clear," Rivers said, "that the members ran across the spectrum in both cities, from an acidly critical stance toward the papers to welcoming acceptance of almost anything the editors chose to present."

At Southern Illinois University, Long and Starck used different procedures in each city. In Cairo, a content analysis of news, editorials and photographs was used to determine the effects of the press council on the *Cairo Evening-Citizen*. In Sparta, the researchers used the Briton-Bush-Newell questionnaire to obtain normative data about readers' attitudes toward the newspaper. Two surveys were made, one before public announcement of the formation of the council and the other in the month of the final meeting, to study audience attitude change, if any, toward the *News-Plaindealer* during the life of the press council.

What resulted from the press council experiments? The results of the tests and a perusal of commentary from the participants indicates that a press council can have three intermingling effects: it can make the publisher more aware of the need for responsible press performance; it can serve a valuable public relations function by acting as a two-way communicative link between the press and public; and, it can enhance the esteem and understanding of the newspaper in the eyes of the public.

The community press council tends to lead the newspaper publisher to a greater awareness of the need for responsible press performance.

Sparta publisher William H. Morgan said, "The council certainly gave me a much better idea of what my readers notice and don't notice in the *News-Plaindealer*." He also said, "We now know more what the community expects from the newspaper, and we've made some changes"—one of which was a more thorough coverage of local government.

Press council criticism in Cairo regarding the scarcity of front-page local news and local editorials "put management on its toes," said Martin Brown, publisher of the *Evening Citizen*. A content analysis of that paper revealed a tendency to devote more page-one space to local news at the end of the experiment than at the start. The findings also disclosed a significant increase in the number of local editorials during the last quarter of the council's existence.

On the West Coast, both publishers said that more than half of the council suggestions were "valuable." The publishers made some changes, but these were modest; for example, they made certain that page numbers are at the tops of pages and used more maps and diagrams.

Generally, Blankenburg found most West Coast council members reticent to engage in sharp criticism of the performance of the newspaper. He cited four reasons: (1) The members were ignorant of journalistic norms and techniques; they spent a good deal of time educating themselves. (2) They felt constrained to be responsible, and not to lash out without data, but they felt little need to gather data. (3) The publishers had good answers for most criticisms. (4) Neither was a bad newspaper.

Bend publisher Robert W. Chandler said: "I cannot point to anything we have done to improve our practices, and I think we were doing pretty well prior to the start of the council."

The "newsmaker" (accuracy) surveys conducted on the West Coast in Nov. 1967 and May 1968 provided a measure of public attitude toward the newspaper as well as a way of detecting changes in newspaper accuracy. The results of the surveys indicated that both newspapers tended to slip downward in accuracy during the life of the council, with the greatest change occurring in Bend. After the experiment had ended, Chandler said: "I would guess we are more aware of the need for accuracy and fairness than we were before the press council started."

Redwood City publisher Ray Spangler commented that the sheer presence of a community press council induces a publisher to reflect more carefully upon his journalistic performance. He said:

Another valuable by-product is a sense of responsibility one enjoys when he knows a problem cannot merely be swept into a newspaper wastebasket if a press council is sitting nearby to ask questions about the ultimate disposition of a problem. Not that the editor would be less responsible without a press council—but with one he might be more certain and immediate.

The community press council serves a valuable public relations function: it allows the publisher to explain newspaper policy and practice to the readers and at the same time, affords citizens the opportunity to make their needs known to the newspaper.

Sparta publisher William H. Morgan cited the value of a press council in affording him "an opportunity to explain" to the members some of the difficulties of production problems. William Rivers noted, "One value for the newspaper is obvious: The opportunity to explain to a group of interested citizens *why* a newspaper operates as it does."

All four community press councils engaged in some discussion of community needs but, particularly on the West Coast, many of the suggestions were "trivial." Blankenburg explained: "Our councils did not do as much of this as they might, because from the start they aimed at criticism."

The sheer presence of the community press council increases the esteem and understanding of the newspaper in the eyes of the council members and the readers.

The results of the pre- and post-press-council attitude surveys in Sparta, using the Brinton-Bush-Newell test, indicated that readers placed more confidence in the newspaper's leadership ... at the end of the council experience than previously.

Similarly, West Coast press council members thought more highly of their newspaper at the end of the experience. Results of the Brinton-Bush-Newell attitude tests done there showed greater change for Redwood City council members. But Robert Chandler of Bend said:

From the newspaper's standpoint, I suspect [the press council] should help us by making our readers aware of the fact that unbiased persons in the community generally feel we are both accurate and fair within the limitations of time, money.... I am not sure we achieved such a result, at least as yet.

The experimental press councils supported by the Mellett Fund were advisory bodies, having no power to impose suggestions on the proprietors of the media. At the end of the pilot projects, none of the publishers felt that his journalistic freedom had been controlled in any way. For example, Martin Brown of Cairo assured others who might adopt a similar press council "not to worry about the loss of control or any inroads on the management's decisions which a press council might make."

In Redwood City, Ray Spangler adopted an unpublicized format because he did not want even the *appearance* that he was giving up some managerial control. He said:

I do not believe that an unpublicized press council such as we had involves an abdication of authority by a newspaper. To the contrary, it established a communications link with the public, valid to the extent that the council is a cross section of the community.

The last of the four major Mellett Fund experimental press councils ended operations in Oct., 1968. Probably the most noteworthy achievement of the projects is that three of the four community press councils have been restarted voluntarily on a permanent basis. The only dropout is Ray Spangler of the *Redwood City Tribune*. "We have not restarted the council," he said, "and would probably do so only for a special project." Spangler, incidentally, has relinquished his post as *Tribune* publisher.

On Nov. 8, 1968, Robert Chandler restarted the Bend Press Council "to see how such an operation can run without the financial hand of a foundation or the guidance of a college professor." Chandler made the following changes: (*a*) Membership is set up on a revolving, three-year basis; (*b*) The council will meet four or five times a year instead of eight; and (*c*) The council will meet, without dinner, in the offices of a law firm.

In southern Illinois, both press councils have been restarted as permanent advisory bodies. William H. Morgan said: "Members of the council have indicated that they would like to make press council in Sparta a permanent thing, and I heartily agree."

William Blankenburg envisions a variety of kinds of press councils: (*a*) one-medium; (*b*) multi-medium; (*c*) local; (*d*) regional; (*e*) lay; (*f*) professional; (*g*) short-term; (*h*) one-problem (e.g., election coverage) and (*i*) general councils.

Suggestions have been made for those who wish to set up press councils in their communities: (*a*) An outside resource person with a knowledge of journalism is necessary in organizing a council, one publisher said; (*b*) "The important factor is the attitude of the publisher," William Rivers said. "A press council is useful if the publisher is open to current and changing experiences;" and (*c*) The initial focus of the council should be on the information needs of the community; criticism should be secondary and come naturally.

What does the future hold for the community press council? At this point in time it is difficult to determine whether the opinions of newspaper publishers will jell in favor or disfavor of the concept. But the fact that Ray Spangler has chosen not to restart his council indicates, perhaps, that all is not well with community press councils.

Spangler mentioned a "considerable anti-press-council opinion" in the United States, although he did not indicate the criticisms or identify the critics. He said there appears to be "considerable alarm" that some Canadian precedents might be followed here. He was presumably referring to the press council ideas that have been discussed during the past two years in Ontario and Quebec. These councils will be modeled after the British Press Council, which handles complaints against the press, issues formal censures and exerts influence through the power of publicity.

Should press councils be the wave of the future? William Rivers said that "a press council is not a necessity in every city. It would have its greatest utility in big cities where a significant portion of the population is at odds with the community power structure."

Mellett Fund president Ben H. Bagdikian warned, to the contrary, that the press must set up a mechanism to judge professional performance or face some sort of accountability. He says that unless *all* newspapers in the country adopt local press councils, there will result some kind of forced intervention similar to that in trial coverage proceedings.

The Mellett Fund apparently has demonstrated that a community press council can function effectively in this country without infringing upon the publisher's freedom. The utility of the press council is seen in alerting the publisher to his responsibilities in areas such as racial coverage and in helping to close the growing "credibility gap" between the newspaper and its readers.

The permanent community press councils that were operating in 1969 represented inchings in the direction of acceptance of the idea that an advisory body, set up to evaluate newspaper performance, can be beneficial to both the public and the press. [Editor's Note: Minnesota started a *statewide* press council in September 1971. See Alfred Balk, "Minnesota Launches a Press Council," *Columbia Journalism Review*, December, 1971.]

STUDENTS AS MEDIA CRITICS: A NEW COURSE

NAT HENTOFF

I have been an obsessive reader of newspapers almost since I could read. And quite early on I began to wonder why newspapers never criticized each other. Or hardly ever. In Boston, where I grew up, the *Globe* would miss or goof an important story, but the paper's dereliction would go unnoticed in the *Traveler*. I moved to New York and saw that process of mutual self-protection at work in this city. I've talked to reporters around the country, and it's the same almost everywhere.

There have been some correctives through the years, notably A. J. Liebling's "The Wayward Press" in *The New Yorker*. Reading Liebling taught me more about the morphology of newspapers—and their failings—than I've learned from any other source. When Liebling died, the press was again almost immune to criticism. The weekly "press" sections in *Time* and *Newsweek* are severely limited as to space, and seldom dig deep or long enough into any particular instance of press misfeasance, obtuseness, or just plain slumber. The professional journalism publications are, by and large, gray and cautious. An exception from time to time is *The Columbia Journalism Review*, but its circulation and impact are limited. For relatively brief periods, WCBS in New York monitored the press, including the magazines—first with Don Hollenbeck and later with Charles Collingwood. These were tart, incisive, knowledgeable essays, but the audience ratings were comparatively low, and so the series was dropped.

In television too, stations and networks do not criticize, do not expose each other. And, except

---

Copyright © 1969 Nat Hentoff.

for Jack Gould of the *Times*, Robert Lewis Shaydon of *The Saturday Review*, and an exceedingly small group of other writers, the level of newspaper and magazine criticism of television is of an order of ingenuousness and laziness that hardly causes anxiety in network board rooms. As a matter of fact, the best television criticism in the country can be found in the opinions of Nicholas Johnson, a member of the FCC, but those opinions are, to say the least, not given wide currency in newspapers or on television. A brilliant, twenty-six-page statement by Johnson in the case of the complaints against WBAI for having Julius Lester on the air received, as I recall, only four paragraphs in the remote vastnesses of the back pages of the *Times*.

Because of a contentious resistance to vacuums in communications—or near-vacuums—I wrote a regular column of press criticism for *The Village Voice* for some ten years. Since I was usually the only game in town, I would get all kinds of leads from reporters about stories they wanted to cover for their papers and couldn't, about whole areas of vital news in the city that were left untouched by the dailies. And doing my own leg-work and telephone checking, I found scores of instances of press distortion and omission. But it is impossible for one man to be anywhere near as comprehensive a critic of the press as necessary. Especially now. The populace at large, according to a recent Louis Harris survey, have "a strong trust in the nation's press," and in television as well. The latter—Tom Jefferson save us all—is "the public's favorite source of news."

The public, moreover, considers itself, according to Harris, "better informed today than they were five years ago." How "informed" do you think the public really is about the Black Panthers, about the Justice Department's war on dissent, about the thrust toward "preventive detention," about the Dickensian nature of the lower criminal courts throughout the country, about the manifold and convoluted conflicts of interest among congressmen, about the specific ways in which huge corporations influence legislation and governmental executive appointments, about the appalling ways in which the schools are failing nearly all children, about the revolutions to come in Latin America and Asia, about the stunning laxness of Federal "regulatory" agencies, about the continuous contempt for "the public interest" in municipal governments and state legislatures? And on and on and on.

It has never been more essential that the media be monitored and corrected and that stories and developments ignored by them be reported. Some of this, of course, is being done—by I. F. Stone, by Andrew Kopkind, and James Ridgeway, by *Ramparts*, by Liberation News Service, by the Newsreel, by various underground papers, by WBAI. But nowhere is there a place devoted entirely to the monitoring of the media, in all its forms.

Such a place is in operation now at New York University's Graduate School of Education. It's only a beginning, but hopefully it will grow, and hopefully similar centers will start in other colleges and universities. At NYU, where I'm now an adjunct professor, whatever that may prove to mean, I am starting with ten graduate students. There will be no lectures, no regular classroom meetings. We may not all meet together more than once or twice during the semester, and that probably in a local bar. I'll be in contact with individual students as they feel the need arises, but weeks may go by before I hear from some of them.

The ten students will be monitoring the media. One or more may focus on *The New York Times*, checking out the stories it runs and the stories it does not run. Others will be examining and comparing the network television news strips. And others will look into magazine reporting or will pursue reportorial interests of their own while noting how much of what they find is unknown to the media. The students themselves will decide the forms in which they'll present their findings. I expect some articles will result and, if they're substantial enough, they'll appear in this and in other magazines. Eventually, a series of broadcasts on the media can be coordinated and produced by the students on WBAI. I would also expect that the publications of the university itself will be under scrutiny.

The possibilities in the years ahead are without limit. I would like, for example, to see a team of students do extended reportage on the schools —all kinds of schools—with a depth of detail and analysis that is alien to, let us say, *The New York Times*' educational reporting. And it has been years since the quality of the judiciary in the New York City courts has been seriously and systematically examined. How did they become judges? On the basis of what qualifications? How much do they really know of—let alone empathize with—constitutional law? What is their "judicial temperament"? What do they know of the prisoners before them? What are the differences in sentences for the same crime? What are the effects of these sentences on a man's family?

How much internal democracy is there in particular unions? What do insurance companies do besides sell insurance? What are their patterns of investments? Who *are* the trustees of various universities and what are the interconnections between *their* interests and the ways in which the universities invest their funds? And how much about these stories—and so many more—do you see in the daily papers and on television? And if not, why not?

What we're starting to do at NYU can so easily be done anywhere else. New buildings are not required. Nor are rigid credential criteria necessary for those faculty who will be resource people for the students. I mean credentials in the customary academic sense. There has been a good deal of rhetoric about introducing professionals from the outside into university life, and this is certainly one area in which only they make educational sense. On a part-time basis, people like Murray Kempton, Andy Kopkind, I. F. Stone, Ralph Nader, Ben Bagdikian, and others can set up basing points for monitoring the media at other universities. There are several former FCC members—Clifford Durr comes to mind—who would be exceptionally useful in terms of radio and television.

Nor need these basing points be limited to colleges and universities. This is a pursuit which would surely interest sizable numbers of high school students and, if they are not bound by arbitrary rules of procedure, they are likely to astonish both themselves and their teachers by the capacity for independent research they reveal as they look into how the newspapers and television stations in their cities function and do not function. As the concept of monitoring the media spreads into the secondary schools, there would finally be a widespread pre-college stimulus for the emergence of large numbers of people who will have been self-trained to read the press and to watch television critically and comparatively.

Centers for monitoring the media would also give support to those newspapermen who would like to vent their frustrations in a wider context than mutual commiseration sessions at bars. Many would volunteer information to such centers—usually with the proviso that their names not be used. And it's also possible that with proliferating independent criticism of the media in schools, newspapermen in some cities will be encouraged to start their own journals in which the objects of the muckraking will be the papers where they work. Just such a publication, the *Chicago Journalism Review,* is already in vigorous operation. It provides a persistently revealing dissection of the regular Chicago press, as well as television stations, and should be both a model and a conscience-prod to newspapermen in other cities. (*Chicago Journalism Review,* 11 East Hubbard Street, Chicago, Illinois 60611. Five dollars a year.)

Equally needed, maybe more so, are independent publications in which television personnel can disclose in detail the restrictions under which they work. And I mean the employees of "educational" as well as commercial stations. In all media, and television more than others, there are infinitely diverse forms of censorship and self-censorship. But as of now, the viewer has no way of becoming aware of how these pressures effectively limit what he is allowed to see. For one example, only after the Smothers Brothers had been fired by CBS, was it revealed that seventy-five percent of their shows during their last season had been censored in one way or another. Those who watched the series had no idea of what had been going on. No words had been blipped out. But whole sequences had been forbidden—two interviews with Dr. Spock, for instance—and innocuous "filler" material had been inserted instead.

In how many cities does the local Red Squad and the FBI have access to all raw coverage of demonstrations and marches? Quite a few, according to information I've been given from inside television newsrooms. But the general public does not know that. Who decides which guests are too "controversial" to appear on local and network talk shows? What are the criteria? Do you know? I don't. But I'm certain lists of the proscribed do exist.

Nor have I seen a carefully researched analysis in any city of the comparative news coverage of television stations and newspapers. How many stations simply take their leads from the morning paper? How much and what kinds of investigative reportage is there on local television? What stories do both newspapers and television miss? How do the combined media cover student rebellions in a given city? To what extent, if any, are student views given equitable expression? When, as is so often the case, the television station and the newspaper are under the same ownership, what kinds of stories and sources are omitted from both media?

As you can see, I have barely sketched the potential range for centers which would monitor the media. Six months or so from now, I'll report on what we've been doing at NYU. If there are any similar media probes going on elsewhere in the country, I'd like to know about them. There is no reason why there should not be hundreds —thousands—of A. J. Lieblings throughout this country. And, among them, teachers—from elementary school on up.

And that's my final point, for now. These centers ought not to be only for those who themselves intend to be reporters, analysts, makers of documentaries. A basically self-directed course in monitoring the media is, it seems to me, essential for anyone in this society who wants to know what the hell's going on. And that includes teachers, professional radicals, radical professionals, all kinds of activists. And, for that matter, even the passive voter.

Last April, a speaker at a meeting in New York of the American Newspaper Publishers Association complained of signs that some among the public were becoming quite hostile to the media. This augury, he said, appeared to reflect an "uninformed and even distrustful public." It is because more and more people are becoming aware of how uninformed they are that they are now increasingly distrustful of all those media which purportedly have been "informing" them all along.

The growth of this therapeutic distrust can be the foundation for much more intensified monitoring of the media to come.

QUESTIONS FOR DISCUSSION

1. Is the government, the media, or the public best qualified to police the media?

2. Why do print media provide some controls such as journalism reviews while electronic media do not? How could similar controls be implemented for electronic media?

3. Do any citizens' review groups exist in your community? If so, evaluate their effectiveness. If not, how might such a group be established and how should it monitor local media?

PROJECTS

1. With a committee of other students, analyze the local newspaper(s) over a seven-issue period to determine whether:
   (a) local news is reported fairly
   (b) coverage of local news is enlightening or confusing
   (c) the editorial pages favor a certain bias in the "Letters to the Editor" column.

MEDIA ENVIRONMENTS PROJECT

As a class project take the top five front-page stories from the local newspaper and select from the members of the class a five-person editorial board for each of the following publications: (1) **New York Times**, (2) A rural newspaper, (3) **Rolling Stone**, (4) CBS network news, (5) your college newspaper. Have each editorial board report to the class on where they would position each story in order of importance to best communicate to the audience of each publication, stating the reasons for each decision.

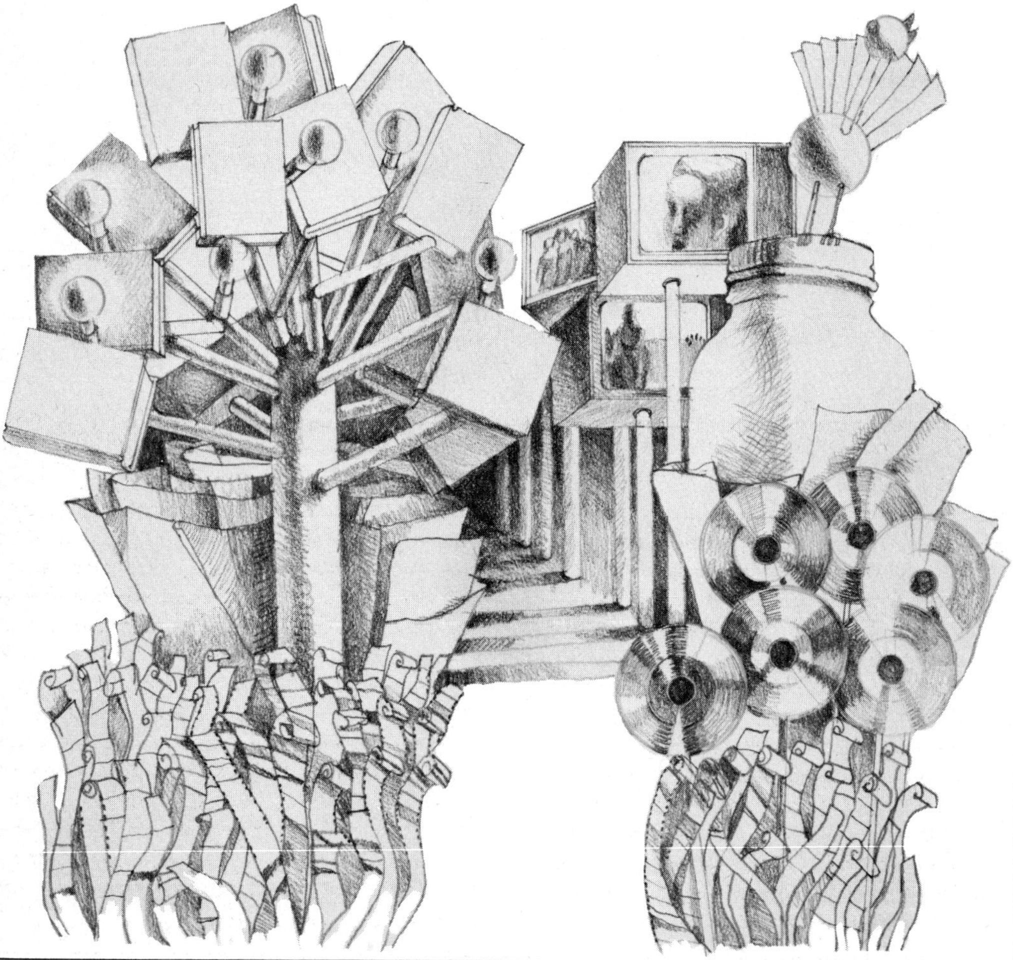

THE LAST WORD

Not long ago Americans had a dream that our advancing technology would usher in a golden age of plenty. Unfortunately, we failed to realize that hardware is not enough. While becoming a nation dominated by technical wizardry, we neglected to pay attention to who was controlling the machine, thereby sacrificing public benefit to a mercantile economy. Our negligence cost us a truly democratic information system; as the demand for such a system grows, its absence becomes more and more evident.

How we resolve our social problems may rest primarily on our ability to communicate. Whether real communication can be attained will depend less on our technology—we are virtually assured of our technical goals—than on our use of hardware to reach and talk with one another.

We must therefore develop a communications system that will utilize technology in meeting human needs rather than limiting its use to economic motivations which usually value products over people.

There has been a meaningful change in the temper of science in the past twenty years, and the focus has shifted from the pure or physical sciences to the life sciences. As a result our colleges and universities are drawn more and more to the study of individuality and the inner person.

This shift places an entirely new set of considerations before the student of mass media.

This closing section provides some valuable insights into what the future of media may hold and what the public, its government, and media operators must do to ensure the establishment of a communications network that does not dominate or enslave any of us, but serves all of us as individuals and as American citizens.

WHAT CAN WE DO ABOUT TELEVISION?

NICHOLAS JOHNSON

Television is more than just another great public resource—like air and water—ruined by private greed and public inattention. It is the greatest communications mechanism ever designed and operated by man. It pumps into the human brain an unending stream of information, opinion, moral values, and esthetic taste. It cannot be a neutral influence. Every minute of television programming—commercials, entertainment, news—teaches us something.

Most Americans tell pollsters that television constitutes their principal source of information. Many of our senior citizens are tied to their television sets for intellectual stimulation. And children now spend more time learning from television than from church and school combined. By the time they enter first grade they will have received more hours of instruction from television networks than they will later receive from college professors while earning a bachelor's degree. Whether they like it or not, the television networks are playing the roles of teacher, preacher, parent, public official, doctor, psychiatrist, family counselor, and friend for tens of millions of Americans each day of their lives.

TV programming can be creative, educational, uplifting, and refreshing without being tedious. But the current television product that drains away lifetimes of leisure energy is none of these. It leaves its addicts waterlogged. Only rarely does it contribute anything meaningful to their lives. No wonder so many Americans express to me a deep-seated hostility toward television. Too many realize, perhaps unconsciously but certainly with utter disgust, that television is itself a drug, constantly offering the allure of a satisfying fulfillment for otherwise empty and meaningless lives that it seldom, if ever, delivers.

Well, what do we do about it? Here are a few suggestions:

Turn on. I don't mean rush to your sets and turn the on-knob. What I do mean is that we had all better "turn on" to television—wake up to the fact that it is no longer intellectually smart to ignore it. Everything we do, or are, or worry about is affected by television. How and when issues are resolved in this country—the Indochina War, air pollution, race relations—depend as much as anything else on how (and whether) they're treated by the television networks in "entertainment" as well as news and public affairs programming.

Dr. S.I. Hayakawa has said that man is no more conscious of communication than a fish would be conscious of the waters of the sea. The analogy is apt. A tidal wave of television programming has covered our land during the past twenty years. The vast majority of Americans have begun to breathe through gills. Yet, we have scarcely noticed the change, let alone wondered what it is doing to us. A few examples may start us thinking.

The entire medical profession, as well as the federal government had little impact upon cigarette consumption in this country until a single young man, John Banzhaf, convinced the Federal Communications Commission that its Fairness Doctrine required TV and radio stations to broadcast $100 million worth of "anti-smoking commercials." Cigarette consumption has now declined for one of the few times in history.

What the American people think about government and politics in general—as well as a favorite candidate in particular—is almost exclusively influenced by television. The candidates and their advertising agencies, which invest 75 per cent or more of their campaign funds in broadcast time, believe this: to the tune of $58 million in 1968.

There's been a lot of talk recently about malnutrition in America. Yet, people could let their television sets run for twenty-four hours a day

---

Copyright 1970 Saturday Review, Inc. By permission of Commissioner Nicholas Johnson, Federal Communications Commission, and author, *Test Pattern for Living* (Bantam 1972).

and never discover that diets of starch and soda pop can be fatal.

If people lack rudimentary information about jobs, community services for the poor, alcoholism, and so forth, it is because occasional tidbits of information of this kind in soap operas, game shows, commercials, and primetime series are either inaccurate or missing.

In short, whatever your job or interests may be, the odds are very good that you could multiply your effectiveness tremendously by "turning on" to the impact of television on your activities and on our society as a whole—an impact that exceeds that of any other existing institution.

Tune in. There are people all over the country with something vitally important to say: the people who knew "cyclamates" were dangerous decades ago, the people who warned us against the Vietnam War in the early sixties, the people who sounded the alarm against industrial pollution when the word "smog" hadn't been invented. Why didn't we hear their warnings over the broadcast media?

In part it is the media's fault, the product of "corporate censorship." But in large part it's the fault of the very people with something to say who never stopped to consider how they might best say it. They simply haven't "tuned in" to television.

Obviously, I'm not suggesting you run out and buy up the nearest network. What I am suggesting is that we stop thinking that television programming somehow materializes out of thin air, or that it's manufactured by hidden forces or anonymous men. It is not. There is a new generation coming along that is substantially less frightened by a 16mm camera than by a pencil. You may be a part of it. Even those of us who are not, however, had better tune in to television ourselves.

Here is an example of someone who *did*. The summer of 1969, CBS aired an hour-long show on Japan, assisted in large part by former Ambassador Edwin Reischauer. No one, including Ambassador Reischauer and CBS, would claim the show perfectly packaged all that Americans want or need to know about our 100 million neighbors across the Pacific. But many who watched felt it was one of the finest bits of educational entertainment about Japan ever offered to the American people by a commercial network.

Ambassador Reischauer has spent his lifetime studying Japan, yet his was not an easy assignment. An hour is not very long for a man who is used to writing books and teaching forty-five-hour semester courses, and there were those who wanted to turn the show into an hour-long geisha party. He could have refused to do the show at all, or walked away from the project when it seemed to be getting out of control. But he didn't. And as a result, the nation, the CBS network, and Mr. Reischauer all benefited. (And the show was honored by an Emmy award.)

There are other Ed Reischauers in this country: men who don't know much about *television*, but who know more than anyone else about a subject that is important and potentially entertaining. If these men can team their knowledge with the professional television talent of others (and a network's financial commitment), they can make a television program happen. Not only ought they to accept such assignments when asked, I would urge them to come forward and volunteer their assistance to the networks and their local station managers or to the local cable television system. Of course, these offers won't always, or even often, be accepted—for many reasons. But sooner or later the dialogue has to begin.

There are many ways you can contribute to a television program without knowing anything about lighting or electronics. Broadcasters in many large communities (especially those with universities) are cashing in on local expertise for quick background when an important news story breaks, occasional on-camera interviews, suggestions for news items or entire shows, participation as panel members or even hosts, writers for programs, citizen advisory committees, and so forth. Everyone benefits. The broadcaster puts out higher-quality programming, the community builds greater citizen involvement and identification, and the television audience profits.

Whoever you are, whatever you're doing, ask yourself this simple question: What do I know or what do I have to know or might find interesting? If you're a Department of Health, Education and Welfare official charged with communicating vital information about malnutrition to the poor, you might be better off putting your information into the plot-line of a daytime television soap opera than spending a lifetime writing pamphlets. If you're a law enforcement officer and want to inform people how to secure their homes against illegal entry, you might do better by talking to the writers and producers of *Dragnet*, *I Spy*, or *Mission: Impossible* than by making slide presentations.

Drop out. The next step is to throw away most of what you've learned about communication. Don't make the mistake of writing "TV essays"—sitting in front of a camera reading, or saying, what might otherwise have been expressed in print. "Talking heads" make for poor television communication, as educational and commercial television professionals are discovering. Intellectuals and other thinking creative people first have to "drop out" of the traditional modes of communicating thoughts, and learn to swim through the new medium of television.

Marshall McLuhan has made much of this clear. If the print medium is linear, television is not. McLuhan's message is as simple as one in a Chinese fortune cookie: "One picture worth thousand words"—particularly when the picture is in color and motion, is accompanied by sound (words and music), and is not tied to an orderly time sequence.

Mason Williams, multitalented onetime writer for the Smothers Brothers, is one of the few to see this new dimension in communication. He describes one of his techniques as "verbal snapshots"—short bursts of thought, or poetry, or sound that penetrate the mind in an instant, then linger. Here are some that happen to be about television itself: "I am qualified to criticize television because I have two eyes and a mind, which is one more eye and one more mind than television has." "Television doesn't have a job; it just goofs off all day." "Television is doing to your mind what industry is doing to the land. Some people already think like New York City looks." No one "snapshot" gives the whole picture. But read in rapid succession, they leave a vivid and highly distinctive after-image.

Others have dropped out of the older communications techniques and have adapted to the new media. These students who are seen on television—sitting in, protesting, assembling—are developing a new medium of communication: the demonstration. Denied traditional access to the network news shows and panel discussions, students in this country now communicate with the American people via loud, "news-worthy," media-attractive aggregations of sound and color and people. Demonstrations are happenings, and the news media—like moths to a flame—run to cover them. Yippie Abbie Hoffman sees this clearer than most:

So what the hell are we doing, you ask? We are dynamiting brain cells. We are putting people through changes.... We are theater in the streets: total and committed. We aim to involve people and use ... any weapon (prop) we can find. All is relevant, only "the play's the thing." ... The media is the message. Use it! No fund raising, no full-page ads in *The New York Times*, no press releases. Just do your thing; the press eats it up. Media is free. *Make news.*

Dr. Martin Luther King told us very much the same thing. "Lacking sufficient access to television, publications, and broad forums, Negroes have had to write their most persuasive essays with the blunt pen of marching ranks."

Mason Williams, Abbie Hoffman, Dr. Martin Luther King, and many others have set the stage for the new communicators, the new media experts. All dropped out of the traditional communications bag of speeches, round-table discussions, panels, symposia, and filmed essays. And they reached the people.

Make the legal scene. Shakespeare's Henry VI threatened: "The first thing we do, let's kill all the lawyers." Good advice in the fifteenth century perhaps. But bad advice today. We need lawyers. And they can help you improve television.

Examples are legion. The United Church of Christ successfully fought *two* legal appeals to the United States Court of Appeals for the District of Columbia, one establishing the right of local citizens groups to participate in FCC proceedings, and one revoking the license of WLBY-TV in Jackson, Mississippi, for systematic segregationist practices. In Media, Pennsylvania, nineteen local organizations hired a Washington lawyer to protest radio station WXUR's alleged policy of broadcasting primarily right-wing political programming. In Los Angeles, a group of local businessmen challenged the license of KHJ-TV, and the FCC's hearing examiner awarded them the channel. [Editor's Note: The challenge was rebuffed by the Commission.] There are dozens of other examples of the imaginative use of rusty old legal remedies to improve the contribution of television to our national life.

For all their drawbacks, lawyers understand what I call "the law of effective reform"; that is, to get reform from legal institutions (Congress, courts, agencies), one must assert, first, the factual basis for the grievance; second, the specific legal principle involved (Constitutional provision, statute, regulation, judicial or agency decision); and third, the precise remedy sought (legislation, fine, license revocation). Turn on a lawyer, and you'll turn on an awful lot of legal energy, talent, and skill. You will be astonished at just how much legal power you actually have over a seemingly intractable Establishment.

Try do-it-yourself justice. Find out what you can do without a lawyer. You ought to know, for example, that every three years *all* the radio and television station licenses come up for renewal in your state. You ought to know when that date is. It is an "election day" of sorts, and you have a right and obligation to "vote." Not surprisingly, many individuals have never even been told there's an election.

Learn something about the grand design of communications in this country. For example, no one "owns" a radio or television station in the sense that you can own a home or the corner drugstore. It's more like leasing public land to graze sheep, or obtaining a contract to build a stretch of highway for the state. Congress has provided that the airwaves are public property. The user must be licensed, and, in the case of commercial broadcasters, that license term is for three years. There is no "right" to have the license renewed. It is renewed only if past performance, and promises of future performance, are found by the FCC to serve "the public interest." In making this finding, the views of local individuals and groups are, of course, given great weight. In extreme cases, license revocation or license renewal contest proceedings may be instituted by local groups.

You should understand the basic policy underlying the Communications Act of 1934, which set up the FCC and gave it its regulatory powers. "Spectrum space" (radio and television frequencies) in this country is limited. It must be shared by taxicabs, police cars, the Defense Department, and other business users. In many ways it would be more efficient to have a small number of extremely high-powered stations blanket the country, leaving the remaining spectrum space for other users. But Congress felt in 1934 that it was essential for the new technology of radio to serve needs, tastes, and interests at the local level—to provide community identification, cohesion and outlets for local talent and expression. For this reason, roughly 95 per cent of the most valuable spectrum space has been handed out to some 7,500 radio and television stations in communities throughout the country. Unfortunately, the theory is not working. Most programming consists of nationally distributed records, movies, newswire copy, commercials, and network shows. Most stations broadcast very little in the way of locally oriented community service. It's up to you to make them change.

You have only to exercise your imagination to improve the programming service of your local station. Student groups, civic luncheon clubs, unions, PTAs, the League of Women Voters, and so forth are in an ideal position to accomplish change. They can contact national organizations, write for literature, and generally inform themselves of their broadcasting rights. Members can monitor what is now broadcast and draw up statements of programming standards, indicating what they would like to see with as much specificity as possible. They can set up Citizens Television Advisory Councils to issue reports on broadcasters' performance. They can send delegations to visit with local managers and owners. They can, when negotiation fails, take whatever legal steps are necessary with the FCC. They can complain to sponsors, networks, and local television stations when they find commercials excessively loud or obnoxious. If you think this is dreamy, pie-in-the-sky thinking, look what local groups did in 1969.

Texarkana was given national attention last year when a large magazine reported that the city's population of rats was virtually taking over the city. Of lesser notoriety, but perhaps of greater long-run significance, was an agreement hammered out between a citizens group and KTAL-TV, the local television station. In January 1969, the Texarkana Junior Chamber of Commerce and twelve local unincorporated associations—with the assistance of the Office of Communications of the United Church of Christ —filed complaints with the FCC, and alleged that KTAL-TV had failed to survey needs of its community, had systematically refused to serve the tastes, needs, and desires of Texarkana's 26 percent Negro population, and had maintained no color origination equipment in its Texarkana studio (although it had such equipment in the wealthier community of Shreveport, Louisiana). But they didn't stop there. Armed with the threat of a license renewal hearing, they went directly to the station's management and hammered out *an agreement* in which the station promised it would make a number of reforms, or forfeit its license. Among other provisions, KTAL-TV promised to recruit and train a staff broadly representative of all minority groups in the community; employ a minimum of two full-time Negro reporters; set up a toll-free telephone line for news and public service announcements and inquiries; present discussion programs of controversial issues, including both black and white participants; publicize the rights of the poor to obtain needed services; regularly televise announcements of the public's rights and periodically consult with all substantial groups in the community regarding their programming tastes and needs.

The seeds of citizen participation sown in Texarkana have since come to fruition elsewhere. Just recently five citizens groups negotiated agreements with twenty-two stations in Atlanta, Georgia, and similar attempts have been made in Shreveport, Louisiana; Sandersville, Georgia; Mobile, Alabama; and Jackson, Mississippi.

In Washington, D.C.,... a group of students under the supervision of the Institute for Policy Studies undertook a massive systematic review of the license applications of all television stations in the area of Washington, D.C., Virginia, West Virginia, and Maryland. They used a number of "performance charts" by which they evaluated and ranked the stations in amounts of news broadcast, news employees hired, commercials, public service announcements, and other factors. The result was a book that may become a working model for the comparative evaluation of television stations' performances.* Citizens groups all over the country can easily follow their example.

I have felt for some time that it would be useful to have detailed reviews and periodic reports about the implications of specific television commercials and entertainment shows by groups of professional psychiatrists, child psychologists, educators, doctors, ministers, social scientists, and so forth. They could pick a show in the evening—any show—and discuss its esthetic quality, its accuracy, and its potential national impact upon moral values, constructive opinion, mental health, and so forth. It would be especially exciting if this critical analysis could be shown on television. Such professional comment would be bound to have *some* impact upon the networks' performance. (The 1969 *Violence Commission Report* did.) It would be a high service indeed to our nation, with rewards as well for the professional groups and individuals involved—including the broadcasting industry. It is not without precedent. The BBC formerly aired a critique of evening shows following prime-time entertainment. It would be refreshing to have a television producer's sense of status and satisfaction depend more upon the enthusiasm of the critics and audience than upon the number of cans of "feminine deodorant spray" he can sell.

These examples are only the beginning. Television could become our most exciting medium if the creative people in this country would use a fraction of their talent to figure out ways of improving it.

Get high (with a little help from your friends). Have you ever made a film, or produced a TV documentary, or written a radio script? That's a real high. But if you're like me,

---

*(IPS, *Television Today: The End of Communication and the Death of Community*, $10 from the Institute for Policy Studies, 1540 New Hampshire Avenue, N.W., Washington, D.C.) Citizens groups all over the country can easily follow their example.

you'll need help—lots of it—from your friends. If you've got something to say, find someone who's expert in communication: high school or college film-makers, drama students, off-time TV reporters, or local CATV outlets with program origination equipment. Bring the thinkers in the community together with the media creators. CBS did it with Ed Reischauer and its one-hour special on Japan. You can do it too. Get others interested in television.*

Expand your media mind. Everyone can work for policies that increase the number of radio and television outlets, and provide individuals with access to existing outlets to express their talent or point of view. Those outlets are already numerous. There are now nearly ten times as many radio and television stations as there were thirty-five years ago. There are many more AM radio stations, including the "daytime only" stations. There is the new FM radio service. There is VHF television. And, since Congress passed the all-channel receiver law in 1962, UHF television (channels 14-83) has come alive. There are educational radio and television stations all over the country. There are "listener-supported" community radio stations (such as the Pacifica stations in New York, Los Angeles, Houston, and Berkeley). This increase in outlets has necessarily broadened the diversity of programming. However, since the system is virtually all "commercial" broadcasting, this diversity too often means simply that there are now five stations to play the "top forty" records in your city instead of two. In the past couple years, however, educational broadcasting has gained in strength with the Public Broadcasting Corporation (potentially America's answer to the BBC). Owners of groups of profitable television stations (such as Westinghouse and Metromedia) have begun syndicating more shows—some of which subsequently get picked up by the networks.

Cable television (CATV) offers a potentially unlimited number of channels. (The present over-the-air system is physically limited to from five to ten television stations even in the largest communities.) Twelve-channel cable systems are quite common, twenty-channel systems are being installed, and more channels will undoubtedly come in the future. Your telephone, for example, is a "100-million-channel receiver" in that it can call, or be called by, any one of 100 million other instruments in this country.

Cable television offers greater diversity among commercial television programs—at the moment, mostly movies, sports, and reruns—but it can also offer another advantage: public access. The FCC has indicated that cable systems should be encouraged and perhaps ultimately required to offer channels for lease to any person willing to pay the going rate. In the *Red Lion* case, the Supreme Court upheld the FCC's fairness doctrine and, noting the monopolistic position most broadcasters hold, suggested that "free speech" rights belong principally to the audience and those who wish to use the station, not the station owner. This concept—which might raise administrative problems for single stations—is easily adaptable to cable television.

If someone wants to place a show on a single over-the-air broadcast station, some other (generally more profitable) program must be canceled. A cable system, by contrast, can theoretically carry an unlimited number of programs at the same time. We therefore have the opportunity to require cable systems to carry whatever programs are offered on a leased-channel basis (sustained either by advertising or by subscription fee). Time might even be made available free to organizations, young film-makers, and others who could not afford the leasing fee and do not advertise or profit from their programing. Now is the time to guarantee such rights for your community. City councils all across the nation are in the process of drafting the terms for cable television franchises. If your community is at present considering a cable television ordinance, it is your opportunity to work for free and common-carrier "citizens' access" to the cables that will one day connect your home with the rest of the world.

Television is here to stay. It's the single most significant force in our society. It is now long past time that the professional and intellectual community—indeed, anyone who reads magazines and cares where this country is going—turn on to television.

---

*A free pamphlet, "Clearing the Air," has been published by Media Ithaca, Department of Sociology, Cornell University, Ithaca, New York 14850. It explains how average citizens can obtain free air time over radio, television, and CATV.

CABLE TV, VIDEOPHONES, SATELLITES, AND DATA NETWORKS WILL SOON CHANGE THE WAY YOU LIVE, WORK, AND PLAY

PETER C. GOLDMARK

The green, rolling landscape in the Windham County region of northeastern Connecticut is quite ordinary-looking as you drive through it. Yet this section, some 350 square miles of rural, slightly underdeveloped countryside with a population of 65,000, seems likely to become one of the most important spots in this country. There we hope to demonstrate in a dramatic way how life can be better—a lot better—for us all. Let me explain:

Since before the dawn of history, men have gathered in cities for defense, trade and commerce, cultural pursuits, entertainment, social contacts. This migration is still in progress, so that today most people in most Western countries live under conditions of extreme density in cities and suburbs. Right now, nine-tenths of the United States population lives on less than 10 percent of the land.

If this trend continues, 200 million of the nearly 300 million Americans in the year 2000 will be crowded into 12 urban centers. More than half of the population—150 million people—will be in the three largest urban concentrations: Boston-Washington, Chicago-Pittsburgh, San Francisco–San Diego.

Reprinted from *Popular Science Monthly*. © 1972 Popular Science Publishing Company.

Many of our troubles today spring from this urban crush. Man is physiologically and psychologically unprepared for the stresses and strains that result from such conditions. In the high-density living areas, the problems of crime, narcotics, pollution, poverty, traffic, education, and so on are greatest. Smaller towns have these problems, too, but they are manageable.

What we propose is to establish an advanced system of communications networks that will do nothing less than give people a choice of where to live—and thus utterly transform our society. Communications technology—through which people will communicate rather than commute to large urban areas—can lay the foundation for this better life.

WHY DO PEOPLE MOVE INTO THE CITIES?

First, for jobs. Then, for educational and medical facilities—universities. And for excitement: theaters, cultural centers, sports arenas.

With our present communications technology we can provide all of these things in small towns.

Let me give you some examples of how this would work. Let's say an insurance company based in Hartford decides it will have to hire an extra 1,000 workers. With two-way television, broad-band cable or microwave, and facsimile, there is no longer any reason why it has to build office space for them in Hartford. It could set up offices in five nearby small towns, each office housing perhaps 200. Two-way TV and facsimile would enable instant communications, more rapid than you have now in a skyscraper office building.

Education? We could establish minicolleges, small colleges with small staffs. A minicollege would be linked by two-way television with a university. Students at the minicollege would participate in all important events at the central university. They wouldn't just sit and look and listen. With two-way television, they could participate, ask questions, enter into discussions.

Entertainment? Through the use of satellites and cables, we can bring anything exciting happening anywhere in the country to every corner of the country: sports events, concerts, anything.

We can do something about medical problems, too. In many depleted areas, it's impossible to keep doctors. In such areas, we could establish telemedicine. With two-way TV, for example, we could have remote diagnosis.

The approach to the new rural society does not mean the de-urbanization of the United States. The main objective is to provide options for 100 million more people, options that today do not exist. This in itself may relieve the pressure on the cities.

To change the nation's living pattern requires more than communications technology alone. Before nationwide planning is undertaken, we are launching an exploratory program on a small scale in Windham County, where population density is low and the need for planned economic development is high. This project is being funded with Fairfield University by the U.S. Dept. of Housing and Urban Development. The study phase, now underway, will be conducted jointly by the university and its president, William C. McInnes, S.J., and my company, Goldmark Communications Corp.

As a test and demonstration we hope to establish broad-band links to Hartford to demonstrate that companies could have employees working just as efficiently in rural settings as in company headquarters. But the first step involves gathering information. Here's what we are doing:

- Studying office practices that result in meetings, memos, letters, presentations, etc., in business, industry, and government. How can these practices be transposed into communications media? The results should indicate how components of business or government could function effectively in rural communities.
- Joining with a number of towns in a given region to explore how to establish standards and limits to ensure the optimum rate and pattern of growth for the highest quality of life. The effort will be coordinated with state agencies to assure that the development program is in the best overall interests of the state. It will also figure out what utilities, transportation, and other resources would be needed.
- Experimenting with a variety of communications equipment that could provide services needed for the business, government, and other aspects of life of the developing community.
- Creating an intergovernment body of federal and state officials to initiate a coordinated, national effort based on experience gained by the study project.

A NEW RURAL SOCIETY WILL EMERGE

Once studies have been made, the building of the communications systems can begin. As we envision it now, it would consist of a number of networks—internal and external. The internal system, strictly within towns, will consist of five basic networks:

Network One: The primary network exists now only in the form of the telephone. It would be expanded into a two-way random-access network for voice, data, and two-way videophone. This would be the most basic urban "nerve system"—as vital as streets, water, or power. The basic purpose: to put everyone in contact with everyone else in the community, no matter how dark the streets or heavy the traffic. Since it will be linked with computers, the same network will provide random access between man and machine, or between machines.

The network can be looked upon as a pipe into every home, office, or library, through which one can not only converse, but also transmit and receive written materials, pictures, data, etc. Its most important contribution is to connect every terminal (telephone, videophone, teletypewriter) with any other.

Network Two: AM-FM radio and television broadcasting. This could consist of one or more local stations, preferably with network affiliations and educational television broadcasting.

Network Three: broad-band cables carrying a multitude of television channels into individual homes. This network would include limited-address narrow-band call-back for purposes of polling or making requests. Such two-way cable-TV systems are already being explored.

As part of this network, general informational services would be made available to individual homes. One important example would be the ability to dial up important municipal events, such as meetings of the various town boards—i.e., Education, Finance, Zoning, Board of Representatives. Through the network's two-way polling ability, public opinion on any issue under discussion could be almost instantly registered. Through a system of "frame freezing," vast amounts of information concerning travel, weather, pollution, shopping, traffic, various municipal and other public services, lists of cultural and entertainment events, could be selected and seen on the home television screen.

Network Four: another broad-band cable system, carrying approximately 30 two-way television channels. These would interconnect the major public institutions of the city: city hall, hospitals and nursing homes, schools and colleges, libraries, police and fire stations, bus and railroad stations, airports, and all other town services. This network would provide informational services among the institutions and key officials, ensuring smooth operation.

Network Five: a town emergency service. This would include the "911" police and fire emergency system, augmented by automatic identification of callers' location and by a system to identify the location of vehicles operated by police, fire, sanitation, ambulance, utilities, and other large fleet operations.

In addition to these internal-communication networks, the city of the future will have *external* systems:

a. Incoming broad-band cable or microwave circuits, which connect the town's business and government offices with operations in other cities or countries. These are permanently wired point-to-point links.

b. Long-distance broad-band circuits interconnecting the town's switched telephone and videophone services with the corresponding switched services in other cities.

c. Common-carrier broad-band and narrow-band services—such as the U.S. Postal Service and Western Union—for transmission of messages, printed material, and data between towns and to other countries.

d. Incoming circuits for educational, cultural, and recreational pursuits. These might include:

- Radio and television broadcast circuits both for private networks and for public broadcasting.
- Two-way broad-band educational-television circuits interconnecting a small local campus with the region's central university.
- Broad-band cable circuit as part of a national high-definition closed-circuit-television network to bring live Broadway, opera, concert, and sports productions to theaters specially geared for such performances. The system would employ high-resolution color television of at least 1,000 lines with cameras and projectors especially designed for live pickup and large-screen projection. The most suitable national distribution method for such signals would be via a synchronous satellite broadcasting several of these high-definition TV signals and received by local high-gain fixed antennas.

THE TASK IS GIGANTIC, BUT IT CAN BE DONE

It will present an urgent challenge to our youth, and all of us must direct our efforts to it. I believe the magnitude of this task will make going to the moon seem like a ferry-boat ride.

But during the remaining 28 years of this century, 50 to 100 million new Americans will join the population. Over that period, the scientific advances we have already produced will, we hope, improve the quality of life, provide everyone with a better ecological atmosphere, unclog our highways, improve health care, and, for the first time, give us a real choice of where we live and work. Such an advance can ensure that in the year 2000 this country will be a wonderful place to live.

HOW COMMUNICATIONS MAY SHAPE OUR FUTURE ENVIRONMENT

BEN H. BAGDIKIAN

In the near future the computer linked to electronic communications will probably alter personal and social life in ways comparable to the combined changes produced by the telephone, automobile and television in the last 90 years, but do it in the life-time of most of us.

It may change the shape of our cities by devising new ways to accomplish many transactions now done face-to-face, but not inherently involving personal closeness. It will probably make education a new force, not only in techniques, but in implementing what is already a compelling fact—that education must be a lifelong activity. It could even reconstitute the family as a tightly knit force by reducing the need to leave the home for largely impersonal acts. It could enlarge the aesthetic and intellectual horizons by making available to everyone in his home the culture and learning stored in distant places.

These forecasts are expressed in the subjunctive mood, the hiding place of all uncertain prophets. There are many "maybe's," not only because these are not completely predictable as technologies, but also because much depends on what society thinks about them, and today society isn't doing enough thinking about them.

We have usually behaved as though the march of technology is an act of nature that human beings cannot tamper with. It has become almost an article of national faith that the music for the procession of technical change must be played under an exclusive union contract by that ubiquitous trio, Mechanical Ingenuity, Mechanisms of the Marketplace and Individual Monetary Profit.

By leaving our environment to the tender mercies of this trinity, we have destroyed the greater water systems of the United States through pollution; we have contaminated our urban atmosphere to the point of threatening life; and we have permitted our inner cities to become horrid traps for the human animal. We may spend the rest of this century discovering whether we can recover from this careless delusion.

At the very least this tells us that human beings must take responsibility for what they do, whether they do it with their own hands or with brilliantly ingenious extensions of their hands. If we urge our adolescents to think ahead before they create little human beings, it shouldn't be an overwhelming task for adults to think ahead before they create little printed circuits.

In thinking about communications and the future, there are some truths that are obvious but often ignored, as obvious things frequently are.

The first is that new communications are agents of change, whether intentional or not. The telegraph and printing techniques in the early 19th century for the first time permitted human knowledge to travel faster than a running horse, and at the time this seemed mechanically fascinating and full of promise for convenience and profit. But if the early users had been told that their new gadgets would change the form of human government all over the world, they would have considered the idea ridiculous. Yet this is what happened.

In the 1950s and 1960s the transistor radio accelerated the world view among the uneducated populations in less developed countries by permitting cosmopolitan information to reach areas without good roads, vehicles or literacy. During this same period television in the developed countries has had revolutionary impacts we are just now appreciating. Novel channels of information carry messages to previously inert audiences and this produces profound change. We should stop being surprised.

Since such changes are inexorable, we need

Copyright © 1969 by Ben H. Bagdikian. Reprinted by permission of The Sterling Lord Agency, Inc., and Journal of the American Association of University Women.

to ask how new techniques can best serve the individual and society. Mechanical efficiency and profit will always be important factors, but they cannot be the only ones. The real power in new technology does not lie in particular gadgets, but in the conceptions men have of their uses. The quality of life must be a part of this conception.

The second obvious truth is that we can use our techniques to meet large-scale social problems not ordinarily thought of as formal communication.

We can look back on our first 20 years of television and envision a more imaginative use of this new instrument. One of the great demographic upheavals of our time has occurred in this period. About 18 million rural people, most of them poorly educated to the point of semi-illiteracy, moved to urban centers. They now constitute an accumulation of despair and alienation that raises doubts whether our cities can survive and whether a democratic consensus is still possible.

A peculiar characteristic of this migration is that most of the adults involved probably would prefer to remain in farming if they did not face starvation and hopelessness.

We might have taken what amounts to about three years of city welfare for a family and loaned it to the same family while it was still in the countryside to buy enough arable land and equipment to become self-supporting. We might have augmented the limited county agent system with televised instruction for the farm family, not in spherical trigonometry or the history of the Hanseatic League, but in land use techniques, maintenance of farm equipment, repair of the home, farm management, literacy, how to fill out tax forms and other elementary arts of coping with the environment.

And what if we had taken the same view of those who migrated to the city, moving into an environment more strange to them than the cities of the nineteenth century were to the foreign immigrants?

What if we offered television instruction in solving their immediate personal problems, like how to read an installment loan contract, job information, how the local bus system works, how to shop in the city, how to maintain a city tenement, what the new and strange city laws were?

And what if we had provided televised instruction for the pre-school children of these migrants, so that they would not enter first grade to find the standard curriculum a total mystery?

It is easier to see these possibilities in retrospect, but at least it tells us that we have not been very imaginative in using our communications to solve practical problems.

The third truth is more difficult and involves the less precise dimension of individual and social needs in aesthetic, intellectual and emotional activity. We need to know more about this because in a short time we must make decisions affecting these needs.

For example, it seems likely that in the future our channels of communication may become an almost limitless resource. Where we now have a maximum of seven VHF television channels in our largest cities, in the future we may have any number of multiples of 20 to 24,000 TV channels in each community.

But the capacity of man to absorb information is not limitless, either intellectually or emotionally. We ought to consider what man needs and society requires. But we must do this without the illusion of looking for the universally perfect single program, since there is none, although our present mass media are largely based on the assumption that there is.

This introduces the philosophical dilemma we will never solve completely, but which we have to cope with: How do we use a social instrument for good as we see it without imposing uniformity and cultural dictatorship?

The need for variety and renewable decisions is not always recognized. Increasingly we hear during troubled times that what we need for survival is uniformity, regularity and order. But the human condition has infinite variety and in the relations among millions of individuals, there are unpredictable combinations of emotions, ideas and values. This human scene is forever creating new situations, and in order for society to survive, it must produce an unending supply of ideas in order to increase the odds that among them will be some that will fit the peculiar circumstances of each moment in history.

The New England Town Meeting that became obsolete when every citizen in the community could no longer fit in the same hall could come back, given large numbers of channels at very low cost, with a capacity for the citizen to respond.

In dealing with the new complexities in communication, we must guard against a mistake we made in the past of permitting access to our educational and communications facilities only to the very highly professionalized experts. We need experts, and we need standards of professionalism in many areas. But we must not let them monopolize the channels of communication.

The rise of the guitar and folk singing reflects the compelling need for nonprofessional communication. Much of hippie culture is a reaction to the exclusion of the individual amateur as a legitimate participant in culture. Without popular culture, High Culture becomes sterile and dies. Without free interchange among all minds, expertise becomes theology.

There is another reason we need to make many TV channels freely available. Dialogue between individuals and the quality of personal communication cannot easily be separated from our mass communications.

The value we put on individual freedom and the right of expression is embodied in our Bill of Rights. At the time this was ratified in 1788, there were only 4,000,000 people in the United States, 95 per cent of whom lived in rural areas where there was no settlement large enough to be called a town. A man presumably communed with his soul and his horse much of the time and with his family the rest. Only one in 20 knew how to read and write, but every time he met another human being, it was an event to be pondered and integrated into his experience. If a man felt the desire to speak to the rest of his community, he could tack a notice on the tavern wall or stand outside the Congregational Church on Sunday or climb on a stump on Saturday and by any of these personal acts communicate with a significant portion of his peers. If he talked to 50 people, he had made a very large impact on his community. Perhaps the whole community.

Today we are 200 million people and 72 million of us live in communities of over 50,000 population, a city size that didn't exist when our Constitution was written. Almost none of us commune with our horses any more, though we do with our souls on occasion, as when we are stalled in traffic or circling Kennedy airport. We still see our families, but only when it happens that all members in their separate outside circuits happen to orbit the dwelling place at the same time. If we feel like communicating with out fellow citizens, we can, if we wish, stand outside one of the 326,000 churches in the country, or get on a soapbox in a public park, but if we manage to speak to 50 people we are lucky and even then we have spoken to less than one-thousandth of one per cent of the people in a community. To make any impression at all we must either have professional access to the systems of mass communication, which is very difficult if not impossible for the ordinary citizen, or else do something spectacular like leap off a tall building or burn our draft card, which may be one reason people attempt to communicate that way.

The attempted withdrawal of a significant portion of our young leadership into hippie and other communities is a warning that something is seriously wrong. Among the reasons for this withdrawal is the one-way quality of mass communication, the implication that the listener or reader is a passive recipient, an empty sack being filled by somebody else's selection of goods.

We integrate new knowledge and experience by reacting to it, by receiving a message and influencing the next person by our response, so that we achieve one basic meaning of communication, which is a collaboration. One cause for hope in the future is that we shall probably have more two-way communications that will involve us in ways that could reduce the undifferentiated scraps of emotions and ideas that collect each evening in the base of our skulls.

It would make sense to reserve some of the many TV channels in every community as soapbox channels, for announcements, gripes or recitations of "Hiawatha." If this is done in neighborhoods, it is feasible that people will be able to respond from their homes in meaningful ways. They might signal applause or tell the performer that his lawn needs cutting.

This sounds strange to us because we know only the present conception of a small number of one-way communications channels serving very large areas. If your neighborhood had 50 channels of its own, it would not be so strange.

Similarly, we are not yet used to the combination of computer and communications channel, but this is already having an impact.

It is quite conceivable, for example, that in the not-too-distant future, the average home will have something like a teletypewriter connected with a computer that is connected with something like a television set that will be connected with every major library, newspaper, town hall, community center and mass access computer in the country.

By typing on the teletypewriter the individual in his home can send messages to particular people all over the world, without using the mails or his telephone. Or he can ask a computerized library for available materials on any given subject. Or his wife can ask for a visual display on the television screen of all children's raincoats in a certain size and price range, and when she sees the one she wants, she can signal and the store will send it to her. And at the moment that she orders it, the computer will instantly deduct the price from her bank account.

Men doing business will communicate this way with secretarial services, with other businessmen and with sources of information now considered so sophisticated that today only the largest corporations and research groups have them available.

The student can get programmed learning, being told what is correct and incorrect, and, more important, pursuing ideas and questions at his own pace and direction, going as deeply and as broadly as he wishes.

Because all this could replace transportation and face-to-face contact for largely impersonal transactions, there would be less need for dense population concentrations in cities. Home would be a more important place, with the need for communication drawing the individual into his home instead of its present tendency to pull him out of it.

If we are wise, we shall make this kind of facility plentiful, so that every neighborhood, every community, every school district will have many channels, often vacant, so that it becomes easy and inexpensive to circulate information, ask questions and get a response on the items of social and political need at the grass roots —communications that are now impossible in systems that have relatively few one-way channels addressing everyone in thousands of square miles.

It is difficult to comprehend the ability of the householder in Minneapolis to reach the files of the New York Public Library and get a printout of any document in its possession, at less cost and in less time than it would take for him to mail a query or drive to the local library.

But look back. When the telephone was first installed, it was a luxury for a few. There were four to 20 people sharing one line, and their combined line went to the local operator who recognized their voices and memorized the few numbers in town. You picked up the telephone, turned the crank and asked Mabel for Charlie Jones the plumber. If you had told this early user that in 1968 his telephone, in seconds, without his ever uttering a word, could connect with any one of 100 million other telephones all over North America, and with most of the 100 million additional telephones all over the world, he would suspect you of being a premature user of LSD. He would have said that no telephone could have 200 million lines attached to it, that no operator could know 200 million numbers, and therefore the job of locating and identifying one phone out of 200 million was impractical. Yet today we take this for granted, and we acknowledge that to lack a telephone is to be forced to do things in a very inefficient way.

We cannot take this computerized development for granted. Nor is it an unmixed blessing. Even if it should reduce the time spent in impersonal contacts and permit deeper personal relations, it would create a new problem that comes with great diversity—the need for some agreement on what the world looks like.

We need greater individuality, but we must maintain some degree of mutuality so that as we all grope toward the future, we do not misinterpret the desires and actions of others.

Rapid change is part of contemporary society, and it will be important that during this perpetual transformation we all have a high level of realistic information. In our times many societies have undergone radical change in a short period, going from the Stone Age to Coca Cola, from the tenth century to the twentieth, from the dugout canoe to motorbikes, all in one generation. Some did it successfully, and some were destroyed by it.

The societies that navigated such changes successfully have generally had some mechanism that kept all segments of their society in touch with each other. Such societies saw the changes coming bit by bit, rather than as a large accumulation. Furthermore, people's motivations and aspirations were known to one another. Differing attitudes were less likely to be seen as malicious or insane, and the close communication led to greater sympathy.

The United States has been fragmenting its population geographically at an ominous rate since the end of World War II. We are separated today by race, by age, by income, by occupation, so that we know less and less about each other and our motivations are increasingly subject to misinterpretation.

Black and brown people tend to live in different kinds of places from white, or to be more exact, orange people. Black people have little idea what motivates orange people, and orange people find much of the behavior of black people incomprehensible.

The same is true of young people and older people. Young people accept the capacity for uninterrupted affluence, and the insanity of nuclear war, without the nagging reminders of those who lived through the Depression, World War II and the Cold War. The young have gone through high-pressure education since Sputnik and are intellectually quite different from their parents.

Blue collar workers are isolated from white collar workers. The affluent and the nonaffluent look at the same phenomenon and react with opposite emotions.

Future society must provide not only a way to give each individual the greatest possible opportunity for personal fulfillment, but it must also give him insight into what motivates others.

It is ironic that, given the growing population of the world, what we call mass communications might—not necessarily will—but *might* permit us to see ourselves as individuals beyond anything possible since the growth of urban man. If it does not permit this, if all we get is more efficient impersonality, then we shall have received a very bad bargain.

In Thornton Wilder's *Our Town*, Emily Webb goes to heaven where she sees all of life spread before her, and chooses to go back to earth for one day, on her 12th birthday, 14 years earlier. To her mother and father this is just another day in their lives, but to Emily it is the only day she has, and to the distracted, matter-of-fact manner of her mother she cries out:

"Oh, Mama, just look at me one minute as though you really saw me ... just for a moment now we're all together ... Let's look at one another."

We can hardly characterize our time today as heaven. But we know just enough about the working of our society to be able to see our past and vaguely what seems to be our future. What remains to be seen is whether we are wise enough to arrange a future world in which we can, like Emily Webb, in Grover's Corners, New Hampshire, "look at one another."

QUESTIONS FOR DISCUSSION

1. Speculate on how we might direct the use of our mass communication systems for purposes of social betterment between now and the next century.

2. Cite what you consider to be the major social failures and shortcomings of our major mass communication systems as they have evolved over the past fifty years.

3. What should be the role of government in the development of major media during the remainder of the twentieth century? For example, what branch, if any, should blueprint the necessary direction of media growth?

4. Speculate on what role print media might play in relation to the predicted visually-oriented information systems in the twenty-first century.

PROJECT

1. With a committee of other students, conduct a study of the local cable television outlet(s) to determine:

    (a) how much minority programming exists
    (b) what original programming exists
    (c) whether available time is being used
    (d) what plans have been made for unique or unusual programming in the future and what policies will guide such programming.

Based on your findings, what recommendations would you make for improving cable programming in your area?

INDEX

ABC Network, 143, 167, 183, 185, 188, 191, 210, 238
Accuracy in Media (AIM), 188
Achorn, Robert C., 53–55
Action for Children's Television, 29, 35, 219, 220
Adler, Richard, 19–26
advertising, 24, 28–36, 50, 58, 61, 63, 68, 127, 128, 133–41, 209, 211, 232, 233, 258; children, 122–23, 216–21; cigarettes, 29, 127, 128; drugs, 30; food, 165; happiness, 122, 124; lies, 134; liquor, 126; marriage, 124; men, 122–23; sex, 122–28; sports, 161–68; truth, 134, 138, 141; women, 122, 124, 127; youth, 124
Advertising Age magazine, 138, 145
Agnew, Spiro, 7, 56, 92, 177, 210–11
American Newspaper Publishers Association, 30, 245, 255
American Press Institute, 149
Antitrust Act, 12
APME New Technology Committee, 55
Argosy magazine, 60
Associated Press, 54, 110, 162, 177, 179
Association for Educational Communication and Technology, 244
Atlantic magazine, 116, 183

Bagdikian, Ben, 11, 47–52, 53, 55, 154, 224, 267–72
Baker, John F., 63–64
Banzhaf Case, 136, 259
Banzhaf, John III, 136, 259
Barcus, F. Earle, 216–21

Batman comics, 93
Beatles, The, 80, 81, 238, 240
Berkeley Barb, 93, 96
Bernstein, Carl, 114–15
Bing Crosby Productions, 244
Bishop, Robert L., 223–31
Black Journal, 152
Black Panther Party, 253
blacks, 98, 113, 181, 210, 238, 260, 262, 272
Blondie comics, 73, 240
Boston Globe, 178, 180, 252
Boston Herald Traveler, 252
Bradlee, Ben, 115, 180
Brando, Marlon, 70
Breitenfeld, Frederick, Jr., 146–47
Brignolo, Donald E., 245–51
British Broadcasting Corporation, 19, 36, 42, 199
Bridges, Jeff, 66
Brinkley, David, 190
broadcasting, 232, 266; commercial, 138, 139; educational, 196; entertainment, 239; news (*see* news); public, 195–201; public resource, 233, 261; regulation, 240
Brown, Les, 22
Buchanan, Pat, 182; 183
Buckley, William, 186, 230
Bundy, George, 38
Bureau of Labor Statistics, 10
Bureau of the Census, 10
Burger, Warren, 186

business, 211, 232, 265, 270; economics, 135, 210, 211; record, 239
Business Week magazine, 59, 60, 61, 133–41, 183

cable television, 259, 263, 264–266
Caldwell Decision, 202, 206
Caldwell, Earl, 206, 207
Cambodia, 113
campaign reform, 193, 194
Canadian Broadcasting Corporation, 19
Canadian Film Board, 30
Cannes, 66, 69
Capote, Truman, 116
Carmichael, Stokley, 7
Carnal Knowledge, 93
Carnegie Commission, 201, 243, 244
Cater, Douglas, 6–13
CATV, 19–26, 35, 224, 225, 226
Cavett, Dick, 185
CBS network, 39, 42, 113, 143, 162, 180, 181, 183, 185, 187, 189, 211, 212, 255, 259–60, 263
censors, 210, 252–55, 259, 269
Charles, Ray, 238
Chicago Daily News, 28, 153
Chicago Sun Times, 161, 162, 163
Chicago Tribune, 51, 148, 150, 161, 162, 183, 236
children, 253; and television, 221, 258, 268
Chisholm, Shirley, 153
Chrysler Corporation, 43, 127
Churchill, Randolph, 11
cinema (*see* film)
civil rights, 151, 233
Cline, Victor B., 212–15
Collier's magazine, 71
Collingwood, Charles, 180
Columbia Broadcasting System, 42, 179, 180
Columbia Pictures, 226
comics, 17, 91–94
Commission on Instructional Technology, 242–44
communications, 19, 63, 258, 260, 264–66
Communications Act, 261
Congress, 38, 82, 110, 112, 233, 234, 253, 261, 263
Congressional Quarterly, 10
Constitution, 111
Coppola, Francis Ford, 69
Corwin, Norman, 71–72
Cosmopolitan magazine, 59
Council of Economics Advisors, 10
Council on Press Responsibility and Press Freedom, 11
counter advertising, 138
Cowles, John, 225
Cox Cable Communications, 224
Cronkite, Walter, 181
Crouse, Timothy, 111
Current magazine, 183

Dallas Times Herald, 225
Dallas Morning News, 183
data networks, 264–66
Defense, Department of, 261
demographics, 264, 268, 269
Detroit News, 183
Dialetic of Sex, The, 144
Dick Tracy comics, 91, 95
Dodd Committee Hearings, 198
Douglas, William O., 191
Drake, Bill, 43
Dragnet, 210, 260
drugs, 39, 89, 92, 265, 270; television as a drug, 258–59
Ducheny, Martin, T., 242–45
Dunaway, Faye, 67
Dun's Review magazine, 183
Dylan, Bob, 79, 80, 90

East Village Other, 92, 93, 96
Eastwood, Clint, 66
ecology, 133, 138, 266
education, 38, 120, 253, 254, 258, 259; 263, 264–66, 267
Educational Media Council, 244
Efron, Edith, 143–45
Epstein, Edward Jay, 105–09
Equal Rights Amendment, 148
equal time principal, 138
Esquire magazine, 116, 117, 162, 183

Fairness Doctrine, 138, 186, 187, 259, 263
FBI, The, 209, 210, 255
Federal Bureau of Investigation, 209
Federal Communications Commission, 6, 21, 24, 25, 29, 30, 39, 85, 107, 108, 146, 147, 153, 185–88, 190, 200, 212, 219–21, 230, 232, 234, 236, 252, 253, 258, 260, 261–63
Federal Government, 29
Federal Trade Commission (FTC), 31, 29, 127, 133–41, 200, 219, 220, 221
Fifth Amendment, 204
film, 73–76, 237–38; violence in, 198
First Amendment, 6, 186, 191, 203, 206, 231, 234
flower people, 239, 269
Forbes magazine, 183
Ford Foundation, 196, 243, 244
Ford Motor Company, 43, 127
Fortune magazine, 59, 61
Fort Worth Star-Telegram, 183
freedom, 263, 269
Friendly, Fred W., 181

Galbraith, K., 9
General Motors, 43
Genesis magazine, 60

Gilliam, Dorothy, 150–55
Glass, Marty, 119–20
GNP (Gross National Product), 9
Goldmark, Peter C., 264–66
Goldwyn, Sam, 70
Gould, Jack, 252
Gourmet magazine, 58
graffiti, 17, 97–99
Graham, Billy, 113
Green Lantern comics, 92

Hackman, Gene, 69
Haldeman, H. R., 225
Hall, Peter, 21, 22
Harper's magazine, 116, 117, 183, 225
Harrington, Michael, 9
Harris, Louis, 252
Hentoff, Nat, 185–92, 252–55
Herblock, 95, 96
Hoffman, Abbie, 260
Hoover, J. Edgar, 92, 211
Horowitz, Irving Louis, 78–81
House of Representatives, 153
Houston, Penelope, 73–76
Howard, Warren E., 150
Hull, Richard, 196
Hunter, Ross, 70
Huntley, Chet, 181

Intellectual Digest, 183
IRS, 230

Jefferson, Thomas, 252
Johnson, Mrs. Lyndon B., 123
Johnson, Nicholas, 30, 252, 258–63
Joint Council on Educational Telecommunications, 196
journalism, 209
Justice, Department of, 252

Kaplan, Stan, 85, 86
Kael, Pauline, 66–70
Kellogg Foundation, 196
Kennedy, John F., 9, 213, 233
Kenyon Review magazine, 183
King, Billie Jean, 150
Klein, Herbert G., 178
Kracauer, Siegfried, 76

Levine, Joe, 70
Library of Congress, 9
Liebling, A. J., 11
Life magazine, 24, 58, 61, 71, 162, 163, 176, 178
Li'l Abner comics, 92
Lindsay, John V., 191
Lippman, Walter, 6, 10

Little Orphan Annie comics, 92, 94
Look magazine, 56, 71, 153, 176, 225
Los Angeles Times, 53, 162, 178, 225, 226
Louisville Courier-Journal and Times, 48, 168

Mad magazine, 57
Madison Avenue, 133–41, 252–53
Mailer, Norman, 117
Marriage magazine, 60
Mauldin, Bill, 95
Mayer, Martin, 20, 22
McDaniels, Charles-Gene, 94–96
McGovern, George, 178, 180, 184, 185
McHugh, Ray, 118
McLuhan, Marshall, 7, 8, 100–01, 130–32, 242, 260
media, 14, 17, 254; monopolies, 234–36; ownership, 243–44; print, 191
metromedia, 263
Miller, D. Thomas, 36–41
Minow, Newton, 196
Minor, Dale, 209–11
minorities, 46, 146, 258, 271
Mitchell, Joni, 66
Mitchell, John, 34, 92, 180, 207
monopolies, 234–36, 269, 301
Moss, Representative John, 138
Ms. magazine, 59, 183
Murrow, Edward R., 180
music, 237–40, 265, 267; black, 238; bubblegum, 78–81; country, 44; promotion, 237, 240; rock, 78–89

Nader, Ralph, 133, 136, 149, 253
Nation magazine, 183
National Advisory Commission on Civil Disorders, 151
National Association of Broadcasters, 29, 217
National Association for Better Broadcasting, 35
National Broadcasting Company, 236
National Enquirer, 36
National Lampoon, 57
National Institute of Education, 243
National Institute of Instructional Technology (NIIT), 242–43
National Organization for Women, 144
National Review magazine, 183
NBC network, 42, 107, 110, 134, 140, 143, 188, 189, 190, 212
New Republic magazine, 183
news, 105–09, 118–20, 178, 209–11, 233, 238
newsmen, 209, 254
Newsday, 149, 162, 178
newspaper chains, 47–52
Newspaper Guild, 150
Newsweek magazine, 48, 58, 153, 162, 180, 183, 252
New York Daily News, 183
New York Herald Tribune, 47, 52

New York magazine, 61
New York Stock Exchange, 180
New York Times, 22, 37, 47, 69, 91, 105, 109, 110, 111, 113, 115, 148, 150, 162, 163, 164, 167, 178, 179, 181, 182, 185, 190, 203, 207, 225, 226, 234, 253, 260
NHK (Japan), 19, 23, 36, 42
Nicholson, Jack, 67
Nielsen ratings, 28, 38
Nielsen Television Index, 213
Nixon, Richard, 34, 112, 113, 115, 118, 120, 173, 174, 176, 177, 178, 179, 185, 225, 236

O'Boyle, Bonnie, 97–99
Office of Telecommunications Policy, 13
Oui magazine, 57

Parrish, Bernie, 163–64, 166
Partisan Review magazine, 183
Pember, Don R., 42–45
Pentagon Papers, 115, 205
Penthouse magazine, 57, 60
Pincus, Walter, 234–36
Playboy magazine, 7, 24, 57, 60, 95
Pogo comics, 92, 94, 95
Polanski, Roman, 67, 119
pollution, 133, 138, 258, 259, 264, 266, 267
Popular Science magazine, 225
pornography, 75, 95
print, 267
Progressive magazine, 183
promotion, 209–10; music, 237–38
propaganda, 209–11
psychology, 91–94, 98–99, 159–60, 258, 262, 264
Psychology Today magazine, 56, 162
Public Broadcasting Corporation, 12, 23, 263
Pullen, Westin, C., Jr., 232–33

radio, 232, 258, 261, 262, 265, 267; AM, 85; records, 237
Radnitz, Robert, 70
RCA, 82, 232–33
Reader's Digest magazine, 24, 58, 63, 162, 183
Red Lion Case, 263
Red Lion Decision, 186
Reischauer, Edwin, 259, 263
Republicans, 165
Reston, James, 53
Reuven, Frank, 107, 190, 191
Rockefeller Foundation, 196
Rolling Stone, 57
Rolling Stones, The, 83, 84
Roosevelt, Franklin, 184
Roosevelt, Theodore, 175, 176
Rubin, Jerry, 7

Salant, Richard, 189, 191
San Francisco Chronicle, 183
Saturday Evening Post, 56, 176
Saturday Review, 56, 183, 252
Schmidt, Benno C., 202–07
Schoenbrun, David, 181
schools, 159, 253, 258, 266
Scientific American magazine, 61
Segal, George, 67
Sergeant Pepper's Lonely Hearts Club Band, 79, 81, 84, 87
Servan-Schreiber, Jean-Louis, 56–64
Sesame Street, 35, 38, 199
Sevareid, Eric, 56, 180
Seventeen magazine, 59
sex, 45, 59, 69; advertising, 100, 122–28, 159
Shain, Michael, 82–87, 237–40
Shirer, William L., 181
Simon, Carly, 66
Sisyphus, 110–13
Skornia, Harry J., 26–36, 195–201, 211
Sloan Commission, 23, 24
Smith, Howard K., 180
Smothers Brothers Show, 211, 255
Spock, Dr. Benjamin, 130, 255
Sporting News magazine, 163, 166, 167
sports, 157–68, 265, 266, 161–78; violence in, 159–60
Sports Illustrated magazine, 162, 166
Squier, Jane M., and Robert D., 192–95
Starr Broadcasting Group, Inc., 230
Steele, Ralph, 196
Stanton, Frank, 143
Stone, I. F., 253
Sunset magazine, 61
Superman comics, 91, 93
Supreme Court, 122, 173, 202, 203, 206, 207, 232–33, 263
Surface, Bill, 161–68
Surgeon General, 30, 198
Surgeon General's Committee, 29
Sussman, Barry, 114

technology, 53, 55, 242, 268; educational, 242
television, 36–41, 133, 159–60, 237, 252–53, 258–63, 264–66, 267–69; commercial, 19, 27, 29, 199, 200; consumerism, 33; drugs, 198–99; energy, 198; ethics, 34; licenses, 261–62; news, 178; nutrition, 199; permissiveness, 33; pollution, 199; public, 36, 195; sports, 34, 159–60; videotapes, 264–66; violence, 29, 30, 212–15; vulgarity, 34
The New Yorker, 116, 183
Time, Inc., 63, 232–33
Time magazine, 38, 50, 59, 63, 109, 133, 176, 183, 230
Time-Life Broadcast, Inc., 224

276 Index

TV *Guide,* 145, 162, 167
Twombly, Wells, 157–58

United Church of Christ, 217, 260
United Press International, 54, 55, 110, 162, 177, 226
US News and World Report, 183

Vietnam, 37, 66, 72, 92, 115, 120, 160, 173, 176, 210, 211, 258–59
Village Voice, 252
Voight, Jon, 68

Wallace, George, 7, 9
Wallis, Hal, 70
Wall Street Journal, 113, 154, 162
Warhol, Andy, 67
Washington Post, 111, 113, 114, 147, 148, 149, 152, 155, 162, 178, 179, 180, 181, 220, 234
Washington Star-News, 55
Watergate, 27, 28, 30, 34, 66, 69, 110–13, 173, 180, 182, 183, 185, 198, 199, 200

Watkins, A. M., 159–60
Welles, Orson, 42
Wells, H. G., 42
Westinghouse broadcasting group, 28
White, E. B., 8
White, Theodore, 173–85
Williams, Mason, 260
Wilson, Woodrow, 112
Winick, Charles, 122–28
Winner, Langdon, 87
Wolfe, Tom, 116–17
Wolper, David, 72
Women's Movement, 93, 143–45, 159
Woodward, Bob, 114–15
World War II, 9, 177
Wylie, Philip, 122

Zap comics, 92
Zappa, Frank, 80
Zurek, Sharon, 28

Mass Media: The Invisible Environment Revisited
was set in 9 point Primer and Trade Gothic Extended
on the Merganthaler V.I.P. by Holmes Composition Service
of San Jose, California, and was printed and bound
by The Segerdahl Corporation of Wheeling, Illinois.

Sponsoring editor was Karl J. Schmidt,
project editor was Barbara L. Carpenter,
designer was Barbara Ravizza,
and artists were Barbara Ravizza and Nan Golub
of grafik eye studio, Woodside, California.

67890/54321